The Pendulum and the Scythe

The Pendulum and the Scythe

A History of Operations Undertaken by
No.4 Group Bomber Command
Between 1939 and 1945

Ken Marshall

**Bomber Command Books
from**

First published in 1996 by Air Research Publications.

This edition published in the United Kingdom 2016 by Mention the War Ltd., Leeds, LS28 5HA, England.

Cover design: Topics - The Creative Partnership www.topicsdesign.co.uk
Cover image by courtesy of the artist, Nico M. Peeters.

A CIP catalogue reference for this book is available from the British Library.

ISBN-13: 9781911255017

Artist's notes: A Whitley of 58 Squadron, returning from a mission over Germany on July 18th 1940, was hit by Flak over Culemborg, Netherlands, where I live. Because the port engine was on fire, the pilot, Flight Sgt. G.J. Ford, urged his crew to bail out but he discovered that his observer, Sgt. E. Jones-Roberts, was wounded and unconscious. Deciding to attempt an emergency landing, he looked for a suitable location. He thought he had found one in the fields behind the dyke, but it appeared to be swampy and the bomber crashed, killing both pilot and observer. Their graves in Culemborg are attended for with love and gratitude up till now, because they gave the ultimate sacrifice for our freedom.

The painting depicts the Whitley, skimming the dyke, moments before the impact. It has a full moon and in the background you can discern searchlights and the bridge over the river Lek, on which borders the community of Culemborg is located.

The painting was commissioned by Culemborger Kees van Hattem, who donated it to Bomber Command Museum in Hendon.

Best regards,
Nico M. Peeters

Other Bomber Command books from Mention the War

Striking Through Clouds – The War Diary of 514 Squadron RAF

(Simon Hepworth and Andrew Porrelli)

Nothing Can Stop Us – The Definitive History of 514 Squadron RAF

(Simon Hepworth, Andrew Porrelli and Harry Dison)

A Short War – The History of 623 Squadron RAF

(Steve Smith)

RAF Bomber Command Profiles:

103 Squadron

617 Squadron

(Chris Ward)

A Special Duty – A Crew's Secret War with 148 (SD) Squadron

(Jennifer Elkin)

Lancasters at Waterbeach – Some of the Story of 514 Squadron

(Harry Dison)

Skid Row to Buckingham Palace

(Ed Greenburgh)

The Boy and the Bomber

(Francois Ydier)

The above books are available through Amazon in print, Kindle and, eventually, audio book format. For further details or to purchase a signed and dedicated copy, please contact bombercommandbooks@gmail.com or visit www.bombercommandbooks.com

About the Author

Ken Marshall was born in South Shields, County Durham, on the first anniversary of VE Day and grew up admiring his father's pretty silver cross with the mauve and white striped ribbon which lived in the china cabinet. This obviously had a greater impact on the child than anyone realised at the time.

An undistinguished grammar school education was followed by an equally undistinguished twelve years as a 'Rigger' (Airframe Fitter) in the Royal Air Force in the UK and Germany before 'Civvy Street' beckoned once more. He retired in 2014.

Ken's interests include RAF history, vintage aircraft and cars, motor sport, drawing and painting. He lives with his wife in Gorleston, Norfolk.

Contents

Bomber Command – A Poem

You knew them when the skies were grey,
these carefree chaps with soul so gay.
You knew them in the local inn,
you took, them home, you asked them in.
You've seen their crazy, happy games,
you knew them all but not their names.
You've seen them rolling back, at night,
'Another crazy airman - tight'.
'But did- you know the 'other' fellow,
cool - though scared he wasn't yellow,
'When as he helped to fly a plane,
he prayed that he'd come back, again.
yes, scared he was but on he flew,
the night was cold and friendless too,
For out there in the inky black,
were foemen waiting to attack
He longed to see this horror through,
he yearned to see his loved ones too,
The home he loves waits his return,
'Pray God, tonight is not our turn.'
He sees the target up ahead,
a stick of greens, the fading red,
The time has come to keep the date,
`Press on you chaps, we can't be late.'
His brow is cold, and yet it's wet.
'It's too damn cold, it can't be sweat."
He feels his pulses beating fast,
how much longer must this last?
A voice speaks - somewhere in the nose,

The Pendulum and the Scythe

Left, left, steady - there she goes.'
The aircraft lifts, the bombs away,
another little debt to pay.
The flak, is rather heavy now,
a little frown is on his brow.
A sudden jar, a burst of flame,
a shell - it must have had his name,
He strives like mad to gain control,
to get back home his only goal
But all his struggles were in vain,
they saw his prang, they felt his pain.
They came back home the tale to tell,
how well he flew, how brave he fell.
Your eyes grow dim, you droop your head,
you can't believe that he is dead
Your soul within you now is stirred
your mind recalls a poem you've heard
He is not dead he could not die,
So young he was and gay,
So gallant and so brave a soul
Could never pass away.'

Written in 1944 by Ken W Marshall whilst on 578 Squadron at RAF Burn, No.4 Group and later dedicated to Sergeant Reg Castlehall; 'Missing in action' - 5th December 1944.

Foreword
by

Group Captain T.G.Mahaddie, DSO, DFC, AFC & Bar, CzMC, C.Eng, FRAeS, RAF (Ret).

I am delighted to be invited to present a Foreword for a new book dealing with my old Alma Mater Group, more especially as 4 Group has been styled as a night-flying group and we were not decimated in the disastrous 1939 sorties when Bomber Command tried to attack German targets in daylight. Whilst 4 Group did suffer casualties, even with the Nickel sorties, we did at least acquire some form of training during this phoney-war period.

I found the early part of *The Pendulum and The Scythe* fascinating in so much as all the names and incidents flooded back to my mind. The AOC, Air Marshal 'Maori' (pronounced Mary) Coningham, a colourful character who awarded me my commission.

Charles Appleton, my CO on 77 Squadron, on whom I tried to model myself when I became a squadron commander and, of course, Leonard Cheshire, a companion Pilot Officer at Driffield, all feature in this early period. Leonard Cheshire actually made Squadron Leader during his first tour, with a DSO awarded when he was still a Flying Officer, to the best of my knowledge, one of only two awards to airmen of this rank throughout the entire war.

My favourite Cheshire story of the war takes place at this time. We 'old' hands who'd come up the hard way were very critical of ex-university entrant aircrew and we never missed an opportunity to correct them in what we called the traditions of the service. To this end, Leonard and his university chums always wore their pilot's brevets some two inches above the top of their left-hand breast pocket. It was pointed out to these over-educated cronies that this was wrong and Cheshire always retorted - 'the gap is meant for the VC, DSO and DFC - with bars, of course!' I am sure that the only reason he didn't mention the Order of Merit was because he hadn't, at that time, heard of it.

There is also a host of other names in other squadrons to the west of the East Riding of Yorkshire mentioned in this book who would seem to have done so much better in the early Forties than we nearer to Bridlington. I recall that I carried out 33 sorties on my first tour and readily admit that a few were leaflet raids, but I cannot place a hand on my heart and swear that I ever bombed a legitimate target, save perhaps the airfield at Stavanger, where oddly enough (as I was to learn after the war), the hangars were cleared of Luftwaffe aircraft in the afternoon before our night attack.

The author has carried out deep research into the early days of Harris' offensive and his comments mirror that of Bill Reid VC after the raid on which he won his little bronze cross. On return to base he said 'I steadied the aircraft and the Bomb Aimer aimed at the T.I.s. We brought back an aiming point picture and I suppose that that is what all the fuss was about.' When I was in orbit throughout the Command I used this quote as an example to all crews to reinforce the message to press-on and bomb the T.I.s, but this took time. In fact it was nearly a year after this before Oboe came on song and they could be absolutely sure that the marked aiming point was exactly where it was supposed to be. My task as Don Bennett's horse-thief at this period, was to describe at squadron level what PFF was trying to achieve and also to recruit those main force crews whose aiming point pictures featured regularly on their squadron and Group league tables.

The conclusions of the Butt Report at the end of 1941caused great concern in Whitehall, but were rejected out of hand by Bomber Command. In turn, the report was welcomed by the Army and, more especially, by the Royal Navy, both of whom were hell bent on sharing between them the few bombers possessed by the Command at that time. In February 1942, not too long after the publication of the Butt Report, Sir Arthur Harris assumed command of theRAF's bomber force. He accepted and was keenly aware of the simple truth of the conclusions laid out by Mr. Butt, in effect - 'approximately only 3% of bombs got within 5 miles of the aiming point.:

Despite the fact that Harris inherited only 374 aircraft, of which fewer than 50 were the new four-engined heavies, he set out to demonstrate to the Chiefs of Staff - and particularly those of the other two services - what strategic bombing was all about, in order to put a stop to the heavy drain of aircraft and trained crews to the Royal Navy (via Coastal Command) and to support the Army in the Western Desert. By calling a temporary halt to training and using as many of his training aircraft and crews as were suitable for ops, and by careful husbanding of all his other resources, he was able, in only three months, to mount the 1,000 bomber attack on Cologne. He was able to do this despite the last minute refusal of the Royal Navy to allow Coastal Command aircraft to be returned to Bomber Command for this one plan. Nevertheless, Harris was able to mount the attack as envisaged and at the end of May 1942 he attacked Cologne, devastated some 600 acres of the centre of the city and showed the Chiefs of Staff what strategic bombing could achieve.

Before Arthur Harris arrived at High Wycombe he made it clear that the debate about a target marking/finding force would not be part of his new command. However, on the 15th August '42 he was forced to accept this concept which he insisted on calling the 'Pathfinder Force' and further demanded that he appoint, as its commander, a young pilot who was at that time the CO of a 4 Group Squadron, but who had been the Flight Manager of the Atlantic Ferry Service earlier in the war. This pilot was Don Bennett, an internationally famous long distance flier known throughout the world as an exceptional airman and the only pilot in the world, to my knowledge, to also possess a first-class navigator's licence and a Post Office licence as a W/Operator, as well as holding every engineers' licence, A, B, C, D, etc. and having over 12,000 flying hours in his Log Book, including a non-stop flight from Dundee to nearly Cape Town, an international seaplane record that still stands to this day.

Despite the Harris objection to the setting up of a Pathfinder Force (PFF), he gave Bennett every facility, particularly with aircraft from selected squadrons from each Group but he made it clear to the Air Ministry that: 'THIS WAS YET ANOTHER OCCASION WHEN THE COMMANDER IN THE FIELD COULD BE OVERRULED BY A JUNIOR STAFF OFFICER (DD OPS(B)) AT THE AIR MINISTRY.'

Whilst Harris was addressing his Command to the directive from the Air Ministry, the 4-engined bombers were coming on stream. The electronic aids were being developed and Bennett was introducing these to bolster his PFF tactics as fast as he could obtain them.

The PFF tactics and equipment were being continually revised in keeping with the measures introduced by the Luftwaffe. At this period the devices that were available to the Command were invariably countered within weeks by the Luftwaffe which is why 'The Pendulum' forms part of the title for this book ('The Scythe' is self-explanatory). A classic example was that the navigational aid GEE was countered and reduced to literally half its range but it was still a valuable aid to getting aircraft back to base in questionable weather.

The Pendulum and the Scythe

It was, however, some considerable time before we discovered that emissions from our H2S were helping the enemy fighters to home on to our bombers and shoot them down. Oddly enough, we never understood why the Luftwaffe did not jam Oboe when I understand it could well have been jammed.

In these final years it always appeared that the facilities available to the Command and the Luftwaffe were on a cat and mouse basis and it is my belief that it seemed that right up to the final year of the bomber offensive, the Luftwaffe was always one step ahead of the Command, save for Oboe having a carefree run.

Thus, after nearly six years of bitter conflict we were astride fortress Europe. From the desperate daylight raids of '39 when we mounted strikes against Kiel and Wilhelmshaven with hopeless results, Bomber Command with its partner, the mighty Eighth Air Force, grew to be masters of the airspace over Hitler's Third Reich and by 1945 operating mainly in daylight. But, it was no walk-over.

I was in Germany on the second day of peace and to my dismay I witnessed squadrons of the Luftwaffe bombers and fighters (including their Me.262 jetfighter) fully serviceable and primed with ammo, but their tanks were bone dry. Please to remember that the plea from the Ministry of Economic Warfare in 1939, when the war started, was 'Bomb oil and you will be home by Christmas.' Sadly, we had the will but were unable to find these German targets. Also, we didn't have the aircraft to carry the weight of bombs needed to destroy these vital targets. In any event, it took the RAF bombers and those of USAAF nearly three years of sustained effort to end the war.

It is worthy of note that in spite of the promises made to Harris, that he would have 3,500 to 4,000 heavy bombers for his task, he could muster only 1,660 aircraft with crews on the final day of the war. Harris's critics would do well to remember that this figure is less than half the number of bombers the Chiefs of Staff Committee considered was necessary to bring Germany to heel, not to mention the same figure that the Eighth Air Force was claimed to require to assist the British offensive.

Nevertheless, the bomber did achieve the essence of the directive which was to destroy the economy and the industrial capacity of the enemy to continue the struggle. There was also a subtle reference to destroy the morale of the population.

Despite the historians having had some 50 years to mull over their researching of the Bomber Offensive, we are told that history seldom evolves within less than 100 years. The great debate that has gone on since the end of the war about Harris' area bombing option versus the USAAF with its precision bombing has raged whenever this issue is raised.

Those of us who served in Bomber Command support utterly the Harris concept, particularly in the final years, when we were able to find those targets that Harris wanted to destroy. Until he died, Sir Arthur embraced this area option without question.

The price was high, 55,500 aircrew of Bomber Command perished; some 11,000 were prisoners of war and there are some still dying from the effects of their wartime service. The Commander-in-Chief viewed these figures with great alarm and my close connection with Sir Arthur after the war humbled me when he would speak of these tragic losses. More especially, whenever it was mentioned, the debacle that was Nuremburg and the loss of 97 aircraft on one target in one night.

I relished the occasion when he would come to some branch of the Aircrew Association and listen to me expound on the Bomber Offensive and I was happy to see him smile whenever I mentioned his 1,000 bomber attack on Cologne, which I styled as the most important 'confidence trick of the entire war.'

Introduction to Second Edition

As the son of a Bomber Command veteran, I have always been interested in the deeds of Bomber Command, but as a youngster I was definitely in the minority. As the first edition of this book was being published I noted that the general public were finally waking up to the achievements of this gallant band of men.

It is therefore with great pleasure that I have seen a most definite increase in this interest, primarily, I think, due to the advent of Social Media. There are now more than a dozen Groups on Facebook dedicated, in one way or another, to Bomber Command and I think I'm a member of most of them. Long may it continue!

Because of this increased interest, Simon Hepworth (my publisher) and I decided that it was the right time to revisit and update 'The Pendulum and the Scythe', hence this second edition, which we hope will find a new audience to add to the old.

I sincerely hope you will get as much enjoyment from the book as I have had in writing and then revising it. It was and still is a labour of love.

In the intervening years, very nearly all of the veterans who helped with the book (including my Dad) have left us for the big 'Squadron Reunion in the sky', but it is still my intention to dedicate this new edition to all of them and everyone who served in Bomber Command from 1939 to 1945.

Gentlemen, thank you all for the freedom in which we live today, your service and dedication will not be forgotten.

'We Will Remember Them.'

Ken Marshall,

Gorleston-on-Sea,

Norfolk.

2016

Introduction to the First Edition.

I was born on the first anniversary of V.E. Day and grew up with my Father's DFC on permanent display in our china cabinet. As a young child and teenager, I made models of Second World War aircraft until my bedroom ceiling would hold no more. I repeatedly asked 'How did you win your medal, Dad?' but, alas, I received little enlightenment. It became obvious to me that Dad did not want to talk about his war experiences. I turned to the local and school libraries and devoured every book I could find on Bomber Command in the hope that, somewhere, I might find some clue as to how aircrew won awards such as the little silver cross that I had admired for so long and I marvelled at the brave deeds of the Bomber men.

At the age of nineteen, I joined the RAF myself and spent twelve years as an Airframe Mechanic and later Fitter - a `Rigger' in service parlance. Being close to 'modern' aircraft (I hate to admit that the Canberras and Lightnings I worked on are now themselves in museums!) only increased my interest in aircraft of the 1939-45 period and I continued to 'research' Bomber Command.

Having reached the ripe old age of 44, I once again asked Dad about his medal and, astounded amazement!!, he actually told me. I finally learned all about the crew, skippered by Geoff Sanders, to which he was so proud to belong. I listened spell-bound as he told me of the things which happened to an `ordinary' crew carrying out their tour of operations around D-Day in 1944.

Since that time I have spent many, many hours researching the activities of 4 Group. I checked into every op which Geoff, Dad and 'the boys' did and amassed as much information as I could. I had my preliminary research typed and I circulated it to the surviving crew members for their personal memories. Once again reticence and modesty came to the fore and it took me some time to cajole some of them into responding.

Whilst chasing my Father's fellow crew members, I was fortunate to make contact with a Welsh wireless operator/air gunner who had been operational in 1940-41 and this gave me the idea of showing the contrast between ops, in 1941 and 1944. Taff (Eddie) Gurmin had flown with Christopher Cheshire, younger brother of the late Lord Leonard Cheshire, and Taff had taken part in the 1941 daylight attack on the Scharnhorst in La Pallice. He put me in touch with the surviving members of Chris Cheshire's crew and

Slim Smalley, the observer, Paul Horrox (second pilot) and Christopher and Taff gave a considerable amount of their time to help me.

I must thank my first publisher, Simon Parry, for the other four chapters in this book. It was he who suggested that I should 'fill in the gaps' left by my initial coverage of 1941 and 1944. Thanks to Simon I have made contact with more 'gentlemen of the shade and minions of the moon' who have helped me to research the years I had not previously intended to cover. I am very glad I did, because I've learned of actual events which I could not have invented, not even in my wildest dreams. Hopefully you, the reader, will be equally pleased to make the acquaintance of the brave men in these pages.

Speaking to these bomber men now, (they are all in their seventies) it is sometimes difficult to remember that at the time they were carrying out these deeds they were only very young men, some of them barely eighteen. Any crew member in his thirties was usually known as 'Pop' or `Grandad'. Most of those who survived their experiences are now 'Pops' and `Grandads' for real, some of them could even be Great-Grandads. This makes it even more imperative to remember the youthfulness of the men in the following pages. Guy Gibson was only 24 years old when he led the Dams Raid. He was only 26 when he died.

Recognition of the courage and bravery of the 125,000 members of Bomber Command in the Second World War is long overdue. Whilst in the early stages of writing this book the Government announced the award of 80,000 campaign medals for the Gulf War. I live in hope that one day we shall hear that the Government has finally agreed to award a Campaign Medal for Bomber Command 1939-45, preferably before all the remaining veterans have left this life. At least 55,573 of them have already gone, they died serving their Country.

In the absence of the country's gratitude for all their endeavours, I submit this book as my personal tribute to their courage and achievements. To all the members of Bomber Command 1939 - 1945, not just those in these pages, please accept this book as a token of my high regard for you all. Gentlemen, I salute you. Thank you for everything we hold dear today.

A Prayer

Teach us, good Lord, to serve Thee as Thou deserveth:
To give and not to count the cost;
To fight and not to heed the wounds;
To toil and not to seek for rest;
To labour and not ask for any reward
Save that of knowing that we do Thy will.

This 'Prayer for Generosity' was written by St. Ignatius Loyola (Founder of the Society of Jesus) in 1548.

It only needs the word 'Lord' changing for the word 'Butch' and it could well have been written for the men of Bomber Command almost four centuries later.

A Toast

So lift up your glasses steady,
Drink a toast to the boys in the sky.
While we drink to the dead already,
Let's drink to the next man to die.

Acknowledgements

(As written for the first edition)

Had it not been for the bravery, fortitude and dedication of all the men of Bomber Command 1939 to 1945, this book could never have been written. Therefore my first acknowledgement must be to those young men who gave so much to ensure victory in the first - and probably the only - strategic bomber offensive.

I should like to specifically thank all those who contributed their memories and allowed me to delve into their past for so much detail they thought they had long forgotten: - to Don Blew, George Riley and Malcolm Lucas for 1939-40 (and to Larry Donnelly for putting me in touch with Malcolm); to Christopher Cheshire, Eddie (Taff) Gurmin, Paul Horrox and Gordon (Slim) Smalley for 1941. To Ray Edghill for 1942-3 and Louis Wooldridge for 1943. To Geoff Sanders, Dick Elliott, Gordon Heard, Jimmy Quaggin and my father, Ken Marshall (the elder) for 1944; and to Bill Strachan, Ted Richards, John Wakefield, Bob Stow and Arthur Tait for 1945 (and to Bluey Mottershead for putting me in touch with this 158 Squadron crew). Thank you gentlemen, one and all, not forgetting Group Captain T.G.Mahaddie - "Hamish" - who did me the honour of reading the manuscript and writing the Foreword to the book.

I must also acknowledge a special debt of gratitude to Jill Rutter for undertaking the Kew Record Office research which I either forgot or ran out of time to record during my own visits there. Also to Jill's husband, Peter, for photographs of pre and early war Whitleys. Both of them gave useful comments on the early chapters and it was Jill who introduced me to Hamish Mahaddie.

On the secretarial front I must thank Jeanette Wilson for typing the original research on my father's tour when I first embarked on this project. That was before my secretary, Helen Sivyer, taught me how to use a word processor and introduced me to its dark and wondrous secrets. Helen also did some typing for me. Sue Minchew came to the rescue towards the end of my struggle - when time was of the essence - typing Chapters 9 and 10 in toto.

Betty Harris at the Yorkshire Air Museum, Elvington and Derek Reed, Managing Director of Pickerings Bookshop in York, have given constant encouragement throughout my endeavours and their unstinting praise has buoyed me up at times when I began to wonder if I would ever be able to finish the book. Dick Teasdale at the Midland Air Museum, Baginton, was another who gave much encouragement and was a great help with information on the Whitley.

Last, but not least, I think I owe my wife and daughters at least one very large apology for all their questions that I must have missed while engrossed in this book. I am sure that, over the last three years, I have spent more time in the Forties than I have in the Nineties. I hope they haven't missed me too much.

To all the above, I give my sincere thanks and appreciation.

Ken Marshall

Warwick 1995

Additional acknowledgement for the Revised 2nd Edition.

It would be remiss of me not to thank Simon Hepworth of 'Mention the War' Publications for volunteering to publish this 2nd edition of 'The Pendulum and the Scythe'. Having seen copies of the first edition on Amazon for £154, we both felt that there must be a demand for it! Simon made this task so much easier than I ever anticipated and because of his assistance I have not had to retype the whole book. My sincere thanks and gratitude, Simon.

Ken Marshall

Gorleston-on-Sea 2016

Bibliography

Adams, Chuck	578 Squadron Operations, unpublished manuscript.
Anon	Bomber Command, HMSO, 1941.
Anon, AP1719C&G	Pilot's and Flight Engineer's notes for Halifax III & VII, HMSO 1944.
Bennett, D.C.T.	Pathfinder, Goodall 1988.
Boyle, Andrew	No Passing Glory, Collins 1955.
Braddon, Russell	Cheshire VC, Evans Brothers 1954.
Cheshire, Leonard	Bomber Pilot, Granada 1979.
Donnelly, Larry	The Whitley Boys, Air Research Publications 1991.
Frankland, Noble	The Bombing Offensive against Germany, Faber & Faber 1965.
Green, William	Famous Bombers of the Second World War, Book Club 1977.
Harris, Sir Arthur	Bomber Offensive, Greenhill 1990.
Held & Nauroth	The Defence of the Reich, Arms & Armour 1982.
Jones, Prof. R.V.	Most Secret War, Coronet 1980.
Mahaddie, T.G.	Hamish, Ian Allan 1989.
Masters, David	So Few, Eyre & Spottiswoode 1941.
Merrick, K.A.	Halifax, Ian Allan 1980.
Middlebrook & Everitt	The Bomber Command War Diaries, Viking 1985.
Middlebrook, Martin	The Battle of Hamburg, Penguin 1984.

Middlebrook, Martin	The Peenemünde Raid, Penguin 1984.
Middlebrook, Martin	The Berlin Raids, Viking 1988.
Middlebrook, Martin	The Nuremberg Raid, Penguin 1986.
Moyes, Philip	Bomber Squadrons of the RAF, Macdonald 1964.
Moyes, Philip	The Armstrong Whitworth Whitley, Profile Publications 1967.
Price, Alfred	The Luftwaffe Handbook 1939-44, Ian Allan 1971.
Roberts, R.N.	The Halifax File, Air Britain 1982.
Saward, Dudley	Bomber Harris, Cassell 1984.
Searby, John	The Great Raids - No. I Peenemünde. No.2 Essen, Nutshell Press 1978.
Smith, Nigel	Tirpitz: The Halifax Raids. Air Research Publications 1994
Webster & Frankland	The Strategic Air Offensive against Germany 1939-45, HMSO 1961.
Public Record Office, Kew	AIR 25 various
	AIR 27 various
	AIR 28 various

Chapter One

Royal Air Force Bomber Command
Formation, Organisation and Rank Structure.

From September 1939, until the USAAF began actively participating in the autumn of 1942, Royal Air Force Bomber Command was the only Allied force capable of hitting back at Nazi Germany. Throughout the Luftwaffe bombing raids of 1940, the bombed-out residents of Britain's cities and towns listened eagerly to their radios for news of the RAFF's' latest attacks on Germany. Whenever they met aircrew from Bomber Command they exhorted them to, 'give those b------s a taste of their own medicine!' and, 'give 'em one from me, mate!' That was exactly what the Command was struggling to do at that time. It was not until much later that the RAF's

Waiting for nightfall: a Halifax Mk.III sits at dispersal.

bomber aircraft were large enough, numerous enough and possessed sufficient high-tech aids to really hurt the enemy and his war machine.

Bomber Command was formed only three short years before the outbreak of the Second World War, although it is necessary to go further back than that to find its true roots. Strategic bombing was begun, by the Germans, in the First World War. Their Zeppelins were sent to bomb targets in the north of England and the Midlands during 1915 and 1916. One or two even managed to reach their prime objective, London. These raids were generally directed at military targets but, navigation being rudimentary at this time, their bombs were dropped largely at random. In 1917 however, the Germans established bomber bases in Belgium and from these they launched their Gotha raids on southeast England. In an attack on Shorncliffe Camp and Folkestone on 25th May 1917 a squadron of high flying Gothas killed ninety-five people and injured a further 195. Seventy British aircraft were sent off to intercept them but only one Gotha was shot down.

London was bombed on 13th June, killing 162 and injuring 432 people. A second raid followed on 7th July. These raids, and others like them, resulted in the War Cabinet appointing a committee of two - the Prime Minister (Mr. Lloyd George) and General Jan Smuts - to review the situation. This committee made three major recommendations that were fully accepted by the Government.

The first, and most far-reaching, of these recommendations was that the Royal Flying Corps (RFC) and the Royal Naval Air Service (RNAS) should be amalgamated to create a single air arm. The second, and most obvious, was the strengthening of Britain's defensive fighter arm. The third recommendation, which was in full accord with the doctrine of the RFC's Commander, Major-General Hugh Trenchard, was that the best form of defence was attack and that Britain should have its own strategic bomber force. Trenchard had already formed (on 17th October 1917) an unofficial independent strategic bombing force based in France and between its formation and 5th June 1918 - when it became an official force - it carried out 57 raids on strategic German targets.

When on 1st April 1918, the Royal Air Force was created from the amalgamation of the RFC and the RNAS. Sir Hugh Trenchard became its first Chief-of-Staff. Political infighting and disagreements very soon drove Trenchard to resign his post, having first learned from his successor that he could return to the command of the independent strategic bomber force, a position in which he remained until the end of the war.

Shortly after the war's end, Lord Trenchard was again appointed Chief-of-the-Air Staff (CAS) and his utter dedication to a strategic bomber force in particular and an independent air arm in general was the driving force of the RAF in its fledgling years. It was due to his firm beliefs that Trenchard was able to counter and block every attempt by the Army and Navy to dissolve his young force and return each component part back to the Generals and their Lordships at the Admiralty. Only Trenchard's vision and determination ensured that the Royal Air Force survived as a fully independent entity and upon his strong foundations was built the force without which Great Britain would not have survived the Nazi onslaught of 1939-45. Truly can Lord Trenchard be known as the Father of the Royal Air Force.

In the twenties Trenchard was encouraging young disciples such as Portal, Harris, Slessor, Saundby and Tedder to follow his belief that, 'The aim of the Air Force is to break down the enemy's means of resistance by attacks on objectives selected as most likely to achieve this end'[1]. He also pointed out that "It is not, however, necessary for an air force, in order to defeat the enemy nation, to defeat its armed forces first. Air power can dispense with that intermediate step, can pass over the enemy navies and armies, and penetrate the air defences and attack direct the centres of production, transportation and communication from which the enemy war effort is maintained." So was the belief in the strategic bomber offensive nurtured.

Something else happened in the Twenties that was to have a tactical bearing on the 1939-45 bomber offensive. While commanding No.45 Squadron out in Mesopotamia, a certain Squadron Leader A.T. Harris and his two flight commanders, Flt. Lt. R.H.M.S. Saundby and Flt. Lt. the Hon. R.A. Cochrane, devised the prone bombing position. This was achieved by cutting viewing panels in the noses of their Vickers Vernon transport aircraft and having their selected crewmen lie on their stomachs to site the target. This system was eventually adopted throughout the air forces of the world and was used until modern electronics and radar/laser guided bombs ultimately rendered it obsolete in the seventies.

---

[1] *Official History. Vol. IV. pp 72-76.*

During the Thirties, Hitler's rise to power and the subsequent rearmament of Germany made the probability of a second world war more likely than ever. Consequently, late but desperate measures were taken in the rearming of the British Forces. The first priority (as always, prior to the Second World War) went to the Royal Navy so that they could safeguard our sea communications. Second priority was given to the RAF Home Defence force to allow us to secure our bases and the air space over Britain and third priority, to enable us to strike back at the enemy, went to our offensive air component.

Royal Air Force Bomber Command was formed on 14th July 1936. Its first Air Officer Commanding-in-Chief (AOC-in-C) was Air Chief Marshal Sir John Steel and Headquarters were situated at Hillingdon House, Uxbridge, Middlesex. Initially Sir John had control of four bomber groups. Nos. 1, 2 and 3 were composed of regular RAF squadrons and No.6 Group, which was then composed of Auxiliary Air Force squadrons. (Not to be confused with No.6 Group RCAF, which was not formed until late 1942).

With typical Service logic, the first of these groups to be formed was No.2, which came into being on 20th March 1936 almost four months before Bomber Command itself, with its headquarters at Abingdon. This group had to wait until 1st August, however, before it acquired its first station, Abbotsinch in Renfrewshire, complete with two squadrons, Nos. 21 and 34, both equipped with Hawker Hind two-seater biplane bombers. On the 1st May 1936, Nos. 1 and 3 Groups were formed, from the Central and Western Areas of A.D.G.B.[2] respectively. The former's HQ was at Abingdon and No.3 Group's HQ at Andover. No.1 Group comprised three stations and ten squadrons: Abingdon with 15, 40, 98 and 104 Squadrons; Bircham Newton with 18, 21, 34 and 39 Squadrons and Upper Heyford with 57 and 218 Squadrons. All these squadrons were also equipped with Hawker Hinds.

By 15th December 1936, No.3 Group had responsibility for six stations and fourteen squadrons. Nos. 10, 78, 97 and 166 Squadrons were based at Boscombe Down and were all equipped with Handley Page Heyfords, as were Nos. 7 and 102 Squadrons at Finningley and No.3 and 99 Squadrons at Mildenhall, although 38 Squadron had just begun to re-equip with Fairey

---

[2] *Air Defence of Great Britain*

Hendons. Driffield had the Vickers Virginias of 58 and 215 Squadrons, Wyton was hosting the Hawker Hinds of 114 and 139 Squadrons while Scampton had 9 Squadron with Heyfords and 214 Squadron with Virginias.

No.6 (Auxiliary) Group consisted of 12 county and city squadrons of the Auxiliary Air Force, the weekend fliers. These squadrons were equipped with Hawker Harts (seven squadrons), Hawker Hinds and Westland Wallaces (two squadrons each) and one squadron of Westland Wapitis.

It was realised at this time that the RAF had no really heavy bombers and that, if Trenchard's dream of a true, strategic bomber offensive was to be properly planned and successfully carried out, then the RAF would need such 'heavy' aircraft. In 1936 the Air Ministry issued specifications to the British aircraft industry that would, in time, produce the Stirling, Halifax and Manchester (the failure of which led to the Lancaster) bombers.

Although the initial build-up of the Command was slow, 1st April 1937 saw the formation of another Group as an offshoot of No.3 Group. This new group was No.4, with Headquarters initially at Mildenhall and its first Air Officer Commanding was Air Commodore A.T. Harris.

On 29th June 1937, 4 Group HQ moved to Linton-on-Ouse, to where 51 and 58 Squadrons were about to relocate (from Boscombe Down) and the Group also acquired 97 and 166 Squadrons at Leconfield; 75 and 215 Squadrons at Driffield; 10 and 78 Squadrons at Dishforth and 7 and 76 Squadrons based at Finningley. The Group had a strange mix of aircraft at this time, Nos. 7, 78, 97 and 166 were equipped with Heyfords, Nos.51, 58, 75 and 215 had Virginias (51 and 78 also had some Ansons) while 76 Squadron was flying Vickers Wellesleys, the aircraft that Barnes Wallis designed before moving onto the Wellington. Only No.10 Squadron had what was then a new, modern aircraft, the Armstrong Whitworth Whitley, displaying the type that was ultimately to equip the whole of 4 Group by September 1939.

Almost two years to the day before the outbreak of the Second World War, on 1st September 1937, No.5 Group was formed, again as an offshoot of 3 Group and again with its HQ initially at Mildenhall. Within a month, however, it had moved to 'St. Vincents' at Grantham (where it would remain until November '43) and taken on responsibility for the Hawker Hinds of 113 and 211 Squadrons based at Grantham (211 Squadron still also had a few Hawker Audax aircraft); those of 44, 50 and 110 Squadrons at Waddington and the Hawker Audaxes and Avro Ansons of 61 and 144 Squadrons based at Hemswell.

Gradually the biplanes and obsolete monoplanes were replaced. By 11.15 am on Sunday 3rd September 1939 when a tired and sad Neville Chamberlain announced (to those households fortunate to possess a 'wireless' set) that ... 'I have to tell you now that no such undertaking has been received, and that consequently this country is at war with Germany ', Bomber Command's equipment had advanced dramatically, in technology if not in numbers, to what were then considered modern aircraft, although many will argue that the Fairey Battle was obsolete before it was built.

Bomber Command went to war with ten squadrons of Fairey Battles in No.1 Group, which immediately became the Advanced Air Striking Force (AASF) and moved to France; No.2 Group possessed seven squadrons of Bristol Blenheims; No.3 had eight squadrons of Vickers Wellingtons, No.4 Group had six squadrons of Armstrong Whitworth Whitleys and 5 Group had eight squadrons of Handley Page Harnpdens. As the Auxiliary Air Force squadrons had all been called up and fully integrated into the RAF 'proper', the No.6 Group of 1936 no longer existed, Instead its name was given to a collection of training units that the then AOC-in-C, Air Chief Marshal Sir Edgar Ludlow- Hewitt, very wisely pulled out of his front line to create a core of experienced personnel to train the Command's new intake of volunteers.

This did not make him popular with the authorities and, by April 1940, he had been replaced by Air Marshal Sir Charles `Peter' Portal. It is only comparatively recently that it has been acknowledged that Sir Edgar's creation of No.6 Group at this time was a spark of genius that certainly ensured the operational longevity of the Command. In September 1939 No.6 Group comprised 13 Group Pool squadrons (2 Hampden, 2 Wellington, 2 Whitley, 3 Blenheim and 4 Battle) and one reserve squadron (also Battles).

Throughout the war Bomber Command expanded, slowly at first but gathering pace as the war progressed. The first of the four-engined bombers entered service in 1940, the Stirling in August with 7 Squadron (3 Group) and the Halifax in November with 35 Squadron (4 Group). In December of the same year the Manchester began its short life when the first examples were delivered to 207 Squadron (5 Group) at Waddington.

The short-lived and unlamented Avro Manchester was considered to be an unmitigated disaster in operational service. However it was the forerunner of what was considered the greatest bomber of the war, the Avro Lancaster.

As already stated, Sir Edgar Ludlow-Hewitt was replaced by Sir Charles Portal as C-in-C on 3rd April 1940 but in October Portal became Chief of the Air Staff and Air Marshal Sir Richard Peirce succeeded him at Bomber Command. The Command's HQ had, meanwhile, moved from Uxbridge to Richings Park, Langley, Buckinghamshire in August 1939 and then to High Wycombe, Bucks, in March 1940. It was to remain at High Wycombe until Bomber Command vanished into Strike Command in 1968 (Strike Command's HQ is now based there).

May 1941 saw the first attempt by the Command to use Boeing B-17 'Flying Fortress', equipping 90 Squadron, initially at West Raynham. It was not a success and the aircraft was withdrawn in February 1942. Conversely, an aircraft that was to be a great success also entered service in 1941, for in December, 44 Squadron at Waddington took delivery of its first Lancasters.

On 8th January 1942, Sir Richard Pierse was posted as C-in-C of the American, British, Dutch and Australian Aircraft Command (ABDA) and thence as C-in-C India and South East Asia. Air Vice Marshal J.E.A. Baldwin became acting A.O.C-in-C pending the arrival, on 22nd February 1942, of Air Marshal Sir Arthur Harris.

The Pendulum and the Scythe

The Mosquito entered service with 105 Squadron shortly after Air Marshal Sir Arthur Harris took over the Command and the next major expansion was the formation of the Pathfinder Force on 15th August 1942. This was commanded by Air Commodore D.C.T. Bennett and initially consisted of five squadrons, one from each Group. These were 156 Squadron (Wellingtons) from 1 Group, 109 Squadron (Wellingtons and Mosquitoes) from 2 Group, 7 Squadron (Stirlings) from 3 Group, 35 Squadron (Halifaxes) from 4 Group while No.5 Group supplied 83 Squadron with Lancasters. These squadrons were located on adjacent airfields within the 3 Group area, namely Oakington (7 Sqn), Graveley (35 Sqn), Wyton (HQ, 83 and 109 Sqns) and Warboys (156 Sqn).

The 25th October 1942 saw the formation of another Group, the third to carry the No.6. title. Initially, only the Headquarters was formed at Allerton Park, Yorkshire, under the command of Air Vice Marshal G.E. Brookes. However, on 1st January 1943, No.4 Group transferred all of the Canadian squadrons it had been forming and collecting since 1941 and No.6 (RCAF) Group became operational.

Seven days later, on 8th January 1943, the Pathfinder Force became a Group in its own right - No.8 (PFF) Group and Don Bennett was promoted to Air Vice Marshal. In April 1943, two more squadrons joined the Pathfinders, 405 (RCAF) Sqn. with Halifaxes from No.6 Group and 97 (Straits Settlements) Sqn. with Lancasters from No.5 Group. At the beginning of June, two more squadrons, 105 and 139, both flying Mosquitoes were added to the force and PFF HQ moved from Wyton to Castle Hill House in Huntingdon.

The last Bomber Group to form was No.100 (Bomber Support) Group, which was formed under the command of Air Commodore E.B. Addison on 8th November 1943. Its HQ was initially at Radlett but moved to West Raynham on 3rd December, followed, on 18th January 1944 by a move to Bylaugh Hall in East Dereham where it was to remain until the Group was disbanded in December 1945. The duties of No.100 (BS) Group were the operation of both ground and airborne Radio Counter Measures (RCM) and control of the long-range fighter interdiction offensive against the German nightfighter force. Both duties were successfully carried out and, although for the first six months of its existence only ground based radio counter measures were undertaken, the RCM campaign especially did much to reduce the casualty levels in Bomber Command. (See description, in Chapter

2, of Kiel Raid on 23/24th July 1944 for an example of No.100 Group's activities).

Until February 1942, a maximum effort could produce a force of about 225 to 250 aircraft for a major raid, but more normal quantities despatched on raids were only in the 50 to 100 range. When Harris took over Bomber Command, he inherited a total front-line night bomber strength of 469. This number was made up of 221 Wellingtons, 112 Hampdens, 54 Whitleys, 29 Stirlings, 29 Halifaxes, 20 Manchesters and 4 Lancasters.

In numbers this was no greater than Peirse had possessed twelve months earlier, but now at least, the build-up of four-engined heavies was beginning. Because of operational losses and the hiving off of complete, trained squadrons to Coastal Command and the Middle East, the numerical strength of Harris' Command was only marginally improving. Just 263 aircraft raided Cologne on 5th/6th April, followed by 272 to Hamburg on 8th/9th of the same month. But, with the future of Bomber Command still in doubt, Harris had to find a way of ensuring its continuance and expansion. His dramatic answer to both worries was the Thousand-Bomber raid. By every means at their disposal, Harris and his Senior Air Staff Officer, Air Vice Marshal R.H.M.S. Saundby, collected and borrowed bomber aircraft from everywhere they could think of. Harris asked his fellow C-in-C's for help. Sir Philip Joubert of Coastal Command immediately offered 250 bombers and crews (most of which had been transferred from Bomber Command in the first place), and Sir William Welsh of Flying Training Command proffered fifty aircraft. In the end, however, most of the aircraft from Flying Training Command were found to have insufficient equipment fitted for operational use and only four operational Wellingtons were eventually forthcoming.

As the raid's planning was nearing completion the Admiralty dropped their bombshell - they would not allow the 250 aircraft from Coastal Command to take part. Bomber Command redoubled its efforts to build up to the magic number. By utilising their own training units, manned by crews composed of `resting' instructors and trainee aircrew, the final number of 1,047 aircraft was arrived at for the Cologne raid of 30/31st May 1942. This was composed of 156 Wellingtons from No.1 Group; 134 Wellingtons and 88 Stirlings from No.3 Group; 131 Halifaxes, 9 Wellingtons and 7 Whitleys from No. 4 Group; 73 Lancasters, 46 Manchesters and 34 Hampdens from No.5 Group; 236 Wellingtons and 21 Whitleys from 91 (O.T.U.) Group; 63 Wellingtons and 45 Hampdens from 92 (O.T.U.) Group and the 4 Wellingtons from Flying Training Command.

After this the future of Bomber Command was assured and its expansion continued, albeit still rather slowly initially. At least the aircraft now joining the Command were the new heavies. Early July saw 325 aircraft despatched to Bremen, while later that same month the number sent to Hamburg rose yet again to 403, followed closely on the night of 31st July/1st August by 630 aircraft despatched to Dusseldorf. Admittedly, 105 of these were from 92 (OTU) Group but that still meant 525 were Bomber Command's own front-line aircraft. This figure was not to be exceeded for almost another year, when on 26/27th April 1943 the Command sent 561 aircraft to Duisburg. Early May 1943 saw a new record of 596 aircraft to Dortmund and by now the average 'maximum effort' would see approximately 450 to 550 aircraft on the battle order. Dortmund again, saw the figure climb even higher on 23/24th May when 826 bombers were despatched.

Henceforth, the Command went on from strength to strength, although there were still setbacks and pitfalls ahead.

The command structure of Bomber Command and the RAF hierarchy changed very little throughout the war although, obviously, personnel filling the various appointments within that structure did move around somewhat. Sir Kingsley Wood had been appointed Secretary of State for Air on 16th May 1938 and was not succeeded by Sir Samuel Hoare until 5th April 1940. Hoare, however, did not stay long, being replaced just over a month later by Sir Archibald Sinclair who took up his appointment on 11th May 1940 and remained in this post for the remainder of the war.

Next down the ladder of command was the Chief of Air Staff and Air Chief Marshal Sir Cyril Newall, who had held this post since the 1st September 1937, retired after just over 13 months of war. His place was taken, on 25th October 1940, by Air Chief Marshal (Later Marshal of the RAF) Sir Charles (Peter) Portal. Under the CAS there were several senior administrative positions; Deputy Chief of Air Staff was a post filled successively by Air Vice Marshals, Richard Peirse (January 1937 - April 1940), Sholto Douglas (April - November 1940), Arthur 'Bert' Harris (November 1940 - May 1941) and Norman Bottomley (May 1941 - May 1942). The title lapsed from May 1942 to July 1943 but when it was reinstated, the position was again filled by Norman Bottomley, now a knighted Air Marshal.

Assistant Chiefs of Staff had many functions and responsibilities, which covered such areas as Operational Requirements and Tactics, Operations, Policy and Intelligence. All these officers were based at Air Ministry, as were the Director of Plans and the Director of Bomber Operations, both of which were misnomers as the officers filling these positions were at least two ranks below that of the C-in-C Bomber Command. Their function was to assist the ACAS to think up ideas for the CAS to appraise and to pass his instructions on to the AOC-in-C.

Within Bomber Command itself, the top man was the Air Officer Commanding-in-Chief and during the war this position was filled by Sir Edgar Ludlow-Hewitt (September 1937 - April 1940), Sir Charles Portal (April - October 1940), Sir Richard Peirse (October 1940 - January 1942) and Sir Arthur Harris (February 1942 - May 1945). The A.O.C-in-C reported directly to the Chief of the Air Staff, although it is now well known that Harris also had a direct line to and from Prime Minister Churchill.

The A.O.C-in-C's right-hand man (at least until February 1943) was his Senior Air Staff Officer (SASO). This post, successively held by Air Commodore Norman Bottomley (November 1938 - November 1940), Air Vice Marshal Robert (Sandy) Saundby (November 1940 February   1943), Air Vice-Marshal R.D. Oxland (February 1943 - February 1944) and Air Vice-Marshal H.S.P. Walmsley. On 15th February 1943, Saundby was promoted to Air Marshal, Knighted and appointed Deputy A.O.C-in-C. Below this, and away from, Bomber Command HQ, were the Groups, each of which was headed by an Air Officer Commanding (see Appendix I). Each A.O.C. had his own Group HQ and his own staff officers to administer all aspects of the Group's activities.

Once a target had been decided upon at a morning meeting in HQ Bomber Command (Harris referred to his target selection meetings as 'morning prayers), it was up to the Command SASO and his team to plan every aspect of the raid - numbers of aircraft from which Group, bomb loads, fuel loads, routes to and from the target., timings, PFF marking methods, etc. Within an hour of the target being selected, Command informed all Groups designated to take part, of the fact that an operation was on for that night, the likely numbers of aircraft required and an indication of bomb and fuel loads. The Groups planning teams then checked all their squadrons' serviceability states to see where they could get the required number of aircraft from. They then notified relevant Station Commanders of the raid and the likely requirement

34

of aircraft and crews from the squadron(s) based on that station. All communications were carried out by simultaneous teleprinter transmission over secure land-lines so that all recipients received their signals simultaneously.

The stations would confirm to Group HQ their resident squadrons' availability of aircraft and crews and they in turn advised Command HQ. By late morning, full details of the raid would be transmitted to all Groups, where the AOC and his staff would check all the details before re-transmitting the operational order to the stations and squadrons. Occasionally someone (at either Group or Station level) would notice that the planned route passed over, or very close to, a new Flak position. This would be passed to the AOC who would call Command to point this out. Command would then modify the route to bypass the new danger and update their maps accordingly. Occasionally the Groups would object to a specific point of the op order (over the route to Nuremburg on the 30/31st March 194. for instance - see Chapter 2) and in cases like these it was not unusual for Saundby and all the AOCs to have a conference telephone call to thrash the problem out.

Thus the decision (whether made by Harris, Portal, Churchill or the Combined Chiefs of Staff) was passed down to squadron commander level. Each station called a 'pilots and navigators only' briefing, in the early to mid-afternoon, at which target details for the night were revealed. This allowed navigators to work out all necessary compass bearings, aircraft speeds and heights, etc., to ensure that their aircraft maintained their position in the stream and reached their objective at the right time and from the right direction. The remainder of each crew did not know the target until the main briefing that was held about two hours before take-off.

Once an RAF station was informed by Group that its squadrons were to operate that night full security measures were instigated. Switchboard operators were informed that all non-official telephone calls, whether in or out were henceforth forbidden. The station's public telephone boxes were chained and padlocked and the station itself was sealed, prohibiting all exits and entrances (except for service personnel returning to the unit). These

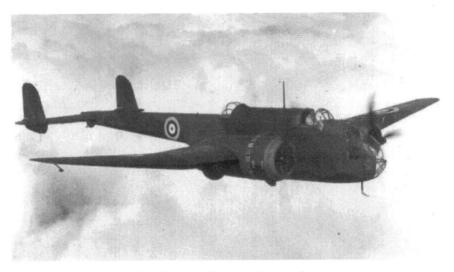

Handley-Page Hampden light bomber.

restrictions remained in force until the time of estimated attack upon the designated target.

At station level (RAF stations were always known as camps ¬and still are) the command structure continued. Most station commanders were Group Captains, but where two or three stations were grouped together into a 'base' organisation later in the war, these were presided over by an Air Commodore. Stations, depending upon their size, had one, two or three squadrons resident, each squadron being under the command of a Wing Commander. Every squadron had two or three flights, each headed by a Squadron Leader. Additionally, each squadron commander selected officers, based on their experience and qualifications, to fulfil the role of aircrew category leader, e.g. Bombing Leader, Gunnery Leader, Navigation Leader, etc., and each of these officers had a deputy. Individual aircraft crews gradually grew in number, from four (pilot, 2nd pilot acting as navigator, wireless operator/air gunner and gunner) in the Hampden to seven (pilot, navigator, bomb aimer, flight engineer, wireless operator and two gunners) in the Halifax and Lancaster.

In the early days the navigator was also the bomb aimer and the pilot looked after his own engine handling on twin-engined aircraft, flight engineers were deemed necessary after the introduction of the four-engined heavies and the decision to eliminate second pilots. Once in the aircraft the pilot was in command of the crew, regardless of his rank and whether any of his crew outranked him on the ground. Group Captains flying as supernumerary crew were subordinate to the aircraft's pilot. Even if he was only a humble sergeant, the 'skipper' was the boss.

Having said that Halifaxes and Lancasters carried a crew of seven, it must also be said that two Groups carried an eighth crew member. No.8 Group (PFF) aircraft usually carried two navigators, one of whom specialised in H2S, while No.100 (Bomber Support) Group carried an additional 'special' wireless operator in its aircraft, as did 101 Squadron when pioneering the Airborne Cigar (ABC) jamming system.

Individual crew member responsibilities were as follows:

Pilot

Control of the aircraft at all times and overall command of the crew.

Navigator

Planning and execution of conformity to the prescribed flight plan. Maintenance of a navigation log to ensure knowledge of aircraft's position at any given time. (Regularly checked after the raid by the Squadron Navigation Leader.)

Bomb Aimer

Primary function was to drop the bomb load on the right target with as much accuracy as possible. Secondary function was to help the navigator by map -reading and route pinpointing. The front gun turret of Stirlings, early Halifaxes and Lancasters or single Vickers Gas Operated nose gun where fitted to later Halifaxes were for the Bomb Aimer's use should the need arise. On some Halifax B.Mk.III aircraft it was also the Bomb Aimer's responsibility to assist the pilot with engine and flap management during take-off and landing, a function that was carried out by the Flight Engineer on most other aircraft.

Flight Engineer

Keep close watch on engine temperature and oil pressure gauges during take-off and landing and during the flight. Maintain a balanced aircraft by emptying fuel tanks in the correct sequence and maintain a flight engineer's log of fuel consumption tank by tank for each engine. In some crews, the engineer took up position in the astrodome while over the target to add another pair of eyes to the constant search for nightfighters.

Wireless Operator

Except in cases of emergency, or when crew was acting as a wind finder, strict radio silence was maintained throughout an operation[3]. The W/Op had, however, to maintain a listening watch for information from Group that was broadcast regularly and had to be logged. Woe betide the Wireless Operator who missed an 'Operation cancelled - Group recalled' message. In addition, it was usually the W/Op who had to throw out the Window throughout the raid. He was ably helped (in Halifax aircraft at least) by the Flight Engineer who had to hump all the bundles of Window from the rest position in the rear fuselage, to the W/Op at the flare chute. Early in the war, Wireless Operators were dual tradesmen - W/Op/Air Gunners - but it was eventually decided that it was quicker (and more economical) to train straight W/Ops and straight Gunners.

Air Gunner

At the beginning of the war most, if not all, gunners were ground crew tradesmen who flew as gunners for the love of flying and/or the princely sum of sixpence per day flying pay (approx. 2.5 pence). They were for the most part, untrained in gunnery and, even when flying on ops, were not excused from their primary ground duty tasks. The Air Ministry eventually realised that this was totally unfair and in May 1940 'air gunner' was made an aircrew category in its own right and thenceforth carried the minimum rank of sergeant. All gunners undertook the same training and, usually, it was not until forming a crew at OTU (Operational Training Unit) that the gunners in a crew decided who was having the rear and who the mid- upper turrets. Once this decision had been taken however, it was very rarely

[3] From about late 1942 certain experienced crews were selected to work out the strength and direction of winds encountered en-route and radio this information back to their Group HQ. These were then averaged out and re-broadcast to all crews for them to use, thus - hopefully - keeping all aircraft heading in the same direction and aiding the cohesion of the bomber stream.

changed. Rear gunners assisted their navigator to establish wind strength and direction by taking a sight on a flare dropped from the aircraft for that purpose.

The crewing up of the various aircrew categories may appear, to modern minds, to be strange and totally disorganised. But the system worked. Shortly after their arrival at OTU, approximately twenty of each aircrew category would be assembled in an empty hangar and told to form themselves into crews.

By the end of the day Bomber Command had twenty new crews, most of whom were quite happy with their new liaisons. Where an OTU was equipped with Wellingtons or Whitleys the crew formation was at this stage short of a flight engineer. These members did not join the team until they reached the Heavy Conversion Unit (HCU), where the missing crewmen were usually detailed to a particular crew, although it was not unknown for transfers to be arranged.

So the men of Bomber Command went to war - superbly backed up by their ground crews who worked long hard hours on the aircraft dispersals, in the open, in all weathers. No account of the activities of Bomber Command should ever omit a reference, however brief, to the care and devotion to duty of the men - and women - who kept their feet firmly on 'terra-firma' (The more firmer - the less terror!). Riggers, Fitters, 'instrument-bashers', Leckies, Armourers and the Photographers serviced, re-armed and refuelled their charges, preparing them for the next op. They 'loaned' their aircraft to the aircrew for each operation and waited on tenterhooks for its return, usually in need of some airframe repairs besides its regular servicing requirements.

The gloom surrounding the ground crew whose aircraft failed to return may have been short lived but was nevertheless deep. They grew to know their usual aircrew more closely than most other station personnel (with the possible exception of a few WAAFs) and there was a mutual trust and respect between both air and ground crew.

Away from the aircraft dispersals there were the non-aircraft tradesmen; the safety equipment section who looked after parachutes and dinghies; the MT drivers who took the crews out to their aircraft; the cooks who fed and watered everyone on the station; the storemen, who supplied all equipment replacements (when the mood took them), even the RAF Police and the

Station Warrant Officers (Bless them all), all had their parts to play in the Strategic Bomber Offensive. Without them there would have been no means of delivering retribution to the enemy.

Never let it be forgotten that the absence of a world war for more than seventy years is due primarily to the threat of what bomber men are now capable of, based upon their past achievements and their new weapons.

Long may this threat continue to preserve us from another and probably final global conflict.

Chapter Two

The Pendulum and the Scythe

A brief combined history of the RAFs Night Bomber[4] offensive against
Germany in the 2nd World War, the German response and the accompanying
technological advances of both sides.

Introduction

The Royal Air Force's strategic bomber offensive during the Second World
War was not only the first proper strategic use of air power. It was also the
first battle in history to depend on advancing technology as well as the tactics
employed and the bravery and courage of its participants. Technological
innovations, by whichever side first introduced them, endowed great
advantage on the initiator's aircrew. They gave a significant saving of lives
for the attackers or an improved interception rate for the defenders, resulting
in a sometimes desperate search for an effective countermeasure by the other
side.

Advancing technology did not only affect casualty and success rates. There
was usually a far-reaching effect on the tactics used by both sides,
occasionally with results unforeseen by the initiator. The introduction of
Window, for example, which was finally given the all clear for the first
Hamburg raid on the night of 24/25th July 1943 after permission had been
withheld by the Air Council for many months on the grounds of there being
no effective countermeasure available in the UK. Only when the AI radar
carried by RAF nightfighters was sufficiently advanced to be relatively
unaffected by Window, was permission given for Bomber Command to
employ this radar deceiving measure. The possibility of the enemy using this

---

[4] *Authors Note: There is no disrespect intended by the omission from this manuscript of the
great deeds of 2 Group. It formed part of the AEAF during the early part of the war, left
Bomber Command in early 1943, carried out most of their attacks by day, and took no part
in the electronic countermeasures battle. It is felt, therefore, its contribution, admirably
covered elsewhere, should be sacrificed to the requirements of brevity.*

countermeasure against us had been foreseen and suitable preventive measures taken.

What wasn't foreseen, but what actually took place, was that because Window was so effective in screening the night bombers from German radar, the Luftwaffe had to totally reorganise its tactics and in so doing created a much more efficient interception and killing machine. It was not until 1945, when the Luftwaffe high command started throwing nightfighters into the day battles and when the allied campaigns against oil and transport really started to bite, that fuel and aircrew shortages resulted in a rapid decrease in the level of interception efficiency.

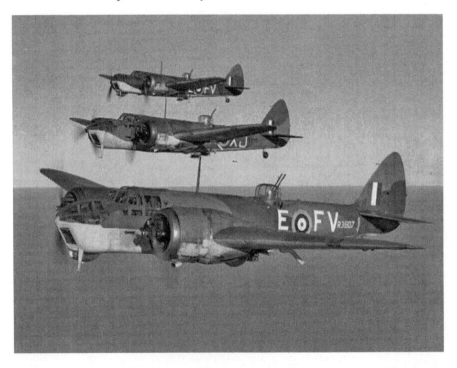

The Bristol Blenheim, considered state of the art at the outbreak of the war, was soon superceded by larger bombers. The Blenheim was also adapted to act as a fighter.

In The Beginning

To review the pendulum effect of technological advances and tactical improvements in true context, we must start in 1939. Shortly after the inevitable declaration of war, on Sunday 3rd September, President Roosevelt appealed to all belligerents to refrain from engaging in unrestricted bombing. Because the French Government felt that they were in the vanguard of the front line and most likely to suffer more from German retaliation, they too requested that the RAF refrain from bombing German land targets. The British Government acceded to both requests - to the satisfaction of the Air Council but to the chagrin of the aircrews. Bomber Command was, therefore, restricted to bombing naval targets, but only then if it could be guaranteed that no bombs would fall on German soil.

These preliminary attacks were carried out in daylight by Blenheims, Hampdens and Wellingtons and continued until December 1939 despite heavy losses - losses that were initially blamed on poor formation keeping by the crews. It was almost three months before the Air Staff could be made to understand that unescorted raids by lightly armed and relatively slow bomber aircraft in the face of determined fighter opposition was tantamount to murder of highly trained crews.

Night activity at this point of the war was restricted to leaflet raids, the first of which was undertaken on the night of 3rd September by ten 4 Group Whitleys of 51 and 58 Squadrons, based at Linton-on-Ouse. These continued until May 1940 but it was not until the night of 19/20 March 1940 that Bomber Command was finally allowed to drop bombs at night. The target was Hornum seaplane base on the island of Sylt and bombing was permitted in reprisal against a German attack on Scapa Flow and only because there were no civilians living nearby.

From September 1939 until May 1940, the night defence of Germany was almost entirely the responsibility of the Luftwaffe Flak arm. The small, ineffective nightfighter force at this time comprised a handful of single engine Messerschmitt Bf109s. These were flown by experienced, specialised pilots who relied on searchlights in the target area to illuminate the RAF bombers for them. These tactics were known as *Helle Nachtjagd* (illuminated night fighting) but, because of the low number of nightfighters and the fact that the few bombers that were operating did so singly, there were few interceptions and even fewer 'kills' during this period. Most RAF losses at this time were caused by bad weather, faulty navigation, mechanical failure or any combination of the same.

The 'Phoney War' finished abruptly on 10th May 1940, when the Germans unleashed their Blitzkrieg against France, Belgium and Holland, during which the Luftwaffe bombed every town and village that stood in the path of the Wehrmacht. This, coupled with the merciless machine-gunning of fleeing refugees, led to many innocent civilian deaths.

Also on that day, Winston Churchill became Great Britain's new Prime Minister and placed immediate pressure on his Government to remove the restrictions on Bomber Command's activities. The following night, 37 aircraft (Hampdens & Whitleys) were allowed to attack Monchengladbach, a town deemed to be very important in supplying the German invasion of the Low Countries. Permission for a full all-out attack however, was still withheld until the Germans bombed Rotterdam on the 14 May. The next night the RAF was finally allowed to initiate the Air Plans, which had been drawn up pre-war, when 99 aircraft (Hampdens, Wellingtons and Whitleys) attacked 16 different oil refinery and railway targets in the Ruhr.

This opening of the Bomber offensive against industrial targets in the German homeland soon showed that Flak defences supported by a handful of fighters were insufficient to protect the targets. This led to a comparatively large scale expansion and reorganisation of the Luftwaffe nightfighter arm, The 1st Nachtjagd division was established on 19th July 1940 under the command of Oberst Josef Kammhuber, who promptly set about building up an integrated night defence system. On 20th July, Oberleutnant Werner Streib of NJG 1 (Nachtjagdgeschwader 1) scored the first victory for *Helle Nachtjagd*.

It is perhaps worth mentioning at this point, Bomber Command's little recognised, but not unimportant, part in the Battle of Britain. During the night of Saturday 24th August 1940, the Luftwaffe inadvertently dropped bombs within the boundary of the City of London, the pilot responsible actually faced disciplinary action for dropping these bombs without Reichsmarschall Goering's permission. Churchill did not hesitate. The following morning the War Cabinet sanctioned the RAF's first raid on the German capital and, that night, approximately fifty bombers were despatched to Berlin. Cloud cover prevented much damage, but the audacity of the attack so incensed Hitler that he ordered the Luftwaffe to discontinue bombing Fighter Command airfields, which by then were in desperate straits and to direct their future attacks on London. This allowed Dowding and Park to recover from the perilous situation in which the defence of Great Britain had been placed and gave the fighter airfields the respite they needed to get back into top shape again. The above is pointed out to set the historical record straight and to recognise the assistance rendered by Bomber Command to Fighter Command in its direst hour of need. It is not in any way intended to denigrate the tremendous efforts of the fighter crews and their ground personnel who suffered and gave so much for so many.

From December 1939 until the end of 1941, bomber sorties were carried out on an almost individual aircraft basis. While perhaps 100 to 150 aircraft might be detailed to bomb a specific target, details such as routes to and from the target and time and height over the target were left very much up to individual aircraft captains and were largely dependent on conditions over the target. In 5 Group, even take-off times were left to aircraft captains although in 4 Group these were more regulated. The number of aircraft required would be notified to Group HQ by HQ Bomber Command. Group HQ would then tell the squadrons how many aircraft they were to operate and the Squadron Commander would then detail specific crews to carry out the operation.

At this stage of the bomber offensive there was no target marking and crews relied upon their individual skills to find their way to and from the target area and to identify the actual target. Moonlit nights offered the best chance of navigation and bombing accuracy, but navigation on dark, cloudy nights was only 'achieved' by ded (short for deduced) reckoning (DR). Thus map reading and bombing errors in the region of 100 miles were not uncommon. This is not to say that there was no accurate bombing.

On the contrary, experienced crews could and did achieve outstanding accuracy on occasions, going over the target at very low level if necessary. During autumn 1941, bombing times became more regulated, but even so there was still no zero hour, no target marking and a raid could last for up to four or five hours.

The month of August 1940 saw the award of Bomber Command's first Victoria Cross. Although Garland and Gray earned their VCs on 12th May 1940, they were serving in the AASF and consequently were not part of Bomber Command. This went to Flight Lieutenant Roderick Alastair Brook

(Babe) Learoyd (a distant relative of Bert Harris) of 49 Squadron, based at Scampton in 5 Group. On the night of 12/13th August 1940 eleven Hampdens from 49 and 83 Squadrons were ordered to make a low level attack on the Dortmund-Ems Canal at its crossing with the River Ems, near Munster. Flight Lieutenant Learoyd had, with other men of 5 Group, made previous attacks on the canal and some damage had been done and repaired. The previous attacks had, however, alerted the Germans to the vulnerability of this bottleneck in their inland waterway system and the anti-aircraft defences had been increased accordingly. On this August night, two Hampdens were shot down while a further eight dropped their bombs successfully despite being damaged by Flak. Flight Lieutenant Learoyd was the last to attack and, regardless of the reception given to previous aircraft, he attacked from a height of only 150 feet. His Hampden (Serial No. P4403) was hit repeatedly, with large pieces of main plane being torn away, while Learoyd himself was almost blinded by the glare of many close-range searchlights. Having completed his attack, Learoyd brought his badly damaged aircraft back to base where, because his flaps were unserviceable and his undercarriage position indicator refused to function, he circled Scampton until dawn before making a successful landing. Babe Learoyd's VC was gazetted on the 20th August.

The Command's second VC followed very shortly and again went to a Scampton airman, Sergeant John Hannah, a wireless operator/air gunner on 83 Sqn. Hannah's pilot, Pilot Officer Connor was one of 155 captains briefed to carry out bomber ops on the night of 15th/16th September 1940. Some aircraft were sent to German targets but the bulk of the force was despatched to the Channel ports to bomb barge concentrations.

Pilot Officer Connor's target was Antwerp docks and, because he couldn't get the right line for a good attack, he aborted his first run and went round again, despite the intense Flak that was now hosing up at his Hampden (Serial No. P1355, OL-W). While on his second approach the aircraft was hit in the wings several times, shaking it badly. Connor had just released his bombs when the aircraft received a direct hit in the still open bomb bay, starting a serious fire that soon enveloped the wireless operator's and rear gunner's part of the fuselage. The rear gunner baled out, but Hannah, despite being aware of the grave risk of petrol from holed wing tanks adding to his problems, promptly set about extinguishing the fire. Grabbing two fire extinguishers, the 18 year old wireless operator fought the flames for ten minutes amid exploding ammunition drums, finally beating out the remaining flames with his log book. The fire had been so intense that the aluminium floor of Hannah's wireless position had been melted away, leaving only the fuselage cross members for him to stand on. But despite serious burns to his face and eyes, Hannah succeeded in putting out the fire. He then crawled forward and, discovering that the navigator had also baled out, he passed the latter's log and maps to Connor so that they could find their way back to base. For his supreme courage, John Hannah was recommended for the nation's highest honour and his VC was gazetted on 1st October 1940. Pilot Officer Connor received the DFC for his coolness in keeping control of the aircraft while Hannah was fighting the flames and then flying the badly damaged Hampden back to base.

As Hannah said afterwards, *'While I was doing my best with the fire, he (Pilot Officer Connor) was sitting up aloft as cool as a cucumber taking no notice of the flames, or the sound of bullets which were either whizzing close to his head or hitting the armour plating just behind it ... if it hadn't been for him I should not have got back."*

Luckily, Hannah's burns healed without leaving any scars to show the extent of his ordeal. Both Learoyd and Hannah survived the war.

During this period there developed a pattern of operations that was restricted by tactical necessity. If our bombers were to be able to return home under the cover of darkness, then far distant targets, such as Berlin, could only be attacked during the long winter nights. During the shorter, summer nights the Ruhr, Cologne, North Sea ports and the like were the farthest they dare go. This pattern continued for most of the war, enabling the Luftwaffe defences to deploy their nightfighters and Flak accordingly.

The Nachtjagd

By the beginning of 1941, the German nightfighter arm was fully manned, organised and equipped for action. The Kammhuber Line of defences (named, by the RAF, after its organiser Josef Kammhuber - now a General) stretched from Hamburg in the north to Luttich in the south. Its searchlight belt was soon to extend as far as Flensburg in the north and Reims in the south. This defensive belt was initially divided into eighteen sections, each thirty miles wide and twenty miles deep. Each section contained a searchlight detachment, three nightfighters and a communications company in conjunction with one Freya and two Würzburg radars. The longer range

The Pendulum and the Scythe

Freya radar detected the incoming bombers, allowing one Würzburg radar (later Würzburg-Riese - 'Giant Würzburg') to lock onto and track an individual bomber while the second Würzburg was used to track the nightfighter. Information from both Würzburgs was fed into Divisional HQ where it was evaluated and converted, via red (the bomber) and blue (fighter) light beams, into the respective aircraft's relative positions on a frosted glass map. This map was originally in the form of a table, but later became a large frosted glass screen that formed a wall in the 'Battle Opera House' as the Division HQ control rooms came to be called.

From the relative position of the bomber and fighter as displayed on the map, the Luftwaffe duty controller (Jagerleitoffizier) directed the nightfighter throughout its interception.

By mid-1941, Germany possessed 250 twin-engined night-fighters (Bf110, Ju88 and Do217) backed by an increasingly effective ground control and reporting organisation. From the middle of 1941 the above system gradually became integrated with the Luftwaffe's Flak arm to create a 'Combined Nightfighting' (Kombinierte Nachtjagd) system around the cities of Bremen, Cologne, Darmstadt/Mannheim, Duisburg, Frankfurt, Hamburg, Kiel and Munich. Flak was normally limited to a height of 4,000 metres, although this could be raised at the discretion of the Division Kommandeur. For various reasons this resulted in quite a few nightfighters being shot down by their own Flak and, not surprisingly, this system was abandoned by the end of the year.

During 1940 the Luftwaffe had also introduced long-range night fighting (Fernnachtjagd). A special, long range fighter Gruppe, I./NJG 2, was equipped with Dornier Do17 and Junkers Ju88 aircraft and commanded by Hauptmann Heyse. Its aim was to loiter in British airspace and attack RAF bombers as they climbed for height after take-off for a raid, or to attack them as they returned to their bases, when they were at their most vulnerable, with tired crews prematurely relaxing after the exertions of the past hours.

These tactics were fairly successful and could have become a source of major trouble had not Hitler ordered their abandonment on 12th October 1941, much to the amazement and disgust of the Luftwaffe hierarchy. The reason behind Hitler's seemingly incredible decision was that only enemy bombers shot down over the Fatherland would show the German people the success and efficiency of their night defences. Despite Hitler's ban, some crews continued to operate occasionally over the UK, but it was not until 1945 that these tactics were officially reintroduced. Fortunately for Bomber Command, this was too late to have any serious effect.

A new system of nightfighting, known as Himmelbett (Four Poster Bed) was introduced during the summer of 1941. A complete network of circular Himmelbett zones was set up next to the searchlight belt and principles began to be evolved that would, with modifications, remain in use until Germany's defeat. These controlled zones were laid out in depth, the radius of each circular zone being equal to the range of its Würzburg radar equipment. (The early Würzburg had a range of 21 miles while the later Würzburg-Riese, which was introduced early in 1942, had a range of 36 to 42 miles).

As previously noted, each Himmelbett station was equipped with one Freya long range radar (90 miles range), one Würzburg to track the bomber, another to track the fighter and the translucent map table (called a Seeburg Table). The operational procedure was as before, with the fighter, already airborne and circling a radio beacon within the controlled area being tracked by the 'Blue' Würzburg. A second fighter, crewed and ready for immediate take off, was held in readiness on the ground, while a third fighter was held in reserve. The fighter control officers, seeing the red (bomber) and blue (fighter) lights on the Seeburg table would then direct their nightfighter until the pilot radioed that he had the bomber in view.

The major disadvantage of this system was that only one fighter could be controlled in a zone at any one time. This was soon recognised by the RAF and led to the introduction of the `bomber stream' tactic, an event that probably first took place against the Billancourt Renault Factory, just west of Paris, on the night of the 3/4th March 1942. General Kammhuber responded by building additional ground stations both in front of and behind his main defensive line, to further extend its depth and thus increase the number of bombers that could be engaged during any one 'stream' attack. The Himmelbett tactics continued to take a steady toll of RAF bombers right up to 24th July 1943. (See The Battle of Hamburg later in this chapter).

Disillusionment and Re-inforcement

Amidst increasing concern over bombing inaccuracy among all those 'in the know' in the UK, the government ordered, in mid-1941, an in-depth bombing survey to be carried out with all speed. This led to the publication in August 1941 of the Butt Report (named after its writer Mr. David M. Butt, a civil servant). This showed, after careful consideration of over 4,000 aiming point photographs, that only one in three crews were managing to bomb within five miles of the aiming point. This was at a time when cameras were not universally fitted to bombers and those that were, tended to be used by the best and most experienced crews.

July 1941 saw the award of the first of three VCs that ultimately went to 3 Group. On the night of 7th/8th July, 49 Wellingtons were detailed to attack Munster. The second pilot of one of them, a 75 (New Zealand) Squadron Wellington IC, Serial No.L7818, was Sergeant James Allen Ward of the RNZAF. The crew had accomplished their mission and were returning over the Zuider Zee when their aircraft was attacked from below by a Messerschmitt Bf110 that secured hits on the Wellington.

Despite being wounded in the foot, the rear gunner managed to get in a good burst of fire at their attacker and the nightfighter was last seen going down, apparently out of control.

Fire then broke out near the starboard engine and, fed by fuel from a damaged pipe, rapidly gained a serious hold, threatening to spread to the entire starboard wing. Through a hole that they cut in the fuselage side, the crew attempted to put this fire out with extinguishers and the coffee from their thermos flasks, but without success. As the aircraft captain warned the crew to get ready to bale out, Sergeant Ward volunteered to attempt to smother the fire with an engine cover that was being used as a cushion. With the navigator's help, Ward tied the rope from the dinghy around his waist, climbed out through the astro-hatch and put on his parachute. Although the aircraft was flying at a reduced speed, the air flow over the wing was still rapid and made the intended action very difficult indeed.

By breaking the fabric to make hand and foot holds as necessary (Barnes Wallis' fabric covered geodetic construction was Ward's greatest ally at this point), Ward made his way down onto and along the wing to the engine and succeeded in smothering the flames. He then returned to the astro-hatch and

50

was helped back into the aircraft by the navigator. The aircraft returned safely to its base at Feltwell despite a sudden flare-up of petrol that had collected by the starboard engine, just as the Wellington was on final approach. Sergeant Ward's Victoria Cross was gazetted on 5th August 1941. James Allen Ward was killed in action on the night of 17th/18th September 1941 while attacking Karlsruhe, only nine weeks after winning this award. His aircraft was the only one, of 38 despatched that night, which failed to return.

On the night of 7/8th November 1941, RAF Bomber Command managed to despatch 392 aircraft to Berlin, Cologne and Mannheim - a new record effort for the Command. Unfortunately bad weather and the increasing efficiency of the Luftwaffe nightfighter arm resulted in the loss of 21 out of 169 aircraft (12.4%) on the Berlin raid and 7 out of 55 aircraft (12.7%) on the Mannheim raid. Only the Cologne raid was loss free, bringing the total loss rate for the night down to 9.4%, the worst since the war began. On November 13th, Air Marshal Sir Richard Peirse, C-in-C of Bomber Command received a directive stressing the necessity to conserve his forces and to avoid heavy losses such as those inflicted earlier in the month. This resulted in the cessation of all long-distance raids and marked the nadir of Bomber Command's fortunes throughout the war.

However, all that had gone before was not wasted. Invaluable experience had been gained in the first two years of war. New tactics were beginning to be developed and, with larger, more efficient aircraft in the pipeline, the outlook for 1942 onwards was considerably brighter. Peirse had performed a great service for the Command by husbanding his resources and pushing for expansion and new aircraft throughout his tenure. On 22nd February 1942, the appointment of Air Officer Commander-in-Chief of Bomber Command was taken over by Air Marshal Sir Arthur Harris (later Air Chief Marshal)

In his post-war dispatch, Air Chief Marshal Sir Arthur Harris, `Bomber Harris' to the public but always 'Butch' to his bomber crews, divided the period of his tenure at Bomber Command into three main parts and it seems politic therefore, to use those same phases in this narrative. The preliminary phase covered the period of February 1942 to February 1943.

When Harris took over Bomber Command he had only 469 aircraft at his disposal, nearly 100 fewer than in November 1941 when Peirse had been directed to conserve his forces. There were two main reasons for the lack of numbers. Firstly, because of the phasing out of the pre-war Blenheims, Hampdens and Whitleys while, as yet, the production of the new larger four-engined types was only proceeding slowly. Secondly, Peirse had been forced to give up many trained, operational squadrons to both Coastal Command and the Middle East.

The decrease in numbers was however, partially offset by a steady improvement in the quality of both aircraft and equipment, an increase in the bomb-loads that could be carried and the development of new operational techniques. The first of the new navigational aids, which the Butt Report had shown were so necessary, also entered service at this point. GEE was a device that received pulse signals from three transmitting stations in the UK, thus allowing the navigator to plot his aircraft's position to within about 1,000 yards. At a height of 20,000 feet, these signals could be received up to 400 miles from the UK based transmitters. Harris and his boffins soon realised that it would only be a matter of time before the enemy discovered the transmissions and, by piecing together the hardware from a crashed bomber, would find a way to jam them.

Another result of the Butt Report was the Air Staff's acceptance that precision bombing by night was generally outside the capability of Bomber Command at this time. Harris arrived at HQ Bomber Command, near High Wycombe, to find an eight-day old directive waiting for him that laid down a new bombing policy.

"The primary objective of your operations should now be focussed on the morale of the enemy civilian population and, in particular, of the industrial workers."[5]

The Air Staff had decided that if individual factories could not be bombed accurately then the whole town in which they were situated should be attacked. This was the order that led to area bombing. In the light of what took place immediately post-war, it is worth stressing that the instruction regarding area bombing was given to Bomber Command over a week before Harris took command of the Bomber force.

---

[5] *The Strategic Air Offensive Against Germany 1939-45: Vol. IV, Page 144*

The Pendulum and the Scythe

The first operational use of GEE, over Essen on the night of 8/9th March 1942, was disappointing. The City's ever-present industrial haze, coupled with lack of experience in using the new device and the enemy's clever use of decoy fires, all combined to ensure that only about 10% of crews managed to hit Krupps, the prime target. GEE had proved to be of great value as a navigational aid but was not, as had been hoped, accurate enough for blind bombing. Success, however, was not long in coming. Harris had a theory (learned from the results of the German Blitz on London and other UK cities) that it was easier to 'burn down' a town or city than to 'blow it up' and it was therefore his intention to increase the percentage of incendiaries in all bomb loads. His search for a suitable target to help prove this theory led to his selection of the Baltic port of Lubeck. This was a medieval town with narrow streets and half-timbered buildings that, in Harris' own words, 'was built more like a firelighter than a human habitation.'

On the night of 28th March Harris despatched 191 bombers, carrying more than 400 tons of bombs, two-thirds of which were incendiaries. Almost 200 acres of the old town were destroyed, including approximately 60 per cent of all buildings. The following month a similar exercise was carried out on Rostock, which was attacked four times between 23rd and 26th April destroying 130 acres, again about 60 per cent of all buildings. Although both Lubeck and Rostock were beyond the range of GEE, the new system gave the crews a good start on the approach flight. Each of these towns was positioned near the mouth of a river and this, in good weather, made their identification relatively easy.

Between the Lubeck and Rostock raids, Butch Harris launched yet another experimental raid. On 17th April 1942, twelve Lancasters, six from each of Nos.44 and 97 Squadron (respectively the first and second squadrons to be equipped with the Lancaster) were despatched in daylight to attack the MAN Diesel engine factory at Augsburg[6]. The six aircraft from 44 Sqn and the raid, were led by Squadron Leader John Dering Nettleton. The raid demanded a round trip of over 1,000 miles, with the outward leg being carried out in daylight. A fighter-escorted raid by Boston aircraft of 2 Group was intended to draw off German day fighter opposition to give Nettleton's force a clear run across France, but all it actually achieved was to stir up a

---

[6] *This attack is well covered in Jack Currie's book "The Augsburg Raid".*

hornet's nest. The six Lancasters of 44 Sqn ran straight into this opposition. Approximately thirty enemy fighters set about Nettleton's formation, shooting down four of them before lack of fuel caused the Luftwaffe pilots to call off the chase and head for their base.

Despite orders to return to the UK in the event of serious trouble, Nettleton elected to carry on to the target, accompanied by his other remaining aircraft. Both aircraft successfully bombed the MAN factory but the other aircraft was shot down by *Flak*. Of the six aircraft from 44 Sqn, only Nettleton's aircraft (Lancaster B.Mk 1, Serial No.R5508, KM-B) returned to the UK, not making its 5 Group base at Waddington.

Squadron Leader Nettleton's VC was announced in the London Gazette of 28th April 1942. It is also worth noting that Nettleton's CO at this time was Wing Commander R.A.B. Learoyd, so, for a brief period, 44 Squadron had the unique distinction of having two VCs serving in the same unit. Squadron Leader Nettleton was killed in action on the night of 12th/13th July 1943, when his aircraft was one of twenty that failed to return from a 374 aircraft raid on Aachen.

Operation Millennium - Portent of the Future

At this point of the war, the major problem being faced by Harris was the continuing drain of trained squadrons to Coastal Command (to help in the fight against the U-boats) and to the Middle East Air Force (to help pulverise Rommel). Harris believed that the only way to stop this dispersal of his force was to prove what could be achieved with a large force. By means of begging and borrowing - he stopped just short of stealing – he managed to amass over 1,000 bomber aircraft and on the night of 30/31 May 1942, 1047 aircraft were sent to Cologne. This raid saw the full implementation of the 'bomber stream' tactic with an additional refinement, the whole force would bomb in the space of only ninety minutes, compared with up to four or five hours for the raids of 1940-41.

The Cologne raid also saw the only Manchester VC of the war. No.5 Group despatched 46 Manchesters from 49, 50, 61, 83 and 106 Squadrons on this attack. One of the 50 Sqn aircraft, L7301, VN-D Dog' was being flown on this occasion by Flying Officer Leslie Manser (D-Dog was not his usual aircraft, having been transferred from 106 Sqn only two weeks before the raid). This was Manser's 14th operation and he soon found that D-Dog's poor performance (it had only been included in the attack because of the maximum effort) coupled with its full bomb load would not allow him to coax her above 7,000 feet, where he, his crew and aircraft would be an ideal target for the Flak. Despite this, Manser elected to continue with the sortie. Over Cologne, Manser held the Manchester rock-steady while his bomb aimer released the load. Just as the bombs left the aircraft, the controls were wrenched from Manser's hands as a direct Flak hit struck the underside of the fuselage. The aircraft immediately went into a dive, coming under a hail of accurate fire from 20mm quick firing ground cannons as it did so. At about 800 feet, Manser regained control but behind him the aircraft was on fire and the rear of the bomb-bay doors had been shot off.

Struggling back up to 2,000 feet, the Manchester wallowed like a drunken duck and then the port Vulture engine burst into flames. The fire spread rapidly, threatening the fuel tanks. Manser had little option but to hope the fire would die out and, incredibly, it did just that. Heading for home it soon became apparent that the Manchester's reputation of being unable to maintain height on one engine was well deserved and that it was obviously not going to get the crew back home. As the crippled aircraft lost height and with its speed only just above stalling, it was obvious that Manser could not control it for much longer. He ordered his crew to bale out. As the last crew member was about to jump, he returned to the cockpit to hand Manser his parachute, but the pilot waved him away and ordered him to jump before it was too late. Seconds later 'D-Dog' ploughed into the ground not far from the Belgian village of Bree. Flying Officer Leslie Manser died in the crash. His navigator, Pilot Officer Richard Barnes was injured but the rest of the crew, second pilot Sergeant Les Baveystock, W/Op Pilot Officer Bob Horsley, second W/Op Sergeant Stan King and gunners Sergeant Alan Mills (front) and Sergeant Ben Naylor all successfully evaded capture and, with the help of the Belgian Resistance, returned to the UK.

From this point on, all attacking aircraft on a raid flew by the same route to and from the target. Each squadron had its specified place and height in the bomber stream and the stream itself was condensed into as short a space of time as possible.

This enabled the bomber stream to smash through the controlled nightfighter lines in no more than four zones (consisting of two zones in width by two zones in depth) assuming all aircraft stayed on track. The result was that the

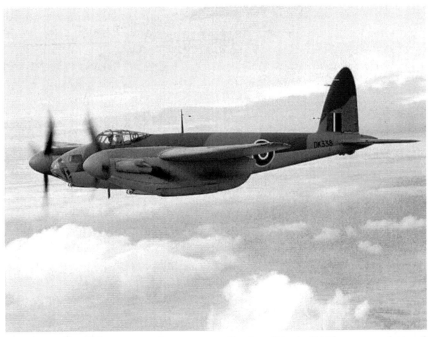

The De Havilland Mosquito was the most versatile aircraft in the RAF's armoury during the war, the various marks acting in the roles of fighter, bomber, reconnaissance and transport aircraft.

single fighter airborne in each zone could only be directed onto one bomber at any given time. Meanwhile, airborne nightfighters in adjacent zones were unproductively patrolling empty airspace. Another reason for condensing the duration of the attack was to swamp the Flak defences and overwhelm the German firefighting services. Thus the fires caused by the incendiary bombs could take hold and spread before the fire teams could start to extinguish them.

Two other portents of disaster for the German nation took place in 1942. Firstly, the USAAF began to join in the bomber offensive, attacking by day and gradually gaining experience in the European theatre of operations. This would eventually lead to round the clock bombing and the total death of the Luftwaffe. The other significant event was the formation of the Pathfinder Force (PFF), due mainly to the strenuous efforts of a staff officer at Air Ministry, Group Captain Sidney.O.Bufton, a pilot with much recent operational experience in 4 Group. Harris was initially against the formation of an elite group of target finders and markers. Nevertheless, when ordered

The Pendulum and the Scythe

The Avro Lancaster became the mainstay of Bomber Command, though not of No. 4 Group.

by the Air Ministry to form the Pathfinders on 11th August 1942, he did so and gave it his full support. Characteristically he gave its command to a very young but highly experienced and efficient officer, Don Bennett, who progressed from Wing Commander to Air Vice-Marshal in the space of one year.

Technological research carried out over the past few years now also began to bear fruit. As already stated, GEE had become operational in March 1942 and, by the end of the year, new technology started to arrive thick and fast. Oboe was the first of the new arrivals. It was a blind bombing device fitted to aircraft, which received transmissions from two ground stations

back in the UK and then re-transmitted the signal back again. The base stations, by timing the gap between their initial transmission and the receipt of the aircraft's signal, could calculate the aircraft's exact position and by means of transmitting yet another signal, tell the aircrew exactly when to release their bombs .

The drawbacks to this system were (i) that the bombing aircraft had to fly straight and level for several minutes, thus making itself highly vulnerable to the enemy defences and (ii) Oboe could only be used by a maximum of 10 bombers in any one hour. Initial Oboe trials were carried out during

The Pendulum and the Scythe

August 1942 by the Wellingtons of 109 Squadron. As the range of Oboe was limited by the curvature of the earth (as with any pre-satellite radio wave transmission) it was soon found that to allow Oboe coverage of the whole Ruhr area, only the new Mosquito bomber had the required altitude. Consequently 109 Squadron became the first operational Mosquito/Oboe Unit and was to become part of 8 Group (PFF). The squadron's first Oboe operation took place over Lutterade, Holland on the night of 20/21st December where the target was a power station. The system soon proved capable of allowing bombs to hit specific factories and one of Germany's major failings in the technology battle was the failure to jam Oboe properly.

The second new arrival, one that was ultimately to be used by nearly all the RAF bomber squadrons, was H2S. Again it was the Pathfinders who received the first sets and 7 Squadron's Stirlings and 35 Squadron's Halifaxes were equipped at the very end of the year, ready for their first operation - to Hamburg – on 30/31st January 1943. H2S was the very first airborne, ground scanning radar set which presented the navigator with an image (at first only a very flickery image) of the ground over which the aircraft was flying. Once reliability problems were ironed out and the crews had more training on and practice with the system, it quickly became invaluable as a navigation aid, replacing ded reckoning and supplementing GEE, which was now being heavily jammed from the eastern half of the North Sea onwards. Eventually, some Pathfinder crews could use H2S for blind bombing with a surprising degree of accuracy, but it was never as accurate as Oboe.

The major disadvantage of H2S, which was only to be discovered much later in 1943, was that because the system emitted radar pulses, it could therefore be monitored and tracked by the enemy.

Two pieces of electronic counter measures equipment also arrived at this point, both designed to counter German radar and radio. The first of these, Mandrel, was initially a UK ground-based device that jammed the radar used for controlling nightfighter interceptions. The second, Tinsel, consisted of a small microphone in one engine nacelle of a bomber, connected to an additional transmitter in the aircraft. The bomber's wireless operator would listen out on his radio for Luftwaffe transmissions and, when he had identified the wave-length and tuned his Tinsel transmitter to match it. He then commenced transmitting the bomber's engine noise in the hope of drowning out the nightfighter controller's instructions. Both of these countermeasures became operational in December 1942 and, while neither caused severe disruption, they were a steady annoyance to the enemy.

On the night of 28/29th November 1942, 228 aircraft were despatched to bomb Turin. Wing Commander G.P.Gibson and Flight Lieutenant W.N.Whamond of 106 Sqn. gave Italy its first taste of 8,000 lbs bombs during this raid. One of the 47 Stirlings taking part in this attack was BF372, OJ-H (Harry), captained by Flight Sergeant Rawdon Hume Middleton, an Australian serving with 149 Squadron based at Lakenheath in No.3 Group. Over Turin, Middleton brought his Stirling down to 2,000 feet so that his bomb aimer could positively identify the target - the Fiat Works. Middleton made three runs across the city, his aircraft being hit many times by light Flak. One shell exploded in the cockpit, seriously injuring both pilots and the wireless operator.

A piece of shrapnel tore into the side of Middleton's face, destroying his right eye and exposing the bone over it. He was rendered briefly unconscious but his co-pilot, Flight Sergeant L.A.Hyder regained control of the aircraft at 500 feet and, when they had regained height to 1,500 feet, the navigator, Royde, released their load on the city below.

Light Flak was still being directed at the Stirling and it was hit repeatedly, the three gunners Mackie (front), Cameron (mid-upper) and Gough (rear) returning fire continuously until the rear turret was put out of action. Flight Sergeant Middleton now regained consciousness and, taking over control of the bomber, cleared the target area and then ordered Hyder back to receive first aid to his head and leg wounds. Hyder returned to the cockpit before his treatment was completed because he knew his captain could see very little and could only speak with great pain and loss of blood.

They set course for base, facing an Alpine crossing and long homeward flight in their damaged aircraft with insufficient fuel and seriously injured crew members. The crew discussed landing in or baling out over northern France but Middleton insisted on trying to get his crew home, despite the knowledge that the time it would take would ensure that his own wounds would probably prove fatal.

Four hours later, flying over the French coast at 6,000 feet, the aircraft was again fired upon and hit by light Flak. Middleton mustered sufficient strength to take evasive action and headed out across the English Channel.

The Pendulum and the Scythe

After crossing the Channel the Stirling only had enough fuel for five minutes flying so the skipper ordered his crew to bale out while he flew the aircraft parallel to the coast. Five of the crew jumped to safety while two remained to help Middleton. The aircraft crashed into the sea shortly afterwards and the bodies of Mackie, the front gunner and Jeffery, flight engineer were recovered the following day. The co-pilot, Flight Sergeant Hyder was awarded the DFM, the other four survivors were also decorated. Middleton's body was eventually washed up on the Kent coast and was buried at Beck Row, Mildenhall, not far from his base. His posthumous VC was gazetted on 15th January 1943.

Bomber Command's resurgence continued in late 1942 with, at long last, an increase in the force of aircraft available for operations. No longer did Harris have to allow his newly formed squadrons to be shunted off to the Middle East or to Coastal Command and the new 'heavies' were really starting to pour out of the factories. 5 Group was now completely equipped with Lancasters, 1 Group became the second to start equipping with this aircraft, while 3 Group had only one squadron of Wellingtons left among its Stirlings.

Three-quarters of 4 Group was now using Halifaxes and most of this aircraft's early problems had, by now, been sorted out – although not completely cured, while the Group's remaining squadrons were still flying the Wellington. Additionally, a completely new group - No.6., which had existed on paper since October 1942 - was getting ready to become operational on 1st January 1943. In this period 4 Group had been collecting all the Canadian squadrons in the command (and forming new squadrons) ready to hand over to No.6 (Canadian) Group's new commander (Air Vice-Marshal G.E.Brooks) in the New Year. The Canadian Government were to meet the full costs of this Group for the rest of the war.

On 8th January 1943, the Pathfinders were promoted to Group status, becoming No.8 Group, continuing under the command of Don Bennett, now promoted to Air Vice-Marshal and their first target indicators were finally being produced ready for their operational debut in mid-January.

The Main Offensive

Ignoring the Thousand-Bomber' raids, the numbers of which were artificially boosted by collecting non-operational aircraft, the average number of aircraft involved in a major raid had been, until the end of 1942, only 250.

From the beginning of 1943 this number was to jump to 450 aircraft, most of which could carry a much larger bomb load than the early war aircraft thus effectively more than doubling the Command's striking power.

In January 1943, Churchill, Roosevelt and the combined Chiefs of Staff met at Casablanca to coordinate the Allied bombing policy, resulting in the Casablanca Directive to both the USAAF and RAF Bomber Command. This directive gave, as a general concept, the overall aim as the, *"...progressive destruction and dislocation of the German military, industrial and economic system and the undermining of the morale of the German people to a point where their capacity for armed resistance is fatally weakened."*[7] Thus making official the policy of bombing cities and towns rather than specific industrial targets contained within them - despite the Government's continued denial in public and evasion of the facts in Parliament. Once again, Harris was instructed to carry out an order in which he had no input.

Just as Harris' 'Preliminary Phase' was drawing to its close and the Command was really ready to start making a serious impact on Germany, there arrived yet another directive that was again to reduce the weight of the attack on Germany. On 14th January 1943, Harris was instructed to attack the U-Boat bases of Lorient, St.Nazaire, Brest and La Pallice - all in France. All these targets had been previously attacked in 1941, since when the German Todt organisation had constructed huge sheltered pens with reinforced concrete roofs that were impervious to any bombs possessed by the Command at this time. Harris pointed out this somewhat major obstacle to the success of the venture but he was ordered to carry it out anyway. The towns of Lorient and St. Nazaire were almost razed to the ground with very little degree of damage being done to the U-Boat pens. The Air Council, finally realising that Harris was right, then cancelled the directive, substituting for it another instructing Harris to attack the U-Boat construction yards in Germany. Even this directive was short lived when Churchill personally urged more attacks on Italian targets. German cities then received their quietest three months of the war.

Harris called the second phase his main offensive. This covered a period of approximately twelve months from the spring of 1943 to that of 1944 and

---

[7] *Official History page 153.*

can be further subdivided into three major campaigns, the battles of the Ruhr, Hamburg and Berlin.

The 'battle' concept was a further extension of Harris' `concentration' theory and was the next logical step after the successful introduction of the bomber stream. The idea was to allow Bomber Command to concentrate their efforts against a particular area, but interspersing the series of raids against that area with additional attacks outside it, thus denying the enemy the opportunity to consolidate their defences in one area.

Thanks to the great skill and drive of its C-in-C, Bomber Command emerged from the winter of 1942/43 increased in strength, technology and bomb lifting capacity, fully prepared to launch a sustained major effort against Germany. In March 1943, Harris gave the order that began the 'Battle of the Ruhr', a battle that was to last for just over four months, during which two-thirds of the 43 major raids carried out were against the Ruhr area. The other third was ranged widely across the rest of Europe.

Despite having the most concentrated Flak and searchlight defences and the most experienced nightfighters in Germany, the Ruhr was the obvious area in which to fight the Command's first major offensive. It was close enough to Harris' UK bases to be within Oboe range and the whole area could be attacked during the shortening spring and summer nights. While the destruction of Berlin was a desirable objective it was at this stage of the war, too difficult a target for the Command, for the converse of the reasons that qualified the Ruhr. The following four months were to be a severe test to both sides and the destruction and casualty figures were about to escalate dramatically.

So the scene was set for the Command's first great battle. An expanding Pathfinder force had its new target indicators and sufficient experience and enough technological support to place them accurately. The Command's new aircraft gave it a larger bomb load per raid than ever before - and was still expanding, while the selected target region was within the range of Oboe. On the night of 5/6th March 1943, Essen received a 40 minute attack by 386 aircraft, the Battle of the Ruhr had commenced. Over the next four and a half months, Bomber Command launched 23,401 sorties, 14,784 of which were aimed at the Ruhr (including Cologne and Aachen).

The Pendulum and the Scythe

This period saw several new 'firsts' achieved. The Essen raid of 3/4th April was the first in which more than 200 Lancasters took part. The attack on Dortmund (23/24th May) was the largest number of aircraft despatched (excluding the semi- contrived 1,000 aircraft raids on Cologne etc.), when the Command detailed 826 aircraft. The 11/12th June raid on Dusseldorf saw the first raid on which more than 200 Halifaxes participated.

Losses were not light and ranged from a low of 2.5% (7 aircraft out of 288 despatched) over Cologne on 8/9th July to a high of 8.0% (12 out of 157) over Bochum on 29/30th March. The average of 4.7% for the whole battle represents a loss of 696 aircraft from a total despatched of 14,784 and is only just below the maximum sustainable loss rate of 5.0%. Aircrew morale however did not appear to suffer, despite these relatively heavy losses; the successful results obtained during the battle seemed to keep the crews' morale high and their courage and perseverance never wavered.

While dealing with aircrew courage, we cannot leave this period of the bomber offensive without mentioning one specific raid. This raid, although positioned in the very middle of the battle, had only a knock-on effect upon it. On the night of 16/17th May 1943, Wing Commander Guy Penrose Gibson led nineteen aircraft from his recently formed 617 Squadron on the now famous Dams raid. This attack has been the subject of several excellent books, starting with Gibson's own and this author cannot attempt to expand on them. Suffice it to say that eight of Gibson's aircraft did not return, a loss rate of 42%, although the participants received many gallantry awards, including a Victoria Cross for Gibson himself.

The Battle of Hamburg and Luftwaffe Reorganisation

Hamburg, in 1943, was not only Europe's largest port but also Germany's second largest city and, long before the Battle of the Ruhr was over, Harris had chosen the target for his next battle. Orders were issued to his Group commanders to start making preparations for a series of heavy raids on this major city of one and three quarter million inhabitants. Although outside the range of Oboe, Hamburg was believed to be a good H2S target because of the wide River Elbe and the city's dock basins. There was also a distinctively shaped coastline only 60 miles away on which the PFF could pinpoint its position en route to the target.

This was to be the first time that the American 8th Air Force would 'join in' an RAF Bomber Command battle, despatching daylight raids to Hamburg on the two days following the RAF's first night raid.

The Battle of Hamburg[8] was also to see the first use of another technological breakthrough. After many months of being denied, Harris finally obtained Air Staff permission to use Window. This was a radar counter measure consisting of strips of tinfoil cut to a specific size, which the aircrew were to unload down the flare chutes of their aircraft at a prescribed rate. The Window would then swamp the enemy radar screens, denying them any precise knowledge of numbers of aircraft, their height or accurate position. Various forms of Window were to be used by the Command's aircraft for the remainder of the war.

The battle opened on the night of 24/25th July 1943, when Harris despatched 791 aircraft to bomb the centre of Hamburg. The Luftwaffe defences were thrown into total confusion by Window and RAF losses amounted to only 1.5% (12 aircraft), a dramatic reduction on the 4.7% average during the previous four months.

USAAF B17's flew 252 sorties to Hamburg during the next two days and the RAF's second attack took place on the night of 27/28th July when Harris despatched 787 aircraft. It was this raid that created the 'firestorm' effect, causing approximately 40,000 German fatalities and encouraging two-thirds of the population to flee the city. Reichsminister Albert Speer was later to remark that had the RAF been able to repeat this sort of attack on five more German cities, then the war would have rapidly become unsupportable by the German nation. Unfortunately, Harris was not to learn how close he had come to realising his ambition of ending the war by bombing alone until after it was all over, nor had he the striking power required to achieve this.

On the following night a further 777 sorties were targeted on Hamburg and on the night of 2/3rd August, 740 aircraft delivered the final raid in this series, although several had to turn back because of atrocious weather.

---

[8] *The author cannot recommend too highly Martin Middlebrook's book "The Battle of Hamburg" for those readers requiring greater detail.*

The Pendulum and the Scythe

The use of Window initially caused tremendous confusion within the German defence but, as pointed out at the beginning of this narrative, it did not take long before the Luftwaffe reorganised their tactics to suit. As an indication of their rapid reaction it is interesting to note Bomber Command's loss rates before and during the series of attacks on Hamburg. Losses during the Battle of the Ruhr, as we have already seen, averaged 4.7%. This dropped to 1.5% (less than one third) with the first use of Window over Hamburg on the night of 24/25th July. Two nights later the loss rate crept up to 2.2% and the next night up to 3.6%. By the fourth Hamburg raid losses had reached 4.1% - almost back to the pre-window period.

As already stated, the initial use of Window swamped all German radar screens, both ground and airborne, with clutter, rendering the Himmelbett system totally useless at one stroke. This led to a sweeping reorganisation of the Luftwaffe nightfighter methods and to the introduction of Wilde Sau (Wild Boar) and Zahme Sau (Tame Boar) tactics. Wilde Sau called for the concentration of single-engined fighters (flown by experienced pilots) over the target area where they could spot and attack bombers illuminated by searchlights. These tactics were the idea of Major Hajo Hermann, a bomber pilot who, during the Battle of Britain, accidentally found his Junkers Ju88 almost at rest on top of a barrage balloon. His flying skill and incredible luck enabled him to disengage his aircraft, regain full control and return to his base in France. Hermann, who had been practicing Wilde Sau tactics on a small scale, found himself rapidly promoted to Gruppenkommandeur of the newly formed Jagdgeschwader 300, equipped with Messerschmitt Bf109 and Focke Wulf Fw190 aircraft and ordered to put his idea into operation.

The radar equipped twin-engined nightfighters could also use Wilde Sau tactics but, to utilise their greater endurance to the full, a system was devised by which Divisional Headquarters scrambled all nightfighters and ordered them to circle the radio beacon nearest to the largest concentrations of Window. When the first nightfighter found the bomber stream the crew would radio back to Headquarters, giving position, height and direction of the stream. This information could then be relayed to all nightfighters who would then chase the stream and attack as many bombers as ammunition, fuel, time and luck would permit. These tactics became known as Zahme Sau and, once the Luftwaffe crews had gained enough experience, were to lead to the running battles that were experienced by the bomber crews from the autumn of 1943 onwards. These included the heaviest losses the

The Pendulum and the Scythe

Luftwaffe ever inflicted upon Bomber Command during the Nuremburg raid of 30/31st March 1944.

Other contributory factors to the Luftwaffe's success from autumn 1943 onwards, were the introduction of new airborne radars. One was Lichtenstein SN-2, replacing the earlier Lichtenstein BC sets and operating on frequencies that were not so badly affected by Window. Two other aids were Naxos, which homed onto H2S transmissions and Flensburg, which homed onto the Monica tail-warning radar that had been fitted to RAF bombers since June 1943.

Another German technological innovation at this time, and one that was to lead to many bombers being shot down without ever seeing their attackers, was Schrage Musik (translated as Jazz Music or Slanting Music). This consisted of two 20mm cannon mounted in the nightfighter's fuselage in an almost vertical position and an additional periscopic gunsight for the pilot to aim them with.

The technique of using Schrage Musik was for the nightfighter pilot to position his aircraft in the blind spot underneath the bomber and to either side of its centre line. The aiming point was the wing, between the engines, where the fuel tanks were situated. Aiming for the fuselage itself was not recommended, especially if the bomber had not yet dropped its bomb load, as the distance at which the nightfighter would open fire (usually no more than 75 yards) was close enough to seriously endanger the attacker. (It is believed that the first use of Schrage Music was during the Peenemunde Raid of 17/18 August 1943).

So the Luftwaffe had, in a few short months, not only developed tactics to circumvent the effects of Window, but had come up with a defence system that actually allowed more of their nightfighters to attack the bomber stream than before the Hamburg raid. The Wilde Sau tactics were only planned to be effective until the new Lichtenstein SN-2 radar sets were operational, but the Zahme Sau tactics were to continue as the Luftwaffe's main method of defence for the rest of the war.

After Hamburg, Butch Harris used the remainder of August 1943 to press his attacks most vigorously to maximise the advantage of Window and the good weather of that month. Most of the effort of the first two weeks however, was directed at Italy rather than Germany. Bomber Command had been ordered to do as much as possible to help the Italians make up their minds about leaving the war, an event that took place on 8th September after 1,346 sorties had been flown, spread over eight raids for a loss of only 19 aircraft (1.4%).

On one of these Italian raids, to Turin on the night of 12th/13th August, the second Stirling VC was won, the first also having been awarded for a Turin raid the previous year. On this night, Bomber Command despatched 504 aircraft to Milan and a further 152 to Turin. One of the No.3 Group Stirlings on the latter target was EF452, HA-O-'Oboe' of 218 Squadron, Downham Market, skippered by 21-year old Flight Sergeant Arthur Louis (Art) Aaron DFM, on his 21st operation.

As Aaron's aircraft approached the target it was hit by a devastating burst of fire from a nervous rear gunner in another Stirling ahead of them. (Aaron's VC citation, dated 5th November 1943, incorrectly states that this fire came from an enemy nightfighter). The windscreen on the port side was shattered, the throttle control pedestal was wrecked - with both inboard engine throttles shot away. The front and rear turrets were put out of action and the elevator controls were damaged, causing the Stirling to become unstable and difficult to control. The Canadian navigator, Bill Brennan, was killed outright with a single bullet through his heart and several other crewmembers were slightly wounded.

One bullet had struck Art Aaron in the face, breaking his jaw and tearing away part of his face. Another bullet pierced his chest and lung and his right arm was almost severed. As he fell forwards over the control column, the aircraft dived several thousand feet, control being finally regained at only 3,000 feet by the flight engineer, Malcolm Mitchem. Amazingly Aaron was still conscious and, by means of signs, made Mitchen understand that he, the flight engineer, had control of the aircraft. It was only as the aircraft turned into the moon that Mitchem could observe Aaron's injuries and see why he had handed over control. He called the crew on the intercom and bomb aimer Allan Larden and wireless operator Jimmy Guy half carried and half dragged Aaron out of the pilot's seat and back into the fuselage where they made him as comfortable as possible with a parachute under his head. Between them they got a shell dressing on Aaron's face and did what they could with his arm, then Larden went back to the cockpit to help Mitchem fly the badly damaged Stirling. Mitchem later administered morphia.

It was clear that they would need more height to clear the Alps, so Larden went down into the nose and jettisoned the bomb load, not realising that a 4,000-pounder had hung up in the racks. The aircraft would still not gain enough height to get across the mountains and after many twists and turns Larden and Mitchem realised that, even if they did find a way through, they wouldn't have enough fuel to get them home.

Larden went back to the navigator's table and discussed their position with Jimmy Guy. A study of the coastline that they were now flying over gave them a pin-point over La Spezia on the North Italian coast. Somehow they had flown through the Maritime Alps. Larden suggested that they make for Sicily, but none of the maps on board covered that area and no-one had any idea which of the Sicilian airfields were still in enemy hands. Guy then suggested flying due South while he tried to get a radio bearing from Bone in North Africa. This was agreed and a course of one-eight-zero was set.

About one hour later, Guy eventually got a response from Bone and, with a minor course alteration to one-eight-four degrees, they continued on their way, reaching Bone some three hours later. The crew decided that as they couldn't get Aaron out by parachute they would attempt to land the aircraft. By this time the drowsiness of Art Aaron's morphia injection was wearing off and, learning what his crew were planning to do, he insisted on being helped back to the cockpit to land the aircraft.

Four times Aaron attempted to land his damaged aircraft but overshot and went round again. At the fifth attempt Larden and Mitchem, now seriously concerned at their remaining fuel state, had to physically restrain Aaron from attempting to overshoot again and Larden managed to belly-land the Stirling without further injury to the crew. Flight Sergeant Aaron died nine hours later. Had he been content to remain at rest in the rear fuselage, without the exertion of trying to land his aircraft, he may well have recovered from his wounds. Arthur Louis Aaron's VC was Gazetted on the 5th November 1943, Allan Larden was awarded the Conspicuous Gallantry Medal and Malcolm Mitchem and Jimmy Guy both received the Distinguished Flying Medal.

Peenemunde

The third week in August provided a break in operations because of the full moon. However, one important raid was carried out on the night of 17/18th August when Harris despatched 596 aircraft to blast the V-1 and V-2 research base at Peenemunde with the dire warning of 'get it right or you'll go back again and again until you do!' Fortunately for the crews it was a case of 'right first time' and sufficient damage was done on this one night, although losses, because of the bright moonlight, were quite high at 40 aircraft (6.7%). Most of these occurred in the last wave of bombers, which were caught by the nightfighters arriving back from Berlin, where a Mosquito diversion had misled the controllers into sending them initially. It is estimated that this raid put the V-2 programme back by at least six months thus protecting the Overlord build up in the UK from horrendous casualties that could well have postponed the D-Day landings indefinitely.

The Peenemunde raid[9] is important for two reasons: it was the first time that the Master Bomber technique, pioneered by Gibson on the Dams Raid, was used on a major raid. The appointed Master Bomber (also known as the Master of Ceremonies), Group Captain John H.Searby of 83 Sqn. PFF controlled both Pathfinders and main force bombers throughout the attack, switching aiming points twice to cover all three target areas successfully.

The second point of note is that this night saw the Luftwaffe's first use of Schrage Musik obliquely mounted cannons. These cannons were fitted to two Messerschmitt Bf110 aircraft and these two aircraft alone accounted for six of the bombers lost on the raid.

Late August 1943 saw a 'false' start to the Battle of Berlin when Harris launched three raids in twelve nights to the German capital. Disappointing initial results and the impending introduction of an improved version of HAS for the Pathfinders, convinced the C-in-C to wait a while.

There followed a period of almost two months during which Harris sent his aircraft out to 'middle distance' targets (i.e. those outside Oboe range, but not as distant as Berlin) on as many nights as the weather allowed. Hannover in particular was attacked three times, but with little success and many casualties.

This period also saw the reliable and much loved Wellington withdrawn from service with the main force. It had flown on operations from the first day of the war, four years earlier and was the last of the early war aircraft to

---

[9] For full details of this raid see The Peenemunde Raid by Martin Middlebrook.

be retired. Although a few Bomber Command squadrons would retain their Wellingtons well into 1944, they only flew limited operations, primarily minelaying.

The Command's strength remained fairly static during this phase of the war. The rapid expansion that had taken place in early 1943 was now ending and the gradual process of modernisation was beginning to make headway. 3 and 6 Groups began to re-equip some of their Stirling and Halifax squadrons with the Mk II Lancaster (Hercules Engines), although production of this version was fairly limited. The Merlin-engined Lancasters were by now pouring off the production lines but the need to replace battle casualties and worn-out aircraft of existing squadrons limited the numbers available to convert squadrons equipped with other, older types.

It was at this point of the offensive that the Command began to introduce diversionary raids, also known as 'spoofs', to try to confuse the German controllers as to the actual target. 8 Group Mosquitoes had been carrying out this type of operation on a relatively small scale for some months, dropping flares and target indicators over cities other than the Command's main target. Unfortunately, due to the small numbers of Mosquitoes available, the German controllers were rarely misled. It was therefore deemed necessary to increase the number of aircraft involved in 'spoofs' to gain the required results, although this increase would be contrary to the 'concentration' principle. The coming year was to see a minor dilution of the main bombing effort because of it.

Additionally, several new devices were introduced at this time. October and November saw the operational trials, first by Mosquito and then by Lancaster, of a promising new blind-bombing aid called *G-H*. The trials were successful but the equipment was withdrawn until enough sets were available to equip a large force. October also saw the radio countermeasures boffins come up with two new pieces of equipment: *Corona* and *Airborne Cigar (ABC)*. *Corona* was the code name for the ground based monitoring and broadcasting stations in the UK from which fluent German-speaking RAF and WAAF personnel would imitate the enemy nightfighter controllers and transmit false instructions to the nightfighters. *Airborne Cigar (ABC)* was a jamming device fitted into the Lancasters of 101 Squadron (1 Group), with which an additional, German-speaking crew member would identify the enemy wavelengths and attempt to jam them. The ABC aircraft also carried bomb-loads and formed an integral part of the bomber stream. The

ABC concept was later expanded to Group strength with the formation of 100 Group.

The night of 3rd/4th November 1943 saw the Command send 589 aircraft to Dusseldorf and a further 62 to Cologne. One aircraft on the Dusseldorf raid was Lancaster B.Mk.III, LM360, QR-O of 61 Squadron, based at Syerston in No.5 Group. Its pilot, a 21-year old Scot, Flight Lieutenant Bill Reid, was on his tenth operational sortie.

Shortly after crossing the Dutch coast at 21,000 feet, Reid's aircraft was attacked from astern by a Messerschmitt Bf110. Due to a fault in his heating system, tail gunner Emerson was too frozen to react instantly and the nightfighter got in an accurate burst before Emerson could return fire. Then he and Baldwin in the mid-upper turret drove the fighter off. Reid's windscreen was smashed; the elevator trim tabs badly damaged, making the aircraft difficult to control and both gun turrets were damaged, leaving Emerson in the rear with only one of his four guns working and having to traverse the turret manually. Baldwin's turret was also hit, leaving him with only one serviceable gun.

Bill Reid himself received wounds to the head, shoulders and hands, while his face and hands were peppered with Perspex fragments from the shattered windscreen. As he momentarily slumped forward over the controls, the aircraft started to dive, but they lost only 2,000 feet before the Australian voice of navigator Alan Jeffries urged Reid to pull back on the control column and regain control. Checking that his crew were all OK, Reid said nothing about his wounds and continued on to the target, steering slightly south of east.

A short time later, both gunners simultaneously warned 'Fw190 on the port beam' but they had both only seen it at the last moment. The Wilde Sau fighter raked the Lancaster with cannon shells before Reid's gunners, with damaged turrets and only one gun each, got in a single burst apiece. The FW190 had caught them broadside. Reid, again wounded by shell fragments all over his body, again lost control and the Lancaster plunged earthward. Welsh flight engineer Norris, despite being badly wounded in the arm, grabbed the control column and helped Reid recover control. Les Rolton, the 19-year old bomb aimer, who had been thrown forward in the nose, looked round to see Reid and Norris struggling with the controls. He forgot his own wounds and hurried to help.

The Pendulum and the Scythe

Alan Jeffries, the navigator was killed in this attack and Mann, the wireless operator, received severe wounds from which he later died. Damage to the aircraft this time included more damage to both gun turrets, total loss of the intercom, hydraulic and oxygen systems, one elevator had been shot away and both compasses were wrecked.

Eventually Reid, Norris and Rolton succeeded in regaining control of the aircraft and, despite his additional wounds, Reid again set course for Dusseldorf, this time steering by reference to the Pole Star. Reaching the target, he held the aircraft steady while Les Rolton dropped the bomb load right in the centre of the target area, taking a perfect aiming point photograph immediately afterwards. Again steering by the Pole Star, Reid set course for home, although now extremely weak from loss of blood and lack of oxygen since the emergency oxygen had now run out. Several times Reid passed out and each time Norris held control as best he could, sometimes with Rolton's help, until Reid recovered again.

Crossing the Dutch coast, the Flak had a go at them but, fortunately, they escaped unscathed. Half way across the North Sea, all four engines suddenly cut out together .Norris, the flight engineer, quickly realised that, with everything else happening and probably due to lack of oxygen, he had forgotten to switch the petrol cocks over. He corrected this and all four engines restarted and the aircraft flew on.

Reaching the English coast, Norris drew Reid's attention to their perilously low fuel state and, although Reid used the emergency air system to lower the undercarriage, one of the undercarriage legs collapsed on landing at the first airfield they came to. Reid had fought his badly damaged aircraft back to the USAAF base of Shipham in Norfolk. For his determination throughout this operation, Flight Lieutenant William Reid was awarded the Victoria Cross. (When he recovered from his wounds, Bill Reid, accompanied by Les Rolton, joined 617 Squadron. He was shot down on 31st July 1944 in Lancaster ME557 on an attack against the V-1 storage site near Rheims. His was the only Lancaster lost out of 104 despatched, but Reid survived as a PoW until the end of the war).

Harris had been campaigning for some time to allow RAF nightfighters to operate over enemy occupied territory. With the very small numbers of German bombers now raiding the UK, he believed that our nightfighters were under utilised. If he could cause the German nightfighter pilots to have to keep looking over their shoulders, the distraction should help to reduce his Command's loss rates. June 1943 had seen the successful trials of Serrate, an electronic device that homed onto the transmissions emitted by the German airborne Lichtenstein radars. It was not until the Berlin raid on the night of 16/17th December 1943, however, that the first Beaufighter and Mosquito Serrate equipped aircraft actually accompanied the bomber stream.

Berlin

The Battle of Berlin[10] proper commenced on the night of the 18/19th November 1943 with the despatch of 440 Lancasters and 4 Mosquitoes. It was to continue for almost four and a half months, during which loss rates varied between 2% (on that first raid) to 8.9% on the night of the 'high winds', 24/25th March 1944.

The second raid of the Berlin series, on 22/23rd November saw Harris send off 469 Lancasters, 234 Halifaxes, 11 Mosquitoes and 50 Stirlings. Losses for the night totalled 26, but the Stirling loss rate, at 10%, finally proved how vulnerable these older aircraft were. They were then left out of all main force raids on Germany and 3 Group were relegated to secondary duties while they continued a very slow conversion to Lancasters.

Once again, an unexpected knock-on effect occurred. With the relegation of the Stirling, the Halifax Mks II and V of 4 and 6 Groups began to receive higher casualties because of their poor performance in relation to the Lancaster. During the eleven-week period from early December 1943 to mid-February 1944 these losses averaged 9.8% of Halifax Mks II and V despatched. Some 4 and 6 Group squadron losses were actually in the region of 15 to 24%. Indeed, on one raid alone during this period, to Leipzig on the night of 19/20th February 1944, the Halifaxes suffered a loss rate of more than 16%. After Leipzig, 'Butch' Harris believed he could no longer expect his Halifax crews to continue facing such odds and a further ten squadrons vanished from his front line strength, although a few Halifax Mk IIs continued to fly with one Pathfinder squadron (35 Sqn).

___

[10] *For a fully detailed account of the Battle of Berlin see Martin Middlebrook's "The Berlin Raids".*

The Pendulum and the Scythe

The failure of the Stirlings and Mk II and V Halifaxes cost Harris almost one third of his total strength (approximately 250 aircraft) and about 20% of his bomb carrying capability. It was a serious reduction at a time of very high effort, which was only partly offset by a steady increase in numbers of new Lancasters and the new Halifax Mk III.

As Bomber Command was losing strength, the Luftwaffe nightfighters, the Zahme Sau fighters in particular, were actually increasing in numbers, with over 400 such fighters in action before the Battle of Berlin was over. This period was to be the high point of the Luftwaffe nightfighters' war. As stated earlier, the Nachtjagd force had been expanding throughout 1942 and 1943. Before the use of Window, the experienced and successful crews (Experten) tended, quite naturally, to get first bite of the cherry in their respective boxes and the junior and newer crews were usually kept in reserve, with very little opportunity to win their spurs against the Terrorfliegers'. (The German propaganda-inspired name for Allied bomber crewmen).

The night of 24/25th July 1943 changed all that. Window unshackled the junior crews earth bonds and gave them as good a chance as the Experten to intercept Harris' bombers. In fact many new crews did not feel the impact of Window as much as their more experienced comrades, because they had so little experience of pre-Window night fighting. By the end of November 1943, the nightfighter crews had yet another bonus. Lichtenstein C-1 radar, which could penetrate Window, had been fitted to nearly all Zahme Sau aircraft, giving all crews the same chance of success. While not all of them became Experten, many developed an aptitude for this kind of warfare and steadily built up their scores.

By now, the German listening service could, by detecting test radio and H2S transmissions from bomber airfields during the day, advise the Luftwaffe defenders of a probable raid that night. They were unable to predict the target, but could tell the approximate number of bombers likely to be involved. With the long range Freya radar on full alert, the impending bomber stream (or rather its Window cloud) would be picked up over the North Sea. Nightfighters would then be scrambled and ordered to circle the most appropriate radio beacons to await the bombers arrival. Special reconnaissance units, flying Junkers Ju88's, would be sent off to try to find the bomber stream as soon as possible. Their role was not to attack but to observe and advise their control of the stream's position, height and direction so that the fighters could be vectored, by means of a running commentary, into the stream at the earliest opportunity.

Harris and his staff followed every German development and attempted to find a successful countermeasure. The old Halifaxes and Stirlings, which had been pulled out of the main stream raids, were sent on mine laying operations in fairly large numbers. They dropped masses of Window in an attempt to simulate a major raid approaching across the North Sea, only turning off to their 'garden' just before reaching the enemy coast. Similarly, the training groups sometimes flew a large exercise over the sea, again dropping Window in an attempt to deceive the defenders into thinking they were the main force. Meanwhile, the actual bomber force was sent by increasingly indirect routes with frequent course changes. The bomber stream was made even more compact so that in the end, 800 bombers could pass over the target in less than twenty minutes (compared to 1,000 in 90 minutes over Cologne - itself an incredible feat of timing in 1942). Also at about this time, Harris was forced to use some of his front line aircraft for diversionary raids on one or more other targets, while the Main Force was making its major attack of the night. This was sometimes carried out by Mosquitoes only, but increasingly, Lancasters and Halifax III's had also to be used. By the end of the main phase of the Battle of Berlin, Harris was having to employ up to 20% of his attacking force on diversionary spoofs.

British radio countermeasures were also increased, with their main objective being to jam the German running commentary. A new group, 100 (Bomber Support) Group, was formed on 8th November 1943 and to it were posted the radio countermeasures squadrons. Several Serrate and intruder Mosquito squadrons were also transferred from Fighter Command so that 'Butch' Harris could have greater control over all his countermeasures activities.

The main offensive against Berlin comprised fourteen major raids, employing 7,397 sorties, from the night of 18/19th November until that of 30/31st January 1944. The collective damage caused, while not the overwhelming success that Harris sought, was actually higher than Bomber Command believed at the time. Many entries in the diaries of both Speer and Goebbels have since confirmed this, but the cost in aircraft and crews was high and increased as the battle proceeded. The loss rate began at 2.0% on 18/19th November, going as high as 8.7% on 2/3rd December and averaging out at 5.2% (386 aircraft) for the main offensive.

Halifax B. Mk.II of 51 Sqn. The aircraft sports the glazed nose fairing.

Halifax B. Mk.I of 10 Sqn.

The Pendulum and the Scythe

There has, in the past, been some talk of a widespread drop in aircrew morale during the Battle of Berlin and there were undoubtedly some units to which this may have applied. But overall, what the Command had to endure during this phase of the strategic offensive was more a decrease in levels of efficiency. This was mainly caused by adverse weather, longer hours in the air and hence tiredness, also a steady drop in experienced crews as losses mounted. All these factors applied to the Pathfinders as well as the main force - the 'Grim Reaper and his scythe' held 8 Group in no more respect than he did the others.

Before moving on from the Battle of Berlin (extended) period, it is worth noting some specific events, which occurred during it. The Berlin raid of 16/17th December was the first on which the main force was accompanied by Serrate Beaufighters and Mosquitoes. The Berlin raid of 15/16 February 1944 was the largest 'non-1000' force despatched to date, with 891 aircraft taking part. It was also the first time that more than 500 Lancasters and over 300 Halifaxes were despatched.

The 24/25th February attack on Schweinfurt (734 aircraft) saw a notable change in tactics. For the first time, Harris and his planners split the force into two halves, one of 392 aircraft and the other of 342, both of which attacked the same target but with a two-hour gap between attacks. The second wave lost only 11 aircraft, against 22 in the first wave, due to many enemy nightfighters having landed to rearm, refuel and rest after chasing the earlier raid.

The last major Berlin raid, on the night of 24/25th March, met with extremely adverse weather conditions, which had not been forecast. An extremely strong wind from the north carried the bombers south of track on every stage of the flight. Not surprisingly, the usual system of selected crews establishing actual wind velocities and vectors and radioing this information back to Group HQ, who averaged and re-broadcast to all aircraft, also broke down. (This system was evolved to help all aircraft steer the same course and thus aid bomber stream cohesion). The system broke down because none of the selected navigators could believe the wind speed they were calculating.

They reduced their calculated wind level to that which they believed to be credible, (of course not all navigators made the same judgement of what was credible). Similarly the Group HQs could not believe the wide variety of ultra-high wind speeds they were receiving and also reduced the reported figures even further.

The winds drove many aircraft over the Ruhr area and flak took a heavy toll. It is believed that of the 72 aircraft lost (8.9%), 50 were lost to flak, while most of the remainder were claimed by nightfighters. Berlin claimed only 14 bombers brought down over the target.

Although not part of the Battle of Berlin, the Nuremberg[11] raid of 30th/31st March 1944, tends to appear as the last raid of the 'Beriin' period. The Nuremberg raid took place during what would normally be the bright moon stand-down period, but the raid was planned on an early weather forecast of high cloud to obscure the moon during the bombers' outward route. (The moon would set before the return journey). The forecast cloud did not materialise but, despite a warning from a meteorological Mosquito, the raid was not cancelled.

Possibly the most controversial feature of this raid was the route chosen, which was much more direct than the Command had been using of late. Both AVM Bennett (8 Group, PFF) and AVM Carr (4 Group) strongly objected to the directness of the planned route, but, without the support of the other Group Commanders, their objections were overruled and the raid stayed as planned.

The Command despatched 795 aircraft (572 Lancasters, 214 Halifaxes and 9 Mosquitoes) on the main Nuremberg attack with an additional 49 Halifaxes minelaying in the Heligoland area and 34 Mosquitoes on additional diversions to Aachen, Cologne and Kassel. Unfortunately the German controller correctly guessed the main raid, ignored all the diversionary forces and assembled his nightfighters over two radio beacons, one either side of the main force route. Because air temperatures were lower than normal at the bombers' usual operating heights on this night, the aircraft were leaving vast contrails in the night sky. This, coupled with the lack of cloud and the bright moonlight, aided the nightfighters' task considerably and the first

---

[11] *Again the author recommends Martin Middlebrook's book "The Nuremberg Raid" for more information on this attack.*

interceptions were made just before the bomber stream reached the Belgian frontier.

A fierce battle developed, lasting for over an hour and leaving 82 RAF Bombers burning on the ground before the stream had left the target area. Fortunately by this time, most of the nightfighters were having to land to rearm and refuel and the running battle abated considerably on the return route. Nevertheless the command lost a total of 95 aircraft (64 Lancasters and 31 Halifaxes), 11.9% of those despatched, the biggest 'chop' night ever and, as was to be discovered later, the penultimate big fling of the Luftwaffe nightfighter force.

This night raid saw the award of the only 4 Group VC, which was also the only Halifax VC of the war. It was awarded posthumously to Pilot Officer C.J.Barton of 578 Squadron, based at Bum just outside Selby. Despite losing an engine and three key members of his crew when his aircraft was attacked by fighters en-route to the target, he pressed on to bomb Nuremberg and brought his damaged aircraft back to England, without his bomb aimer, navigator or wireless operator. Unexpected winds took Barton's Halifax (LK-E: LK797) steadily up the North Sea and the English coast was finally reached near Sunderland. Running out of fuel, Barton had to make an emergency landing, managing to avoid all but the last house of a row of miners' houses and his aircraft crashed in Ryhope Colliery. Barton remained alive for about half an hour, regaining consciousness only briefly - when his one concern was the safety of his remaining crewmen. He died having been informed that they were all safe with but minor injuries. (See Chapter 3).

Army Support

For the next four and a half months, most of the Command's efforts were to be in support of the preparations for and execution of Overlord, with only occasional excursions into Germany. 'Butch' Harris expressed grave misgivings over completely stopping the raids on Germany for this lengthy period. He felt that his bombers' absence over the enemy heartland would give them a much needed opportunity to repair their factories and replenish their depleted war stocks. Fortunately, Bomber Command had, by this time, destroyed so much of Germany's war production capability that even Albert Speer - the Third Reich's super-organiser - could make little headway on the road to recovery.

The Pendulum and the Scythe

The official date for the transfer of Bomber Command to the control of Eisenhower and Tedder was 14th April 1944, but Harris had, by then, already started to hit the new list of targets. As early as the night of 2/3rd March the Command had attacked an aircraft factory fifteen miles outside Paris and French targets continued to be attacked throughout the month.

After a brief rest following the Nuremburg raid, Harris resumed his attacks in and around the invasion area. Despite his misgivings, he was pleasantly surprised to learn that the accuracy of his crews had so improved that worries over heavy French civilian casualties proved to be needless. Targets during this period included railways, military camps, ammunition depots and armament factories in France and Belgium. As much bomb tonnage was being dropped outside the invasion area as within it, to deceive the German defenders. On nights when Bomber Command was not required to attack pre-invasion targets, Harris despatched aircraft to German targets, but only when conditions were favourable. Now was not the time to take chances with valuable crews and aircraft.

It was during this period that the Master Bomber system really came into its own, with the Master Bomber keeping very tight control of the main force, ensuring both accuracy of bombing and minimal civilian casualties. Also, with Harris' force now being sufficiently large, he was often able to attack three or four targets in one night. The night of 20/21st April was just one such case. Cologne was attacked by 379 aircraft, 269 more went to La Chapelle (a railway target that was used as the first major test of 5 Group's new 'offset' marking technique led by Wing Commander Leonard Cheshire of 617 Sqn.), 196 aircraft raided railway yards at Ottignies and 175 aircraft bombed more railway yards at Lens. These four attacks, together with various RCM, Serrate, Intruder and minelaying sorties brought the total effort for this one night to 1,155 sorties, a new record for the command - and with a loss rate of only 1.3% (15 aircraft). During this phase of the offensive, 5 Group started to become established as a semi-independent force, as would 3 Group later in the war. This was the beginning of the development that Harris had envisaged when he opposed the formation of the Pathfinder Force back in 1942.

Despite a general belief to the contrary, Harris did send his aircraft to attack the ball bearing factories at Schweinfurt. On the night of 26/27th April 1944, the Command despatched 226 bombers from 1 and 5 Groups to this 'panacea' target. One 5 Group aircraft was Lancaster B.Mk.I. serial no. ME669 ZN-O from 106 Squadron based at Metheringham. The aircraft captain was Canadian Fred (Miff) Mifflin and he and his crew, with one exception, were on their 30th operation and looking forward to a spot of leave before transferring to the Pathfinders The exception was the flight engineer, Sergeant Norman Cyril (Jacko) Jackson, who had managed to get one op ahead of the rest of his crew.

Shortly after dropping their bomb load and while flying at 20,000 feet, the Lancaster was attacked by an FW190 nightfighter. A fire started near a fuel tank on the upper surface of the starboard wing, just inboard of the inner engine. Jacko immediately pressed the extinguisher button on his flight engineer's panel and the fire subsided considerably. A few moments later however, the fire was as strong as ever. Stuffing a fire extinguisher into his battledress top, Jackson donned his parachute and then pulled the ripcord, allowing the 'chute to spill out into the aircraft. Assisted by the bomb aimer Maurice Toft and navigator Frank Higgins who were to hold onto Jackson's parachute rigging lines and pay them out to him as required, Jacko proceeded to climb out of the astro hatch, just aft of the cockpit, onto the wing to put out the fire.

Unlike James Ward, who had done the same thing in a Wellington in July 1941, Jackson could not kick foot and hand holds in the aircraft fabric. The Lancaster was all metal so Jackson could only use whatever holds there were already on the aircraft. He held tightly to the rim of the hatch until his feet were firmly on the wing and then threw himself forward making a grab for a small air intake in the leading edge of the wing. He made it and then proceeded to fight the fire with his extinguisher. Just as he was winning and the flames were almost doused, Jackson felt the aircraft bank to port. He hung on grimly wondering what the hell was happening. Then he heard cannon fire and knew - the nightfighter had found them again. Seconds after hearing the cannon fire he felt stabs of pain in his back and legs and the next moment the airflow snatched the fire extinguisher from his hands. Within seconds the fire was burning as fiercely as ever and he felt his grip on the air intake loosening. Jackson was flung from the wing and was being dragged along only a few yards behind the rear turret. Toft and Higgins were frantically feeding his parachute out into the night air before the fire caught it and so that they themselves could abandon the aircraft before it blew up.

Thanks to the assistance of his fellow crew members, Jackson's damaged parachute was at last released from the aircraft and he was able to make a safe, if somewhat faster than normal descent. The only additional injuries received on landing being one broken and one severely sprained ankle. For Jacko 'the war was over' and he spent ten months in a German Hospital.

Of the rest of the crew, Toft and Higgins, together with wireless operator 'Sandy' Sandelands and mid-upper gunner 'Smudger' Smith successfully baled out but pilot Fred Mifflin and rear gunner Hugh Johnson were killed. The story of Jackson's gallantry did not come out until after the war so his Victoria Cross was not gazetted until 26th October 1945.

From 14th April 1944, when French and Belgian targets became the norm, it was decided by the air staff that attacks on these targets would only count as one third of an operation towards a full tour. But the Mailly-le-camp raid of the 3/4th May reversed this decision. Harris despatched 346 Lancasters and 14 Mosquitoes of 1 and 5 Groups plus two 8 Group (P.F.F.) Mosquitoes to attack a German military camp situated close to the French village of Mailly. Unfortunately the attack did not go as planned and while the target marking was accurate and on time, the main force controller could not transmit the order to bomb because his VHF radio (which was slighty off station) was being drowned out by an American Forces broadcast. Eventually, the Deputy Controller realised something was wrong and passed the Marker Leader's instruction to bomb on to the Main Force

In the meantime however, German nightfighters arrived in the target area and 42 Lancasters (11.6% of the force) were lost. This was the Luftwaffe's last well-known triumph over Bomber Command, but it did not stop approximately 1,500 tons of bombs decimating the German military. From this date, bomber losses began to drop quite sigmificantly.*

This is not to say that losses ceased after the Mailly-le-Camp raid. Average losses did start to drop quite dramatically, but there were still occasions when the Luftwaffe managed to inflict serious damage. The following raids were particularly expensive in lost aircraft and crews with casualty rates of more than 5%:

21/22.6.1944	361 despatched	46 lost	12.7%.
28/29.6.1944	230 despatched	20 lost	8.7%
7/8.7.1944	634 despatched	34 lost	5.3%
28/29.7.1944	1,126 despatched	61 lost	5.4%
12/13.8.1944	329 despatched	27 lost	7.1%
Same date[12]	297 despatched	20 lost	6.7%.
11/12.9.1944	226 despatched	12 lost	5.3%
23.12.1944	30 despatched	6 lost	20%
12.1.1945	33 despatched	4 lost	12.1%

The 23rd December raid on Cologne/Gremburg was the occasion on which Squadron Leader Palmer won his Victoria Cross.

On 5th June, the night before D-Day, Bomber Command flew 1,211 sorties, the greatest total of the war so far. Gun emplacements, radar stations, ammunition dumps, oil storage depots and E-Boat bases were attacked, in fact anything that would hinder the German's rapid reaction to the D-Day landings. Besides this, 617 and 218 Squadrons, under the command of Leonard Cheshire, carried out the now famous 'large convoy simulation' by dropping dense, accurate clouds of Window that they slowly advanced across the channel.

Just after D-Day, while invasion support sorties were still the main task of Bomber Command, 'Butch' Harris sent 671 aircraft to attack communications targets, mainly railways, on the night of 12/13th June 1944. Targets were situated at Amiens/St.Roch, Amiens/Longueau, Arras, Caen, Cambrai and Poitiers. The aircraft came from Nos.4, 5, 6 and 8 Groups (303 aircraft of Nos.1, 3 and 8 Group were attacking Gelsenkirchen this same night) and Pilot Officer Andrew Charles Mynarski was the mid-upper gunner in one of 6 Group's Lancasters on the Cambrai raid. The aircraft

---

[12] *Losses from other raids brought the overall percentage down to 4. 2%.*

concerned, a Mark X Serial No.KB726 VR-A was from 419 (Moose) Squadron, Royal Canadian Air Force, based at Middleton-St. George.

During this sortie, the aircraft was attacked by a nightfighter that knocked out both port engines, setting fire to the port wing and the fuselage between the mid-upper and rear turrets. The flames soon became very fierce and the skipper ordered the crew to abandon the aircraft. Pilot Officer Mynarski left his turret and went towards the rear escape hatch. As he did so, he saw that the rear gunner was trapped in his turret - the loss of the port engines had caused a failure of the hydraulic system and in his haste to escape the gunner had broken the manual winding gear.

Without hesitation Mynarski fought his way through the flames to the rear turret to help his crewmate to escape. While doing so, his clothing up to the waist and his parachute were set on fire. All Mynarski's efforts to free the rear gunner were in vain and eventually the rear gunner waved him away telling him to jump himself. Mynarski returned to the escape hatch but, before jumping, turned to his rear gunner and, standing to attention in his flaming clothing, he saluted the man trapped in the rear turret. He then left the aircraft. Mynarski's flaming descent was watched by French civilians on the ground who promptly started a search for the seriously burnt airman.

Eventually they found him, but his burns were so severe that he died in their care shortly afterwards.

Amazingly, Mynarski's rear gunner survived the crash to become a PoW for the rest of the war. Once repatriated, it was his testimony that resulted in Mynarski's VC being the last of the Second World War awards to be gazetted, on 11th October 1946.

Back to Germany - More Power, Greater Accuracy

Once the landing had been successfully made, the army support tasks required only a part of Harris' force. Additional directives were issued, one of the more important of which was a renewal of the offensive against the German synthetic oil industry, in support of the USAAF, which had started bombing these targets in May. Again Harris argued against attacking another 'panacea' target at the instigation of MEW (Ministry of Economic Warfare). With hindsight it is easy to see that on this occasion Harris was wrong, but

The Pendulum and the Scythe

at the time, with MEW's record of unmitigated foul-ups and totally incorrect estimations of the enemy's weak-spots, Harris deserves every sympathy for his then current opinion. Despite the best efforts of the Chief of Air Staff, Sir Charles Portal, Harris could not be made to agree with MEW's conclusions, but he nevertheless devoted much his Command's effort against oil targets. (Actually 13% of the bombs dropped in the last six months of the war, only 1% less than that devoted to attacking Transport targets.)

Seven days after the D-Day landings, on the 13th June 1944, the first V-1 exploded at Swanscombe, near Gravesend, Kent. Bomber Command now acquired a new set of targets, the first attack taking place on the night of 16/17th June when four V-1 sites in the Pas de Calais area were accurately bombed by 405 aircraft with no losses. The campaign against the V-1 would last until late August when advancing Allied troops overran most of the launching sites.

Germany escaped any major raids in June, but the moonless period of July saw five attacks on German cities. The need for extreme accuracy on the French targets, be they V-1 sites or Army Support missions, led to the re-introduction of daylight raids despite misgivings by Harris who well remembered the resulting casualties from the early war daylight missions. All went well however, since the Command operated within the range of the overwhelming Allied fighter cover. Initially, most daylight raids still used the night-bombing techniques involving Pathfinders, Master Bomber and Main Force. In fact the Command just seemed to imagine that they were night bombing - except that the crews could now see what was going on around them! More sophisticated methods of daylight bombing were on their way however, the most important of which were the Oboe-leader and G-H formation methods. Oboe-leader, where two or three aircraft would formate on an Oboe-equipped aircraft and bomb when it did, proved to be the most accurate of these methods. However, G-H was more flexible because there was no limit to the number of aircraft that could be fitted with the G-H system, allowing much larger bombing formations.

This was a very intense period for everyone in Bomber Command, planners, air and ground crew. Aircrew sometimes flew two sorties in twenty-four hours, bombing German troops in front of Allied lines by day, returning to base for a brief rest. Ground crew rearmed, refuelled and repaired the aircraft, and the crews attended another briefing before taking off again to bomb marshalling yards or an oil refinery in Germany at night. The

Command's average weekly sortie rate during this period, at 5,000 plus, actually equalled the total sortie rate for the 9-month period of September 1939 to May 1940!

A daylight attack on the V-1 storage sites at Bois de Cassan and Trossy-St-Maxim on the 4th August 1944 saw the first award of a Victoria Cross to an airman of No.8 Group (PFF). Squadron Leader Ian Willoughby Bazalgette, DFC, was the captain of Lancaster B.Mk.III, Serial No.ND811, F2-T and was taking part in the all 8 Group attack on Trossy-St-Maxim. While approaching the target Bazalgette's aircraft was hit by Flak, which knocked out both starboard engines and set fire to the starboard mainplane and the fuselage. He continued on his course and released his markers and bombs on the target. (Bazalgette's VC citation incorrectly states that he was the master bomber of this attack).

On leaving the target, the Lancaster, now well alight, dived steeply, almost out of control, but Bazalgette managed to regain control of his stricken bomber. As he did, the port inner engine failed and the pilot ordered those members of his crew who could do so to bale out. (The bomb aimer had been badly wounded and the mid-upper gunner had been overcome by fumes). Four crew members abandoned the aircraft and Bazalgette then made a good crash-landing in an attempt to save the remaining members of his crew. Unfortunately the Lancaster exploded shortly after landing and all three airmen perished. Squadron Leader Bazalgette's VC was not promulgated until 17th August 1945, presumably after his four surviving crew members had been repatriated and told their story.

One month and four days later another VC was awarded. This one was not for one specific act of valour but for an extended bomber career of continuous bravery and dedication. The officer concerned had, at the time of his award, just relinquished command of 617 Squadron., had completed four tours of bomber operations, undertaking at least 102 ops and already received three DSOs and a DFC. Wing Commander Geoffrey Leonard Cheshire was informed of his award personally by Butch Harris and it was gazetted on 8th September 1944. As the citation said `Wing Commander Cheshire has a reputation second to none in Bomber Command.'

By mid-September 1944, SHAEF had released Bomber Command back to Air Ministry control. Its future operations would still have to comply with overall Allied planning and it had to remain ready to answer all calls for assistance from the ground forces, a requirement that Harris was ever ready to fulfil. The only remaining question at this point of the war, was how best to use the vast resources that Harris now had at his disposal. There were three schools of thought, the Air Ministry's Oil campaign, Tedder's Communications plan or that which Harris favoured, the continued general attack on German industrial towns and cities. A successful all-out attack on oil targets would remove the Germans' ability to wage any form of mobile war in the air or on the ground. As already proved by the combined RAF/USAAF interdiction sorties in Normandy over the last few months, a successful campaign against railways, road junctions, canals, etc., would also immobilise the German forces. Harris' handful of supporters for the continued attack on German cities could not prevail. On 25th September 1944 both the USAAF and the RAF bomber forces were instructed to attack the petroleum industry (including storage) as a first priority, with rail and waterway transport systems and tank and motor vehicle production as joint second priorities. German cities only rated a late mention for general attack when weather and tactical conditions were unsuitable for attacks on primary objectives.

This directive took the Command into the final phase of the Bombing offensive and, despite Harris' disagreement with the objectives as set down, he proceeded to direct his force with his usual degree of efficiency.

(See Chapter 10 of Harris' Bomber Offensive for full details of his views on 'Panacea Targets'). The Command's strength was now increasing steadily and the number of front line aircraft increased by 50% during 1944, most of which took place in the last six months of the year. Every group saw expansion, the wholly Lancaster equipped 1 and 5 Groups were each able to drop as much bomb tonnage in late 1944 as had the whole of the Command in 1942. The Canadian 6 Group became a mixed Lancaster and Halifax force with almost 300 operational aircraft. The all-Halifax 4 Group received the further improved Mk VI version to add to the Mk III's that had turned the Halifax's reputation around so completely from the under-powered, overloaded earlier Marks. The new aircraft was much faster, more capable and, with its reliable Hercules-engined versions, it could actually out-climb the Lancaster in a time-to-height race. Admittedly the Lancaster had a higher ceiling than the Halifax, but not by much and there were few, if any, Halifax pilots who would swap their Halifax for the 'Woolworth's Bomber' as they called the Lancaster.

The Pendulum and the Scythe

The resurgence of 3 Group was probably the biggest improvement in the regular groups. Having borne the brunt, as already described, of the Command's early war effort with their Wellingtons and then having suffered so grievously with the Stirling. By the end of 1944 the Group would be fully equipped with Lancasters, many of which would also have or be about to have the new G-H blind bombing device fitted. G-H enabled aircraft to bomb accurately in any weather as long as the cloud tops did not reach the Lancaster's operational height (the aircraft formating on the G-H leader needed to see the bomb release signal). The Pathfinders (8 Group) received the improved Mk III H2S and an increase in Mosquitoes for the Light Night Striking Force while 100 Group was steadily increasing in numbers and technical ability to hoodwink the Germans.

With 3 and 5 Groups now operating independently with their own target marking as and when required, the main force - which was still capable of operating up to 1,000 aircraft for a maximum effort - consisted of 1, 4, 6 and 8 Groups.

The Home Straight

So the curtain was raised on the finale of the Bomber Offensive. The Luftwaffe nightfighter force was in decline. Bomber Command's losses were decreasing while its accuracy, bomb lifting capacity and size were increasing beyond anything previously known. By the end of August 1944 daylight raids were resumed as a regular event and several German cities, which had previously defied the Command's best efforts, finally succumbed. Old targets also took another bashing and there was, in fact, a second Battle of the Ruhr. What remained of the German war industry disappeared underground or to distant locations in the east to escape the unwelcome attentions of Bomber Command, but with the great success of the Oil and Communications plans, German logistics became one of Speer's biggest nightmares.

Eventually, as might be expected, Harris ran out of large cities to attack and so moved his attention to smaller, less industrialised towns like Darmstadt and Bremerhaven, while all the time, despatching smaller forces to deal with synthetic oil refineries and Tedder's transportation targets. Variety was certainly the bomber crews 'spice of life' during this final phase of the war. Flying by night or day - and sometimes both – they attacked such diverse targets as enemy gun batteries or strong points of resistance holding up allied troops, V-1 and V-2 launching and storage sites, canals, railways, important road junctions, well-known targets like Essen or Cologne plus some towns in Germany they had never even heard of. The last nine months of the war would see the Command drop approximately 46% of the total war tonnage!

As an example of the Command's sophistication at this time, it is worth taking a closer look at just one raid, against Kiel on the night of Sunday/Monday 23/24th July 1944. This was the first major raid on a German city for two months and Harris despatched 519 Lancasters, 100 Halifaxes and 10 Mosquitoes (total 629) on the main raid, with elaborate deception and Radio Countermeasures operations. These, combined with the unexpected return to a German target, so confused the defences that only four aircraft, all Lancasters, were lost. A loss rate of only 0.6%.

Kiel suffered heavily in this raid, its first since April 1943 and its heaviest RAF raid of the war. As far as the Luftwaffe nightfighter controllers were concerned, the bombing force appeared suddenly from behind a Mandrel radar jamming screen and the German local radio warning system only reported it as a minelaying force. 612 aircraft then bombed the port in a concentrated raid lasting only 25 minutes. All parts of Kiel were hit, but damage was particularly heavy in the port areas and all of the important U-Boat yards and naval facilities were hit. 315 people were killed and 439 injured. The presence of around 500 delayed action bombs and unexploded duds caused severe problems for the rescue and repair services. There was no water for three days, no trains or buses for eight days and no gas for cooking for three weeks.

In addition to the raid on Kiel and as part of the deception plan for this raid, 119 aircraft (100 Halifaxes, 14 Lancasters & 5 Mosquitoes) of 6 and 8 Groups, attacked the oil refinery and storage depot at Donges, by St. Nazaire near the mouth of the River Loire, while 116 aircraft (102 Halifaxes, 2 Lancasters and 12 Mosquitoes) of 4 and 8 Groups bombed the V-1 sites at Les Catelliers and Les Hauts Buissons. Twenty-seven Mosquitoes of the Light Night Striking Force (LNSF) made the long haul to the big city - Berlin - and four Oboe Mosquitoes (of the five dispatched) dropped high explosive bombs on Duren.

Two Stirlings and six Lancasters were gardening in the Brest and Kiel areas respectively, 180 aircraft from training units were on a diversionary sweep over the North Sea while other O.T.U. crews dropped leaflets over France.

The Pendulum and the Scythe

Thirty-nine Fortresses, Halifaxes, Stirlings and Wellingtons of 100 Group were supporting these operations. Thirteen operated the Mandrel screen, eight dropped a new kind of 'window' over Kiel, 13 operated Jostle and two Fortresses were operated ABC (Air-borne Cigar).

These elaborate plans were all designed and carried out to protect the Kiel force from the nightfighters based in Holland, Belgium and France by out flanking them over the North Sea.

As the 6 Group force, heading for Donges, crossed into Brittany at midnight, the Mandrel screen was operating over the North Sea. This was extended northwards to conceal the Kiel force that was flying at only 2,000 feet (to keep below the German radar) and assembling 30 miles north of Texel. From this point the Kiel force climbed to operational height while the Berlin Mosquitoes flew a parallel course nearer to the enemy coast. At this time the Mandrel screen was allowed to 'break down' gradually at its southern end, revealing the OTU diversionary force approaching Flushing. The German controllers, thinking - as they were intended to - that the OTU force was bound for the Ruhr, deployed five Gruppen of nightfighters to meet the threat, while the remainder were sent to oppose the 6 Group force heading for Donges.

Isolated interceptions were made as the Kiel force crossed the enemy coast and Wilde Sau single-engined fighters were seen over the target. No casualties were sustained, however, until the force was homeward bound - and, as previously stated, only four Lancasters were shot down.

December 1944 and early 1945 saw three more acts of selfless bravery that resulted in the award of Victoria Crosses. On the 23rd December, 27 Lancasters and 3 Mosquitoes of 8 Group were detailed to attack the Gremberg railway yards in Cologne. The force was split into three formations, each led by an Oboe-equipped Lancaster with an Oboe Mosquito as reserve leader, but the whole raid went very badly. Two Lancasters of 35 Squadron collided over the French coast, killing all on board. On nearing the target it was found that the forecast cloud cover had cleared. Orders were given for the bombers to break formation and bomb visually as the formations would have been very vulnerable to Cologne's Flak defences on their long, Oboe-controlled run in.

90

Unfortunately the order to abandon the Oboe run was not received by the leading Lancaster, a B.Mk.III, Serial No.PB371, 60-V, a 582 Squadron aircraft based at Little Staughton. This aircraft was piloted by a 109 Squadron pilot on loan to 582, Squadron Leader Robert Anthony Maurice Palmer, DFC who was on his 110th operation. He continued with his Oboe approach, although his aircraft had already been damaged by Flak. At this point, enemy fighters, who were being directed to intercept an American raid, appeared on the scene and, ignoring their orders to seek the USAAF, attacked Palmer's formation.

Squadron Leader Palmer's aircraft continued on its bombing run and dropped its load on target. It then spiralled down in flames, only the rear gunner managing to abandon the aircraft before it crashed. Squadron Leader Palmer's VC, the only Oboe VC of the war was gazetted on the 23rd March 1945, by which time two more VCs had been won.

The first of these was earned on New Year's Day 1945 during an attack on the Dortmund-Ems canal, the second VC to be won over this target. It was awarded to the only wireless operator to be awarded the nation's highest decoration for gallantry (Sgt.John Hannah was a W.Op-A/G). Flight Sergeant George Thompson was the wireless operator in the 9 Squadron crew of New Zealander Flying Officer Harry Denton. Their aircraft, a

Lancaster B.Mk.I, Serial No.PD377, left its 5 Group base of Bardney to join another 101 Lancasters and 2 Mosquitoes, al from 5 Group, to attack a stretch of the canal near Ladbergen, which the Germans had again just repaired. Only 2 Lancasters were lost, one of them being PD377.

Flying Officer Denton's aircraft was hit by two rounds of 88mm Flak shortly after bombing. The first blew a hole five or six feet square in the floor of the fuselage just forward of the mid-upper turret and set fire to the whole rear section of the aircraft. Fractions of a second later, the second shell shattered the nose compartment, setting fire to one engine and blowing large holes in the pilot's canopy.

Thompson, sitting in the wireless seat to the rear of the navigator's position, peered down the fuselage. He saw the mid-upper gunner, Ernie Potts, slumped in his blazing turret with ammunition exploding in all directions and Thompson at once made his way over the gaping hole in the fuselage. With almost superhuman strength and a superb sense of balance, Thompson extracted the unconscious Potts from his turret and carried him a little further down the fuselage. Because the wireless operator's position was the warmest in the aircraft, George Thompson was not wearing gloves, but using his bare hands, he beat out the flames on Pott's clothes. By this time Thompson's trousers had been almost completely burnt off and his legs were burned but, having settled Potts down, he set off through the flames to rescue Haydn Price in the rear turret. Price had already tried to bale out of his turret but, on opening the doors, the flames had burnt off his hair and blistered his ears. He promptly shut the doors and, realising that his parachute was in the flames in the rear fuselage, sat back to await his fate.

A few minutes later, Price was astounded to hear someone knocking on the rear doors of his turret and, on opening them again, saw a charred figure crouched there. 'Come on, Taff, said a voice he recognised as Thompson's, 'you'd better come out of there'.

Standing again among the flames, Thompson half carried and half dragged Price clear of his turret and set him down next to Potts. Again he beat out his fellow crewman's flaming clothes with his bare and by now badly burnt hands. Still Thompson did not think his self-imposed task finished. The Skipper needed to know what had happened in the rear fuselage, so Thompson set off to the front of the aircraft, again crossing the gaping hole in the fuselage floor. This time, however, the task was much more difficult. Thompson's badly charred hands and legs were of little assistance to him, but somehow, by using his elbows, knees and body he made it over the hole and stumbled up to the cockpit.

Appalled at Thompson's condition, navigator Ted Kneebone and flight engineer Hartshorn protected him as best they could from further exposure to the icy wind blowing through the fuselage while Harry Denton struggled to keep the Lancaster airborne long enough to reach allied lines. Denton eventually crash-landed the aircraft in a Dutch field, from where the injured were taken to hospital. Potts quickly lapsed into unconsciousness again and died the next day but Price was well enough to be flown home to a hospital in England ten days later.

Three weeks after Thompson's bravery and despite excellent nursing, he succumbed to pneumonia and died. His posthumous VC was gazetted on the 20th February 1945.

The next VC was the last of the war and the only award to a South African. Captain Edwin Swales DFC was a pilot on 582 Squadron, part of 8 Group and based at Little Staughton, as had been Squadron Leader Palmer. Captain Swales was the designated Master Bomber on a 380 aircraft attack on Pforzheim on the night of 23/24th February 1945. While over the target, his Lancaster B.Mk.III, Serial No. PB538, 6O-M, was twice attacked by an enemy fighter. The first attack knocked out one engine and the rear turret, while the second took out another engine. Despite this damage, Swales continued to circle Pforzheim directing the attack until the end of the raid, which due to his instructions, was extremely accurate and damaging. (The postwar British Bombing Survey team established that over 80% of the town's built-up area was destroyed).

Only then did Swales set course for base, the two shot-up engines seriously reducing his speed. After an hour's flying, the aircraft entered thin-layered cloud but shortly this changed to heavy turbulent conditions. Swales was, by now, over allied territory and, as the turbulence seriously reduced even further his somewhat slender control over the Lancaster, he ordered his crew to bale out. Using all his strength, Captain Swales kept the severely damaged aircraft steady enough for all his crew to escape but, before he himself could escape, the Lancaster plummeted to earth and Swale's body was found still at the controls.

His award was gazetted on 24th April 1945 and the citation read 'He did his duty to the last, giving his life that his comrades might live.'

Dresdenitis

The final phase of the bomber offensive led, unfortunately, to the controversy over the Dresden raid, a raid ordered by politicians who promptly headed for cover when the storm broke, leaving 'Butch' Harris and his 'boys' to take the blame. This resulted in the denigration of all their tremendous efforts and outstanding bravery throughout the course of the war. To this day, we, as a nation, heap annual honour on the airmen who fought in the Battle of Britain but totally ignore the honour more than due to the 125,000 aircrew of Bomber Command.

This was the case for many years, but as this second edition is being revised, it is now the author's great pleasure to be able to say that, on 28th June 2012, Her Majesty Queen Elizabeth II unveiled a superb Memorial in Green Park, London which is dedicated to the 55,573 Airmen of Bomber Command who gave their lives for our freedom.

It is still worth pointing out that Bomber Command lost more airmen in the single raid on Nuremberg on 30th/31st March 1944 than Fighter Command lost in the whole period of the Battle of Britain. While our fighter pilots received a special Battle of Britain clasp to affix to the ribbon of their 1939-45 Campaign Star, the bomber boys received nothing - except a letter of appreciation from Butch. This remained the case until 2013, when the then current Government finally decided to award a 'Bomber Command' Clasp which was also to be affixed to the ribbon of the 1939-45 Star. Unfortunately this far was too late for many of the Veterans who were no longer with us. At least the next of kin could apply for the deceased's Clasp.

Granted, the Air Crew Europe Star was awarded to bomber crews who completed a set number of ops before D-day, but the rest of 'the boys' received only the France & Germany Star and the Victory medal, as given to anyone who served in the armed forces, whether or not they saw action.

In 1985, Lady Harris and Air Vice-Marshal Don Bennett, in conjunction with the Bomber Command Association, issued their own medal which qualifying aircrew could purchase. Thousands of Bomber Command veterans from all over the world paid £18 for their 'Campaign' medal.

It is therefore worth reviewing the facts surrounding the Dresden raid so that we may banish the myths that persist to this day.

From late 1944 the Air Ministry had been considering a series of very heavy attacks on specific German cities. This was with the intention of causing such confusion as to finally and irrevocably break down the enemy war machine and civil administration, to end the war as quickly as possible. The cities so listed for these raids were Berlin, Chemnitz, Dresden and Leipzig. The codename for this series of heavy attacks was Operation Thunderclap, but although preliminary planning was carried out, it was decided not to carry out the operation until the military situation in Germany was deemed to be critical.

The Pendulum and the Scythe

By late January 1945, all four of these cities were just behind the front line on the eastern front and all were vital supply and communications centres for the front. Packed as they were with refugees from the east and wounded military personnel from the front, it was obvious that both military and civilian administration systems would be close to absolute saturation. At the end of January, Air Ministry issued a directive to Bomber Command to carry out Operation Thunderclap.

Webster and Frankland describe how Churchill himself took a direct hand in the operation's final planning (Official History, Vol.IV, pages 112-113) and at the Yalta Conference on 4th February, the Russians asked for this kind of raid to take place. The Americans also agreed to help and it was planned that the Dresden attack should open with an American raid on 13th February. Bad weather over Europe on that day however, prevented the Americans from operating so it was left to RAF Bomber Command to start the battle.

On the night of 13th February 1945, Harris despatched 796 Lancasters and 9 Mosquitoes in two separate raids, the first by 5 Group alone and the second, three hours later, by 1, 3, 6 and 8 Groups. Between them they dropped 1,478 tons of HE and 1,182 tons of incendiaries which caused a firestorm similar to that caused in Hamburg in July 1943. This burned out large areas of the city. The Dresden casualty list has never been precisely determined, but it is believed that deaths in the city may have exceeded 50,000, although this has been revised downwards in recent years by the authorities in Dresden itself, to approx 25,000. Bomber Command lost six Lancasters with a further three crashing in France or on return to the UK

The next day, on the 14th February, 311 American B17 bombers dropped 771 tons of bombs on the city. Also, their Mustang fighter escort was ordered to strafe any traffic found on the roads around Dresden, but it is generally accepted that it was the RAF night raid that caused most damage.

The controversy began when an American officer who took part in the daylight raid leaked to an American war correspondent that the Dresden attack was pure, merciless, terror bombing. The American press quickly picked this up (sensationalism was a major reporting criteria with some newspapers, even in 1945) and the furore broke. Churchill immediately tried to distance himself from the events of the 13/14th February by writing a memo that effectively left Harris and his Command out on a limb. Harris, via Portal, had the memo withdrawn and a milder version substituted, but, unfortunately, the damage had been done. Harris and his 'boys' were left to carry the can for a raid that had long been planned by the British Prime Minister, backed by the US President, requested by Stalin and ordered by the Prime Minister through the Air Ministry. They are still suffering this wrongly directed ignominy, to a certain extent, today, seventy years later.

If one wished to be truly pedantic, one could argue – with considerable justification - that the Dresden raid was actually a tactical operation in support of Russian ground troops and should therefore be excluded from the records of the RAF's Strategic Offensive against Nazi Germany. This would then remove what stigma remains, however unjust!

Mercy Missions

Some Bomber Command critics, who seem to forget that but for Harris and his 'old lags' they would not be in any position to criticise, also ignore two major operations of a more humane nature carried out by the Command just before the end of the war. The first was Operation Exodus, the repatriation to the UK of prisoners-of-war recently liberated by the advancing allied armies. These men were taken to Brussels where, within twelve days, Bomber Command flew 469 sorties between 26th April and 7th May 1945 to bring 75,000 men back home as quickly as possible.

At almost the same time as Exodus, Operation Manna (29th April to 7th May) saw 124 Mosquito marking sorties and 2,835 Lancaster sorties taking place in western Holland, which was still under German occupation. The Lancasters dropped over 6,500 tons of food to the starving Dutch people during a cease-fire negotiated with the local German Commander. The Dutch have never forgotten this and, to this day, still thank Bomber Command for saving countless lives.

Victory in Europe was announced on 8th May 1945. The allied armies had successfully defeated the enemy and liberated the whole of Western Europe in just eleven months of fighting. The British Army had lost fewer than 40,000 men in this whole period, mainly because of the supreme efforts in ground support by the Air Forces. Bomber Command's losses for this same period amounted to 2,128 aircraft and approximately 10,000 airmen killed.

Final Reckoning

Air Chief Marshal Sir Arthur Harris, in his own book 'Bomber Offensive' says that approximately 125,000 aircrew served in the squadrons, OTUs and Conversion Units of Bomber Command, during the period September 1939 to May 1945. It is now generally accepted that bomber aircrew deaths while on operations or while prisoners of war totalled 47,268. Figures for aircrew killed whilst still in training vary between just under 8,200 to just over 8,300. It is now agreed that the total Bomber Command aircrew fatality figure of 55,573 is the definitive number. If we add to this, the number of airmen taken prisoner (many of them wounded) at 9,838, the number of wounded in returning damaged aircraft (4,200) and the number wounded while in training (4,203), the total casualty list amounts to almost 74,000, which is almost 60% of the total number of aircrew in the Command. No other branch of the country's armed forces suffered so heavily or received so little recognition for their sacrifices.

The major reason that the army, both UK and US, were loath to attack a defended area in Normandy was the fear of heavy casualties. Nearly all of the allied army commanders had been junior to middle ranking officers during the First World War. Without exception, they had promised themselves that the wastage of life seen during the pitched battles of the Somme, Arras, Loos, etc., would not be repeated. So, in nearly every case of an assault being required against a fortified position, the RAF were called in to 'soften up' the enemy. It is of some significance that the 55,573 aircrew killed during the Second World War, exceeds the 38,834 officer losses of the total British Empire during the First War by almost 45%. When one realises that the RAF was called in to save army casualties among the "cream of the nation's youth" (the class from which both army officers and RAF aircrew were drawn) then Bomber Command's sacrifices are really put into perspective.

Bomber Command commenced operations at 12.03 hours on 3rd September 1939 and fought with the equipment it had and the tactics that this equipment dictated right through to its last bombing mission on the night of 2/3rd May 1945. It was the Command's job to take the war to Germany when no other allied force could do so and, in the early years of the war, it was Britain's only offensive weapon. By 1943, the force had improved beyond all recognition and did tremendous damage to the German war machine. It steadily caused such a huge diversion of enemy resources, especially in anti-aircraft defences (the famous 88mm anti-aircraft gun was also Germany's best Anti-tank weapon and the retention for home front usage of over 20,000 of these guns was a major contribution to Russian success on the Eastern Front) and the number of able-bodied men (between 1 and 1.5 million) who had to be retained in Germany to deal with air raid precautions and bomb damage repair, all of whom could have been well used to counter the Russian offensive.

Well might Albert Speer say: *"The real importance of the air war consisted in the fact that it opened a second front long before the invasion of Europe. That front was the skies over Germany .., every square metre of the territory we controlled was a kind of front line. Defence against air attacks required the production of thousands of anti-aircraft guns, the stockpiling of tremendous quantities of ammunition all over the country, and holding in readiness hundreds of thousands of soldiers, who in addition had to stay in position by their guns, often totally inactive, for months at a time."*

Apart from the German home front requirements mentioned above, RAF bombing caused a considerable reduction in German war material production. In guns, there was a 10% shortfall against production target in 1943 and 20% in 1944. In aircraft, it is worth noting that in January 1942, 62.2% of the total German aircraft production was of bombers, while only 17.7% were fighters. By January 1945, 80.8% were fighters and only 5.3% were bombers. Albert Speer has stated that, without the allied bombing, German bomber production would have remained at a minimum of 53% - twice the number of fighters - and that all these bombers would have been used against the UK.

Despite the impression gained by the casual observer, Harris' efforts against the enemy's oil production also reaped a good result. With the USAAF attacks (it is not possible to separate out respective results) German oil production and reserves were reduced from approximately 987,000 metric tons in April 1944 to 150,000 tons by December 1944. By January 1945 there was no military vehicle fuel production at all and only 12,000 tons of aviation fuel were produced, with absolutely no reserves remaining. It only remains to be said, that the argument over Oil between Portal and Harris could have been totallt avoided had Harris been party to the Enigma decrypts. It seems absolutely ridiculous that the Leader of the RAF's Bomber Offensive was not included in the select band that were in on the Enigma secret.

The Pendulum and the Scythe

Dudley Saward's biography of Harris (Bomber Harris) says that between 3rd September 1939 and 3rd May 1945, Bomber Command carried out 389,809 sorties for a total loss of 8,655 aircraft (2.2%). This total was made up of 336,037 bombing sorties (dropping 955,094 tons of bombs), 19,025 mining sorties (947,307 mines at 33,237 tons) with the balance comprising countermeasures, decoy, intruder, fighter support, met flights and drops to and pick-ups of agents in occupied countries.

From February 1942 to May 1945, the period of Harris' tenure at Bomber Command, the totals were 331,001 sorties dropping 906,973 tons of bombs and 45,428 mines. The USAAF dropped an additional 621,260 tons during the period 1943-45.

While it is realised that most people today find the thought of area bombing distasteful it must be appreciated, even by Bomber Commands' most severe critics, that, in time of war, it would be suicidal not to use one's only weapon in self-defence, even if that 'defence' is a form of attack. The speaker at the 1961 Royal United Service Institution lecture, Dr. Noble Frankland, (co-author of the Official History of the Strategic Bomber Offensive and himself a Bomber Command Navigator with a DFC) summed up the situation extremely succinctly: *"The great immorality open to us in 1940 and 1941 was to lose the war against Hitler's Germany. To have abandoned the only means of direct attack which we had at our disposal would have been a long step in that direction."*

Therefore those who still consider Bomber Command's unsurpassed contribution to the Second World War as immoral, which this writer will strenuously deny, must consider the effect of the 'greater immorality' had the British Government not had the moral strength to take the decision to area bomb Germany and had Bomber Command not had the courage and skill to carry it out. And let us not forget that the decision for an all-out bombing offensive was not taken by the British Government until well after Warsaw, Rotterdam, Coventry and London had suffered severely at the hands of the Luftwaffe.

To paraphrase Harris' own words, the Germans sowed the wind and they reaped the whirlwind.

Map 1, RAF airfields in Yorkshire.

Chapter Three

From Whitleys to Whitley's

Bombing up a Whitley Mk.V. The scale of the operation appears very small in comparison with the much larger loads carried by the later 'heavies'.

No.4 Group was formed from parts of No.3 Group on 1st April 1937. Its first Air Officer Commanding (AOC) was Air Commodore A. T. Harris and its Headquarters, initially at Mildenhall, was relocated to Linton-on-Ouse, just outside York, on 29th June that same year. On its formation the Group acquired five stations and ten squadrons; 51 and 58 Squadrons were about to move their Vickers Virginias from Boscombe Down to their new base at Linton-on-Ouse, 97 and 166 Squadrons had their Handley Page Heyfords at Leconfield and the Virginias of 75 and 215 Squadrons were based at Driffield. Finningley was host to the Heyfords of No.7 Squadron and the Vickers Wellesleys of 76 Squadron, while the Heyfords of 78 Squadron shared Dishforth with No.10 Squadron, the only unit in the Group to be equipped with a modern aircraft - the Armstrong Whitworth Whitley - which had only entered service on 9th March. At this time 51 and 58 Squadrons also had a few Avro Ansons on unit strength but they were soon to go.

At the outbreak of war the AOC was Air Vice-Marshal A. (Maori, pronounced Mary) Coningham and the Group had only four stations, having handed Finningley over to 5 Group. Only three were actually in operational use, since Leconfield was at this time under 'Care and Maintenance' and was to be transferred to 13 Group, Fighter Command, before September was out. The Group's squadrons had been reduced to five operational units plus one Group Pool (Training) Squadron by 3rd September 1939, but they were, at least, all equipped with the Whitley. No.10 and 78 Squadrons were still based at Dishforth, although 78 was the non-operational Group Pool unit referred to previously. Driffield now housed 77 and 102 Squadrons, while 51 and 58 remained at Linton.

The only Group in Bomber Command to have been specifically trained for night operations, primarily due to Air Commodore Harris' insistence on night flying, No.4 was in action from the very first night of the war. Ten Mk.III Whitleys of 51 and 58 Squadrons were despatched to drop leaflets (codenamed Nickels) over Bremen, Hamburg and the Ruhr. Leaflet dropping, or Nickelling as it came to be known, was to be the Group's major contribution to the war effort for several months and was to continue, to some degree or other, throughout the war. 'Butch' Harris has since gone on record as believing that the only achievement of this Air Ministry inspired task was to provide Germany and the occupied countries with sufficient toilet paper to see them through the war.

These early Nickelling missions did, however, allow the Whitley crews to learn their way about a blacked-out Europe, albeit with no guarantees of 100% accuracy for much of the time. Much valuable experience was gained in navigational methods including ded (short for Deduced) reckoning (DR), wireless direction bearings, general crew co-operation and, of course, the enemy's infant night defence systems. All of this was to bear much fruit in later years. The Group's aircraft losses during this 'phoney war' period were comparatively light and most were due to mechanical failure, bad weather, getting lost and running out of fuel or by any combination of the three, rather than as the direct result of enemy activity. This however, in direct comparison to the heavy losses being sustained by the rest of the Command

A 77 Sqn Whitley Mk.V at Driffield in 1940.

who were still carrying out unescorted daylight raids - 3 and 5 Groups until 12th April 1940 and 1 and 2 Groups until well after Dunkirk. There were in fact, no 4 Group losses at all between 10th November 1939 and 16th March 1940, although there were some close calls.

On the night of 15/16th March for instance, a 77 Squadron Whitley Mk.V., Serial No.N1387, `KN-L for Love' was returning from a very long Nickelling trip to Warsaw under the control of its pilot and captain, Flight Lieutenant Tomlin. Flying in bad weather and running low on fuel Tomlin decided to land as soon as they had crossed the Franco-German border to sit out the inclement weather and to organise some more fuel. Having crossed the border (or so they thought) they touched down in a large field, climbed out of the aircraft and engaged in conversation with the local peasantry. It did not take long for them to realise that they had made a slight navigational error and they quickly established that France was actually about another two miles further along their previous flight track. It was at about this time that one of the crew observed the approach of German troops on bicycles. A hasty climb on board ensued, followed by a rapid double engine start and an equally rapid take-off that was achieved in a hail of rifle bullets from the enemy troops who were now within range. Flight Lieutenant Tomlin dragged the Whitley into the air and over the border on the last dregs of his petrol, setting his aircraft and crew safely down once more, this time on the right side of the border.

Meanwhile the Group's operational strength increased in October 1939 when 78 Squadron became fully operational after a move to Linton-on-Ouse. In between Nickelling raids the Group had been allowed to drop real bombs onto naval targets but only if the crews could be certain that none of their bombs would accidentally land on German soil. Finally, on the night of 19/20th March 1940, the Group was given the go-ahead to drop bombs regardless of their opportunity to strike dry land. The target was the Hornum seaplane base on the island of Sylt and the objective was to stop enemy aircraft taking off to lay mines in British territorial waters. The raid was undertaken by thirty Whitleys of 10, 51, 77 and 102 Squadrons, of which 26 claimed to have found the target, supported by 20 Hampdens of 5 Group, fifteen of which made the same claim. The 4 Group Whitleys dropped 46,300 lbs. of bombs on and around Hornum. Although subsequent reconnaissance showed that very little damage had been done.

It was not until May 1940 that the night bomber offensive `proper' was allowed to begin, although the Hampdens of 5 Group and the Wellingtons of 3 Group had been transferred to night operations with effect from 12th April after a disastrous daylight raid against shipping at Stavanger, Norway, when nine out of sixty aircraft were shot down by enemy fighters.

On 15th May the Luftwaffe bombed Rotterdam and the War Cabinet at last allowed RAF Bomber Command to cross the Rhine and attack the German heartland. The bomber commanders could at long last begin to implement their pre-war plans and the strategic night bomber offensive truly began. That night 99 aircraft attacked sixteen different industrial targets in Dortmund, Sterkrade and Castrop-Rauxel. A further twelve aircraft attacked German communications in Belgium. Thirty Whitleys from 4 Group took part in these attacks and it was the first time the Command had launched over 100 sorties in one night.

For the next five nights the attacks on Germany continued with bombs falling on industrial targets in Bremen, Cologne, Hamburg and the Ruhr. But the tactical situation in France was such that bombing operations then had to be redirected against bridges and communications targets near the battlefront.

Throughout the Battle of France, Bomber Command devoted 70% of its efforts against German oil targets but, despite optimistic forecasts, with very little effect. It was also during this period that bomber aircraft were tasked with dropping Razzles over German forests while en-route to their main targets. Razzles were small flat sandwiches of pills of phosphorus encapsulated by thin celluloid and covered in gauze which, once dried out, would burst into spontaneous fire. For this reason they were carried in sealed cans of water until just prior to dropping, at which time the foil lids were removed and the Razzles, complete with the accompanying water were poured down the flare chute. Unfortunately, they had a nasty habit of lodging in the bomber's elevators or rudders and, having dried out in the aircraft's slipstream, they proceeded to ignite. They set fire to more RAF aircraft tailplanes than they ever did German forests, but there were several recorded instances of unsuspecting German civilians picking them, or their smaller counterparts - Deckers - up and pocketing them, only to have the unpleasant surprise of their trousers erupting into flames as the Razzle or Decker dried out.

On the night of 21/22nd May 4 Group provided 52 Whitleys (their largest contribution to date) as part of a record 124 aircraft attacking various German railway targets, mainly in the Aachen area. Five aircraft, including one Whitley, did not return. Later the same month thirteen Whitleys joined 34 Wellingtons in attacks on German positions near the perimeter defences of Dunkirk. Usually, however, the longer ranging Whitleys were sent to targets in Germany, leaving the Dunkirk support operations to the Blenheims by day and the Hampdens and Wellingtons by night. Bomber Command's effort on the night of 3/4th June resulted in a force of 142 aircraft being despatched to attack industrial and communications targets from Hamburg to Frankfurt. This was another 'largest raid to date' and 4 Group contributed 48 Whitleys. It was also during June that the Group gained a new station when Leeming opened. This new base was to house 10 Squadron from July and 102 Squadron in August.

Italy declared war on Great Britain and France on 10th June 1940. The following night (11/12th.June) 36 Whitleys left their bases in Yorkshire, landed in the Channel Islands to refuel and then took off again to bomb Turin. On reaching the target, crews were amazed to find the city still lit up as in peace-time, but the lights were soon doused when the Italians realised what was happening. Two Whitleys crashed in France on the return flight. Another ten Whitleys joined Hampdens and Wellingtons in attacks on various targets in Germany and occupied France on this same night and one of these also failed to return. The next night 4 Group supplied 34 Whitleys to help the Command reach another all-time high of 163 sorties in one night, this time the targets were all communications related. The Command's efforts were beginning to grow.

The Pendulum and the Scythe

The night of 25/26th August saw the Group involved in the first bombing raid against the German capital and, on 7/8th September, attacks began on the barges being amassed for Operation Sealion, the German invasion of England. Meanwhile the Group had lost the use of its base at Driffield. Luftwaffe raids on 15th August resulted in the station being closed for repairs until the end of the year, at which time it was briefly transferred to 13 Group (Fighter Command) and did not return to 4 Group until April 1941. Driffield's squadrons were transferred to Linton-on-Ouse (77 Squadron) and Leeming (102 Squadron). On the credit side 4 Group opened up two new stations in September. These were Melbourne and Topcliffe and 77 Squadron relocated to the latter almost immediately.

On 17/18th September the Command set another record for numbers of aircraft dispatched when 194 bombers took off, two-thirds of them destined for the barges gathered in the Channel ports. Five nights later the Command tried a new tactic when, for the first time, it concentrated its total force for the night on a single target. One-hundred-and-twenty-nine aircraft attacked eighteen separate aiming points in Berlin. The aiming points comprised railway yards, power stations, gas works and aircraft component factories. Three aircraft, including one Whitley, failed to return (see Chapter 5, Pilot Officer A. W. Dunn). The Group took part in eight attacks on Berlin during August and September.

It was a 4 Group Whitley, based at Linton-on-Ouse, Which became the first victim of a Luftwaffe nightfighter intruder operation over the UK. On the night of 20th October 1940, the 58 Squadron aircraft, flown by Pilot Officer E. H. Brown, had just taken off to participate in an attack on the Skoda Works in Pilsen, Czechoslovakia, when it was attacked and shot down by a fighter from 1./NJG 2 flown by Hauptmann Karl Hillshoff. The Whitley crashed near Thornaby-on-Tees with only one survivor.

The 5th November 1940 gave a portent of things to come with 4 Group receiving the first of its truly 'heavy' bombers when 35 Squadron was resurrected as a Bomber unit. It was detached to Boscombe Down to be the first squadron to equip with the Handley Page Halifax. The unit's CO was Wing Commander R.W.P.Collings and the first Halifax (L9486) arrived on 13th November. 35 Squadron moved back to Leeming, in 4 Group territory

P/O Leonard Cheshire's Whitley P5005, DY-N before and (lower photo) after being sliced open by flak over Cologne.

on the 20th November before settling into Linton-on-Ouse on the 5th December. This unit was to remain with 4 Group for almost two years before becoming one of the founder squadrons of the Pathfinder Force.

On the night of 12/13th November, while over Cologne, a 102 Squadron Whitley Mk.V., Serial No.P5005, DY-N ('N-for-Nuts'), had the port side of the fuselage blown open by Flak as if cut open by a tin opener. The damage extended from above the port wing back almost to the crew entry hatch (see photograph). The Flak also detonated a flare in the flare chute, temporarily blinding the wireless operator. The pilot, one Pilot Officer G. L. Cheshire, successfully brought his badly damaged aircraft and its injured crew member home. For his skill and determination Cheshire was awarded the DSO, a most unusual award for one of such lowly rank (Hamish Mahaddie believed that this award was one of only two awarded to such a low ranking officer). Leonard Cheshire was to go on to complete over 100 operations and to be awarded a further two DSOs, a DFC and ultimately, when serving with 5 Group later in the war, the Victoria Cross, the country's highest award for valour.

It was around this time that the argument in favour of 'area bombing' first began to be voiced. This was based on two major and very relevant points. Although the difficulties in finding and identifying targets were not yet fully appreciated, the first point was that because of the doubts about navigational and bomb aiming accuracy in general, it was proposed that area bombing would make more effective use of the bomber force in that, while a primary industrial target might be missed by some of the force, stray bombs would at least hit some smaller industrial premises in the town under attack. Secondly, the War Cabinet, urged on by the UK's civil populace, felt that raids of this nature would be fully justified in the light of recent heavy and apparently indiscriminate bombing of British towns and cities by the Luftwaffe, in particular those attacks on Coventry and Southampton.[13]

This policy was however, firmly rejected at that time with but one exception, a raid by 134 aircraft on Mannheim on the night of the 16/17th December. Probably one of the more interesting operations of this period of the war, the

---

[13] *While the Coventry raid has often been referred to as an indiscriminate terror raid, it was, in fact, a remarkable feat of precision bombing. The targets were all small factories engaged upon aero-engine production and every one was hit with an average bombing error of around 100 yards - at a time when the primitive equipment issued to the RAF gave an average error of around five miles.*

Mannheim raid was authorised by the War Cabinet as a purely retaliatory attack for the exceptionally heavy German raids on Coventry and Southampton already mentioned. The raid was officially termed a `General attack on the centre of the city' and, under the codename of Operation Abigail, was planned to utilise 200 aircraft. Weather forecasts, however, indicated that conditions over and around some of the Command's base airfields were set to worsen and in the event only 134 aircraft, including 35 Whitleys from 4 Group, were despatched.

For the first time in the war, crews were instructed to aim at non-military and non-industrial targets. Also for the first time it was decided to illuminate the target with incendiary bombs dropped by experienced crews ahead of the main force. This first attempt at pathfinding was not, unfortunately, to be greeted with the success the idea merited. The early Wellington fire-raisers were not accurate and the largest fires were away from Mannheim's centre. This resulted in scattered bombing by the main force, although 240 buildings were destroyed or damaged by incendiary bombs and a further 236 by high explosive bombs, thus rendering 1,266 people homeless. Although irrelevant at this distance in time, one is tempted to wonder why the 4 Group Whitley crews, who had been operational at night from the very beginning of the war, were the only bomber crews who had trained for the task before the war and obviously had more night flying experience, were not tasked with the early fire raising sorties.

The new year of 1941 started with the opening of a new 4 Group aerodrome, the fourth since the war began but the first outside Yorkshire. Middleton-St. George, in County Durham, was situated mid-way between Darlington and Stockton-on-Tees. Although opened in January the station did not receive its first squadron until March, when 78 Squadron moved in from Dishforth.

At this period of the war Sir Richard Peirse, the C-in-C, used to try to plan one big raid every month, timed to coincide with the new moon. The bulk of the remainder of the Command's effort comprised small attacks by relatively small numbers of aircraft against various oil targets as per the directive issued to him on 15th January.

Two of the Group's units were involved in a non-bombing mission on the 10th February, when aircraft and crews of 51 and 78 Squadrons took part in Operation Colossus. This was the first allied airborne operation of the war and the Whitleys transported and dropped British Paratroops who then blew up the Acquedetto Puliese at Tragino in Southern Italy. The whole mission was a total success - an unusual occurrence at this stage of the war.

Despite the loss of the services of most of these two units, that same night (10/11th February) the Command reached a new high when 265 aircraft were despatched, 222 of them (including 30 Whitleys of 4 Group) to Hannover and 43 to Rotterdam. This latter attack saw the operational debut of the Short Stirling with No.3 Group (7 Squadron).

Having prepared his Command for the previously mentioned oil attacks, Peirse soon found himself distracted from his course by another Air Ministry directive, dated 9th March 1941. This instructed him that, until further notice, the Command's main operational effort was to be directed at all and any threats to British shipping. Because of the huge losses amongst the ships that were providing Great Britain's lifeline to America, Bomber Command was to attack the bases of German capital ships, U-boats and the long range Focke Wulf Fw200 Condor.

Peirse, like Harris after him, was not happy to be taken off the strategic bombing of Germany, especially as the coming spring heralded better weather for such attacks. Eventually the Air Ministry obtained approval from Churchill (who had instigated the 'Shipping Directive' at the request of the Admiralty) for Peirse to continue to devote a proportion of his effort to the oil campaign.

The second of the new 'heavies', the Handley Page Halifax, made its operational debut on the night of 10/11th March 1941, when six of 35 Squadron's aircraft joined eight Blenheims in an attack on Le Havre. This operation was marred by the shooting down, by a British Beaufighter nightfighter, of one of the returning Halifaxes. Only the pilot, Squadron Leader Gilchrist, and the Flight Engineer, Sgt. Aedy survived. Two nights later Halifaxes and Manchesters made their first attack on a German target when seven of them (4 Halifaxes from 35 Squadron, 3 Manchesters from 207 Squadron) joined 81 other aircraft in an attack on the Blohm and Voss U-boat yards at Hamburg.

On the 14th March, four months after the formation of 35 Squadron, No.4 Group formed its eighth unit. Based at Driffield, 104 Squadron was equipped with Vickers Wellingtons, a type that was obviously indicative of a short stay in the Group, for after only eleven months it became one of the many Bomber Command units sent out to the Middle East.

The night of March 30/31st was the beginning of the naval support campaign detailed above. Peirse despatched 109 aircraft, including 24 Whitleys, to attack the Scharnhorst and Gneisenau (known to the RAF crews as 'Salmon and Gluckstein') in Brest Harbour. This offensive was to continue until 8th May when it was briefly suspended, recommencing on the night of 7/8th June after the Prinz Eugen had entered the same harbour. These raids continued sporadically until 7th July, although the anti-capital ship campaign was to recur so often during the war that RAF Bomber Command was to sink more enemy capital ships than the Royal Navy.

No.4 Group formed another new squadron on the 23rd April when 405 (Vancouver) Squadron became the Group's first Canadian unit. It was equipped with Wellingtons and was based initially at Driffield. The next unit to appear in the Group was 76 Squadron, the second unit to be equipped with the Halifax. The squadron was transferred from No.6 (Training) Group in May 1941 and was based at Linton-on-Ouse for a month before moving to join 78 Squadron at Middleton-St. George in June.

104 Squadron was ready for its first operation on the night 8/9th May when it despatched six Wellingtons as part of a force of 133 attacking Bremen. On this same night the Command also despatched 188 aircraft to Hamburg, 23 to the Kiel Canal a Bremerhaven and a further 20 on minor operations, a grand total of 364 aircraft and a new record effort for the Command.

During June 1941, the Group opened its eighth base when 405 Squadron moved into Pocklington and then carried out its and the Royal Canadian Air Force's - first operation on the night of 12/13th June when it despatched four Wellingtons to join 80 Whitleys in an attack on Schwerte. This same night 76 Squadron also made its operational debut, their aircraft forming part of the force of eleven Halifaxes and seven Stirlings that attacked Huls. The total number of sorties on this night, at 102, was No.4 Group's best effort of the war to date.

Later the same month, on the night of 27/28th June, the Group despatched 35 Whitleys on a raid to Bremen. Joining 73 Wellingtons, the force encountered severe storms with bad icing conditions and, as recorded in Command records for the first time, 'intense nightfighter attacks'. This combination of bad weather and a spirited enemy defence resulted in the loss of eleven Whitleys (31% of those despatched) and three Wellingtons, the heaviest night casualty rate of the war so far. Two days later, on 30th June, No.35 Squadron despatched six aircraft to Kiel in the first Halifax daylight raid of the war. One Halifax failed to return.

On 24th July No.4 Group were ordered to despatch 15 Halifaxes of Nos.35 and 76 Squadrons on an unescorted daylight attack against the Scharnhorst at La Pallice (Operation Sunrise). The force met fierce fighter and Flak opposition resulting in the loss of five aircraft (33.3%) and damage to the surviving ten. The raid was led by the CO of 76 Squadron, New Zealander Wing Commander Jarman. The Halifaxes managed to achieve five direct hits on the ship, but three of the bombs, being armour piercing, passed straight through the ship leaving only small holes in the hull. The other two hits caused only light damage but the raid made the Germans decide that the Scharnhorst should return to Brest, which had superior Flak defences and better repair facilities. Despite her hull containing between 3,000 and 7,000 tons of water due to the armour piercing bomb hits, the Scharnhorst sailed for Brest that same night. (See also Chapter 6).

The damage caused during this attack necessitated some four months of repair work. The raid can thus be deemed a success. On the evening of the raid the BBC radio announced not only the news of the successful daylight attack on the Scharnhorst but also officially disclosed the existence of the new Halifax four engined bomber to the British public.

The Halifax undertook its first trip to Berlin on the night of 25/26th July when two of them joined seven Stirlings in an attack on the German capital. Two Stirlings and one Halifax failed to return, the single Halifax that did return was flown by Leonard Cheshire, now a Squadron Leader on 35 Sqdn.

The Group had a change of commanders on 26th July 1941 when Air Vice-Marshal Arthur Coningham followed so many of the Command's bombers out to the Middle East where he was to win fame - and the undying gratitude of the Eighth Army - as the commander of the Desert Air Force. His place at Heslington Hall (No.4 Group HQ) was filled by Air Vice-Marshal C. R. (Roddy) Carr, a New Zealander who would remain in command of 4 Group until almost the very end of the war.

Although not directly concerned with 4 Group at this time the night of 11/12th August saw the first operational use of the new navigational aid, GEE, by two Wellingtons of 115 Squadron on an attack on Monchengladbach. The following night Leonard Cheshire's younger brother Christopher failed to return from a raid to Berlin. (See Chapter 6). The next 4 Group occasion of note was the opening, in October, of the most northerly Yorkshire base. Croft was a satellite of Middleton-St. George and received the Whitleys of 78 Squadron almost immediately it had opened. This same month a new record number of sorties in one night was also set when the Group despatched 54 Whitleys and nine Halifaxes, forming part of a 152 strong force attacking Nuremberg on the night of 12/13th. The Group lost one aircraft of each type.

Another 4 Group base opened in November 1941 when Dalton became a satellite of Topcliffe and 102 Squadron moved in with their Whitleys; No.10 Squadron became the third unit to be equipped with Halifaxes and the Command launched its largest number of sorties in one night so far in the war. On the night of 7/8th November, 392 aircraft attacked targets in Berlin, Mannheim, the Ruhr, Ostend, Boulogne and Oslo. Thirty-seven aircraft failed to return from these attacks, twenty-five of them running out of fuel due to exceptionally strong headwinds encountered on the return flight. Working on the assumption that it was silly to fight both the enemy and predicted bad weather this prompted Churchill (via Portal) to order Peirse to conserve his forces and to carry out raids at a reduced scale only until further notice. This instruction marked the nadir of both the Command's and Peirse's fortunes.

A daylight attack on Brest that took place on the 18th December became the largest Halifax force to date when 18 of them joined 18 Stirlings and 11 Manchesters on yet another raid on this unfortunate French port. One Halifax failed to return.

Operationally, 1942 got off to a quiet start with Churchill's conservation order still in effect. Because of the ongoing successes of the German U-boats, a lot of the Command's - and thus the Group's - efforts were to continue to be directed at the enemy's naval threat. Thus the Scharnhorst and Gneisenau in Brest Harbour, the Tirpitz in Trondheim and other naval associated targets in Hamburg, Bremen and Wilhelmshaven all appeared on the target list with monotonous regularity.

January did, however, see 102 Squadron begin their conversion to Halifax aircraft, an undertaking that was completed during February, the month when the 'Channel Dash' occurred. The Scharnhorst and Gneisenau were joined by the Prinz Eugen in leaving Brest harbour and making a dash up through the English Channel in broad daylight on their way to German ports. This daring undertaking, which was completely covered by a Luftwaffe air umbrella, initially met with the success its boldness deserved and the Royal Navy was left with considerable egg on its face, despite the extreme bravery of their airmen under Lieutenant Commander Eugene Esmonde of No.825 Squadron. Only the mines dropped in the path of the escaping ships by RAF aircraft - and the damage they caused - had any effect on their progress, but they nevertheless made it to the safety of German ports, even if they were not the ports intended them. Now they were in the Fatherland's ports they were, at least, a lesser threat to Atlantic shipping than they had been whilst based in Brest.

Meanwhile, the Group lost 104 Squadron to the Middle East, although their ground echelons remained in the UK to form a new unit, 158 Squadron, on the 14th February. The unit was initially equipped with Wellingtons but would convert to Halifaxes within six months. Also on 14th February (inappropriately St. Valentine's Day) Bomber Command HQ, at High Wycombe, received Portal's 'Area Bombing' Directive. Eight days later, on 22nd February, Air Marshal Arthur (Bert) Harris took over the running of Bomber Command. On this date No.4 Group consisted of 54 Whitleys in 51, 58, 77 and 78 Squadrons; 29 Halifaxes in 10, 35, 76 and 102 Squadrons and approximately 30 Wellingtons in 158 Squadron and 405 (RCAF) Squadron.

Five days after Harris took over at High Wycombe, one of 4 Group's squadrons was involved in another Combined Operation on behalf of Professor R.V.Jones of British Scientific Intelligence. This operation, codenamed *Biting*, took place on the night of 27/28th February and was undertaken by twelve Whitleys of No.51 Squadron under the command of Squadron Leader. Percy C. (Pick) Pickard. Pick was already known to the British public although not by name - as the pilot of Wellington F for Freddy' in the film 'Target for Tonight'. Operation Biting was a paratroop raid on the German Wurzburg radar unit situated near Bruneval in France. The raid, by 'C' Company, 2 Para, accompanied by an RAF radar mechanic, Flight Sergeant C. W. H. Cox, was under the command of Major J. D. Frost, the total force dropped was about 120 strong and the raid was a complete success. 'Pick' Pickard was later to die on the famous Amiens Prison attack

(Operation Jericho), which he successfully led as a Group Captain, on the 18th February 1944.

The night of 3/4th March saw a raid that was really the Command's first truly precision night attack of the war. No.4 Group contributed 20 Halifaxes, 23 Whitleys and a few Wellingtons to a total force of 235 that bombed the Billancourt Renault Factory, just west of the centre of Paris. During this raid many records were broken, for both Command and for 4 Group. It was the greatest number of aircraft ever sent to one target, it was the best concentration of bombers over a target - at an average of 121 per hour, it bettered the previous record by 41 per hour - and a record tonnage of bombs (approximately 450) was dropped. It was also the largest Halifax force despatched to date. A significant innovation on this attack was the foreshadowing of later Pathfinder techniques by opening the raid with the mass use of flares to illuminate the target for selected experienced crews to place their incendiaries accurately in order to get the attack off to a good start. Renault's production was halted for four weeks and it was several months before final repairs were completed. Only one Wellington failed to return.

During March 1942, 78 Squadron converted onto the Halifax, the fifth so to do. The general introduction of the new navigational aid GEE occurred on an attack on Essen during the night of 8/9th and, on the night of 27/28th of the month, the Group despatched 35 Whitleys to join 27 Wellingtons in an attack on German positions around St. Nazaire in support of the joint Commando/Royal Navy raid to destroy the dry-dock gates in the port. In the event only four aircraft bombed because of 10/10ths cloud. One Whitley was lost in the sea. The largest Halifax force to date (34) was sent to bomb the Tirpitz in a fjord near Trondheim on the night of 30/31st March, one of which did not make it back to its base.

The month of April was quite eventful. A 4 Group aircraft dropped the Command's first 8,000 lb. bomb during an attack on Essen on the night of 10/11th. The aircraft was a 76 Squadron Halifax B. Mk.II, serial no. R9487, MP-A flown by Pilot Officer Mike Renaut. His aircraft was one of eight that helped to make up a total force of 254 aircraft, fourteen of which - including one Halifax - failed to return. On the 20th April the aircrew category of Air Bomber was introduced and that of Observer was renamed Navigator, although Observers already qualified were not required to replace their 'O' brevets.

The Pendulum and the Scythe

The Group's Whitleys carried out their last attack on a German target as part of a front-line unit when five of them joined another 104 aircraft in a raid on Rostock on the night of 26/27th April and the following night two of the same 58 Squadron Whitleys made their last front-line sorties of the war. Their target was Dunkirk and both aircraft returned safely. From the first night of the war No.4 Group's Whitleys had carried out 9,169 sorties for the loss of 288 aircraft. Operational Training Units would carry out a further 558 sorties, including participation in the three Thousand Bomber' raids, but this night marked the full and final disappearance of this old stalwart from 4 Group's front-line strength. Their crews suffered severely from the cold during the winter months, a level of suffering that was admirably summed up, in 1991, by veteran Whitley pilot Peter Rutter. Peter and his wife Jill were donating a piece of Whitley fuselage to the Midland Air Museum at Baginton, Coventry (where Armstrong Whitworth built the Whitley), which was attempting to rebuild an example of the type. The piece of fuselage had spent over forty years on a Welsh mountainside being used as a goat shed. Peter was heard to remark that he had every sympathy for the goat - he knew just how bloody cold it could be in a Whitley in the winter.

The Tirpitz was once again the target on the night of 27/28th April[14]. No.4 Group sent 31 Halifaxes to join 12 Lancasters in another attempt to remove this permanent thorn in the flesh of the Royal Navy. The attack cost the Command one Lancaster and four Halifaxes, two of which are worthy of further comment. One of the missing Halifaxes was that of the CO of No.10 Squadron, Wing Commander D.C.T. Bennett who, despite having difficulty keeping control of the aircraft, managed to do so long enough to enable his crew to parachute to safety before rapidly following them out of the escape hatch. Having landed safely Bennett hid his parachute and walked to Sweden from where he returned to his squadron in only five weeks. Another of the missing Halifaxes was W1048 of 35 Squadron, flown by Pilot Officer Donald McIntyre. It crash landed on the frozen surface of nearby Lake Hoklingen and all the crew managed to scramble clear before it sank through the ice. In 1973 an RAF Sub-Aqua Club team located and recovered the aircraft and it now resides in the RAF Museum as the only 'surviving' example of a Halifax B.Mk.II. We as a nation are fortunate that the

[14] For the full story of the 4 Group attacks on the Tirpitz and of Halifax W1048 `S-Sugar', see "Tirpitz: The Halifax Raids" by Nigel Smith.

Yorkshire Air Museum at Elvington, just outside York, has now built a full size replica of a B.Mk.III for posterity.

In May the last three Whitley squadrons left the Group. No.58 Squadron was transferred to Coastal Command never to return, while Nos.51 and 77 Squadrons were detached to it for six months, returning in October and immediately commencing to re-equip with Halifaxes. On the night of the 30/31st May 1942, Harris launched the first of his Operation Millennium thousand bomber raids, with Cologne as the target. Of the 1047 aircraft that took part, 4 Group contributed 131 Halifaxes (the first time that the one hundred number had been reached), nine Wellingtons and seven OTU Whitleys, a total of 147. Losses for the night amounted to 41 aircraft, of which 3 Halifaxes and one Whitley belonged to 4 Group.

Operation Millennium II took place on June 1/2nd, when the Group contributed 127 aircraft to the total of 956 attacking Essen. Eight of the Group's aircraft failed to return.

On the 25th June the Group gained its second Canadian unit when 425 (Alouette) Squadron formed at Dishforth with Wellingtons. This was the start of a considerable amount of new squadron activity, which was to reach a crescendo at the end of the year, as No.4 Group collected existing Canadian squadrons from the other Groups and formed new units in preparation for the formation of No.6 (Royal Canadian Air Force) Group. On the night of the 25th June Harris again mounted a 'thousand bomber' attack and 4 Group contributed 124 Halifaxes to the Bremen raid. It is worth pointing out that whilst the Group managed to muster over 100 Halifaxes for each of the `Millennium' raids, this was the result of a 'maximum, maximum' effort. The more usual Halifax availability at this stage of the war was in the region of thirty to forty aircraft.

The Group opened another airfield, its eleventh, at East Moor and 158 Squadron moved there from Driffield almost immediately. This new opening was offset, however, by the closure for repairs of Topcliffe's satellite, Dalton, which would not re-open for business until November. Having moved to East Moor, 158 Squadron began to convert, in July, to

Halifaxes, the aircraft type with which it was to see out the rest of the war. One of this unit's aircraft, LV907, coded NP-F, was known on the squadron as 'Friday the Thirteenth'. This aircraft was not named after the day on which it arrived on the unit, as is commonly believed, because it arrived on Friday 10th March 1944 and was originally held as a spare before carrying out its first op, to Nuremberg, on 30th March 1944. This aircraft, a B.Mk.III, was to complete 128 operations - more than any other Halifax aircraft. Bearing in mind the horrendous losses suffered by the Command on the night of its first operation, LV907 obviously had a charmed life from the very beginning, but that didn't stop it being scrapped at the end of the war!

During July there was also a change of command for 78 Squadron at Middleton-St. George, when Wing Commander J.B.(Willie) Tait took over. Willie was later to take over command of 617 Squadron from Leonard Cheshire in July 1944. On the night of 19/20th July the Group put up a normal effort when it despatched 40 Halifaxes to join 31 Stirlings and 28 Lancasters on an attack on the Vulcan U-Boat yards at Vegesack. Three Halifaxes failed to return. The number despatched increased to 73 Halifaxes for a 403 aircraft attack on Hamburg on 26/27th of the month, but this time eight of the Group's aircraft failed to return.

No.76 Squadron received a new C.O. in August with the arrival of Wing Commander G.L.Cheshire. `Chesh' was to stay with this unit (on which his younger brother, Christopher, was serving when shot down twelve months previously) until April 1943 when he was promoted to Group Captain and posted to Marston Moor as Officer Commanding the station. It was from Marston Moor that he begged to be put back on operations and willingly dropped back a rank to take over command of 617 Squadron from Squadron Leader Micky Martin in November 1943. Martin had been placed in temporary command of the unit after Wing Commander George Holden was killed on the first Antheor Viaduct raid on the 16th September.

The build-up of Canadian units continued in August with 419 (Moose) Squadron joining the Group from No.3 Group, bringing its Wellingtons to Topcliffe, while 420 (Snowy Owl) Squadron brought its Wellingtons from 5 Group to the newly opened airfield of Skipton. August 15th was the date on which the Pathfinder Force was formed and the man that Harris selected to lead it was 4 Group's D. C. T. (Don) Bennett.

From March to August 1942 the Group had lost 109 Halifaxes from 1,770 sorties. This was a loss rate of 6.2%, which was well above the 5% that Harris considered to be the maximum sustainable rate. Not surprisingly the aircrews' confidence in the aircraft was shaken and morale in the seven

W/C Leonard Cheshire (seated centre) with the 76 Sqn football team. Norman Frankish (4th from right, standing) serviced the Halifaxes flown by both Cheshire brothers. (Norman Frankish)

Halifax squadrons had fallen. The aircraft were virtually grounded for four weeks and the units rested while 76 Squadron's CO, Wing Commander Leonard Cheshire, helped the Air Ministry boffins to find out what the problems were. At no small risk to himself, `Chesh' undertook various tests, including spin checks, in order to determine the cause or causes of such high losses. Apart from the fact that too much rubbish had been hung on the poor Halifax's airframe, thus reducing its aerodynamics and power-to-weight ratio at the same time, it was discovered that due to the triangular shape of the fin, the twin rudders were over-balancing if fully deflected, a not uncommon occurrence when a pilot was undertaking desperate corkscrew manoeuvres to avoid an attacking nightfighter. This led to a redesign of the fin and resulted in the bigger, slab sided D' fin that was eventually to be retro-fitted to most operational aircraft in service and was fitted to all new aircraft during production.

In September, 35 Squadron left the Group to become one of the founder members of the Pathfinder Force. This was not in the least offset by the arrival of another Canadian unit, 408 (Goose) Squadron, which moved its Hampdens into Leeming from No.5 Group. These were the only Hampdens to serve in 4 Group and, although the unit commenced re-equipment with Halifaxes in October, 408 Squadron was never to carry out an operation under the 4 Group banner.

The Pendulum and the Scythe

Forty-nine Halifaxes took part in the 479 aircraft raid on Dusseldorf on the 10/11th September and three of the Group's aircraft were lost. It was during this attack that the PFF first used the 4,000 lb. Pink Pansy marker bomb, which was soon to become a familiar sight to all bomb aimers.

The last three months of 1942 were unusually hectic for the opening of new bases and the movements of units in and out of the Group. 158 Squadron and 405 (Vancouver) Squadron were both detached to Coastal Command, 158 returning in December while 405 continued its detachment until February 1943, although its 'ownership' was transferred to 6 Group on the 1st January. When Kiel was raided on 13/14th October the number of Halifaxes for a normal 'non-1000 bomber' raid rose to 78, of which one failed to return. On the following day, the 15th October, the Group formed three new units, two Canadian and one Australian. 424 (Tiger) Squadron formed at Topcliffe, 426 (Thunderbird) Squadron at Dishforth and 466 (RAAF) Squadron at Driffield. All were equipped with Wellingtons.

The Group also received two new stations in October, with the opening of Elvington and the handing over, from 1 Group, of Snaith. In November, 77 Squadron moved to Elvington and 51 Squadron arrived at Snaith when both squadrons returned from their detachments to Coastal Command and began Halifax conversions. Another unit to re-equip with this four engined heavy during October was 408 (Goose) Squadron based at Leeming. Rufforth and Burn also opened in November and Dalton re-opened after the completion of repairs. 428 (Ghost) Squadron formed at Dalton on 7th November and 431 (Iroquois) Squadron formed at Burn on the 11th, both equipped with Wellingtons. Rufforth was to remain unoccupied until December.

Three more Wellington squadrons were also formed on the 7th November, 196 at Driffield, 427 (Lion) Squadron at Croft and 429 (Bison) Squadron at East Moor. In December, Leconfield returned to the 4 Group fold after more than three years when it re-opened as a modern bomber base and accepted 196 and 466 Squadrons as its resident units. At the same time Rufforth greeted the return, from Coastal Command, of 158 Squadron, which immediately began conversion to the Halifax. Another unit to commence re-equipping with this aircraft was 419 (Moose) Squadron, which also made a December change of base, moving to Middleton-St. George from its satellite, Croft.

No.4 Group had operated one Canadian unit (405 Squadron) since April 1941 but since June 1942 it had been forming new, or collecting existing Canadian squadrons from other Groups in the Command. On the 1st January 1943 all these squadrons and nine of 4 Group's stations were transferred to No.6 (Royal Canadian Air Force) Group. The new Group took control of Dishforth with 425 and 426 Wellington Squadrons; Leeming with 408 Halifax Squadron; Topcliffe with 424 Squadron (Wellingtons); Middleton-St. George with 419 (Halifaxes) and 420 (Wellingtons); Croft with 427 Squadron and East Moor with 429, both equipped with Wellingtons. No.6 Group also received Skipton-on-Swale, which was unoccupied, and Burn with its resident Wellingtons of 431 Squadron. Burn was to be returned to 4 Group twelve months later. This mass exodus of units left No.4 Group with seven Halifax Squadrons (10, 51, 76, 77, 78, 102 and 158) and two Wellington units (196 and 466 (RAAF) Squadrons).

During the course of 1943 the average strength of the Command's nightly force was to rise from 250 to circa 450 aircraft, but the average bomb load was to more than double from one ton to approximately 2.25 tons as a result of the availability of more four-engined heavies. No.4 Group's nightly availability was to double from around 50 to more than 100 plus aircraft during the same period, despite the loss of so much of its strength to 6 Group.

The Pathfinder Force gained Group status on 8th January 1943 as No.8 Group and on the night of 16/17th, the Command's newest Group made the first use of the 250 lb. Target Indicator on Berlin. The 21st was the date of issue of the Casablanca Directive (see Chapter 2) and the night of 30/31st saw the first operational use of H2S over Hamburg by the Halifaxes of 35 Squadron and 7 Squadron's Stirlings.

In February the Group opened another new station, Lissett, and 158 Squadron moved there from Rufforth. Meanwhile the Halifax force (including 6 Group) was expanding rapidly. Eighty-four were despatched to Hamburg on the 3/4th February, increasing to 96 for an attack on Lorient ten days later. On the night of the 16/17th, the total rose to 103 for another Lorient raid and increased yet again, to 110, for Wilhelmshaven on the 19/20th February.

Following 158 Squadron's move from Rufforth this station left 4 Group's front-line in March to become the home of 1663 (Halifax) Heavy Conversion

Unit and as such played a major role in training Halifax crews for the remainder of the war.

Harris opened the Battle of the Ruhr on the night of 5/6th March with a 442 aircraft attack on Essen. This figure included 94 Halifaxes, 74 of which came from 4 Group. Three Halifaxes failed to return. The Halifax contribution to Command total sorties continued to rise during the Battle of the Ruhr; 114, for the loss of one, to Duisburg on the 26/27th March; 124 (4 lost) to Berlin on 27/28th March; 124 again on the 10/11th April, this time to Frankfurt with the loss of three; 141 with 12 lost to Dortmund 4/5th May and 199, again to Dortmund on 23/24th May, but this time with a loss of 18, not far short of 10%.

During this latter attack, Bomber Command dropped, for the first time, over 2,000 tons of bombs in one raid. Throughout the Battle of the Ruhr the Halifax contribution amounted to 3,624 sorties for the loss of 225 aircraft (6.2%).

In June 1943 the Group acquired two stations from No.1 Group: Breighton, to which 78 Squadron moved from Linton-on-Ouse, and Holme-on-Spalding Moor, into which 76 Squadron moved from the same base. Linton was being cleared of the Group's units in preparation for its hand-over to 6 Group in July. Also in June, work began to rebuild Driffield as a modern heavy bomber base, but 462 Squadron remained resident, carrying out its operations from among the excavators, cement mixers and road rollers. The total number of Halifaxes despatched exceeded the 200 figure for the first time on 11/12th June, when 202 of the type joined 581 other aircraft in an attack on Dusseldorf. On the 18th June, RDF (Radio Direction Finding) officially became known as Radar (RAdio Direction And Ranging), the first of the many new acronyms that were to creep into RAF usage as the impact of the American build-up was felt.

There was also a little-known, or mentioned, all-Halifax precision raid at this point of the war, when 134 aircraft of 4 Group and 31 from 8 Group (the latter being 35 Squadron - ex-4 Group) attacked the Peugeot factory in the suburbs of Suchaux at Montbeliard, near the Swiss border on the 15/16th July. Unfortunately the centre of the group of markers dropped by PFF was 700 yards beyond the factory and approximately 123 civilians were killed.

The Battle of Hamburg (Operation Gomorrah) opened on the night of 24/25th July with a new record number of 246 Halifaxes despatched as part of a total force of 791 aircraft. Throughout this battle 4 Group were to contribute 601 Halifax and 61 Wellington sorties over the four raids. 578 crews successfully bombed the target but eighteen Halifaxes failed to return and one further aircraft, from 76 Squadron, crashed on return to the UK. One crew from 51 Squadron, skippered by Sergeant Fletcher, succeeded in shooting down a Dornier Do217 nightfighter that had attacked them. This was confirmed as destroyed. Operation Gomorrah cost the Group 110 men killed and 20 taken prisoners-of-war.

Also in June, 196 Squadron was transferred to 3 Group, leaving 466 (RAAF) Squadron as the only Wellington unit in 4 Group, while, on the 12th of the following month, the Group received its second Australian unit when 462 (RAAF) Squadron reformed at Driffield.

The 'Master Bomber' technique, pioneered by Guy Gibson on the Dams Raid, was applied to a main force attack for the first time on the night of 17/18th August. The target was Peenemunde, the German V-1 and V-2 research and development base. The master bomber was Group Captain John Searby and, for the first time, the Pathfinder squadrons were able to use a new marker bomb, the Red Spot Fire. The 596-strong force for this raid included 145 Halifaxes from 4 Group and another 73 from Nos.6 and 8 Groups. The 4 Group contribution was the largest in the Command this night, exceeding the next strongest Group by twenty-eight aircraft. No Wellingtons, including those of 466 Squadron, were detailed to participate in the Peenemunde attack. The Group lost three Halifaxes with 20 men killed and two taken prisoners-of-war.

Five nights later, on 23/24th August, the Command despatched 727 aircraft to Berlin and the Halifax content, at 251, was another new record for the type. Berlin was the target again on the night of 31st August/1st September when the Luftwaffe nightfighters first used flares to illuminate the bomber force from above. Later in September, on 22/23rd, Harris was finally forced into increasing the number of aircraft used in his 'spoof raids in order to make them more convincing to the enemy controllers. He therefore despatched 29 Lancasters and Mosquitoes of No.8 Group to Oldenburg, with orders to drop flares and markers as if in preparation for a major attack. Meanwhile the main force of 711 aircraft (including 226 Halifaxes) attacked Hannover. The spoof worked well and losses were negligible.

The Pendulum and the Scythe

During October 1943, 466 (RAAF) Squadron - the last Wellington unit in the Group - began converting to the Halifax and the 7/8th October attacks on Aachen and Stuttgart marked the first use of G-H (by a 139 Squadron Mosquito) and ABC (by a 101 Squadron Lancaster) respectively, whilst on the following night the 'old faithful' Wellington undertook the Command's last front-line sorties. Corona was used for the first time during a raid on Kassel on the 22/23rd October and on the 8th November the Command gathered all of its radio countermeasures activities together with the formation of No.100 Group.

The Battle of Berlin began on the night of the 18/19th November 1943 and was to continue for over four months. No.4 Group contributed 1,183 Halifax sorties over nine of the attacks and lost 92 aircraft (7.8%). Casualties were 487 men killed and 226 taken prisoners-of-war. Four shot-down aircrew managed to evade capture, all from the same 76 Squadron crew, captained by Pilot Officer G. G. A. Whitehead. Their aircraft, a Halifax B.Mk.V, serial no. LL116 and coded MP-X, was badly hit in the nose by Flak while over Berlin on the night of 20/21st January 1944. The bomb-aimer, Flying Officer H. D. G. Morris, was killed and the wireless-op, Sergeant L. Stokes, was wounded. The navigator, Warrant Officer J. M. Trach, lost all his charts when the Flak struck and the aircraft compasses and one engine were put out of commission. The Halifax steadily lost height on the return journey and, when it was down to 4,000 feet, the pilot gave the order to abandon aircraft. Whitehead, Trach and both gunners, Sergeants J. M. Fisher and B. Compton, all landed safely by parachute and successfully evaded capture. The Halifax crashed five kilometres west of Lens in France.

During the Berlin battle several new firsts took place. On the night of 19/20th November, the FIDO (Fog Investigation and Dispersal Operation) system was used to assist aircraft to land in thick fog for the first time when four Halifaxes of 35 Squadron landed safely at Graveley. FIDO was fitted at two of the Group's airfields, Carnaby - the emergency landing ground (ELG) - near Bridlington, and Melbourne. This system ultimately equipped eleven Bomber and one Coastal Command airfields and enabled 2,486 aircraft to land safely in conditions that would otherwise have resulted in their total loss with, no doubt, many casualties.

A new era for 4 Group dawned on 1st December 1943, with the Hercules-engined Halifax B.Mk.III carrying out its first operation when twelve of this new type belonging to 466 (RAAF) Squadron, based at Leconfield, went mining off Terschelling. On 16/17th December, Beaufighter and Mosquito nightfighters carried out intruder patrols for the first time as a fully integrated component of Bomber Command, while a 650-aircraft raid on Frankfurt on the night of 20/21st December brought the Halifax force to a new high of 257, although casualties, at 27 Halifaxes, were tragically excessive.

The new year of 1944 opened with the formation, Within 4 Group, of two new units, 640 Squadron on the 7th and 578 Squadron a week later on the 14th January. Both squadrons were equipped with the Halifax B.Mk.III from the outset and were in the thick of the battle almost immediately, 578 Squadron, for instance, carried out its first operation (to Berlin) on the 20th January, only six days after being formed and only four days after taking its first aircraft on charge! This unit, based initially at Snaith, despatched six aircraft (two more aborted) as part of the 769-strong force that attacked the 'Big City' that night. This raid also saw the Halifax force increase to 264, with 22 of them failing to return, Pocklington's 102 Squadron losing 5 out of 16 despatched.

The Halifax force increased yet again on the night of 15/16th February when 314 of them formed part of the Command's largest (non-Millennium) force of 891 aircraft. Seventeen failed to return. The last attack on Berlin (as part of The Battle') took place on the night of 24/25th March, the night of the 'strong winds' (see Chapter 2) and the Halifax component lost 28 aircraft out of 216 despatched. Fifteen of these were from 4 Group alone. 51 and 640 Squadrons lost two each, five more were lost from 78 Squadron, one each from Nos. 76, 158 and 466 Squadrons and three from 578 Squadron. Additionally one aircraft from each of Nos. 78 and 158 Squadrons crashed in the UK on return. The greatest casualty rate in the Group during the Battle of Berlin was borne by 77 Squadron, which lost fifteen aircraft from 146 sorties (11.2%).

The Nuremberg raid of 30/31st March 1944 was the most costly, in terms of lost aircraft and aircrew, ever undertaken by Bomber Command in the whole five-and-a-half years of the Second World War. Air Chief Marshal Sir Arthur Harris despatched 572 Lancasters, 214 Halifaxes and 9 Mosquitoes on the main attack and of these 795 aircraft, 64 Lancasters and 31 Halifaxes, failed to return. Additionally, a further ten aircraft crashed on return to the UK and many more returned with severe damage and with dead and wounded crew members aboard.

Of the 214 Halifaxes despatched on this raid, No.4 Group put up 119 of them and 77 and 102 Squadrons sent a further ten on mining operations. Eighty-one of the Halifaxes despatched to Nuremberg dropped their bombs but twenty failed to return and a further three were wrecked in crashes on their return to the UK. No.51 Squadron suffered the Group's worst casualties of the night, losing five out of seventeen despatched, with another aircraft crashing on return. Only 466 Squadron escaped unscathed with all sixteen of their aircraft returning safely. No.10 Squadron lost one out of thirteen, 76 Squadron lost three out of fourteen while both 78 and 640 Squadrons lost three out of sixteen and 158 Squadron lost four out of sixteen. 578 Squadron lost only one out of eleven despatched although another two were wrecked in crashes and one more returned badly damaged. In total the Group lost 115 men killed, with 21 taken prisoner-of-war. Four were injured in crashes and a further two were wounded in action but returned home in their aircraft. There was one Victoria Cross awarded for the Nuremberg raid and, not surprisingly in view of the casualties, this award was made posthumously. The recipient, Pilot Officer Cyril Joe Barton, was a member of 578 Squadron, based at Burn near Selby and this award was the only VC ever awarded to a Halifax crew member, or indeed to a member of 4 Group during the whole war. (Leonard Cheshire was in 5 Group when his VC was awarded, although most of his ops were carried out in 4 Group.)

578 Squadron had been formed from 'C' Flight of 51 Squadron, at Snaith, on the 14th January 1944 and moved to Burn on 6th February. The CO of 51 Sqn, W/C D. S. S. Wilkerson, took command of 578 Squadron on its formation. The Squadron had not had an easy introduction to operations as five out of their first six operations had been to Berlin. They had the misfortune to be formed during the middle of the Battle of Berlin and very quickly became blooded the hard way. On the night of 30th March 1944 the Squadron had detailed fourteen Halifax B.Mk.III aircraft for the Nuremberg raid but two failed to take off because of engine trouble. Of the remaining 12 aircraft, LW473, F (Flight Sergeant G.M.Henderson) was attacked by a fighter at 20.05 hours. The starboard inner engine, aircraft nose and the hydraulic system sustained damage, which caused the pilot to jettison the bomb load and abandon the mission. The aircraft landed at Elvington With a wounded Flight Engineer (Sergeant R.C.Corker).

LW469, A, flown by 'A' Flight Commander Squadron Leader H Harte-Lovelace, suffered an engine failure en-route to the target and the mission was abandoned, the aircraft landing at Snetterton Heath complete with bomb load.

A third aircraft, LW471, X, skippered by Flight Sergeant J. A. Malvern also abandoned the mission. This is hardly surprising when it is learnt that the starboard outer engine oil pressure began to fluctuate erratically shortly after take-off, the starboard inner propeller managed to feather itself, thus effectively losing that engine and the mid-upper gunner found his guns frozen and unable to fire. As if this wasn't enough, having made the sensible decision to forget Nuremberg and return to base, the crew then found that they could not jettison their bombs because the fuse controlling the bomb release circuit was missing! The aircraft landed back at Burn complete with bomb load.

The nine remaining aircraft are all listed in squadron records as having bombed the primary target but it is now known that at least one bombed Schweinfurt (as did many other aircraft on this night, including some Pathfinders) and it is highly probable that MZ508 'N' never quite made it to the target area. This aircraft, piloted by Sergeant A. E. Pinks, was shot down and crashed at Kunreuth, near Ederbrighausen, approximately 22 kilometres north of Nuremberg, with the loss of all on board. It was the 79th aircraft shot down that night.

Eight aircraft returned to the UK. Two landed at Elvington, one each at Breighton, Melbourne and Riccall and one landed back at Burn. The seventh aircraft, LW478, S, flown by 'B' Flight Commander Squadron Leader McCreanor, had eight men on board including Sergeant A. W. McClennan, who was undertaking an experience flight as second pilot, a thing most squadrons tried to do with pilots fresh from HCU. This aircraft attempted to land at Silverstone but, on overshooting to go round again, the aircraft's undercarriage struck the fire section roof and some trees and crashed. Only the navigator, Pilot Officer T. A. Evans survived.

The eighth aircraft, LK797 `E-Excalibur, was flown by Pilot Officer C. J. Barton. Pilot Officer Cyril Joe Barton, known as 'Cy' to his crew and other friends, was 22 years old at the time of the Nuremberg raid and was fairly untypical of the general public's idea of a bomber pilot. Barton had the face of a boy much younger than his 22 years and was a quiet-living and intensely devout Christian who even managed to get his hard-bitten and cynical crew to attend services at the local village church.

He is reported to have confessed that he had to gather up his courage to kneel at the side of his bed every night in order to say his prayers in the presence of the two other young officers with whom he shared a bedroom. Barton's crew consisted of:

Navigator: Pilot Officer J L Lambert (Len)[15]

Bomb Aimer: Pilot Officer G W Crate, RCAF (Wally)

Wireless Operator: Sergeant J A Kay (Jack)

Flight Engineer: Sergeant. M E 'Trousdale (Maurice)

Mid-upper Gunner: Sergeant H D Wood (Timber) – later Flying Officer

Rear Gunner: Sergeant F Brice (Fred)

Barton and his crew had originally been with 78 Squadron at Breighton but were then posted to Snaith to help form a nucleus of 'C' Flight, 51 Squadron, which in January 1944 became 578 Squadron. Nuremberg was to be the new squadron's 22nd raid, all but three of which had been against Germany's major cities, including six visits to Berlin and three to Stuttgart. It was Cy Barton's 18th operation with his crew.

While waiting for transport to take the crew out to the aircraft, Cy Barton used his torch to test his gunners on their emergency Morse intercall signals that they had devised during their training for use in the event of intercom failure. Barton had not tested them in this before and none of the crew had any idea what made him do it then.

LK797 (Squadron code letters 'LK', aircraft identification letter E-Excalibur) took off from Burn at approximately 22.10 hours and, setting course for the first leg of the outward flight, began to climb to operational height. The crew's main worry was the bright moonlight that was not exactly what 'met' had promised and was making the scene around the ascending Halifax as clear and as light as day.

---

[15] *Len Lambert had been commissioned on 21st March 1944 but was unaware of the fact and, at the time of the Nuremberg raid, was still wearing his sergeant's chevrons.*

The Pendulum and the Scythe

The aircraft crossed the enemy coast to the usual welcome from the Flak and searchlights and was lucky enough to be unmolested along the whole length of the long leg. Several times, however, the gunners witnessed combats between bombers and nightfighters taking place and many bombers were seen to go down in flames. This was very worrying as early in the flight their Monica tail warning radar, which detected aircraft approaching from the rear of the Halifax, had become unserviceable.

About seventy miles from the target Barton reiterated need for everyone to keep their eyes peeled as they were now turning onto the final approach to Nuremberg. Barton made the turn steeper than usual to allow the gunners an extra good look at the normally blind spot underneath the aircraft and just at that moment there was a series of loud bangs. The rear gunner, Fred Brice, called out for evasive action as the Halifax shuddered and went into a slight dive. Cy Barton pushed his aircraft into a tight corkscrew as the intercom went dead. `E-Excalibur had been hit in the nose and the starboard inner engine.

On hearing the call for evasive action, Timber Wood automatically rotated his mid-upper turret to face aft raising the barrels of his four .303 machine guns as he did so and fired blindly to the rear of the aircraft. Only one gun actually fired, the other three had frozen up. As the aircraft was in a turn to port, Sergeant Wood spotted a Junkers Ju88 beneath the Halifax and fired a long burst at it with his one functioning Browning. The nightfighter vanished into the darkness.

With the intercom out of action, Timber Wood used the emergency flashing light system to advise Cy Barton that it was now safe to resume course. Only seconds later, the Ju88 reappeared and the mid-upper gunner signalled for another corkscrew manoeuvre. During this corkscrew a Messerschmitt Me210 also attacked the Halifax, but from in front of the aircraft. Fortunately, because of Barton's evasive action the fire from the Me210 went over the top of the aircraft.

Finally, having lost both nightfighters, Wood again signalled his pilot to resume level flight. During the running battle, the Halifax had lost about 12,000 feet in height and was now flying at only 9,000 feet. It was now that they discovered that the navigator, bomb aimer and wireless operator were no longer in the aircraft. The howling gale from the open nose hatch told the story that they must have baled out.

The Pendulum and the Scythe

Following the crew drill, navigator Len Lambert folded up his navigational gear as his skipper made the turn onto the final approach to Nuremberg. It was their normal practice for navigation over the target area to be taken from notes on the navigator's knee-pad and from sightings by the bomb aimer, Canadian Wally Crate. Lambert's seat was directly over the escape hatch in the nose and, for obvious reasons, access to the hatch must not be obstructed.

Up in the nose, the rear gunner's shout for evasive action remained unfinished as the intercom went dead in the hail of cannon shells that peppered their forward compartment, miraculously without hitting any of them. The Halifax went into a steep dive and, from their windows in the nose, they could see that one engine was on fire. The emergency warning lights, which were being operated by the gunner's push buttons, were blinking on and off and all three crew members in the Halifax's nose misunderstood the signals, believing them to be an order to bale out. In this sort of situation, where the difference between life and death could be measured in fractions of a second, they can hardly be blamed for donning their parachutes and jumping.

It is now known that Len Lambert had not intended to bale out quite when he did. Having folded away his seat, he picked up his chest-type parachute to fasten it to his harness prior to opening the escape hatch. Unfortunately, with the aircraft bouncing about all over the sky, Lambert inadvertently picked his chute up by the D'-ring of the rip-cord, causing the drogue to spill out into the aircraft.

Fastening the chute to his harness and clutching the spilled drogue chute to his chest, Len now tried to open the escape hatch. It wouldn't budge. He kicked it - it still wouldn't move, finally he jumped on it with both feet. The next thing Len Lambert knew he was falling in space.

Quite amazingly Lambert was not injured during his unplanned departure from LK797 and his main concerns, once he found himself swinging under his open parachute canopy, were that the canopy was damaged and that it was bitterly cold.

Once Lambert had cleared the escape hatch, albeit very unconventionally, Wally Crate and wireless operator Jack Kay followed their navigator out into the cold night air. Len Lambert landed, shaken but unhurt, in a hard-frozen German field. Hiding his parachute and flying gear, he walked all night through heavily wooded countryside and then hid all through the following day. His second night on the march brought him to a farmhouse close to the railway line between Bamberg and Stassfurt, about fifty miles northwest of Nuremberg and, while attempting to steal food, Lambert was caught and taken to a Luftwaffe base at Schweinfurt. From there he was transported to the interrogation centre at Oberursel, near Frankfurt, where he was re-united with Wally Crate and Jack Kay, but all three feared the worst at the non-appearance of their skipper, flight engineer and two gunners.

Meanwhile back in 'E-Excalibur' and having discovered the loss of three important crew members, Cy Barton made the decision to continue on to the target. Seeing the target indicators, Cy made a determined effort to drop his bombs as close as possible and flew on well past the blazing target before setting a course for home. It was not until well after the war that it was discovered that the bombs had been dropped on Schweinfurt. While in the target area, the starboard inner engine, which had been vibrating quite badly since the attack, finally shed its red hot propeller. Fortunately this flew away from the aircraft rather than into the fuselage. The engine threw back sparks for a short while but mercifully, did not catch fire.

Barton and his crew had once before landed a damaged aircraft at the Woodbridge emergency landing ground and it is believed that it was Barton's intention to head there again. Using his captain's map and steering by the stars and his compass Pilot Officer Barton flew his Halifax back across enemy territory, carefully avoiding Flak and searchlights as he went and managing to get the damaged aircraft back up to 13,000 feet.

Well into the return journey, flight engineer Maurice Trousdale worked his way back to Timber Wood in the mid-upper turret and informed him of the situation, Wood's first concern was for their fuel state, wondering if they had enough to get them home, Trousdale's response in the affirmative came as a great relief and between Wood, Trousdale and Barton the decision was taken to make the effort to get back to the UK. Shortly after this, Barton sent instructions to Wood to leave his turret, then go and tell Fred Brice in the rear turret what was happening. Then he was to come up front to see if he could work the GEE equipment or the radio.

Cy Barton had always insisted on each crew member having a basic understanding of at least one other crew job and Timber Wood had, in the past, had some success with GEE. Unfortunately, the cannon shells that had

131

peppered the nose compartment had smashed the GEE box, the radio, the IFF and had chewed up all the maps in the navigators drawer. There was nothing that Wood could do.

It was still dark as they crossed the enemy coast and, after what seemed like an eternity over the dark, foreboding sea, someone voiced the opinion that perhaps although they were flying due west, if they had left the coast further south than they had intended, they could be flying out into the Atlantic and miss England altogether. Cy Barton therefore decided to turn north for a while (had he but known, his aircraft was at this point, only twenty minutes flying time away from his intended landing ground at Woodbridge). The Halifax flew north until it crossed some lights on the sea and taking these to be a convoy in the North Sea, Barton once again turned to fly due west. The grey dawn was gradually getting lighter when a Beaufighter appeared quite close, the flight engineer hurriedly fired off distress flares from the Very pistol but the Beaufighter, having identified the Halifax as friendly (British radar would have picked up an incoming aircraft with no IFF transmission and despatched a fighter to intercept) had already turned and left the Halifax alone.

As they crossed the English coast, the ground defences, in their usual inimitable way, failed to recognise the damaged Halifax as belonging to the RAF. They decided to try to add a few more holes, but Cy Barton about-turned and flew back out to sea. Timber Wood then went into the nose, taking great care when crossing the open escape hatch, to connect up the Aldis lamp. Barton turned back towards the UK and, with Wood flashing an SOS and a message that the Halifax was friendly, the ground gunners relented and allowed the aircraft to cross the coast.

Timber Wood then started his return down the fuselage and, just as he reached the cockpit, Barton shouted at him to get aft the crash position as quickly as possible; they were about to crash.

Unknown to the crew, the nightfighter's gunfire had severed the fuel pipes from the last tanks to the engines. As Maurice Trousdale switched over to these tanks, the fuel ran out into the slipstream instead of to the engines. All three remaining engines cut out just as Wood was alongside Cy Barton, hence Barton's shout. Wood rushed down the fuselage, over the main spar and had just taken up his crash position with his back to the spar as the first bump arrived.

The Pendulum and the Scythe

Two or three miles south of Sunderland (in County Durham as it was then) is a little mining village called Ryhope (the mine has long since closed). Barton's fuel finally ran out just as his aircraft was approaching the village at about 1,500 feet. As his remaining crew members took up their crash positions, Cy Barton, with only diving speed left to manoeuvre his damaged Halifax, attempted to land. Immediately in the path of LK797 were four rows of miners' cottages and Barton lifted the Halifax's nose to clear them. Unfortunately this robbed the young pilot of his last remaining speed and control and, clipping the last cottage in the last row, the aircraft flopped heavily onto a hillside, running over a railway line and into the yard of the local coal mine before coming to rest in several large pieces, unfortunately killing one miner on the way.

Timber Wood was knocked out by the crash. When he recovered, it was to hear Maurice Trousdale telling Fred Brice to 'Get off me bloody leg'. Looking up he saw Fred trying to climb out of the escape hatch in the top of the fuselage above the crash position. Maurice Trousdale, who had taken up his position on the starboard side of the fuselage, had been quite badly injured by the flap hydraulic accumulator exploding during the crash and was on the danger list for several days. Fred Brice and Timber Wood escaped with cuts, bruises, back injuries and shock.

The three survivors were helped out of the wrecked fuselage by a group of local miners and taken to the mine's first aid room, where they were looked after and given cups of sweet tea. Using the colliery telephone, Wood eventually managed to get through to the Squadron CO, Wing Commander Wilkerson, and advised him of their experiences of the night, not knowing at that time that Cy Barton had just died. Wood, Brice and Trousdale were then transferred to a local hospital for further treatment. Cy Barton survived the crash for thirty minutes, only briefly regaining consciousness to ask how his crew were before he died.

The letter that he left behind at Burn, to be sent to his Mother in the event of his death, was a further testimony to this young pilot's faith in God. His mother allowed it to be published and it was widely circulated at the time:

"Except for leaving you I am quite prepared to die. Death holds no terrors for me. I know I shall survive the judgement because I have trusted in Christ as my Saviour... All that I am anxious about is that you and the rest of the family will come to know Him... I commend my Saviour to you."

Three months later, in the London Gazette of 27th June 1944, came the announcement of Cy Barton's Victoria Cross for '... *gallantly completing his last mission in the face of almost impossible odds....*' The only Halifax VC, the only 4 Group VC. But, as his Mother said, "It won't bring him back, will it?"

In April, with D-Day on the horizon, the Command was officially attached to SHAEF. This came into effect from the 14th, so after a brief pause to recuperate from the Nuremberg raid the crews found themselves attacking shorter range French targets on a regular basis. There were still, however, a few trips deep into the Third Reich. The Brunswick raid of the 22/23rd April saw the first use of the thirty-pound liquid filled incendiary 'J' bomb, while within 4 Group the rebuilding of Driffield was completed.

The last of No.4 Group's new operational stations, Full Sutton, opened in May and 77 Squadron moved in from Elvington, where it had been based since October 1942. The reason for this move was that Elvington had been earmarked as the base for the French squadrons within the RAF and their first unit, 346 (Guyenne) Squadron formed there, as part of 4 Group, on 16th May. On the night of 22/23rd May the Command launched its largest number of sorties in a single night since the Millennium raids when 1,023 aircraft were despatched to Dortmund (375 aircraft from 1,3,6 and 8

Groups), Brunswick (235 aircraft from 1 and 5 Groups), Le Mans (132 from 6 and 8 Groups) and Orleans (128 from 4 and 8 Groups). The total Halifax force on this night was 230, 112 from 6 Group on the Le Mans raid and 108 from 4 Group on that to Orleans. One Halifax failed to return from each of these attacks.

Five days later, on the 27/28th May, the total sortie number rose to 1,111, exceeding the Millennium total of 1,047 for the first time. It had taken the Command two years, all bar three days, to finally surpass the amazing total of aircraft that Harris and Saundby had scraped together for that dramatic Cologne raid of so long ago. Targets for these 1,111 aircraft included Bourg Leopold, Aachen, Nantes, Rennes, Berlin, Dusseldorf and five coastal batteries in addition to various RCM, Serrate and Intruder sorties, minelaying and OTU sorties and drops to the Resistance. 316 Halifaxes were involved in these raids, 267 on the Bourg Leopold attack and 49 on those on the coastal batteries. Nine of them failed to return. It was during May that the Halifax B.Mk.II carried out its last front-line operations within 4 Group.

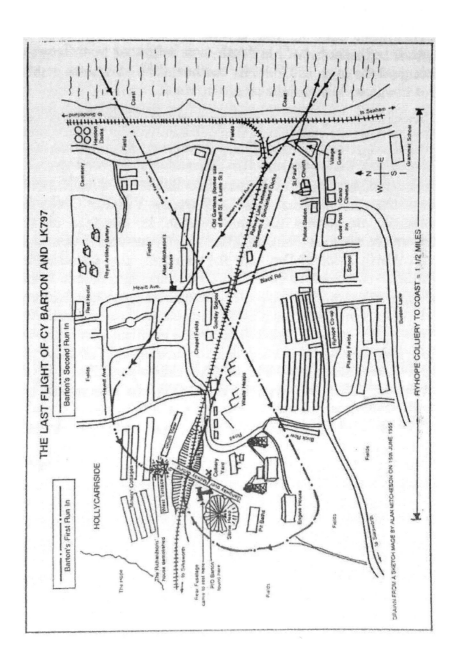

The detached port wing of Halifax LK797. (Alan Mitcheson)

The gangway over the railway cutting. The cross (top right) marks the place where Barton's body was found; the E by the railway line shows where one engine came to rest. (Alan Mitcheson)

The Pendulum and the Scythe

The Ryhope crash. The rear section of LK797 of 578 Sqn in which Trousdale, Brice and Wood survived. The young boy (circled lower right) is Alan Mitcheson, who has done much in the Ryhope area to commemorate Braton's gallantry. Top, inset: The newly-commissioned Cyril Barton in December 1943. (Alan Mitcheson)

The last of the Group's units to use them were 77 and 102 Squadrons. The Mk.IIs were then pensioned off to the HCUs.

On the eve of `D-Day', 5/6th June, the Halifax force exceeded 400 for the first time when 412 of them formed part of a 1,012 aircraft attack on Normandy coastal batteries. The Command dropped at least 5,000 tons of bombs this night, the largest tonnage in one night in the war so far. One Halifax and twelve Lancasters failed to return. Back in 4 Group, the second French unit, 347 (Tunisie) Squadron, formed at Elvington on the 20th June and it was during this month that the Group set a Command record when its bomber aircraft claimed to have shot down a total of thirty-three enemy nightfighters.

Harris' force returned to German targets in strength on the night of 23/24th July when 100 Halifaxes joined 529 other aircraft in an attack on Kiel. This unexpected return to Germany took the enemy defences by surprise and only four Lancasters were lost. During July also, the last front-line operations (within 4 Group) of the Mk.V Halifax took place, the last user unit being the French 347 Squadron. On the 3rd August the Command set another new record for total sorties when 1,114 aircraft, including 492 Halifaxes, attacked V-1 and oil storage sites in daylight for the loss of only six Lancasters. Two days later this record was broken again when 1,148 aircraft, including 469

137

Halifaxes, made further attacks on V-1 and oil storage sites, again by day. This time only three aircraft were lost, two Lancasters and one Halifax (0.3%).

Harris was now allowed a full return to German targets and on the night of 16/17th August he despatched 462 Lancasters to Stettin and 348 other aircraft (including 144 Halifaxes) to Kiel; seven Lancasters and three Halifaxes failed to return. On the 27th August, 216 Halifaxes of 4 Group, led by fourteen Mosquitoes and thirteen Lancasters of No.8 Group, made the first major daylight penetration of Germany with an attack on the Rhein-Preussen synthetic oil refinery at Meerbeck, Homberg. The bomber force was escorted by nine squadrons of Spitfires on the outward flight with a further seven covering the withdrawal. One Messerschmitt Bf110 was seen and swiftly driven off by the Spitfire escort and, despite severe Flak over the target, all aircraft returned safely. During the month of August No.4 Group carried out 3,629 sorties in twenty-two operations, the highest monthly figure for the Group during the whole war.

On 25th September, seventy Halifaxes from 4 Group commenced a series of urgent delivery flights from the UK to Belgium in order to alleviate the severe fuel shortage being experienced by the British Second Army. On every flight each Halifax could carry approximately 165 jerricans containing roughly 825 gallons of petrol, the Group flying 435 sorties over an eight day period. The squadrons delivered in excess of 350,000 gallons, those taking part in this operation included 77, 346 and 347 Squadrons. No aircraft were lost. It may, however, cause a wry smile when it is learned that, in order to deliver these 350,000 gallons of petrol to the Second Army, the squadrons involved used 350,000 gallons of petrol!

In October 1944 the Group contributed to some of the heaviest raids of the war when Operation Hurricane was launched on the 14[th.] The Command despatched 1,013 aircraft (including 474 Halifaxes) on a daylight attack on Duisburg, losing only thirteen Lancasters and one Halifax. At the same time, the US Eighth Air Force sent 1,252 heavy bombers with a 749-strong fighter escort to Cologne. That night the RAF returned to Duisburg with 1,005 aircraft, split into two forces, two hours apart. This force lost only seven aircraft, but Duisburg received nearly 9,000 tons of bombs in twenty-four hours. This attack did not involve 5 Group, because the Command was now so strong that while over 1,000 aircraft were involved in the Duisburg raid Harris was still able to despatch a further 240 Lancasters and Mosquitoes of

The Pendulum and the Scythe

No.5 Group to carry out a separate attack on Brunswick, losing only one aircraft in the process. This, along with other support and minor ops, brought the night's total sorties up to 1,572 for the loss of only ten aircraft (0.6%), giving an amazing total for twenty-four hours of 2,589 sorties with a loss rate of only 0.9% (24 aircraft) During this period a staggering 10,050 tons of bombs had been delivered by the Command. These totals would stand as records for the whole war. The tide had definitely turned.

On the night of the 23/24th October Harris launched the greatest number of aircraft to a single target in one night when 1,055 bombers attacked Essen for the loss of eight aircraft. The Halifax contribution was 463, of which three failed to return.

In an attack on Bochum on the night of the 4/5th November, one of the French units, 346 (Guyenne) Squadron, lost five out of sixteen Halifaxes despatched. They formed part of a 749-strong force that caused severe damage. A further eighteen Halifaxes and five Lancasters were lost in this last major attack of the war on this target. On the 16th November, the Command carried out 1,188 sorties in attacks near the German front lines at the request of the American 1st. and 9th. Armies. 413 Halifaxes, 78 Lancasters and 17 Mosquitoes of 4, 6 and 8 Groups attacked enemy communications in the Julich area. The USAAF carried out a further 1,239 sorties. Other RAF targets on this day were Duren and Heinsburg.

During October/November No.3 Group commenced operating as a separate force, utilising G-H, and Harris started to split his force in order to hit many targets at the same time. On the night of 21/22nd November, for instance, he despatched 283 aircraft from 1 and 8 Groups to bomb railway yards at Aschaffenburg, 273 aircraft from 1, 6 and 8 Groups to the oil refinery at Castrop-Rauxel, 270 aircraft to the synthetic oil refinery at Sterkrade, while 5 Group sent 142 aircraft to breach the banks of the Mittelland Canal near Gravenhorst and a further 128 to the Dortmund-Ems Canal near Ladbergen. Sorties for the night totalled 1,345 for the loss of only fourteen aircraft (1.0%).

On 12/13th December, No.4 Group sent 163 Halifaxes to join 377 aircraft from 1 and 8 Groups in yet another attack on Essen. All the Halifaxes returned safely but six Lancasters were lost in what was to be the last heavy night raid of the war on this target. Albert Speer paid the Command a compliment after this attack, saying that its extreme accuracy caused surprise.

One of the Group's two Australian units, 462 Squadron, Was screened from operations on the 22nd December, pending a move to 100 (Bomber Support) Group that took place on New Year's Day. During the course of 1944, air gunners from No.4 Group had claimed to have destroyed a total of 73 enemy nightfighters.

Because of bad weather, January 1945 was less hectic than preceding months, but 4 Group opened the year with a 105 Halifax attack on a benzol plant at Dortmund during the night of 1/2nd January. Although led by the Pathfinders, bombing was unfortunately scattered and the plant escaped damage, although all aircraft returned safely. The Group participated in raids on Ludwigshaven the following night and on the 5/6th the first raid on Hannover since October 1943 took place. This was an attack that caused unusually high losses for this period of the war when 23 Halifaxes and 8 Lancasters failed to return, a loss rate of 4.7%.

On the night of 6/7th January the Group took part in a 482 aircraft attack on an important railway junction at Hanau, destroying approximately 40% of the town and, on the night of the 13/14th January, it contributed to the 242 strong Halifax force that caused extremely accurate and effective damage at Saarbrucken. One of the Halifaxes that took part in this raid was 51 Squadron's Y-Yorker', a B.Mk III, Serial No MZ465 `MH-Y'. Flown by Flying Officer A. L. Wilson and his crew, this aircraft was involved in a mid-air collision with another bomber after leaving the target and nine feet of the nose, from the windscreen forward, was completely chopped off, killing the bomb aimer and the navigator. Immediately after the collision the aircraft dived 1,500 feet but Wilson regained control and coaxed the damaged aircraft back up to 11,000 feet, at which point it promptly stalled. Once again the pilot regained control of his aircraft and, by experimentation, discovered that he could maintain height at 7,000 feet. The wireless operator had managed to transmit an SOS, giving details of what had happened and approximate damage to the Halifax, within a short time of the accident occurring but, because of electrical shorting - blue sparks were playing all around the aircraft - the radio and all other electrical equipment had to be switched off shortly thereafter. Damage to the aircraft was quite extensive, in addition to the obvious loss of the nose section, the Halifax was also without intercom, airspeed Indicator, DR compass and most of the remainder of its navigation and flying instruments. Despite this, and the howling gale roaring down the entire length of the fuselage, Wilson managed to keep `Y-Yorker' in the air long enough to reach an emergency landing ground at which he succeeded in landing without further mishap.

The Halifaxes suffered heavy casualties during a night attack on Magdeburg on 16/17th January. Losses amounted to seventeen out of the 320 despatched (5.3%), but 44% of the target's built-up area was destroyed. Other targets attacked on this night were the Braunkohle-Benzin synthetic oil plant at Zeitz, near Leipzig, and other oil plants at Brux (Western Czechoslovakia) and at Wanne-Eickel. These, together with other minor operations, brought the Command's total effort for the night up to 1,238 sorties. Five nights later, on 22/23rd January, it was an altogether different story when 4 Group sent 107 Halifaxes to join 29 Lancasters and Mosquitoes of 5 and 8 Groups to carry out a small area attack on Gelsenkirchen. 'Moderate' damage was caused to residential and industrial areas of the town and all aircraft returned safely. The Group also contributed to the 316-strong Halifax contingent that helped to make a 602 aircraft attack on Stuttgart on the 28/29th January. The attack was split into two waves, separated by three hours and was to be the last heavy raid of the war on this city.

February opened with the Group's participation in an attack on Mainz on the first night of the month. 340 aircraft, including 293 Halifaxes of 4 and 6 Groups, had to bomb on PFF sky markers because of 10/10ths cloud and bombing was scattered. All aircraft on this raid returned safely but other attacks carried out on this night, to Ludwigshaven and Siegen, resulted in the loss of ten aircraft. Total Command sorties this night were 1,273.

The following night (2/3rd) the Command launched 1,252 sorties to Wiesbaden, Wanne-Eickel and Karlsruhe, losing 21 aircraft in all. No.4 Group's aircraft attacked two of the three targets hit on the night of 4/5th February, sending squadrons to Bonn - with aircraft from 6 and 8 Groups and a further 96 Halifaxes to Gelsenkirchen with the Pathfinders. All Halifaxes returned safely.

No.4 Group received a new AOC on 12th February. In fact three of the Command's Groups had new commanders during this month. There was no hint of criticism in these changes however, just a desire to allow a new generation of senior officers to gain experience of higher command before the war's end. Air Vice-Marshals Rice, of 1 Group, Carr of 4 Group and

Cochrane of 5 Group all handed over the reins to younger men. The new AOC of No.4 Group was Air Vice-Marshal J. R. Whitley. John Whitley had been the Station Commander at Linton-on-Ouse in late 1942, when the two Halifax units, 76 Squadron commanded by Leonard Cheshire, and 78 Squadron - commanded by Willie Tait, were the resident units. He was shot down over Northern France in April 1943 but, by dint of meticulous preparation before take-off and cool courage after landing in occupied France, he successfully evaded and returned to England. The Group had started the war with a Whitley -and it was also to end it with one!

Operation Thunderclap was launched on the night of 13/14th February with Dresden as its target (see Chapter 2) but the aircraft of 4 Group were not involved. Instead, 326 Halifaxes of 4 and 6 Groups, together with 34 Lancasters and Mosquitoes of the PFF, attacked the Braunkohle-Benzin synthetic oil plant at Bohlen, near Leipzig. Unfortunately bad weather was encountered and the 10/10ths cloud to 15,000 feet containing severe icing caused both the Pathfinders' marking and the Halifaxes' bombing to be scattered. Thunderclap's second phase took place the following night, with Chemnitz as the objective. This time the Halifax force was included and 218 of them took part, losing five in the process.

The Command again split its force on the night of 20/21st February, when it attacked Dortmund (514 aircraft), Düsseldorf (173 aircraft), Monheim (128) and the Mittelland Canal (154).

These raids, together with diversionary and minor operations, amounted to a total sortie figure of 1,283, twenty two aircraft failing to return. No.4 Group sent 156 Halifaxes on the Düsseldorf raid, successfully halting all production at the Rhenania Ossag refinery in the Reisholz district of the city.

A synthetic oil plant at Bergkamen, just north of Kamen, was attacked several times during late February and early March. On the 24th February 340 aircraft, including 290 Halifaxes of 4 and 6 Groups raided it and 153 Lancasters of 3 Group made a G-H attack on it the following day. They had another go at it on the 1st March, while on the night of 3/4th - the 2,000th night of the war - 33 Pathfinder aircraft led 201 Halifaxes from 4 Group to finally finish it off. This ended production at the plant for the rest of the war. It was on this last attack on Kamen that two of the Group's Halifaxes both logged their 100th operation. LW587, LK-A and MZ527, LK-D, both from 578 Squadron, went on to complete 104 and 105 trips respectively, but unfortunately this achievement saved neither of them from the scrap heap. At least two more Halifaxes are known to have carried out at least 100 trips, LV907 (NP-F, Friday the 13th.) of 158 Squadron, which has already been mentioned (see Chapter 2) and LV937. This latter aircraft served on 578 Squadron as LK-X between March and late August 1944 when it was transferred to 51 Squadron, becoming MH-J initially and then being subsequently re-lettered 'M' and then 'E'. It reached its century in April 1945. It seems a little unusual that, of the four Halifaxes to top the 'ton', three of them should have served on the same squadron.

Handley-Page Halifax B. Mk.II, Series I (Special) of 10 Squadron, fitted with the Tollerton nose fairing.

Operation Thunderclap continued on the night of the 5/6th March when 760 aircraft were despatched on a second attack on Chemnitz. 256 Halifaxes participated and the centre and south of the city suffered severe fire damage. The Command despatched 1,079 aircraft, the largest number to one target in the war so far, when Essen received 4,661 tons of bombs through 10/10ths cloud on 11th March. This raid was led by Oboe controlled aircraft and was extremely accurate. The city was virtually paralysed until US troops entered it some time afterwards. This was the last RAF raid on the city, most of which now lay in ruins. The pre-war population of 648,000 had been reduced to 310,000 by April 1944 and, while 7,000 had died in the ruins, the remainder had departed to less dangerous areas of the Fatherland. The following day, Dortmund was the recipient of 4,851 tons from 1,108 aircraft, also through cloud.

This was to be this city's last attack and the 1,108 sorties to one target was to be the largest of the whole war.

March was a busy time, with both daylight and night attacks. The Command dropped a greater tonnage of bombs (63,637 tons) than in any month of the war, a tonnage that was equal to all bombs dropped from September 1939 to July 1943. No.4 Group contributed 8,294 tons from 2,727 sorties for the loss of only fifteen aircraft. By the end of March the strategic bomber offensive was virtually over, the majority of April's targets being of a strictly military nature. The last 4 Group attack took place on the 25th April when it and 6 Group contributed 308 Halifaxes to the raid on the Wangerooge coastal batteries. Five Halifaxes failed to return. On Monday the 7th May 1945 all units in 4 Group, except for the French squadrons - 346 and 347 -were transferred to Transport Command. The next day, the 8th May, was V-E Day.

Many aircrew members who later won fame in Bomber Command started their operational careers in No.4 Group. Probably the most well-known of them was Leonard Cheshire (Group Captain the Lord Leonard Cheshire, VC, OM, DSO**[16], DFC.), who started as a Pilot Officer on 102 Squadron, at Driffield, on the 6th June 1940, ending the war as a Group Captain with over 100 operations under his belt. Sergeant T. G. (Hamish) Mahaddie began his ops on 77 Squadron in 1940 and went on to command No.9 (Pathfinder) Squadron. He had completed two operational tours before being promoted to Group Captain and becoming chief 'Horse Thief' for No.8 (PFF) Group. His 'boss', Air Vice-Marshal D. T. C. Bennett - A.O.C. of 8 Group, went to 4 Group as C.O. of 77 Squadron (Whitleys) in December 1941 after completing his early war role in organising and pioneering the ferrying of new aircraft across the Atlantic from America. It was with 77 Squadron that Don Bennett first learned the dangers of operational flying, but it was not long before he was moved on to command No.10 Squadron, newly equipped with Halifaxes. It was while flying with this unit that he was shot down while attacking the Tirpitz and,as already related, made his way home via Sweden in only five weeks. Bennett's own chief, Air Chief Marshal Sir Arthur Harris, was yet another ex-4 Group man, having been the Group's first A.O.C. in 1937. The Dam Busters, 617 Squadron, also had several connections with 4 Group.

---

[16] *The two asterisks denote two bars to Cheshire's original Distinguished Service Order.*

The Officer Commanding RAF Scampton, the base from which the unit launched its famous raid, was Group Captain J. N. H. Whitworth. As a Squadron Leader, in June 1940, Whitworth was the commander of 'B' Flight on No.10 Squadron and in January 1941 was the CO of 78 Squadron based at Dishforth. He also taught Leonard Cheshire to fly at Oxford University Air Squadron in the late Thirties. Squadron Leader H.M.(Dinghy) Young, the Skipper of AJ-A; ED877/G, who failed to return from the Dams Raid, served as a Pilot Officer - with Leonard Cheshire - on 102 Squadron at Driffield in 1940. The wireless operator in Flight Sergeant Bill Townsend's Lancaster, AJ-O; ED886/G, one of the specially modified aircraft that took part in the raid, was Flight Sergeant George Chalmers. George flew his first operations as an aircraftsman, complete with the winged bullet on his arm, in the Whitleys of 10 Squadron in 1939-40. He was awarded the DFM for his part in the attack on the Dams. Two of 617's Commanding Officers were also ex-4 Group. Leonard Cheshire (November 1943 to July 1944), as previously mentioned, and Wing Commander J.B. (Willie) Tait (July to December 1944). Willie had previously been a Squadron Leader on 51 Squadron before becoming CO of 78 Squadron.

The officer who did most to promote the 'Pathfinder' concept (see Chapter 2) was Group Captain S. O. Bufton. In July 1940 Syd Bufton was C.O. of 10 Squadron and later the first CO of 76 Squadron when it reformed with Halifaxes in 1941. Yet another member of 'Shiny Ten' at around that time was Sergeant George Dove, a wireless operator/air gunner, who having already been awarded a DFM, went on to win one of the war's few Conspicuous Gallantry Medals while on an attack on Milan on the night of 14/15th February 1943, whilst serving with 101 Squadron. Dove's skipper, Sergeant I. H. Hazard, and three other members of his crew also won the CGM on this mission, the only time in its history that this decoration was awarded to five members of the same crew at the same time. Ex-Cranwell 'brat' Dennis Witt served as a Sergeant pilot on 10 Squadron during 1939-40. He ended the war as a Wing Commander with a DSO, DFC and DFM, having completed over 100 operations. One CO of 35 (PFF) Squadron used to indulge his somewhat 'gallows' sense of humour by hanging a large axe over his desk, greeting all newcomers to his unit with the warning 'That's what you'll get here! The chop!'. His name was Pat Daniels and he had carried out his first operations with 58 Squadron between September 1940 and May 1941.

No.4 Group was the only one of Bomber Command's Groups never to have its own crest. Despite this lack of recognition it contributed a total of 57,407 sorties to the Command's war effort. It dropped almost 200,000 tons of bombs and laid 7,000 mines, losing 1,509 aircraft (2.6%) in the process. The Group carried out 94% of all Whitley sorties, 6.1% of all Wellington sorties and 57.3% of all Halifax sorties that were undertaken during sixty-eight months of war. These percentages represent 9,169 Whitley, 2,901 Wellington and 45,337 Halifax sorties. Losses amounted to 288 Whitleys (3.1%), 97 Wellingtons (3.3%) and 1,124 Halifaxes (2.5%). The Group started the war with six squadrons, reached its peak of nineteen squadrons in December 1942, just before it handed over all the Canadian units to No.6 Group and ended the conflict with eleven squadrons. Having been transferred to Transport Command on the 7th.May 1945, it remained part of it until February 1948 when the Group was finally disbanded.

Chapter Four

The Aircraft of No.4 Group

During the course of the Second World War, four aircraft types served in No.4 Group. In chronological order, these were the Whitley, Halifax, Wellington and the Hampden. The last named aircraft served only very briefly, equipping only the Canadian 408 (Goose) Squadron during the month of September 1942. As this unit carried out no Hampden operations during its four month sojourn with the Group and given that it re-equipped with Halifaxes in October 1942, this author deems it sufficient to merely acknowledge that the Hampden did, in fact, serve in 4 Group, however briefly and to leave its coverage at that.

Armstrong Whitworth Whitley

The Armstrong Whitworth Whitley was the first of the RAF's trio of 'heavy' bombers and all 1,814 of them were built at Baginton, Coventry. The Whitley was named after the area of Coventry in which the main Armstrong Whitworth factory was located. Known in the design office as the AW.38, the aircraft was built to Air Ministry Specification B.3/34, issued in July 1934. It was designed by the Armstrong Whitworth design team under the Chief Designer, Mr John Lloyd and the prototype (Serial No.K4586) flew from Baginton for the first time on 17th March 1936, with the Company's Chief Test Pilot, Mr.Alan Campbell Orde at the controls. Powered by two Armstrong Siddeley Tiger IX 14-cylinder, two-row radial engines, which were slightly supercharged, the aircraft was the first to be fitted with De Havilland three bladed, two position, variable-pitch propellers. K4586 attained a maximum speed of 192 mph at 7,000 feet and 186 mph at 15,000 feet. Its maximum range was 1,250 miles, its service ceiling was 19,200 feet and it took 27.4 minutes to reach 15,000 feet. Seven months before the prototype flew the Air Ministry had decided to re-equip the RAF's heavy bomber squadrons with the Whitley and in August 1935 they placed an order for 80 aircraft.

The first production aircraft, Serial No. K7184, was, naturally enough, a Mark I and it left the assembly line in March 1937. It was issued to No.10 Squadron at Dishforth on 9th March to start the replacement of their ageing Heyfords. The Mk.I was powered by the same engines as the prototype, had a wingspan of 84 feet, a length of 71 feet 3 inches and an empty weight of 14,275 lbs. Its normal loaded weight was 21,660 lbs. with a maximum of

23,500lbs. The bomb doors were opened by the simple expediency of the weight of the released bombs bearing down upon them and were closed after bomb release by elastic bungee cords. Not exactly 'high-tech', even for 1937, but it was simple and it worked. Defensive armament comprised manually operated nose and tail turrets, each containing a single .303 Vickers machine-gun. At an early stage of its production life it was found desirable to introduce dihedral on the outboard wing panels (from outboard of the engines to the tip) in order to improve overall stability. This modification was applied to all aircraft, including those which had already left the factory. The 26th production aircraft (K7208) was modified to permit operation at an all-up weight of 33,500 lbs., an increase of 10,000 lbs. above the normal maximum and extra fuel tankage increased the aircraft's range to 1,940 miles. This aircraft, together with the 27th production aircraft (K7209) were later converted as prototypes for the Merlin engined Mk.IV, while the 29th aircraft (K7211) was modified as a prototype for the Mk.III and then subsequently as a Mk.IV.

Only thirty-four Mk.Is were built, equipping 10, 58 and 78 Squadrons, before production changed over to the Mk.II, around which A.M. Specification B.21/35 had been written. This entered service with 58 Squadron at Boscombe Down in January 1938. No.51 Squadron was next in

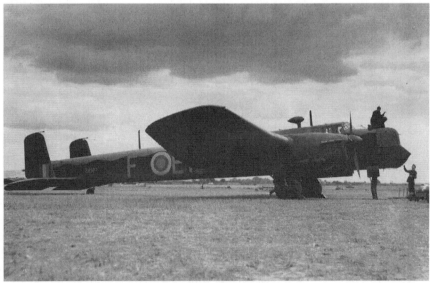

A Whitley Mk.V of 78 Squadron.

line, followed by No.7 Squadron in March and 97 Squadron in July the same year. Forty-six Mk.IIs were built, the balance of the original order for 80 aircraft. The main difference between the two Marks was the fitting to the Mk.II of 920 hp Tiger VIII engines with two-speed superchargers. These increased the maximum speed to 215 mph at 15,000 feet, with a cruising speed of 177 mph at the same altitude. Maximum range was 1,315 miles and the service ceiling was boosted to 23,000 feet. The climb to 15,000 feet was reduced by almost four minutes to 23.5 minutes.

Air Ministry Specification B.20/36 and Contract No.522438/36, both issued in 1936, resulted in the building of 80 Mk.IIIs. This Mark's most notable differences from its predecessors were mainly confined to changes in defensive armament, with the replacement of the manually operated nose turret by a similarly armed Nash and Thompson powered turret and the addition of a retractable ventral 'dustbin' turret armed with two .303 Brownings. This 'dustbin' had a full 360 degree traverse and could be manually wound up and down. Unfortunately it weighed half-a-ton and, when the extra weight was added to the tremendous drag it induced when in the down position, it drastically reduced the aircraft's speed at a time when as much speed as possible was needed to enable it to escape the unwelcome attentions of an attacking fighter. It was soon proved that while the concept of this ventral turret was admirable, the practicality was much less so. The 'well' into which the dustbin was fitted had been built in to all the previous Marks of Whitley and would, in fact, continue on later Marks. It was subsequently to prove useful as a dropping hatch for paratroops. The other visible external difference of the Mk.III was an increase in dihedral on the wing outer panels, while internally, it was fitted with new bomb racks capable of accommodating larger bombs.

By the time the eightieth Mk.III had been delivered, the Whitley had taken on a new lease of life with a change of engines. Contract No.522438/36, issued in 1936, ordered forty Mk.IV aircraft fitted with Rolls Royce Merlin IV engines (rated at 1,030 hp for take-off and 990 hp at 12,250 feet) driving Rotol constant speed propellers. The first one was delivered to No.10 Squadron at Dishforth in May 1939. Another vast improvement on the Mk.IV was the replacement of the single Vickers-armed, rear manual turret with a powered Nash and Thompson unit equipped with four Browning .303 machine guns. This was the most powerful defensive rear armament of any bomber extant at that time. Two additional wing tanks, of 93 gallons capacity each, increased the Whitley's fuel load to 705 gallons and the characteristic

Plexiglass 'chin' extension was fitted to replace the earlier flat Bomb Aimer's sighting window in the nose. The Merlin engines made a marked improvement in performance, maximum speed rising to 245 mph at 16,000 feet, while maximum cruising speed went up to 220 mph at 15,000 feet, an altitude that could now be reached in only 16 minutes. The new Mark's normal cruising range was 1,250 miles but this could be extended to 1,800 miles by fitting auxiliary fuel tanks in the fuselage. Empty weight was now 17,250 lbs. and normal loaded weight was 25,900 lbs.

The Mark IV retained the docile handling characteristics of the Tiger-engined versions in the air, but could be something of a handful on take-off, with a marked swing to port that could not be held on the rudders alone, needing some careful juggling of the throttles to correct it. On the night of 1st October 1939, three Mk.IVs of No.10 Squadron became the first RAF aircraft to fly over Berlin.

With the availability of the Merlin X engine, with a further increase in power (1,075 hp for take-off and 1,130 hp at 5,250 feet) these engines were installed in the last seven Mk.IV airframes (K9049 to K9055), which were then redesignated the Mk.IVa, all seven of which served on 78 Squadron.

The largest pre-war production contract for a bomber aircraft was placed in 1938. This was Contract No.75147/38 and called for 312 Whitley Mk.V aircraft. This mark was to become the most extensively produced version of the aircraft with 1,466 of them leaving the Armstrong Whitworth factory. Like its immediate predecessor, the Mk.V was powered by two Merlin X engines but its fuselage was 15 inches longer than the Mk.IVa, the extra length being added at the rearmost frame, thus putting the rear turret further aft to give the tail gunner a better field of vision and fire. The tail fins and rudders were also redesigned, becoming less angular and slightly increasing the aircraft's keel surface in order to further improve directional stability. BTR rubber de-icing boots were fitted to the leading edges of the wings, fuel capacity was again increased, this time to 837 gallons (normal) or 969 gallons (maximum) and the D/F (Direction Finding) loop was reduced in size and housed in a streamlined fairing. The Mk.V had a slightly increased normal cruising range over the Mk.IV (1,500 miles compared to 1,250 miles) but, being some 2,100 lbs heavier than its forerunner, it suffered a loss of 15 mph on top speed and 10 mph on cruising speed. Climbing time to 15,000 feet remained unchanged, however, at 16 minutes.

Although effectively obsolescent at the outbreak of war, it was the Mk.III that undertook the Command's first night operation of the conflict when, on the night of 3/4th September, three Mk.III's from 51 Squadron (K8938, K8941 and K8982) and seven from 58 Squadron (K8964, R; K8969, G; K8990, L; K9006, E; K9009, M; K9013, W and K8973, K, the last being flown by the raid leader, Squadron Leader Sutton) took off from RAF Leconfield (they were actually based at Linton-on-Ouse) to drop six million leaflets (also known as 'Bumphlets') on Bremen, Hamburg and the Ruhr. On the 3rd September 1939 only 77 Squadron was equipped with Mk.V Whitleys, although it still had some Mk.IIIs on strength. The rest of 4 Group's operational units were still flying Mk.IIIs (51, 58 and 102 Squadrons) or Mk.IVs (10 Squadron). 78 Squadron, which was at this time a 4 Group Pool (Training) unit based at Dishforth had a mixed bag of Marks I, IVa and V although, as far as the Mk.Vs were concerned, they were only fitting the first ten of them with operational equipment prior to handing them over to 77 Squadron in the front line. The RAF's total Whitley strength at the start of the war was 32 Mk.Is, 43 Mk.IIs, 76 Mk.IIIs, 33 Mk.IVs, 7 Mk.IVas and 5 Mk.Vs, 196 in total, equipping six of 4 Group's squadrons and two of 6 (Training) Group's units. By the time that Bomber Command was finally allowed to carry out its first real bombing attack, on the night of 19/20th March 1940, most of the Group's front line squadrons were almost fully equipped with the Mk.V, Nos.10 and 51 Squadrons having started to re-equip that month.

Although not relevant to this book, it is worth mentioning that one other Mark of Whitley was produced. This was the Mk.VII, a version of the Mk.V especially built for Coastal Command of which 146 were produced. The Whitley was also used as a paratroop transport (initial trials were carried out with a Mk.II; Marks III, IV and V were used for training and operations) and as a glider tug (Mk.V only). Chapter Three details two of the Whitley's successes as a paratroop transport.

The Whitley enjoyed great affection from its crews, although it was sometimes seen as a strange beast to the uninitiated Most surviving Whitley pilots will now admit to never having actually been in full control of the aircraft throughout the duration of a flight, but it was at all times so docile that it could be left largely to its own devices. It never, ever did exactly what its pilot requested of it, but, by and large, the things it did concede to do were usually reasonable and not uncomfortable. The Whitley's arrival on the ground was a unique affair of its own. With its Merlin engines singing their own individual songs - they could rarely be synchronised for more than a few minutes at a time - the pilot would motor gently onto the grass (no hard runways in the early days) on the mainwheels and then attempt to get the tail down. At this point the Whitley would ignore all control inputs from the pilot and, in its own time, allow its tailwheel to quietly and gently kiss the ground.

As mentioned earlier, take-offs could be somewhat 'hairy'. The pilot had to use the throttles as well as full rudder to counter the swing to port, which the power of the Merlins induced. It was not unusual to see a Whitley floating crab-wise into the air. In flight the Whitley always gave the visual impression that its wings and fuselage were travelling on different flight paths. This was due to the 8.5 degree angle of incidence on the wing that was designed into the aircraft at an early stage of the design concept, at a time when flaps were a very rare fitment on aircraft. The addition of flaps to the aircraft, before production commenced, would probably have rendered this large angle of incidence superfluous, but apparently no-one thought to reduce it. Because of this the aircraft flew with a decidedly 'nose-down' attitude, but it was, nevertheless, as steady as a rock. The Whitley was a docile, matronly aircraft which, for the most part, behaved like the lady she was.

The Whitley had many impressive firsts to its credit. It flew the first night raid of the war (3/4th September 1939), it was the first aircraft to fly over Berlin (1st October 1939), dropped the first bombs on German soil (Hornum 19/20th March 1940 accompanied by Hampdens) attacked the German mainland (Monchengladbach 10/11th May 1940) and raided Italy (11/12th June 1940). It also carried out the first British paratroop raid of the war (see Chapter 3.) This grand old aircraft carried out its last front-line operation with 58 Squadron on the night of 27/28th April 1942 but, as part of the OTU force, it also participated in all three of the Thousand Bomber attacks, by which time it had carried out 9,868 sortie's for the loss of 317 aircraft (3.22%), of which No.4 Group undertook 9,169 for the loss of 288 aircraft (3.1%).

Vickers Armstrong Wellington

Although the next 4 Group aircraft in chronological order is the Halifax, the longevity of this type kept it in service throughout the war. It is therefore more logical to consider next the Vickers Armstrong Wellington. This aircraft was initially conceived as a daylight heavy bomber, but early war daylight raids soon proved that the idea of self-defending bomber formations was totally impracticable in the face of a determined attack by modern fighter aircraft. After a final and disastrous armed reconnaissance to the Schillig Roads and Wilhelmshaven on 18th December 1939, in which twelve out of twenty-four Wellingtons were lost and another six were badly damaged, the aircraft was, through no fault of its own, relegated mainly to night bombing, although some daylight sorties were carried out up to April 1940.

The Wellington, Vickers Type 271, was designed by Barnes Wallis and Vickers Chief Designer, Rex K. Pierson. It incorporated Wallis' geodetic construction previously used in the successful R100 airship and the Vickers Wellesley long range monoplane and utilised the lessons learned from the latter. Designed to meet the requirements of Air Ministry Specification B.9/32, issued in September 1932, it was intended that the aircraft should be fitted with steam cooled Goshawk engines. The Goshawk, however, failed to come up to expectations and the specification was relaxed to allow the fitment of Bristol Pegasus X engines and the prototype (Serial No.K4049) flew for the first time on 15th June 1936, with test pilot 'Mutt' Summers at the controls.

Although destined to be almost completely re-designed before emerging as the Wellington Mk.I, the Type 271 was a major step forward in British bomber design, with a well streamlined fuselage and a fairly high aspect ratio wing (8.83:1) for a twin-engined aircraft. Type 271 had a wingspan of 85 feet 10 inches, a fuselage length of 60 feet 6 inches and a crew of four/five. Air Ministry Specification B.29/36 issued in 1936, was written around this prototype and was accompanied by an order for 180 aircraft,

Wellington production was initiated at the Vickers Weybridge Works at Brooklands, with the first, production aircraft (L4212) flying on 23rd December 1937. Vickers later established two shadow factories, the one at Broughton, near Chester, flying its first machine (L7770) in late August '39 and Squires Gate, Blackpool, whose first production Wellington, a Mk.Ic (X3160), flew in 1940. The first production Wellington was fitted with Bristol Pegasus X engines and had Vickers-designed Fraser Nash powered nose and tail turrets, fitted with a single machine gun in the nose and two in the tail and was equipped with a ventral turret. Its wingspan was 86 feet 1 inch and its length was 61 feet precisely. Meanwhile, further development of the Pegasus engine resulted in the Pegasus XVIII, offering 1,000 hp and these were fitted to L4212 and test flown on 23rd April 1938. All subsequent Mk.I aircraft were then similarly fitted.

The Mk.Ia featured Nash and Thompson nose and tail turrets, both fitted with two .303 Brownings and the crew was increased to six. Also, the aircraft was fitted with an astrodome for the navigator and larger wheels to cope with its higher gross weight of 28,500lbs. The Mk.Ib was not proceeded with and the Mk.Ia was therefore succeeded by the Mk.Ic on which the 12-volt electrical system was replaced by one of 24 volts and the ventral turret was deleted in favour of a Vickers gas-operated `Ic' gun mounted in either side of the fuselage.

By September 1939, the Weybridge factory was achieving its target of one aircraft per day, having produced the initial order for 180 Mk.Is before going on to the Mk.Ia. The Chester works built three Mk.Is, then seventeen Mk.Ia s when it then switched to the Mk.Ic. Squires Gate's production commenced with the Mk.Ic. The first Mk.Is reached No.9 Squadron at Stradishall in October 1938 and by the outbreak of war six units were so equipped. The early Wellington development had not, however, gone unpenalised. While the Mk.I was capable of a maximum speed of 267 mph at 15,500 feet, the Mk.Ia was 16 mph slower because of the ventral turret, while the heavier Mk.Ic could only manage a top speed of 250 mph

The Mk.II Wellington was fitted with two Rolls Royce Merlin engines and the prototype (L4250) first flew on 3rd March 1939, while the Mk.III had Bristol Hercules III engines and this prototype (L4251) took to the air for the first time on 16th May that same year. Production of both these types was delayed however, so as not to disrupt the flow of Mk.Is. Both types eventually went into large scale production during late 1940, reaching Bomber Command early in 1941. All the 585 Mk.II's produced were built at Weybridge, while the Mk.III's were initially built at Chester, followed first by Weybridge and then by Squires Gate. By September 1940 the three plants were turning out 134 Wellingtons per month. It was a couple of modified Mk.II Wellingtons (W5389 and W5439) that dropped the RAF's first 4,000 lbs. blockbuster bombs over Emden on the night of 31st March/1st April 1941.

The Wellington Mk.X was an improved version of the Mk.III and went into production in 1942, a total of 3,500 of them being built. They had a wingspan of 86 feet 2 inches, a length of 64 feet 7 inches, a wing area of 753 square feet and weighed in at 26,325 lbs., with a normal loaded weight of 31,500 lbs. The maximum fuel capacity of 1,236 gallons gave a range of 1,885 miles at the normal cruising speed of 180 mph, while carrying 1,500 lbs. of bombs. Sacrificing fuel for bomb-load gave a range of 1,325 miles with 4,500 lbs. of bombs at the same speed. The Mk.X's maximum speed was 250 mph at 600 feet or 255 mph at 14,500 feet. Its service ceiling was 24,000 feet and it took 27.7 minutes to reach an altitude of 15,000 feet.

Of the 1,047 aircraft that participated in the first 'Operation Millennium' thousand bomber raid to Cologne on the night of 30/31st May 1942, over half (599) were Wellingtons and, during the period of 1941-42, no fewer than 21 of Bomber Command's squadrons were equipped with the type. During its front line service with the Command the Wellington carried out 44,139 sorties and dropped approximately 42,440 tons of bombs for the loss of 1,369 aircraft. It carried out its last operational mission, to Hannover, on the night of 8/9th October 1943. Throughout its production life a total of 11,461 Wellington aircraft were built.

No.4 Group's first Wellington unit was 104 Squadron (formed 1st April 1941), closely followed, three weeks later, by 405 (Vancouver) Squadron, RCAF. In February 1942, 104 Squadron was transferred to the Middle East Air Force, but its Merlin engined Mk.IIs remained in the UK to be taken on charge by the newly formed 158 Squadron, which used them until it converted to Halifaxes in July 1942, 405 having already re-equipped with the Halifax in April. With but two exceptions (196 and 466 Squadrons) all other 4 Group Wellington units were Canadian squadrons, only one of which (419 Squadron) converted to the Halifax prior to leaving the Group[17].

No.196 Squadron kept its Wellingtons throughout its service in 4 Group, being transferred to No.3 Group in July 1943. The last Wellington unit in 4 Group was 466 (RAAF) Squadron, which did not convert to the Halifax until October 1943. Four of the Canadian Wellington units (419, 426, 428 and 431) did not undertake any operations while with 4 Group, while 427 Squadron carried out only one operation during its three-month sojourn in the Group. In total, No.4 Group carried out 2,901 Wellington sorties for the loss of 97 aircraft and its usage of the various Marks of Wellington breaks down as follows:-

Mk.II:

104 Squadron   Apr 1941 - Feb 1942

158 Squadron   Feb 1942 - Jul 1942

405 Squadron   Apr 1941 - Apr 1942.

Mk.III

419 Squadron   Aug 1942 - Nov 1942

420 Squadron   Aug 1942 - Dec 1942

424 Squadron   Oct 1942 - Dec 1942

---

[17]*One other Canadian unit converted to Halifaxes prior to leaving 4 Group. This was 408 (Goose) Squadron, which had come from 5 Group, equipped with Hampdens.*

425 Squadron   June 1942 - Dec 1942

426 Squadron   Oct 1942 - Dec 1942

427 Squadron   Nov 1942 - Dec 1942

428 Squadron   Nov 1942 - Dec 1942

429 Squadron   Nov 1942 - Dec 1942

466 Squadron   Oct 1942 - Nov 1942 (for training only)

Mk.X

196 Squadron   Nov 1942 - Jul 1943

431 Squadron   Nov 1942 - Dec 1942

466 Squadron   Nov 1942 - Sep 1943

Handley Page Halifax

The longest serving aircraft in No.4 Group during the war was the Handley Page Halifax. Specification B.3/34 which resulted in the Whitley, was less than a year old when the Air Ministry issued Specification B.1/35 in a search for the Whitley's replacement. Handley Page was one of several manufacturers submitting designs. Like the Manchester/Lancaster, the Halifax also started its design life as a twin-engined aircraft, the HP55, powered by two Bristol Hercules engines. As a safeguard, alternative versions featuring two Merlins or two Vulture engines were also studied. The HP55 was not the successful entrant and the order for B.1/35 went to Vickers with their 'Warwick' development of the Wellington.

By 1936 the Air Ministry was beginning to appreciate the need for four-engined heavy bombers, Specification B.12/36 resulted in the Short Stirling while P.13/36, for an all metal cantilever mid-wing monoplane powered by two Rolls Royce Vulture engines, resulted in the placing of two development contracts. One went to A.V. Roe (for the Manchester) and the other, placed in April 1937, went to Handley Page, calling for two prototypes of their HP56 design. During August 1937, when it became obvious that the Vulture engine was not developing its intended power or reliability, the Air

Ministry asked Handley Page to re-design the HP56 to take four Merlin engines. This re-design emerged as the HP57 and thus, the Halifax was born.

A 'fresh from the factory' Halifax B.Mk.III

The HP57 was ordered into production in January 1939, a full nine months before the prototype (serial no. L7244) first flew on 25th October at the hands of Major J. L. Cordes. The second prototype (L7245) flew on 17th August 1940 and the first production aircraft (L9485) joined its two predecessors on the Boscombe Down test programme in October 1940. The Halifax B.Mk.I had a 22 feet long bomb bay in a fuselage measuring 70 feet 1 inch, with further bomb cells in the wing centre section. Its wingspan was 98 feet 10 inches and it was powered by four 1,145 hp. Merlin X engines driving Rotol constant speed, three bladed, wooden propellers, giving a maximum speed of 265 mph at 17,500 feet. Normal range, with 2,242 gallons of fuel and a 5,800lbs. bomb load, was 1,860 miles. Maximum bomb load was 13,000lbs.

Defensive armament comprised two Boulton Paul power operated turrets, that in the nose containing two .303 Browning machine guns whilst that, in the tail housed four. These were supplemented by two beam guns in the sides of the rear fuselage.

Production of the Halifax was ultimately carried out by an organisation known as the 'Halifax Group'. This was a large conglomerate of companies comprising the parent company, Handley Page, English Electric, the London Aircraft Production Group (LAPG) consisting of Chrysler Motors, Duple Bodies and Motors, Express Motor and Body Works, Park Royal Coachworks and the London Passenger Transport Board, Rootes Securities and last, but by no means least, Fairey Aviation. During its peak production period the Halifax Group had 41 factories and dispersed units, 600 sub-contractors and 51,000 employees who together produced one complete Halifax aircraft every working hour. A total of 6,176 Halifaxes were ultimately built. 4,046 of them being produced between October 1940 and mid-1944. Not a single, solitary one of them was preserved for posterity.

On Guy Fawkes Day, 5th November 1940, No.35 Squadron was resurrected as a bomber unit within 4 Group and detached to Boscombe Down for equipping with the new Halifax. The Squadron's Commanding Officer was Wing Commander R. W. P. Collings. One of the unit's crews, captained by Flying Officer M. T. G. Henry DFC, collected the Squadron's first aircraft (L9486) and took it back to Boscombe Down on 13th November. The Squadron's training task was not to be an easy one however, for no-one had any experience of flying large four-engined bombers and crews were very much thrown in at, the deep end. The task was somewhat alleviated by the fact that all the squadron crews were skippered by operationally experienced pilots, all of whom wore the ribbon of the DFC or DFM. Initial progress was also hampered by a lack of aircraft and a series of moves to Leeming on 20th November and then to Linton-on-Ouse on 5th December.

The Halifax undertook its first operation, to Le Havre, on the night of 11th March 1941, an operation that was marred by the shooting down of one Halifax (L9489, TL-F) flown by Squadron Leader Gilchrist. This aircraft was intercepted on its return to the UK by an RAF Beaufighter nightfighter whose crew mistook the new bomber for an enemy aircraft and shot it down in flames over Surrey. As already mentioned (Chapter 3) only Squadron Leader Gilchrist and his Flight Engineer, Sergeant Aedy, survived this tragic event. It was not until July 1941, following the daylight attack on the

Halifax B. MkIs of 35 Sqn take off from Linton-on-Ouse

Scharnhorst at La Pallice, that the existence of the Halifax was announced to the British public. By this time a second Halifax unit was not only extant but also operational, having taken part in the La Pallice raid with 35 Squadron. No.76 Squadron was formed from 'C' Flight of 35 Squadron at Linton-on-Ouse on 1st May 1941. It was also equipped with the B.Mk.I and was placed under the command of Wing Commander S.O.Bufton.

Immediately after Handley Page had completed the initial production batch of 84 aircraft, production switched to building the B.Mk.II, starting with L9609. The major technical difference between the Mark I and Mark II was the fitting of more powerful Merlin XX engines, while the main visual differences were the deletion of the rearmost wireless aerial mast and the substitution of a Boulton Paul C.Mk.II dorsal turret (without any doubt the biggest, ugliest mid-upper turret ever designed) fitted with two .303 Brownings in place of the Mk.I's waist guns. The addition of this turret promptly negated any improvement that might have been imparted by the Merlin XX engines.

Further units were formed or re-equipped as Halifax production increased, with Nos.10 and 102 Squadrons replacing their Whitleys with B.Mk.IIs in December 1941, followed by 78 Squadron in March 1942 and 405 Squadron in April. No.158 Squadron swapped its Wellingtons for B.Mk.IIs in May and 408 Squadron its Hampdens for B.Mk.Vs in September, which were replaced with B.Mk.IIs in December. Halifax B.Mk.IIs also went to 77 Squadron in October and to 51 and 419 Squadrons in November.

The B.Mk.V, which equipped 408 Squadron, was basically a B.Mk.II with a Dowty lever suspension undercarriage in place of the Mk.II's Messier telescopic units. This was a measure taken in late 1941, due to doubts over British Messier being able to keep their production rate up to that of the Halifax. The Dowty undercarriage was actually smoother over bumpy ground and gave improved handling on take-off, but there was a not. inconsiderable weight penalty, despite the more solid Messier units looking to be the heavier of the two.

Unfortunately, the addition of the bulky C.Mk.II mid-upper turret was to prove to be the straw that broke the camel's back At this time, despite the fitting of Merlin XX engines, the Halifax was still underpowered. The extra weight and drag of the new turret resulted in an alarming tendency for the aircraft to spin uncontrollably when fully loaded. During 1942, Halifax accidents and losses began to mount steeply and an analysis of these revealed that a large percentage were due to rudder overbalance, a feature that had been present, to some degree, since the Halifax's entry into service. Many modifications were carried out in order to cure this, including limiting the rudder travel by fitting larger stops and bulbous noses were fitted to the rudders themselves. The problem was not really cured, however, until the whole airframe was cleaned up by removing the very rough (and thus high drag inducing) matt black night paint finish, the enormous asbestos exhaust shrouds and some other unnecessary appendages that had been hung on the poor Halifax since its entry into service and replacing the original triangular fins with the larger D' fins. Other modifications that were incorporated to help reduce accidents and improve performance were the total deletion of the nose turret (operational research showed that it was hardly ever used) and its replacement with, initially, a metal fairing. This change, together with the deletion of the ugly C.Mk.II mid-upper turret, was redesignated the B.Mk.II (or V) Series 1 (Special). The next stage was to redesign the aircraft's front end, incorporating a streamlined perspex nose housing a single Vickers gun (this was sometimes removed on the squadrons) and to fit a much smaller, lower profile and lighter mid-upper turret (the Boulton Paul A.Mk.VIII), fitted with four Browning machine guns, which restored the Halifax's defensive capability. An aircraft in this state of modification was designated the B.Mk.II (or V) Series 1a.

Between November 1942 and August 1943 the bulk of Halifax production went to re-equipping the Canadian units in No.6 Group. Therefore it was not until the 12th August that No.4 Group received sufficient new aircraft to equip the reforming 462 (RAAF) Squadron at Driffield. This was followed by 466 (RAAF) Squadron converting from Wellingtons to the B.Mk.II.

Although the Merlin-engined Halifaxes did commendable work with Bomber Command, from their introduction into service in November 1940 right through to mid-1944, they were always underpowered. When fully loaded they were incapable of reaching their designed operational height and this made them easy prey for both Flak and Luftwaffe nightfighters, not to mention from bombs from higher flying aircraft! The first version of the Halifax to redress this serious problem was the B.Mk.III. Fitted with Bristol Hercules XVI radial engines of 1,615 hp, almost 500 hp more per engine than the Merlin XX, the B.Mk.III could not only operate at a new maximum all-up weight of 65,000 lbs. (3,500 lbs more than previous marks) but it also had a quite remarkable all-round improvement in performance.

Handley Page had retained a B.Mk.II (R9534) for use as a test aircraft and, by late 1942, this had been cleaned-up to a Series 1 (Special) modification state except for still being fitted with a C.Mk.II mid-upper turret and not yet having the larger `D' fins. In late 1942 it was this aircraft that was first fitted with four Hercules VI engines, followed by the fitting of a retractable tail wheel in early 1943 but it did not receive the new 'D' fins until May 1943 making the aircraft ready to commence test flying the radial engines on 1st June. Now redesignated as the B.Mk.III prototype, R9534 found its test flying intensifying greatly on the 17th July.

The first production B.Mk.III (HX227) flew on the 29th August 1943 and was delivered to Boscombe Down for service testing, where it quickly gained approval and praise while the first deliveries to operational squadrons took place on 3rd November. The first units to receive the new Mark were 6 Group's 433 Squadron and 466 RAAF Squadron in 4 Group. It was the latter unit that was the first to achieve operational status on the type when they took them minelaying on the night of 1st December 1943.

In January 1944 two new 4 Group units formed with the B.Mk.III. These were 640 Squadron, from 'C' Flight of 158 Squadron on the 7th and 578 Squadron from 'C' Flight of 51 Squadron on the 14th. By early May all the 4 Group squadrons had re-equipped with the new mark. No.346 (Free French)

Squadron was then formed on 16th May, at Elvington, initially with B.Mk.Vs. The second French unit, 347 Squadron, formed at the same base on 20th June, also with B.Mk.Vs, just as its sister unit was converting to B.Mk.IIIs. 347 followed suit in July, at which time the re-equipment of No.4 Group with the Mark III was completed for a second and final time.

From a pilot's point of view, the Halifax B.Mk.III was a beautiful aircraft to fly, apart from being very slightly heavy on the ailerons. It had excellent visibility and an initial rate of climb (960 feet/minute) that left all its contemporaries, including the Lancaster, standing. Many pilots who flew both the Halifax B.Mk.III and the Lancaster have expressed a strong preference for the 'Hallie'. Its performance was at least as good as that of the Lancaster, matching it for speed (280 mph) and service ceiling at maximum load (20,000 feet), although this official ceiling figure was frequently exceeded by both types, the Halifax was capable of reaching at least 24,000 feet.

Apart from the superior initial rate of climb already mentioned, the B.Mk.III had a slightly longer range (1,030 miles) than the Lancaster (985 miles) when both were carrying a 13,000lbs bomb-load.[18] It must be said, however, that due to the internal construction of their respective bomb bays the Lancaster was capable of carrying larger bombs than the Halifax. In some cases this was achieved by the adaptation or modification of the airframe structure, as was the case in the equipping of the Lancaster to carry the splendid collection of large bombs designed by Barnes Wallis, Upkeep (the Dam Busters mine), Tallboy and finally Grand Slam.

Towards the end of the war, two further Marks of Halifax entered service alongside the B.Mk.III. The B.Mk.VI started to join 4 Group squadrons in February 1945 and the B.Mk.VII entered service primarily with 6 Group. Both of these Marks had a pressure-transfer fuel system with fuel tanks grouped for each engine. They also had additional fuel tankage, special filters over the carburettor intakes and the H2S radar scanner housing was a permanent fixture. The B.Mk.VI was fitted with 1,675 hp. Hercules 100 engines giving a maximum speed of 312 mph at 22,000 feet, and, despite an increased all up weight of 68,000 lbs., the new engines gave this Halifax an

---

[18] *These performance figures are taken from Royal Air Force 1939-45, Volume III. by Hilary St.G.Saunders. (HMSO)*

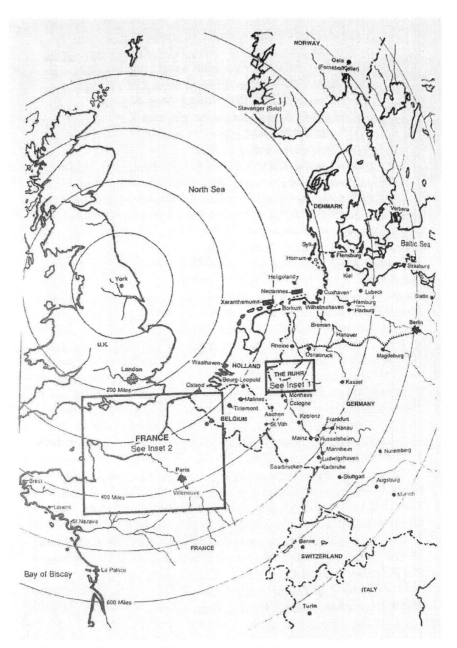

Map 3: Bomber Command Operational Area. For inset maps see opposite page.

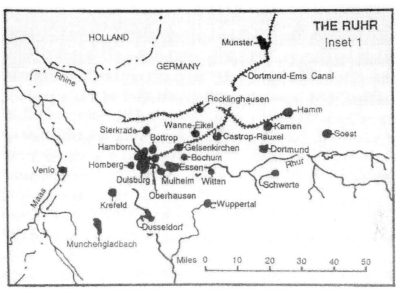

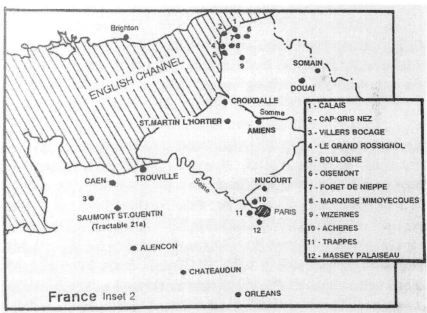

165

even better performance than the B.Mk.III. The B.Mk.VII only came into being because airframe production of the B.Mk.VI exceeded the supply of Hercules 100 engines and thus the surplus airframes were fitted with the same Hercules XVI engines as the B.Mk.III, hence the new Mark number. The B.Mk.VI served, in smallish numbers, with 76, 77, 78, 102, 158, 346, 347 and 640 Squadrons in 4 Group, but the Mark was only starting to get established when the war in Europe ended.

From 1942 onwards, much of the wartime media coverage of Bomber Command was focused upon the Avro Lancaster, to the extent that even attacks made by forces in which the Lancaster was in the minority were reported as '500 Lancasters and other aircraft' This was taken to such lengths by one of the popular tabloid newspapers of the day that some Halifax aircrew renamed the Lancaster the 'Daily Mirror Bomber'. Its other nickname in 4 Group was the 'Woolworth's Bomber' because the standard of its build quality and internal fitments was seen by the Halifax air and ground crews to be considerably cheaper than those of their own aircraft. This wartime focus of attention has continued ever since and thus the main, if not the only, four-engined British bomber of which the general public are aware is the Avro Lancaster. The Halifax, and indeed the Stirling, seem to be remembered only by those who flew or serviced them. It is not this author's intention to denigrate the Avro Lancaster in any way, it was an excellent aircraft and without doubt one of the finest of the wartime bombers, but it was not the **only** bomber.

It must also be pointed out that, while the Lancaster served only as a bomber operating from the UK, the Halifax successfully and effectively fulfilled every role, in every theatre of war, that was asked of it. Bombing attacks, Coastal Command patrols (Halifax crews sank at least eight enemy submarines), transport tasks, glider towing, paratroop dropping, supplying Resistance groups with arms and dropping secret agents into enemy occupied territory for the SOE (Special Operations Executive), all came within the Halifax's remit and it carried out some or all of these duties not only from the UK, but also from the Middle East and Far East.

Throughout the strategic bomber offensive against Germany, Halifax aircraft of Bomber Command carried out a total of 82,773 sorties for the loss of 1,884 aircraft. These losses, 2.28% of all operational missions despatched, mean that of the total number of Halifax aircraft produced (6,176), no fewer than 30.5% of them were lost while their crews carried out what they, both individually and collectively, believed was their duty to their country.

Individual Group Halifax Sorties and Losses

Group	Sorties	A/c Lost	Percentage
No.1	137	12	8.8%
No. 4	45,337	1,124	2.5%
No. 6	28,126	508	1.8%
No. 8	2,106	77	3.7%
No.100	3,383	23	0.7%
H.C.U.s[19]	58	4	6.9%

---

[19] *Heavy Conversion Units.*

Chapter Five

1939 and 1940: Early Days but far from Early Nights

Don Blew joined the RAF in late 1936 on a Direct Entry Short Service Commission and did his Initial Flying (ab initio) Training on Miles Hawks (the predecessor of the Magister) at Woodley Aerodrome with predominantly civilian instructors. From there he went briefly to Uxbridge for kitting-out with uniforms, etc., before going on to Flying Training School (FTS). Don's junior FTS term (in June 1937) was at Digby, next door to Cranwell. For the senior term he and his fellow pupil pilots moved to Brize Norton. Brize was, at this time, still under construction - a sea of mud with temporary wooden huts. The hangars had no roofs and the Hawker Harts and Audaxes of the FTS were kept in First World War canvas Besseneau hangars until the proper hangars were completed. Don Blew's course and their instructors were the first RAF personnel to be based there. He finally arrived at Honington in Suffolk to join No.77 (Bomber) Squadron in January 1938 and learned to fly their Vickers Wellesleys. In July the same year he accompanied the unit when it moved to Driffield in Yorkshire with its sister unit 102 Squadron.

RAF Station Driffield was one of the new 'permanent' stations with proper brick-built accommodation for all residents. There was no bar in the Officers Mess and all drinks were served in the ante-room by stewards. Although Driffield had opened in September 1936, the airfield had been in use during the First World War under the name of Eastburn. All in all it was an extremely comfortable place to live, especially in the light of the conditions that would prevail on the wartime 'economy' stations built during the Command's expansion later in the war.

In October 1938 their sister squadron was re-equipped with the Armstrong Whitworth Whitley Mk.III and 77 Sqn received their first Whitleys the following month. During the Munich crisis 77 Squadron's Wellesleys carried the codes 'ZL' but, on the outbreak of war, their Whitleys were coded `KN'.

Although 78 Squadron was the first unit to equip with the Mark V Whitley, this unit was at that time a Reserve (Group Pool Training) Squadron. It fitted these first Mk.Vs with operational equipment, before handing them over to 77 Squadron during September and October 1939. Don Blew's unit was

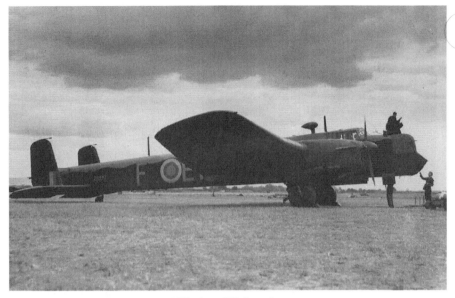

A Whitley of 78 Squadron.

therefore the first operational squadron to fly this much improved, Merlin-engined variant.

At the outbreak of war 77 Squadron's Officer Commanding was Wing Commander J. Bradbury and he ensured that his unit was as battle ready as any. It undertook its first operation on the night of 5/6th September when it despatched three aircraft to drop leaflets over the Ruhr and carried out its second, to the same area, on 8/9th of the month. Pilot Officer Don Blew undertook his first operational flight on the night of 14/15th September, as second pilot to Flying Officer Hullock. They took off at 23.30 hours in Whitley Mk.III, Serial No.K8953, with sealed orders and once safely airborne Flying Officer Hullock opened these and informed the crew:- Pilot Officer Don Blew, Sergeant Tom Atchison (observer), Aircraftman Poad (wireless operator) and Aircraftman Silverwood (Rear Gunner) that they were off to drop Nickels in the Ruhr area. After reading the sealed orders further he then told them that they were now returning to base. They returned to Driffield and landed at 00.50 hours, a frustrating end to their first trip after what had been a prolonged, stomach-churning build up. The sealed orders had been part of a ploy, the facts of which emerged a few days later.

A Whitley Mk.III, believed to be at the factory at Bagington.

At this early stage of the war one of the general worries was over the possible activities of fifth columnists and 'spies'. RAF Intelligence had become aware that aircraft operational movements were regularly becoming general knowledge in the Yorkshire area and it was believed that a spy, or at least a German sympathiser, was operating in Betty's Bar in York. In order to test out this theory, 77 Squadron were instructed to send a couple of aircraft out with the sealed orders as if they were going on a raid, but none of the crew members were let in on the ploy for obvious security reasons. To this day Don has no idea whether this subterfuge was effective or not but Betty's Bar was put 'out of bounds' for a while.

Things were fairly quiet, operationally at least, for a few weeks with aircraft only going out in ones and twos on Nickel raids. It was not until 11.40 in the morning of Saturday 14th October that Don Blew found himself lifting Whitley Mk.III, K8959 (KN-K) into the air on his way to Villeneuve (official codename Little Sister, but referred to as plain 'sister' on the squadron) in France, where they arrived at 15.45 hours to refuel prior to standing by to fly a nickel raid. The order never arrived, so at 10.30 the following morning, he flew his crew back to Driffield with all their leaflets still on board. Once again Don Blew had geared himself up to carry out an operation over enemy territory only to have it fail to materialise.

The Squadron received their pre-war OC back on 1st November when Wing Commander C.H.Appleton took over from Wing Commander Bradbury. As a Squadron Leader he had been OC 77 Squadron at Honington when they were still equipped with the single engined Wellesley. 'Regulations' decreed that the Officer Commanding a squadron of twin-engined aircraft must be of Wing Commander rank, so the arrival of the Whitleys meant the departure of Squadron Leader Appleton. Now promoted, he was given a very warm welcome back by 77 Squadron. Charlie Appleton was nicknamed 'Ambrose' because his dark features and black 'patent-leather' shiny hair gave him a strong resemblance to the dance band leader of that name.

The leisurely pace of the early war operations continued however (77 Squadron only operated on two nights between 14th October and 10th November) and it was not until 10.05 hours on Friday 10th November that Don Blew, now a Flying Officer, once more flew to Villeneuve, now flying a Whitley V, N1353 (KN-M). He once again refuelled and made ready to drop a load of nickels. This time the order came and, as one of five crews detailed, Don took his second pilot Sergeant Samson, observer Tom Atchison, wireless operator Aircraftman 'Boy' Poad (an ex-Halton Apprentice and a brilliant wireless operator) and rear gunner Aircraftman White out over the Ruhr to supply the Nazis with another delivery of toilet paper, also known as `Bumph' (short for Bum Fodder).

The squadron despatched one aircraft to drop Nickels over Wilhelmshaven on the night of 24/25th November, but it was not until 21.15 hours on the night of Monday 27th November that Don took the same crew in N1351 to reconnoitre Cuxhaven and Heligoland. The weather was horrendous, with severe icing, electrical storms and very low cloud. It was also extremely cold. In fact, the whole seven and a quarter hour trip was a freezing waste of time but for a couple of moments of unmitigated terror, Just as they were leaving the target area the rear gunner reported that they were being shadowed by three enemy fighters. Don very quickly slipped the Whitley into something more comfortable - a big bank of thick cloud - and that was the last they saw of them. Several hours later, Don was relieved to identify Flamborough Head under a layer of low cloud and set course for Driffield.

The Pendulum and the Scythe

Suddenly the gunner reported, 'Enemy fire from small arms, Sir!' After well over six hours of flying in such atrocious conditions, Don was in no mood for ground gunners, be they Fish-heads, Pongos or LDV (Look, Duck and Vanish the Local Defence Volunteers, Home Guard or 'Dads Army') who couldn't distinguish their Arado from their elbow. Don ordered his rear gunner to return fire. The 'enemy' fire ceased forthwith and N1351 sailed serenely on to join the circuit at Driffield where it landed at half-past-four in the morning. No mention of this latter incident was made at debriefing and nothing was ever heard about it thereafter.

Three of the squadron's Whitleys operated in daylight on the 10th December but it was a fortnight before Don Blew operated again. With the same crew yet again, he lifted Whitley N1362 into the air at 13.40 hours on Tuesday 12th December as one of six squadron aircraft detailed to carry out security patrols in the Sylt and Borkum areas. The squadron aircraft took off in pairs every two hours and covered the target area in patrols of two hours duration from 16.00 to 23.59 hours. The crews were all briefed to attack any observed movement of enemy seaplanes (minelaying aircraft). Despite the cloud base in the patrol area being as low as 600 feet, the crew of N1362 encountered searchlights but no Flak. The long return to base over the North Sea was always a worry but, about fifty miles into the journey, 'Boy' Poad, who was still only seventeen, came on the intercom and said to his Skipper, 'Sir, I don't know if you're interested, but I've got Harry Roy and his Dance Band loud and clear on the radio, would you like to listen?' 'Yes please', answered Don - and the Whitley swayed gently all the way home. Apart from relaxing frayed nerves, there was another advantage to listening to the BBC Home Service on the way home. As long as the signal kept getting stronger you knew you were at least heading in a westerly direction. They landed safely at base at 20.10 hours.

Christmas 1939 and New Year of 1940 came and went before the same crew found themselves on the Operations Order again, the squadron had despatched just twenty sorties on seven raids since Don had last operated. Their briefed objective was to drop Nickels on Hamm and Osnabruck and they took off in KN-N (N1371) at 21.00 hours on the night of Tuesday January 9th. It was a very dark night and neither of their objectives could be positively identified so Don took his crew on a general reconnaissance of the Ruhr area, landing back at Driffield after eight hours and thirty-five minutes in the air.

The Pendulum and the Scythe

On the 10th January the squadron sent two aircraft on a daylight anti-shipping sweep over the North Sea in which Don Blew was gladly not involved. With the heavy losses experienced by the Blenheim, Hampden and Wellington squadrons prior to Christmas, daylight anti-shipping sweeps were not top of anyone's list of 'things to do'. The next night, January 11th, Whitley N1366 with Flying Officer Don Blew and crew on board was airborne at 17.10 hours on its way to carry out another security patrol over Borkum and Sylt. Flying over the North Sea at about 1,500 feet Don saw below him a huge, wide white streak. He knew they were too far away from any land for this to be waves breaking on the beach so he dropped down to about 500 feet and circled this phenomenon. He had never encountered anything like it before and, with his curiosity aroused, he decided to follow it. After a short while the streak stopped and there beneath the Whitley was a very large and totally blacked-out ocean liner. Quickly climbing back up to 1,500 feet Don circled the ship several times, firing off the colours of the hour - no response. He tried signalling the vessel in morse code with his downward identification light - still no response. Don took his aircraft up to a safer height and instructed 'Roy' Poad to radio base with this sighting and the ship's position but, no acknowledgement was received. Don's mission was to prevent enemy minelaying sea planes from taking off and he was under strict orders not to bomb anything other than a seaplane or its flarepath. He resumed his course for Borkum and left the unidentified liner alone. They saw absolutely no activity whatsoever near the target islands although they saw some lights south of Terschelling. They completed their patrol and returned to Driffield at 23.40 hours.

Two days later, the newspapers carried a story about the return to Hamburg of the German ocean liner Bremen. It had been in New York at the outbreak of war and had been waiting to choose its time and best route home in order to avoid the Royal Navy. It managed to achieve this despite Don Blew's signal to base. Had Don's signal been acknowledged and acted upon, the Bremen may not have been so successful in its return to Hamburg.

Between January 21st and the 17th February there was severe winter weather with very heavy snowfalls over most of the UK in general and the

bomber airfields in particular. This prevented night operations until 17/18th February, when 77 Squadron managed to send two aircraft on a daylight reconnaissance of the Heligoland area. This was far from a rest period as virtually all station personnel were out trying to clear the snow from their airfields. They had very little success; as fast as it was cleared, more snow fell.

The unit despatched two aircraft to Prague and Pilsen on the night of 23/24th February and another two on security patrols over Hornum and Borkum the following night. Early March operations were confined to five leaflet sorties on the night of 7/8th. On Sunday March 10th, with a new rear gunner (Aircraftman McKenzie) and two ground crew (Corporal Young and Aircraftman Lamplugh), Don Blew took to the air in Whitley N1366 bound once more for Villeneuve, this time as a reserve aircraft for a Nickel raid on Warsaw. Two aircraft were despatched but Don and crew were not required for the operation. Their ground crew passengers were, however, needed at Metz to repair another of the squadron's aircraft that had gone unserviceable so Don and crew flew them over to Metz where N1366 went unserviceable in sympathy with the other Whitley. They finally returned to Driffield on Wednesday March 20th. Although they had not carried out any operations in the air during their French sojourn they did make several ground sorties into Metz and Rheims.

The next night, Don was detailed to fly as second pilot to his friend Flying Officer 'Polly' Parrott for a nickel raid on the Ruhr. Unfortunately the engines of their allocated aircraft (KN-L; N1387) refused to start because of the intense cold and they were forced to scrub the operation, leaving only two of the squadron's aircraft to carry it out. 'Polly' Parrott had been second pilot to Flight Lieutenant Tomlin on 15/16th March when they'd mistakenly landed inside Germany on their return from Warsaw. (See Chapter 3).

Although he had been flying as an aircraft captain since October 14th, Flying Officer Don Blew now found himself in the somewhat invidious position of reverting back to second pilot status because the squadron had somehow accrued a surplus of qualified captains. Don found himself teamed with Polly Parrott and, although they were both Flying Officers, Polly had a few months seniority. He was thus officially listed as captain but, in practice, they shared the flying equally. Also unusual for this period of the war, Polly and Don found themselves with what was an 'almost permanent' crew. This comprised Sergeant Shaw as observer, Leading Aircraftman Poad as wireless operator (Boy Poad had been promoted to Leading Aircraftman on his eighteenth birthday) and Aircraftman Jones as rear gunner.

Whitley V N1387 of 77 Sqn at Villeneuve in 1940. F/L Tomlin is in the cockpit and F/O Polly Parrot is standing behind.

Neither Polly nor Don were called upon to take one of the five squadron Whitleys despatched to the Ruhr on 27/28th March. It was not until the unit's next operation, on Thursday April 11th, that the crew found themselves detailed to fly KN-N (N1371) on an armed reconnaissance of ports near Flemburg, along with Sergeant Fletcher and his crew in KN-O (N1372). Five other 77 Squadron aircraft were detailed to attack shipping between Kiel and Oslo, one of which was captained by another of Don's friends, Flying Officer George Saddington (KN-E: N1347). While carrying out this armed reconnaissance Polly and Don dropped four 250 lb. bombs on Stralsund Harbour, thereby being the first British aircraft to drop bombs (albeit only small ones) on a German town. Until now this 'first' was believed to have taken place on and around Monchengladbach on the night of 11/12th May.

Although there is no mention of this incident in the Squadron Operations Record Book (ORB) this author has no reason to doubt the veracity of Don Blew's statement on this matter, nor the entry written in his log book at the time. It is likely that any report of bombs being dropped on mainland Germany prior to official sanction by the British Government would, in any case, have been omitted from all official records - no names, no pack-drill.

Polly, Don and crew returned safely and uneventfully to Driffield after an eight hour and twenty minute flight, as did Sergeant Fletcher, but Don and Polly were perturbed to learn at debriefing that George Saddington had radioed back to base at 03.05 hours stating that he was ditching in the sea approximately sixty miles from the coast. An intense search was carried out throughout the next few days by both the RAF and the Royal Navy but no trace was ever found of George and his crew.

A couple of days later, while carrying out 'circuits and bumps' with Polly in the driver's seat, Don decided to take a walk down the 'back end'. As he was level with the rear entry door the Whitley hit a spot of turbulence and Don was thrown against the door. Instinctively he put his hand out to steady himself and inadvertently caught hold of the door handle, moving it down and unlocking the door which, with a sound like a rifle shot, promptly vanished in the slipstream, leaving a somewhat apprehensive pilot with no parachute, teetering on the edge of a gaping void to a long drop! On return to terra firma, a still white-faced and shaken Flying Officer Blew reported the near-fatal incident and, as a result, all the Squadron's aircraft had their door handles modified to pull upwards to open rather than push down. We shall hear more of Don Blew's intimate knowledge of the workings of the Whitley door handle later.

Germany had invaded Denmark and Norway on 9th April and 77 Squadron was ordered, on the 15th, to move to Kinloss to take part in the air support for the Norwegian campaign. At half-past-seven the following night, Don, Polly and crew in N1371; N-Nuts, were one of five crews that took off to attack Vaernes aerodrome. 'N-Nuts' had an uneventful trip, returning to Kinloss at 03.30 hrs on 17th April. Squadron Leader Mark Hastings, in N1387; KN-L, was not so lucky. 'L- London' ran short of fuel while returning and the Squadron Leader ordered his crew to bale out. This they did and Hastings then force-landed the Whitley near Grantown on-Spey, Morayshire, where the Whitley's port wing hit, a tree and the bomber was wrecked. Mark Hastings escaped unscathed and his crew were all safely gathered in and returned to Kinloss. (Squadron Leader Hastings failed to return from an attack on the Hochst Explosives Factory in Frankfurt on the night of June 29/30th. He and his crew were all killed and are buried in the Rheinberg War Cemetery).

Observer Sergeant Shaw had a night off on 18/19th April and his place was taken by Sergeant Prescott when the crew borrowed N1420; DY-L from 102 Squadron. With two 77 Squadron aircraft, they were detailed to attack shipping in Trondheim Fjord before carrying out a reconnaissance of the aerodrome (Vaernes) and seaplane base in the area. The trip was an uneventful washout apart from spending almost ten hours in a freezing Whitley. None of the nine Whitleys (three each from 10, 58 and 77 Squadrons) involved in this raid were able to bomb due to extremely lousy weather in the Trondheim area.

On the 22/23rd April the squadron sent a further two aircraft to Trondheim with the same result. Sergeant Tom Atchison returned to Don's crew on Thursday 25th April, when the squadron despatched five aircraft to attack shipping in Oslo Fjord and neighbouring waters, oil storage tanks near Oslo and the aerodromes at Fornebo and Kjeller (both at Oslo). These aircraft were captained by Pilot Officer Hamish Mahaddie, Flying Officer Peter Rutter (see Chapter 3), Flying- Officer G.L.Raphael[20], Flying Officer Polly Parrot and Flight Lieutenant B.S.Tomlin (he of landing in Germany fame). Polly and Don reconnoitred off Oslo Fjord before bombing the oil storage tanks from 12,000 feet in bright moonlight. They then descended to 600 feet over the Fjord and attacked a merchant ship with their two remaining 250 lb. bombs and the rear gunner let rip with his four machine-guns as they left the area. They landed back at Kinloss just before five am on 26th April after eight hours and five minutes in the air.

On the last night of April, 77 Squadron sent six aircraft to Stavanger but Polly and crew were not invited to join the party. The next night (1/2nd May), Polly Parrot went to Fornebo aerodrome as second pilot to the Squadron CO, Wing Commander Appleton. They flew together again on 9th May when

---

[20] *Gordon Raphael, who in February 1940, became the first Canadian to be Mentioned in Despatches, transferred to nightfighters in December with 96 and later 85 Squadrons. He ended his career as a Wing Commander DSO, DFC* with at least seven confirmed 'kills'. He was himself killed on 10th April 1945 when his Spitfire collided with a Dakota.*

their target was Stavanger (Sola) aerodrome but they were recalled before they'd crossed the North Sea. During this short period most of the Squadron returned to Driffield, leaving only a few aircraft and crews at Kinloss.

Several things happened on Friday May 10th. The rest of 77 Squadron returned to Driffield, Winston Churchill became Prime Minister and the 'Bore War'[21] ended when the Nazis shouted 'BANG' in all directions. Sitzkrieg turned to Blitzkrieg in no more than a few hours and the Wehrmacht, most ably supported by the Luftwaffe, fell upon the Low Countries. That night 4 Group despatched nine Whitleys (four from 77 Squadron and five from 102 Squadron, both based at Driffield) to drop 'real' bombs on road and rail communications in the Cleve area.

Three Whitleys were detailed by 77 Squadron to attack main roads around Monchengladbach on the night of Saturday 11th May. They were to form part of a total force of thirty-seven aircraft (19 Hampdens and 18 Whitleys - six from each of No.10 and 102 Squadrons, three each from Nos 58 and 77 Squadrons), some of which were to carry out the first (official) raid of the war on a German town. The 77 Squadron contingent comprised the CO, Wing Commander Appleton in N1388, Flying Officer D.D.Pryde in N1356 and Flying Officer Parrot in N1366. Flying Officer Polly Parrot's crew consisted of Flying Officer Don Blew, Sergeant Tom Atchison, Leading Aircraftman 'Boy' Poad and Aircraftman Jones. As usual, Don and Polly shared the flying and so it was that Don Blew eased N1366 off the Driffield grass at 20.25 hours and flew it all the way to the target area without any untoward incidents. Crossing the Dutch coast on their way in they passed close to Rotterdam aerodrome, still burning from the pounding it had taken from the Luftwaffe during the day. The whole area was still a mass of flame and thick smoke, although the misfortunes of the Royal Dutch Air Force did at least give Tom Atchison a first class positional fix on their track to the Dutch/German border where their target lay.

About twenty minutes after passing Rotterdam Don Blew prepared to hand over control to Polly Parrot. The night was pitch black and none of the crew

---

[21] *The term 'Phoney War', referring to the war prior to 10th May 1940, was not used until later in the war. The contemporaneous terms used for the period were the 'Bore War' or the 'Funny War' - 'Funny' being used to mean peculiar, rather than humourous.*

could see any ground detail at all. While Don and Polly prepared to carry out a rapid left-hand seat change, Polly asked Don to go through the tunnel under the main spar to the rear fuselage and drop some parachute flares for them. Because there was no intercom point by the flare chute (there was only one oxygen point there too, which made it difficult when two crew members were required down there to drop out leaflets) they arranged that, when Polly wanted a flare released, he would tell Tom Atchison and Tom would flash his torch down the fuselage at Don. Don unstrapped from the left hand seat, leaving his seat-type parachute for Polly to sit on and then quickly vacated the seat as Polly Parrot hopped into it. Don then wormed his way down the fuselage, taking a spare chest-type parachute with him - although to this day he still knows not why, he'd never bothered in the past.

After he'd been crouched by the flare chute for about ten minutes he received the first torch flash from Tom. Down the chute went flare number one. No sooner had the flare departed the Whitley than the Flak opened up. He couldn't see any of what was going on outside, but he could certainly hear it and Polly began to take very energetic evasive action. Every so often Don got another torch flash from up front and down the chute would go another flare. N1366 was not fitted with a flare rack and they were just laid loose on the fuselage floor. So, as Polly's evasive tactics got wilder and wilder, Don was having his work cut out just trying to catch a flare, never mind balancing himself while he removed the safety clip before dropping it down the chute. Just to add to his troubles his parachute kept getting tangled up with the flares. In desperation, he trapped it with his foot as it passed him for the third or fourth time and clipped it onto his harness out of the way. Another torch flash, down went another flare. Another torch flash - even before the last one had time to light up. 'Polly must have found the target', thought Don as he dropped yet another flare down the chute. Then another torch flash and another and another - Don was catching flares, removing their safety clips and heaving them down the flare chute as fast as he could go. It was only in 1993, when he was recounting this event to the author that Don suddenly realised that most of the 'torch flashes' were more probably the light from exploding Flak shells or tracer entering the aircraft through the bomb aiming panel in the nose).

Seven or eight flares had gone down the flare chute when there was an almighty bang, the Whitley heaved, filled with swirling smoke and the sickening smell of cordite. Where Don had previously been in darkness he could now see the Flak explosions and tracer through myriad holes in the

The Pendulum and the Scythe

Whitley's fuselage. He could also see small blue flames, similar to St. Elmo's fire, curling back from the wings and around the centre fuselage. Worse still, he could now smell petrol - and then he could see the stuff, pouring out of the main tank into the fuselage.

Don decide to go back to the cockpit to help Polly and started to move forward. He was level with the fuselage door when there came an enormous 'Whoomph' and a huge ball of fire came down the fuselage towards him, engulfing him in the flames in less than a second. Don couldn't breathe, he couldn't see, the heat was unbearable. He had to get some air, he must breathe, he must get out... Reflex action and training took over. His hand reached out to the door handle, his sub-conscious brain remembered the handle modification his near accident had been responsible for and his hand moved the handle up. The door went off into the slipstream and Don Blew followed it. He would have gone even if he had not been wearing his parachute, no-one could survive in that inferno.

As his parachute opened, Don's first realisation was that he could at long last breathe again and that he was once again cool. Then he noticed how light it was - very light. In fact it was almost as light as day. Looking around he realised that this was due in part to the searchlights and the Flak still pumping up into the night sky but that there was also a neat string of parachute flares stretching out behind him, each one slightly higher than the one behind it and all shining like miniature suns.

Don searched the sky for N1366, finding it over his left shoulder. Jiggling his parachute harness straps, he turned himself around to watch the Whitley, praying that he'd see some more of the crew bale out. But his prayers went unanswered. The Whitley was just a ball of flame in which no human being could possibly hope to survive. The only other parachutes Don could see in the sky were those attached to the flares he had so recently released from the confines of the Whitley's rear fuselage. N1366 crashed to earth near Krefeld, there were no other survivors. This aircraft was the first bomber to crash inside Germany while carrying out a bombing operation on a German town. Flying Officer Don Blew became a prisoner-of-war for five long years. But at least Don could return home in 1945. The rest of the crew are buried in the Reichswald Forest War Cemetery.

The wreckage of Whitley Mk.V N1366 is examined by Germans after being shot down on 12th May 1940, the first bomber to crash in Germany whilst carrying out a bombing operation on a German town.

In his book "Bomber Pilot", Leonard Cheshire wrote: "Andrew, the tall, blonde, mad Irishman who crowded more laughter into 5 weeks[22] than anyone would have thought possible. People said he was looking for trouble and gave him a DFC. But Andrew was not satisfied with looking for trouble in the skies. He resorted to the roads and an MG and, because he was asking for it, ended up by breaking the car up. Somehow he escaped himself. I can see him so clearly, laughing his wild laugh and afraid of neither man nor machine."

When the rest of 77 Squadron returned from Kinloss on Thursday the 9th May, they found a new pilot waiting for them. Pilot Officer Andrew Dunn, from Larne, Northern Ireland, had arrived at Driffield on 23rd April and had been kicking his heels waiting to get operational. He did not have to wait for much longer. That, very night Flying Officer Tony Meade, who occupied the next room to Don Blew in the Officers Mess, took young Andy Dunn to bomb bridges across the Rhine at Rees and Wesel while other Whitleys attacked columns of road transport near Goch and Geldern and thirty-six Wellingtons attacked Waalhaven airfield. Tony Meade's observer for this six hour and five minute trip in KN-J (N1373) was Sergeant Thompson, while the wireless operator was Aircraftman Kenny and rear gunner was Aircraftman Crawford. Four nights later the same crew took KN-X (N1355) to join another eleven Whitleys in an attack on communications targets around Monchengladbach, landing back at Driffield at 04.15 hours in the morning of Wednesday 15th May after an uneventful six and a half hour flight. It was Command policy at this period of the war to give all new pilots some operational experience with at least two different aircraft captains. So, at 20.35hrs on Saturday 18th May, Andy Dunn found himself airborne in KN-G (N1348) under the command of Flying Officer David Pryde, who occupied the room on the other side of what had been Don Blew's room until the 12th May. Along with Sergeant Thompson and Aircraftmen Kenny and Crawford, as previously. They were off to bomb an oil refinery at Hannover, In all sixty aircraft operated this night, twenty four Whitleys, twenty-four Wellingtons and twelve Hampdens, with targets including various oil refineries and railway yards in the Fatherland and enemy troop concentrations in Belgium. Two Whitleys failed to return; MH-K (N1408) of 51 Squadron, flown by Squadron Leader Turner DFC and crew who all

---

[22] *Cheshire only knew Dunn for 5 weeks while 77 and 102 Squadrons shared RAF Driffield.*

became prisoners of war and KN-R (N1388) of 77 Squadron, flown by Flight, Lieutenant Gordon Raphael.

P/O Andrew Dunn's Whitley, KN-O is overflown by three other aircraft of the same type.

While heading towards the Dutch coast on their way to Hannover, Raphael's Whitley was attacked by a Messerschmitt Bf110 and badly damaged. Raphael was wounded in the foot but his rear gunner, Aircraftman Parkes, got in a good long burst from his four Brownings and claimed to have shot the Messerschmitt down into the sea. Despite his somewhat painful wound, Flight Lieutenant Raphael made a successful ditching in the North Sea. Lady Luck was certainly smiling on the crew of 'R-Robert' this night, for this whole encounter was seen by another 77 Squadron aircraft that was in the vicinity and the pilot, Flight Lieutenant J. A. Crockett, immediately got his observer to pin-point N1388's position before he turned back to meet a British destroyer (HMS Javelin) he'd passed a short while before. Thanks to Crockett's prompt action the Royal Navy was able to fish Raphael and his crew out of the 'oggin' after only four hours in their dinghy. Flying Officer David Pryde, Andy Dunn, et al, in N1348, landed safely back at Driffield after seven and a quarter hours in the air. Two nights later, on the 20th May, the same crew in Whitley N1384 took off at 20.36 hours. They were one of ninety-two aircraft operating on this night. The force comprised twenty-four Whitleys, thirty-two Wellingtons, eighteen Hampdens and eighteen Blenheims. The latter were being tried out on night operations in an effort to avoid the crippling losses that had been experienced in daylight. All were despatched in an attempt to delay the German breakout. Seventy-seven of the ninety-two aircraft sent out successfully bombed their targets and three Whitleys and one Wellington failed to return. Messrs Pryde, Dunn, Thompson, Kenny and Crawford in N1384 were one of the missing Whitleys, but fortunately they were all unhurt in a crash-landing near Abbeville (Somme) in France and soon returned to Driffield none the worse for their experience.

On Sunday, 2nd June, David Pryde was awarded the DFC and promoted to Acting Flight Lieutenant. That night he attacked Soest and Hamm with Aircraftsmen Kenny and Crawford, another observer - Sergeant Saville and Pilot Officer T. G. (Hamish) Mahaddie as second pilot.

Pilot Officer Andrew Dunn was rated as an 'exceptional' pilot. This is made obvious by the fact that after only four trips as a second pilot he was detailed

77 Squadron Officers at Driffield June 1940.
Includes P/O Akroyd-Stuart - P/O G.A.Elliott - P/O P.Eldridge - P/O I.M.H.Brownlie
P/O Saltzgeber - S/Ldr Howard - W/Co J.C.MacDonald - W/Co G.T.Jarman - F/O Meade -
P/Off R.M.Pinkham - P/O A.W.Dunne - P/O McGregor - Others not identified.

as an aircraft captain on the 3rd June. On this night the Command despatched 142 aircraft (48 Hampdens, 48 Whitleys and 46 Wellingtons) to attack many targets from Hamburg to Frankfurt, although a few of the Wellingtons made a last attack on German positions near Dunkirk. Dunn, flying Whitley N1476 with Pilot Officer C. J. D. Montagu as second pilot, Sergeant Malcolm Lucas as observer, Aircraftman Kennedy as wireless operator and Aircraftman Martin in the rear turret, took off from Driffield at 21.15 hours and set course for Gelsenkirchen. Here Malcolm Lucas released their bombs from 7,000 feet, scoring direct hits on fires that were already burning. They returned to base unscathed but tired after eight and three quarter hours in the air, Dunn's longest operation to date.

It seems that Andy Dunn was hooked on operational flying, for he kept volunteering to do extra operations. In the early years of the war it was most unusual for aircrew to undertake more than one or two sorties in a week. Dunn was to carry out four between the 3rd and 10th of June. At 20.30 hours on Wednesday 5th June, Andy Dunn, again with Pilot Officer Montagu, Malcolm Lucas, Kennedy and Martin, lifted N1476 off the grass runway at Driffield. They were to join ninety-one other aircraft in attacks on railways in Germany and communications targets in the Somme area. Dunn's target was to be roads in the area of Bapaume but N1476 didn't get there. About thirty minutes after take off, when near Finningley, a flare in the rear fuselage self-ignited. Despite the best efforts of Pilot Officer Montague and Malcolm Lucas, who did everything possible to extinguish the fire, it soon became obvious that the Whitley was doomed. Dunn ordered his crew to abandon the aircraft, then, when he was sure that they'd all jumped safely clear, he landed the flaming Whitley on Finningley aerodrome at 21.15 hours and, rapidly 'vacating the premises', watched it burn itself out before the fire crews could do much about it. Most of the crew escaped injury but Aircraftman Kennedy sustained slight damage to his back that required a brief stay in hospital.

Malcolm Lucas landed in the grounds of Bawtry Hall (which in July 1941 was to become No.1 Group Headquarters). It was dusk, but on his way down he observed several people armed with shotguns awaiting his arrival on the ground. He then noticed that he was heading straight for some high-tension electricity cables and, having had enough shocks for one night, had to resort to some drastic pulling on his parachute lines to avoid them. As a result of this he landed rather heavily and, while still lying on his back gazing up at the sky and recovering his breath, suddenly found himself staring up the two very large, round black holes that were obviously the business end of a double-barrelled shotgun. He was just beginning to wish he'd stayed in bed that morning when, to his great relief, a lady clutching a bottle of Scotch to her bosom appeared as if by magic. Turning on the intrepid holder of the aforementioned lethal weapon, she asked him why on earth he couldn't see that Malcolm was 'one of ours' and what the blazes he thought he was playing at (or words to that effect). She then offered Sergeant Lucas a swig from the bottle of Scotch. Being a gentleman, even if not an officer, Malcolm could not possibly refuse such a kindly offer and bravely sank at least three fingers of the amber liquid. Malcolm never did discover .from whence this vision of kindly benevolence conjured herself, but he was 'bloody glad she did!'

On the 7th June Driffield was visited by the 'Grand old man' himself, Lord 'Boom' Trenchard. Flight Lieutenant David Pryde was detailed to act as Personal Assistant. Trenchard's visit coincided with another event, and one that was long overdue. At long last wireless operators and air gunners got their just deserts - promotion to Sergeant and proper aircrew brevets. It had only taken nine months from the outbreak of war for the Air Ministry to wake up, but approximately two hundred and eighty 'part-time' aircrew of the rank of Corporal and below had died on operations during this time.

The following night Andy Dunn with the same crew - only now Kennedy and Martin were Sergeants - lifted KN-O (N1372) into the air at 20.10 hours on their way to bomb roads and/or railways in the Hirsen region. This operation was part of a concentrated three-night attack on German communication targets in support of the 'Battle of France' that resulted in 336 sorties over the period of the 7th to 10th of June. Malcolm Lucas released their bombs on a road running northeast from Hirsen, seeing several hits.

The same crew, in the same aircraft, were airborne at 20.27 hours the following night (9th June) continuing the raids on German communications. They had been detailed to attack bridges in the Somme area, but their starboard engine was hit by Flak on their way to the target and they were forced to abandon the sortie. (The Merlin engines fitted to the Whitley at this time were not as powerful as they would be by 1941 and it was almost impossible to maintain height on one engine at this stage). Malcolm Lucas jettisoned the bomb load over the channel on their return journey and then repeated the procedure to ensure that there were no hang-ups. This was a technique he had learned while training to be an armourer before volunteering for aircrew. As 'O-Orange' was passing over Abingdon the damaged engine burst into flames and, seeing their predicament, Abingdon switched its airfield lights on despite there being an air raid in the locality. This time Andy Dunn gave his crew the option of baling out again or riding the Whitley down to the deck with him. As they'd all played that game only four days earlier, to a man they elected to stay.

As Andy Dunn started his landing approach to Abingdon, Malcolm Lucas realised that there were better places to be than in the foremost part of a Whitley that was about to attempt an emergency landing with a burning engine. It was quite obvious to him that he'd be much better off down the back end. Unfortunately, the level of activity in the cockpit was such that he couldn't get past the two pilots without causing further consternation to them, not to mention the unspoken implication that he didn't have exactly 100% confidence in his survivability factor. Somewhat disappointedly, he turned about and headed back to whence he'd come. Looking carefully for impending disaster through his bomb-aiming panel in the nose, Malcolm was suddenly alarmed to see a line of red lights running across their direction of travel. As this indicated that the Whitley had just passed the total amount of runway available and that, with only one functioning engine they could not possibly go around and have another try, Malcolm decided that discretion was most definitely the better part of valour and opened the front hatch to lower himself out when the aircraft had slowed sufficiently for him to do so.

This was the plan. He dangled his legs through the hatch, still watching the Whitley's progress through the nose clear view panel. He then lowered his torso through it, taking his weight on his forearms, ready to drop out at the first indication of impending doom. He was still looking through the clear view panel, awaiting the right moment to drop clear when he experienced several stabbing pains in his thighs and found himself involuntarily dragged out of the aircraft before he was ready. His legs had been caught by the barbed-wire fence surrounding the bomb dump. As he had been hauled out so unceremoniously, 'O-Orange' also came to an abrupt halt on its nose on the edge of the bomb dump itself, with the tail wheel just above Malcolm's head! Fortunately the Whitley decided to stay on its nose and, as the fire in the engine and wing spread, the rest of the crew swiftly vacated the aircraft and its immediate vicinity at a great rate of knots.

Happily for Malcolm Lucas, his predicament was seen in the light of the burning Whitley by Flight Lieutenant Cattell, an ex 77 Squadron officer now stationed at Abingdon. Cattell helped Malcolm to disentangle himself from the barbed wire and get to safety, despite the rear turret's ammunition exploding all around them. Sergeant Kennedy received further damage to his back, which he had injured baling out on the 5th June, but apart from some cuts and bruises and a severe shaking up, the rest of the crew had escaped relatively unharmed. All that, remained of 'O-Orange' was, the tail turret, some very badly burned aluminium and, despite Malcolm Lucas' double jettison, two 500lb. bombs! The crew were all detained in Station Sick Quarters for a couple of days, just to make sure they were alright and then they returned to Driffield and duty by train. This had been Andy Dunn's third crash in exactly one month of operational flying. It was also Malcolm Lucas' second crash in only four flights with Andy Dunn and on his return to Driffield four days later was not unrelieved to learn that the CO felt he'd done enough. He was classified as 'Tour completed' and reverted to his pre-aircrew trade of armourer, retaining his Sergeants chevrons and his Observer's brevet[23]. As a matter of passing interest, it was on this night that one Pilot Officer G. L. Cheshire undertook his first operation (as second pilot) with 102 Squadron.

While Dunn and crew were recovering at Abingdon and then travelling back to Driffield, the squadron operated in smallish numbers every night but one for the next six nights. This was followed by two rest nights so it was not until Monday the 17th of June that Dunn was called upon to operate again. With Sergeant Savill replacing Malcolm Lucas and Sergeant Dawson replacing Sergeant Kennedy, the crew took off at 21.17 hours as part of a force of 139 aircraft destined for Northern Germany and numerous targets in the Ruhr. Dunn's specific target was Gelsenkirchen but the aircraft's radio and intercom went unserviceable only thirty minutes into the flight so Dunn returned early, as did Squadron Leader Mark Hastings in N4948 for exactly the same reason.

Pilot Officer Dunn was 'on' again the next night, but with a new wireless operator, Sergeant Dunn (no relation) and, most unusual for 1940, a commissioned rear gunner, Pilot Officer Watt. From the beginning of June, No.4 Group began to receive aircrew members of the RAF Volunteer Reserve (RAFVR) who were just completing their operational training at 10

---

[23] *Malcolm Lucas was commissioned into Flying Control Duties later in the war.*

The Pendulum and the Scythe

OTU, Abingdon. Some of these VR aircrew were commissioned and it is believed that this is why Pilot Officer Watt was that exceedingly rare creature, a commissioned air gunner. This night, that of the 18/19th June, 77 Squadron despatched seven Whitleys to oil plants at Sterkrade and Hannover, forming part of a total force of sixty-nine aircraft attacking oil and railway targets throughout Germany. Approaching Sterkrade, the target was already well alight and could be soon from some distance. Andy Dunn's crew added their bombs from 10,500 feet and returned safely to base.

Sergeant Dawson was back with them on the night of 19/20th June when they took KN-N (N1371) to the Wanne-Eickel oil refinery. They were the recipients of an extremely intense flak barrage en-route to the target and tried to go around it. As they started their run up to their aiming point, 'N-Nuts' was attacked from astern by two Messerschmitt Bf109s which, on their first pass, scored many hits on the fuselage and port wing, wounding the observer, Sergeant Savill and the wireless operator, Sergeant Dawson, who was in the front turret at the time;. It was a bright moonlit night and as one of the '109s bore in for a second attack Pilot Officer Watt, in the rear turret, gave it a really good burst from his four Brownings as it tried to pass under the Whitley's tail. Watt's shooting was spot-on for Andy Dunn saw the '109 flop over onto its back and go straight down out of control. The remaining Messerschmitt obviously didn't fancy the same treatment and wasn't seen again. In spite of this attack, Dunn pressed on with his bomb run and Sergeant Savill released their load from 8,000 feet, revealing a blast furnace in all its red-hot glory as the Whitley's bombs demolished the building in which it was housed.

During the return journey the damage caused by the fighter attack started to tell and the port engine burst into flames. Dunn and Montagu shut the engine down, feathered the propeller and set off the built-in fire extinguisher, which successfully put the fire out. Continuing on their homeward flight on only the starboard engine the Whitley gradually lost height so, in order to try to regain some altitude prior to crossing the Dutch coast, Dunn restarted the port engine. It coughed once or twice and then began to run reasonably well, allowing 'N-Nuts' to recover a little of its lost height but it then burst into flames again. Dunn immediately shut it down for the second time and hoped that the fire would go out of its own accord -the built-in extinguishers only worked once - and, as luck would have it, that is exactly what it did.

The four-gun rear turret as fitted to the Whitley V.

They were now approaching the Dutch coast with very little height in hand for a single-engined crossing of the North Sea. Andy Dunn asked his crew whether they wanted to abandon the aircraft over Holland or try to make it home over the sea. Without the slightest hesitation the vote was unanimously in favour of heading for home. 'N-Nuts' crossed the North Sea at no more than 400 feet but, because their compass had also been damaged during the fighter attack and they hadn't fully realised this fact, their navigation was adrift. They finally ran out of petrol and had to ditch the Whitley in the sea just off Hastings Pier. Needless to say they were all quickly rescued and Sergeant Savill was taken to a local hospital for treatment to his bullet wound. The rest of the crew returned to Driffield by train on June 21st and were promptly sent on 'survivors leave'. For Pilot Officer Dunn this was his fourth crash in five weeks! (In 1993 an amateur diving team recovered an undercarriage leg from this aircraft.)

On Friday the 12th July 1940, Pilot Officers Dunn, Montagu and Watt were all awarded the Distinguished Flying Cross, while Sergeants Dawson and Savill received the Distinguished Flying Medal. Savill was fit again by the time the crew were next called upon to operate. Their target on the 19th July was to be an aircraft factory at Kassel but only half an hour into the trip the radio and intercom in KN-O (N1435) went 'on the blink', so Dunn returned to Driffield.

They were briefed for Kassel again on the 21st July but `O-Orange' just didn't want to go there. This time she stubbornly refused to even start her engines so Dunn and Company never even got airborne. They were, however, definitely going to Kassel, whether N1435 wanted to or not, for this was once again the target for the night of 23/24th July. Except for the replacement of Sergeant Dawson by Sergeant Silverwood, it was the same crew as two nights previously and it was the same reluctant Whitley, 'O-Orange'. After a good stiff talking to from the ground crew, 'O-Orange' allowed her engines to be started and she lifted off the grass runway at Driffield at 21.00 hours. By the time they arrived over Kassel the weather had clamped right down and the crew couldn't even see the ground Disappointedly, Andy Dunn set course for home and O-Orange gathered up her skirts and smirked all the way back to Driffieid where they landed at 04.37 hours after jettisoning their bombs in the North Sea on the way back. The whole crew felt that they had just wasted the last seven and a half hours, but O-Orange, just clicked quietly to herself.

Bomber Command detailed 166 aircraft for seven Ruhr targets and some Dutch airfields on the night of Thursday the 25th July. Dunn was once again allocated 'O-Orange' and, with yet another wireless operator, Sergeant Bain, they were airborne at 21.15 hours. Their target was the synthetic oil plant at Bottrop in the Ruhr and Dunn dropped his bombs from a height of only 5,000 feet (absolutely no future in that in 1943-44). Because of intense Flak and searchlight activity, they were unable to observe any results but at least they made it safely back to Driffield, landing at 04.30 hours.

Three nights later the same crew took N1390 to attack an aircraft factory at Wismar, leaving base at 20.40 hours and heading out across the North Sea. They experienced difficulty in locating the target, a small town about thirty miles due east of Lubeck, so Sergeant Bain went down the rear fuselage to drop some flares. This enabled them to find the aircraft factory but one of the flares exploded prematurely while still in the flare chute and wounded Bain in the leg. Bearing in mind the injuries that Pilot Officer Leonard Cheshire's wireless operator was to receive over Cologne on 12/13th November (he was badly burned about the face and hands and temporarily blinded for several weeks), Bain was actually remarkably lucky, although he probably didn't think so at the time. Dunn released his bombs from 10,000 feet but no results were observed. They landed back at Driffield at 5 am after a long eight hours and twenty minutes in the air and Sergeant Bain was taken off to hospital.

191

The Pendulum and the Scythe

On Friday the 2nd August, 'B' Flight of 77 Squadron, to which Andy Dunn belonged, received a new Flight Commander in the shape of Squadron Leader G. T. (Bull) Jarman who was posted in from 10 OTU, (See Chapter 6 for more of G. T. Jarman). Andy Dunn was briefed for operations again on the 3rd August, the next night the squadron was called upon to operate but, as Pilot Officer Montagu had now qualified as an aircraft captain, Dunn was to have a totally new crew. They were all Sergeants. Harrison as 'second dickie', Amos as observer, Coull as first WOp/AG and Hopkins as second WOp/AG in the rear turret. They took KN-U (P5004) to Monheim, in the Ruhr, to attack an oil storage depot and, following the release of their bombs, observed many explosions and fires. This was a long eight and a half hour slog that was made worse on their return to the UK by very bad weather that caused many diversions.

The squadron did not operate again until six nights later (9/10th August) when Dunn took KN-U to Ludwigshaven. The only crew change was the second pilot who, on this occasion, was Pilot Officer Bailey. They took off at 21.00 hours but en-route to the target they were picked up and coned by a large concentration of searchlights that held them for over thirty minutes. Miraculously, the associated Flak did not cause any major damage to the Whitley, but their evasive action cost them so much time and fuel, and so disorientated the crew (not to mention scaring them all witless) that they decided to call it a night and head for home.

Probably as part of his 'getting to know the chaps' routine, Squadron Leader Jarman detailed Andrew Dunn as his second pilot for the night of Monday 12th August. The rest of the crew were all sergeants, Charlton (observer), Sawyer (wireless operator), and Edmonds (rear gunner) and they were to fly KN-K (P5042) to attack an aluminium factory at Herinjan. Unfortunately they were unable to identify their target because of 10/10ths cloud and so KN-K returned to base with its bombs still on board. This was the night on which Flight Lieutenant `Babe' Learoyd won his VC over the Dortmund-Ems Canal near Munster. (See Chapter 2).

On the 14th August the unit's CO, Wing Commander Macdonald, was posted to 82 Squadron and Squadron Leader Jarman took temporary command of 77 Squadron. The following day, the Luftwaffe attacked RAF Driffield in some strength, hitting four hangars - three of which were burnt out. Two of the Airmen's barrack blocks, one wing of the Officers Mess and the hutted Sergeants Mess were destroyed, as were nine Whitleys, four from 77

Squadron and five belonging to 102 Squadron.. In addition, fifteen men were killed and twenty wounded.

Sometime between the Op on the night of 12/13th August and their next Operation, the flight's aircrew were in their local hostelry along with some of the crews from 102 Squadron. Being Irish, Andy Dunn was very particular over who was allowed to sing 'Danny Boy'. Unfortunately, Squadron Leader Jarman wasn't amongst the chosen. After his second attempt at murdering Andy Dunn's favourite song, he took his Flight Commander by the throat and threatened to strangle him if he didn't desist. (This was witnessed by Leonard Cheshire – amongst many others!) It is known that Jarman was a very strict disciplinarian and it wasn't overly difficult to upset him! So it was perhaps no great surprise to all concerned when Pilot Officer Andy Dunn found himself detailed as second pilot to Sergeant Coogan for the night of 16/17th August. On this occasion they had another of those rare beasts, a commissioned Rear Gunner – Pilot Officer Shotter. Sergeant Sawyer was the wireless operator, Sergeant Savill DFM was to be the observer for his first flight with Dunn since their trip to Bottrop on the 25/26th July. They flew KN-A (N1474) to Augsburg but nothing of any note happened and they returned safely to Driffield after 10¼ hours in the air, a long trip in a Whitley.

Andrew Dunn now had what, was, for him, an exceptionally long break from operations and his name did not appear on the operations list again until 24th August,. This was mainly because the squadron only operated on one night in the intervening period, that of 18/19th when they sent four Aircraft to Milan. Again Dunn was detailed as second pilot to Sergeant Coogan, still with Sergeant Savill as observer but with Sergeant Erickson as wireless operator and Sergeant Darbisher in the rear turret. They were to fly KN-J (N1373) and their target was again Augsburg. This Sunday night the Command despatched twenty-nine Whitleys and thirty-nine Wellingtons to five different targets in Germany, the principle of concentration of effort was still some way off yet. KN-J released its bombs from 8,000 feet, starting fires at the northern end of the target area. This trip must; have been by a more direct route than that employed nine nights earlier, as at 'only' nine hours duration, it was seventy-five minutes shorter. Either that, or they had a huge tail wind in both directions!

On return to Driffield, Dunn would have been upset to learn that his friend and second pilot of twelve trips had failed to return. Pilot Officer Montagu and crew, in Whitley N1473, crashed close to Haarlemmeer Ijweg, Vijhuizen

Damaged Whitleys at Driffield after the second raid by the Luftwaffe.

in Northern Holland at 03.00 hours. The whole crew:- Pilot Officer C. J. D. Montagu DFC, Sergeant J. W. Ward, Sergeant R. T. Penny, Sergeant A. F. Webber and Sergeant E. J. Clarke were all killed and are now buried in the Amsterdam General Cemetery.

The Luftwaffe had hit RAF Driffield again on the night of 24th August and inflicted more damage, making operating from the station very difficult indeed, so on the 26th of the month it was closed for repairs and its resident units moved elsewhere. No.102 Squadron joined 'Shiny Ten' at Leeming, while 77 Squadron moved to Linton-on-Ouse to share with 58 Squadron.

Before the aircraft moved to Linton, however, the Command detailed twelve Whitleys to fly to Abingdon for refuelling prior to taking off for an attack on Turin and Milan. Andy Dunn was one of the twelve aircraft captains detailed for this raid. Once again 'Master of his own fate', Dunn lifted N1390 off the Driffield grass at 13.30 hours and set course for Abingdon to refuel before making the long haul over the Alps. Unfortunately, Dunn landed at Abingdon rather more heavily than usual and badly damaged a tail beam. Consequently N1390 did not participate in this Italian operation.

Having settled in to their new base, the squadron operated from Linton-on-Ouse for the first time on the night of the 30/31st August. The Command despatched eighty-seven aircraft to five targets in Germany and airfields in France, Holland and Belgium. Andrew Dunn was detailed to fly KN-O (N1435) with Pilot Officer Wiltshear as second pilot, Sergeant Hutchinson as observer, Sergeant Everest - wireless operator and Sergeant Oddy in the rear turret. This was the same crew he had taken to Abingdon on the 26th August. They left Linton at 20.35 hours, bound for an oil storage depot in Berlin where they obtained direct hits on the storage tanks and watched as their incendiaries started considerable fires. On the return flight they encountered intense Flak over Hannover and Bremen and O-Orange landed back at base at 06.30 hours with many holes in the airframe. Another long flight at just five minutes under ten hours.

Sergeant Savill DFM was crewed with Andy Dunn again for the night of 5/6th September. The rest of the crew consisted of Sergeant Gibbons as second pilot, Sergeant Allen on the wireless and Sergeant George Riley, a wireless operator-gunner in the rear turret. They were to take N1365 to the Fiat Works in Turin. Theirs was one of eighty-two aircraft that the Command sent to many targets from Stettin to Turin. Dunn and crew attacked from 8,500 feet and the explosion of their bombs was followed by what Dunn described as 'a colossal explosion' followed by a dense column of smoke rising up to 5,000 feet. This 'colossal explosion' was corroborated by all the other pilots over Turin at the same time. N1365 landed safely at Linton-on-Ouse at five in the morning after a nine hour five minutes trip.

The squadron was on again three nights later when the same crew in KN-O (P5046) was one of only two Whitleys detailed to attack barges in Ostend. Despite much searching of the Ostend area they were unable to locate their target and were not helped in their search by severe icing. 'O-Orange' returned to Linton at 05.15 hours on Monday the 9th September with its bombs still on board after a fruitless six and three-quarter hours in the air.

On the night of the 10/11th September, 106 aircraft of all types were despatched to attack the collection of barges in the Channel coast ports. Seventeen Whitleys were however sent further afield, to Potsdammer Station in Berlin and to Bremen Docks. Andrew Dunn with exactly the same crew as for two nights previously and also with the same aircraft, O-Orange was detailed for the Bremen raid. Sergeant Savill released their first stick of bombs from 6,000 feet and then Dunn took O-Orange down in a gliding attack on the Docks, dropping their second stick from 3,500 feet. The crew observed the breakout of several fires and some heavy explosions were seen to follow. The inadvisability of dropping as low as 3,500 feet over Bremen was re-inforced by the local Luftwaffe gunners who delivered an extremely heavy barrage, damaging the Whitley's front turret and narrowly missing Sergeant Savill. Two Whitleys failed to return from the Bremen raid, one from 58 Squadron, the other, KN-K (P5042), from 77 Squadron, was captained by Sergeant J. A. G. Deans. Both crews survived but were taken prisoner. Deans was later to achieve fame for his leadership while a PoW and was awarded an MBE in recognition of this.

Barges were to be the target for Dunn and company on the night of Friday the 13th September but KN-Y (P5091), the aircraft allocated to them, was found to have an unserviceable rear turret during the crew's pre-flight inspection and their trip was scrubbed. Bearing in mind the day and the date, it is doubtful if anyone was unduly upset!

By Sunday the 15th September the Flak damage to 'O-Orange' had been repaired and it was once again allocated to Pilot Officer Dunn DFC, for his fourth trip with the same crew. This night brought to a close the day that had seen the climax of the Battle of Britain, although very few people, if any, realised it at the time. Bomber Command despatched 155 aircraft on widespread operations but by far the largest effort was once more against the barges being assembled in the Channel ports for Operation Seelowe (Sealion). This was also the night that on which the Command's second VC was won, that of Sergeant John Hannah of 83 Squadron (see Chapter 2). All of our aircraft returned safely. Pilot Officer Dunn bombed his quota of barges in Ostend Harbour from 6,700 feet and saw direct hits on several of them. He then took O-Orange down to 100 feet on their way out of the harbour and Sergeant Savill in the front turret and George Riley in the rear, machine-gunned numerous barges.

Messrs Dunn, Gibbons, Savill, Allen and Riley, together with KN-O, were a team yet again on the night of 18/19th September. Yet while the bulk of the Command's efforts was once more focussed on barges in the Channel ports, 'O-Orange' was off to Soest, five miles east of Hilversum in Holland. Dunn bombed a factory just outside the town, releasing the bombload from only 2,000 feet, but low, patchy cloud prevented the crew from assessing the damage with any accuracy. They landed safely at Linton at 05.30 hours after eight hours and twenty minutes in the air. Eight of the 117 aircraft despatched failed to return, among them were three Whitleys, two of which belonged to 77 Squadron. KN-E (N1425), flown by Pilot Officer Eldridge, with Sub-Lieutenant P. O. Williams as observer, failed to return from the Soest raid, whilst KN-T (P4992), flown by Pilot Officer R. P. Brayne, went missing during an attack on Antwerpen. All ten crew members from both of these aircraft lost their lives. The third missing Whitley, from their sister unit at Linton - 58 Squadron, was GE-M (P5008).

After a five night rest the 'team' was on the operations order once more and again they were allocated O-Orange and the night of 23/24th September, was to be unique for this period of the war. For the first time Bomber Command decided to concentrate its main strength on an attack on targets in just one German city - and where else to go but Berlin which, even this early in the war, was becoming known as 'The Big City'. One hundred and twenty-nine Hampdens, Wellingtons and Whitleys were dispatched to eighteen separate targets in the German capital. These comprised seven railway yards, six electrical power stations, three gas works and two aircraft component factories. One hundred and twelve aircraft reported having bombed in a three-hour period from heights between 4,500 and 16,000 feet but many searchlights and a ground mist made target identification in the city very difficult. Three aircraft, one of each type, failed to return. The missing Whitley was P5046, KN-O.

This 58 Sqn Whitley flown by F/L Fleming from Linton-on-Ouse lost her ailerons and much of her wing surface to flak over the enemy coast in 1940.

Andrew Dunn and his crew had the Spandau aircraft factory as their target and, as they flew across Germany, the weather conditions were not too bad, despite a few clouds. George Riley kept a sharp lookout in the darkness constantly moving his rear turret from side to side searching for enemy nightfighters, but these were not to be their problem this night. As they approached their target on the outskirts of Berlin, the enemy searchlights began to reach their long fingers of light into the night skies, quickly fastening onto 'O-Orange'. Dunn briefly took avoiding action but the target was coming up fast and Sergeant Savill wanted to start the bombing run. Sergeant Allen dropped a couple of flares down the flare chute as Dunn straightened the Whitley and roared over the Spandau works, flying right through the Flak barrage that was now accompanying the searchlights. George Riley advised his skipper and observer that the flares were directly over the factory so Dunn brought O-Orange around in a tight turn and let Sergeant Savill begin the bombing run into the target. Again the Luftwaffe gunners concentrated their efforts on the lone Whitley, which was regularly buffeted by exploding shells and shrapnel hits. Dunn held his course while Sergeant Savill lay in the nose giving small directional changes as the target slowly crept up his bombsight. After what seemed like a lifetime the crew heard the prayed for 'Bombs Gone' over the intercom and Dunn immediately recommenced his evasive action. George Riley watched the aircraft factory explode as their bombs struck home, starting a good sized fire.

Unfortunately the Flak had found its target. At least one large piece of shrapnel had holed one of the Whitley's fuel tanks badly enough to cause a serious leak. As they started for home, it soon became apparent that they were losing petrol at a considerable rate. Economising on the aircraft's fuel consumption as well as he could, Andrew Dunn flew the damaged Whitley back across Germany. By the time they had reached the Dutch/German border it was obvious that they had insufficient petrol remaining to get them to the English coast. Flying over Holland, Dunn tried to coax as much height as possible out of the damaged Whitley so that, when the fuel finally ran out, he could try to stretch their glide to the maximum. As they approached the Dutch coast, Dunn, for the second time in his operational career, gave his crew the choice of landing in Holland to almost certain capture, or to try to get as near to home as possible and hope that the rescue services could find them quickly. All four of his crew went for the second option and Andrew Dunn continued on his flight path out over the North Sea, closely watching the rapidly dropping needles on his fuel gauges as he did so.

They knew they had no chance of reaching the English coast; it was just too far away for the petrol they had left. At about thirty miles out from the Dutch coast Dunn got Sergeant Allen to send a radio message to Linton-on-Ouse advising them of their predicament, its obvious prognosis and their current position, speed and heading. They flew on, gradually losing height as Dunn eased back on the throttles to economise on their dwindling fuel state as much as possible. They were all hoping against hope to see a Royal Navy ship on the seas below them, but, just like policemen and buses, there's never one around when you want one.

Eventually they were flying just above the waves. The sea was heaving ominously and Dunn's windscreen was regularly slashed with salt spray. George Riley, still in the rear turret, had serious doubts about their chances of surviving a ditching in such terrible conditions. Finally, Andrew Dunn had to surrender to the obvious and ordered his crew to their ditching stations. Sergeant Gibbons left his co-pilot's seat and crawled under the main spar to the rear fuselage where he and George Riley chopped off the escape door to enable them to launch the aircraft dinghy and clamber into it without delay. Sergeant Savill, who had been constantly monitoring their position, passed the latest one to Sergeant Allen who immediately transmitted it to base before they both followed the co-pilot under the main spar to the rear fuselage where they all took up their ditching positions and braced themselves for what was obviously going to be a very tricky landing on an exceptionally rough sea.

Andrew Dunn was left alone in the cockpit. All their lives were now in his hands as he made his final preparations to land the Whitley on the heaving water just below. He had ditched a Whitley before, but that was in the relatively calm waters off Hastings Pier. Their current predicament was a totally different kettle of fish - and a kettle of fish was exactly what they'd be sharing if he got this ditching wrong. As first the port and then the starboard engines died for lack of petrol, the ominous silence served as a warning for the four crew members in the darkness of the rear fuselage to brace themselves for the inevitable impact. There was nowhere else to go but down and inexorably the Whitley sank closer and closer to the heaving waves. Andrew Dunn's last bit of flying proved what an exceptional young pilot he was. The crew were thrown about inside the fuselage as 'O-Orange' hit the higher waves, bounced once and then settled down on the water, but no-one was hurt and the Whitley remained in one piece. Dunn quickly unstrapped himself and scrambled under the main spar to join his crew who were busy launching the inflatable dinghy. George Riley had grabbed the Very pistol and some cartridges and stuffed them inside his shirt in the hope of keeping them dry, Sergeant Allen had brought his packet of biscuits and Sergeant Savill had picked up a water bottle. As Dunn joined them to cries of 'Well done Skipper' and 'Bloody marvellous landing, Sir' they quickly launched the dinghy, with Dunn and Riley in the water hanging on to the ropes ready to push it away from the aircraft. George Riley unleashed the mooring rope and they pushed themselves away from 'O-Orange' before she sank.

The weight of their sodden flying boots was dragging Dunn and Riley down so they both kicked them off in the water and then the three men in the dinghy helped them aboard. Sergeant Savill reckoned they were about eighty miles from the English coast when they ditched at 05.50 hours. George Riley was absolutely certain of the time because he had banged his wrist watch when they'd hit the sea and the impact had stopped it. The heavy seas gradually took them further away from their Whitley and they could only catch occasional glimpses of it when they were on the crest of a wave. Eventually they could see her no more, the sea had irrevocably claimed Whitley P5046.

Someone plonked their great flying-booted foot on one of Andy Dunn's stockinged feet, causing him to yell out. He then ordered the rest of the crew to remove their flying boots. These were used in an effort to bail out the dinghy but the waves swept in faster than they could ever hope to throw the sea out. In any case they needed to hold on with both hands just to stay in the dinghy.

From that moment on, a surprising amount of the resources of both the RAF and the Royal Navy were concentrated upon the rescue of the Whitley crew. Within minutes of the receipt of Sergeant Allen's last radio transmission, a Hudson of Coastal Command was ordered to commence the search. It failed to locate them but, at 10.50 hours on 24th September, exactly five hours after the ditching, another Hudson came across the little yellow dinghy in the rough seas. It was then one hundred miles east of Hartlepool and the search aircraft immediately radioed this position back to its base while continuing to circle the dinghy until it was relieved by another Hudson at 12.35 hours. This, in its turn, was relieved by another at 14.00 hours.

On seeing the first Hudson, George Riley immediately tried to fire the Very pistol. Unfortunately the cardboard cartridges had swollen due to their immersion in the sea and would not fit into the chamber. While George was frantically stripping off the outer layers of cardboard, Andy Dunn grabbed the hand-held flare that was provided in the dinghy - it didn't work. George Riley finally managed to get a cartridge into the chamber and pulled the trigger - the flare went all of ten feet into the air before falling back into the sea!

Upon receipt of the Hudson's radio message, a high speed rescue launch was despatched to pick up the crew of O-Orange but, at about midday, the weather deteriorated considerably, and heavy sea hid the dinghy from view. Worse still the wind swung round from the southwest to northwest, thus changing their direction of drift by a full ninety degrees. The weather worsened to such an extent that the rescue launch began to ship a lot of water and had to turn for home, radioing its base as it did so. Shortly after this radio message all contact with the launch was lost.

Meanwhile, the rough seas that were making life so difficult for the High Speed Launch were making much more misery for Andy Dunn and his crew in their little rubber craft. Waves continually broke over them, keeping the dinghy permanently flooded, soaking the five crewmen to their skins and considerably lowering the temperature of their bodies. In an effort to warm themselves they partook of their emergency rum ration, but this didn't go far between the five of them and, on empty stomachs made them feel a little light-headed, while the rough seas were making them all feel pretty sick anyway.

Having waved like lunatics at the first Hudson to find them, they were now wondering how long they would have to wait before they were actually picked up. Now that the adrenalin generated by the attack on Spandau, the drama of the subsequent return flight and their ditching had worn off, they realised how exhausted they were. Some of the crew started to doze as hypothermia set in without them realising what was happening. As conditions worsened, the circling Hudson lost sight of them. Despite another search by a further Hudson and a second launch, which lasted for over an hour and a half, no trace of the downed airmen could be found and the searchers were driven back to their respective bases by the worsening weather. Yet another Hudson was sent out and, fortunately, this was lucky enough to rediscover the drifting airmen. Corning in as close as possible, it dropped a container of emergency rations only ten yards away from the dinghy. It might just as well have been ten miles away for, despite their frantic paddling, the five had to watch broken-hearted as the heavy seas took their succour further and further away from them, until it finally disappeared from view altogether.

The Hudson crew carefully noted their position and dropped a flame float in order to work out the direction of their drift and watched long enough to work out that they were drifting at about three knots. Then, short of fuel, the

Hudson headed back to land. Once again the elements conspired against their rescue, with the wind swinging round yet again, this time to almost due north, changing the direction of drift so carefully calculated by the last Hudson. Yet again, the worsening weather caused a temporary overnight halt to the continuing search for the forlorn crew of Whitley P5046. And there was still no word from the missing High Speed Rescue Launch.

The continual pounding of the seas was beginning to tell on the bedraggled airmen. One of the crew grew lightheaded and fell overboard, but his four companions managed to drag him back into the dinghy. Shortly afterwards, he fell into the sea again and again his fellow survivors managed to haul him back on board. Yet a third time he fell out of the dinghy and for the third time the rest of the crew dragged him back into their little yellow craft. The exertion that this caused, linked to their continued exposure to the elements, resulted in them drifting off to sleep and George Riley awoke just too late to reach this crew member as he went overboard for a fourth time. Despite his arousing the other three men from their slumbers and some frantic paddling by them all, they had to watch their crewman drift away like the emergency food container until they could see him no more.

During the course of that day they had finished their flask of water and eaten a couple of biscuits each, now they were cold and thirsty as they huddled closely together and exhaustedly dozed their way through their first full night adrift in an open dinghy. Just after 06.00 hours on the morning of Wednesday September 25th, four Hudsons took off from their base and set off to continue the search. A prolonged hunt along the presumed track of its drift from its last known position yielded no results On the sea below them, two Royal Navy destroyers - HMS Ashanti and HMS Bedouin - were also doing their bit to find the missing airmen, but with the same results. One Hudson did however sight the missing High Speed Launch limping back towards land and was at least able to radio that piece of good news back to base. Their search along the dinghy's projected track being fruitless, the Hudsons commenced a square search and, at 11.00 hours that morning, one of them finally came across the bedraggled remainder of the Whitley crew. Circling low, it dropped another canister of food but again, the rough sea and their weakened state prevented the downed airmen from reaching it. The Hudson's navigator fixed their position with the utmost diligence before its pilot flew off to find the destroyers to lead them back. It was just at this critical point in the renewed rescue bid that shortage of petrol forced the Hudson to head for base before it could find the destroyers.

Acting on the radio messages transmitted by the last Hudson, another one rendezvoused with Ashanti and Bedouin and directed them to look in the area reported by its fellow search aircraft. But once again they could find nothing. Yet another Hudson finally came upon the little rubber craft just after 11.15 hours and circled it until 13.00 hours when it was relieved by a fourth aircraft. On its way back to base it came across the destroyers about sixteen miles from the dinghy and, using its Aldis Lamp, signalled directions for them to reach the crew of `O-Orange'.

When the first Hudson of that day had come across the dinghy, all four remaining crewmen had waved to it. By the time the third one arrived at 13.00 hours, they could only see one man making any movement at all. Circling round the dinghy, the aircraft dropped some flame floats and another parcel of emergency rations but, again, the sea carried this succour beyond the reach of the drifting airmen. By now it was impossible to see the dinghy from anything further away than 400 yards and as the Hudson came round again it lost sight of the tiny craft in a squall and the rough seas. The destroyers were now only eight miles away, so the Hudson flew off to attract their attention. Sadly, they too disappeared in the rapidly deteriorating weather at about 14.30 hours.

Still the Hudson stuck doggedly to its search. It sighted two Heinkel floatplanes and immediately set to seeing them off. They saw him coming and rapidly disappeared into the clouds. Another Hudson and two Ansons were sent out to join the search and hundreds of square miles of tossing sea were covered but the little yellow dinghy containing the four exhausted airmen could not be found. The sea was getting worse by the minute and when the circling Hudson finally lost sight of the dinghy it was drifting at more than four knots. George Riley clearly remembers this aircraft.

"A Hudson found us and dropped flares. It stayed with us for a long time. We sighted a destroyer later that afternoon and the Hudson seemed to be directing it to us, but as soon as the Hudson flew off we lost sight of the destroyer."

So near, yet so far away.

Once again night closed over the little group of airmen still drifting at the mercy of the waves. Lack of sustenance and protracted exposure were seriously sapping their strength. During that night a second crew member rolled over the low side of the dinghy and was lost beneath the waves, so that when they awoke on the morning of Thursday the 26th September they were only three - Pilot Officer Andrew Dunn, Sergeant D Allen and Sergeant George Riley. Of the three, only George Riley was in any state to take any action, while the other two were in a very comatose condition despite George's attempts to revive them and keep them awake. For over forty-eight hours the RAF and Royal Navy had spared nothing in their search for the missing airmen and at dawn on the third day five more Hudsons took off to renew the search. They were detailed to cover an area some ninety miles long by sixty miles wide off Flamborough Head - a total area of over 5,000 square miles! All morning they carried out this search, fighting now and then with German aircraft that tried to interfere. On one occasion a Hudson helped to drive off two Heinkel He 115's that were thinking about attacking Ashanti and Bedouin who were also continuing their part in the search. The Hudson promptly sailed into the attack and the Heinkels cleared off in the direction of Germany at a fair rate of knots.

A Blenheim also went out to join in the search, but a motor launch, also engaged in the hunt, was so badly battered by the heavy seas that she sprang a leak and was obliged to return home. Throughout that morning of the 26th September, the third day of the search, the Hudsons fought short, sharp engagements with the Luftwaffe who kept escaping into cloud. From dawn until the early afternoon they continued their mission of mercy but nothing did they see of the dinghy from `O-Orange'. Just after 14.00 hours, shortage of fuel again forced them to return to their bases and they were replaced by four Ansons. They too, failed to find the three remaining survivors. Despite the apparent hopelessness of the search, neither the RAF nor the Royal Navy would yet abandon it.

At dawn on Friday. September 27th, the fourth day of the search, five Hudsons and four Ansons resumed the task in hand. Visibility was poor, the sea was still rough and, as these aircraft flew low over the water, their windscreens were covered in brine. At last, a Hudson spotted the dinghy but was only able to keep it in sight for five minutes before losing it again in yet another squall. What its crew did notice however, was that the dinghy now contained only three men and that only one of them seemed to be moving. The little yellow craft's position was carefully marked once again and, at 11.15 hours, another Hudson flew to this position and searched the seas around it. It could find nothing! One hour later another aircraft searched the same area with exactly the same result. Disappointedly they returned to base, while a further three continued the search. These found Ashanti and Bedouin and escorted them to where the dinghy was last reported. They too found nothing but an empty, heaving sea.

One Hudson took off again at 13.00 hours to resume the search. Another followed it thirty minutes later. Just after 14.00 hours, almost on the point of giving up, the pilot of one of these aircraft finally spotted the missing dinghy. Coming down very low he dropped a flame float and with it a watertight container of rations. He was an excellent shot, it landed almost right next to the dinghy and George Riley quickly reached out and grabbed it. Although very weak after four days adrift in an open dinghy, George was in much better shape than either of his companions, Dunn and Allen, who were both lying unconscious in the bottom of the dinghy. The first thing George did on opening the emergency rations was to take a good swig of brandy that revived him to some extent. He then tried to rouse Dunn and Allen by holding them up and trying to get some of the brandy down their throats, but could not be sure if he had been successful. George made his crewmates as comfortable as he could and then lit up his first cigarette for almost ninety hours.

This Hudson pilot was absolutely determined that the dinghy would not be lost again and continued to circle it very closely indeed. One hour later, the second Hudson also arrived and for hour after hour the two aircraft played 'follow my leader' round and around the dinghy. By 15.00 hours they watched helplessly as one of the crew fell overboard and then saw George Riley use almost the last reserves of his strength to pull him back on board. The exertion had obviously tired the airman out, for very shortly after this he appeared to fall asleep. At 16.00 hours, while George Riley was still asleep, the watching Hudson crews saw the same airman fall out of the dinghy once again and vanish below the waves. Although they did not know it, they had just witnessed the last moments of Pilot Officer Andrew Dunn.

So from 14.00 hours, first one and then two Hudsons circled the dinghy and the last two remaining airmen in it. A tiny little circle of yellow rubber that the Royal Navy and the RAF had sought for four days. The Hudson crews were determined not to lose it again. At last Ashanti and Bedouin steamed up in answer to the Hudson's signals. The aircraft dropped flares by the dinghy and kept diving over it to lead the destroyers to the exact position. At 17.35 hours, HMS Bedouin lowered a boat and George Riley and Sergeant Allen were gently lifted from their little rubber craft and taken on board. The

Hudsons waited for Bedouin to signal the state of the survivors and at last it came, 'One fair, one very ill.' The Hudsons turned for home, their mission completed.

Sadly, Sergeant Allen died within an hour of being rescued. Only Sergeant George Riley survived this horrendous ordeal. After being picked up the only thing he could vaguely remember about HMS Bedouin was being asked by the naval doctor if he wanted anything. George asked for a cigarette but fell asleep before it was lit for him. The next thing he remembered was waking up in The Royal Naval Hospital at Rosyth the following day. George Riley had been drifting for eighty-four hours. In that time the dinghy covered a distance of about ninety miles.

The intensive search detailed above was first recounted in a book entitled 'So Few'. This is a collection of true short stories about all Commands of the RAF written by a gentleman called David Masters and first published in 1941. Masters had interviewed George Riley while he was still in Rosyth Hospital and quickly added the story to his book. In one of his final paragraphs, Masters claims that this rescue "will go down in history as an act of true democracy because, in his view, the search was not for an officer of very high rank, but for a crew whose highest ranking member was a humble Pilot Officer."

One must understand that books written during the war had a duty to boost morale and they usually contained at least some surreptitious propaganda, so it is perhaps not surprising that neither the rescue search for Andrew Dunn and his crew, nor Master's book, actually went down 'in history'. It does however, seem very sad that this story of true dedication has been all but lost for over fifty years before the first edition of this book appeared.

Additional Notes to Chapter 5.

1) **Pilot Officer Andrew Dunn DFC** was operational from 10th May to the 23rd September 1940, a period of just four and a half months. During this period 77 Squadron lost sixteen Whitleys on operations - Andy Dunn was in five of them. Allowing that he carried out the business end of his last operation (and we know from George Riley that he did), Dunn carried out twenty-four operations in a very short

time. This was an extremely high rate of operations for this period of the war and my research has shown that Dunn volunteered for far more than his fair share. His first four operations, as a second pilot, were outside his control but were nevertheless undertaken every other night that the squadron operated. He missed only six of his unit's operations after his first crash and most of this time was taken up with returning from France. Once he started operating as an aircraft captain he missed only one squadron operation until his third crash, when 77 Squadron operated on four nights without him. He then carried out three on the trot until he ditched off Hastings Pier, after which he was sent on survivors leave, because it was exactly one month before he appeared on the operations order again - he'd missed ten op-nights!

From the 19th July, until his final trip on 23rd/24th September, Andrew Dunn missed only five of his squadron's operational nights, a phenomenally high rate of operations, especially for 1940 when one sortie every four nights was considered to be a fairly high average. It is tragic that such a keen and dedicated young pilot should die in such a manner but, unfortunately, that is war. We shall never know what it was that drove him, it was too early in the war for him to have lost family or close friends in the Blitz, for that was just starting to intensify when he died. Some may think that Dunn was a 'death or glory' boy and the cold hard facts could be interpreted in that way. I prefer to believe, however naively, that he was just very determined to 'do his bit' to defeat Nazi Germany. Whichever view you, the reader, take, I believe we can say that Andrew Dunn was a brave man.

2) **Sgt. George Riley** fully recovered from his experience and returned to 77 Squadron to find his CO had decided that George's first tour was deemed to be completed, despite the fact that he'd only carried out seven operations. He was sent as an instructor to Cumbria and then to 14 OTU at Cottesmore. At the end of 1942 he volunteered for a second tour and was posted to 106 Squadron at Syerston in 5 Group. Here he carried out fourteen operations before he was allowed home on leave because his Father was seriously ill. George's Father died only three hours after he arrived at his bedside

and, being the only son, His leave was extended by his CO so that he could make all the neccesary arrangements.

On his return to Syerston, George was saddened to learn that his crew had been shot down on a trip to Hannover and had all been killed. Once again George was the sole survivor of a bomber crew. He was expecting to have to complete his second tour as a 'sparebod' and didn't fancy the idea one little bit - then he had an idea. While at Driffield, he had met Leonard Cheshire who was then a Pilot Officer on 102 Squadron. Now George knew that Chesh had just taken command of 617 Squadron so he decided to phone him to ask if 617 had a vacancy for a wireless operator. George's luck held. Not only did Chesh remember him but, yes, 617 did require a replacement wireless operator and Wing Commander Cheshire ordered Warrant Officer Riley to pack his bags and report to Coningsby forthwith and that he, Chesh, would sort out the paperwork. George Riley carried out a further 28 operations with 617 Squadron, including all the Tirpitz raids, as part of the crew of Flight Lieutenant Paddy Gingles. Altogether, George Riley carried out 49 operations, finishing the war as a Warrant Officer and never even got a sniff at a gong!

Chapter Six

1941: Not the "Glorious Twelfth"

In 1941, bomber crews were not permanently 'crewed up' as they would be twelve to fifteen months later. However, it was not unusual for senior captains on a squadron to have 'first claim' on two or three key crew personnel with whom they had a rapport, thus forming a nucleus of a semi-permanent crew. At this stage of the war it was the norm for aircrew to take their leave entitlement as and when they could fit it in, or as they needed it for personal reasons, rather than at regular intervals as would become the standard practice later in the war.

Also at this time, all "heavy' bombers still carried a second pilot who would undertake between five and twelve operations with at least three different captains. In this way they could gain valuable experience themselves and, having seen how different captains approached operations, decide on which operational methods and style suited them best. Having gained the necessary experience and satisfied the Squadron Commander of their suitability for more responsibility, they were cleared to fly as first pilots and captains. They could then start to look around for crew members who had no 'semi-permanent' liaisons with the senior captains. All this meant that, on any given Operation, on any given night, it was very unlikely, if not impossible for all the members of any single aircraft's crew to have carried out the same number of operations.

So it was with the crew of a 76 Squadron Handley Page Halifax B.Mk.I, serial no. L9530, coded 'MP-L for London', on the night of Tuesday the 12th August 1941. The captain and first pilot, Flight Lieutenant Christopher Cheshire (known to his intimates as 'Chris' or `Chesh) was on his 25th operation. His observer Sergeant Gordon (Slim) Smalley was on his 26th and wireless operator Sergeant Eddie (Taff) Gurmin was on his 29th, but had decided to stay with Slim and Chesh until they finished their tours. All three were near to being screened at the end their tour. The flight engineer, Sergeant Reggie Wash, was on his sixth operation and the second pilot, Sergeant Paul Horrox, was on his fifth. The gunners represented the most and the least experienced members of the crew. The rear gunner, Flight Sergeant Timber Woods, had already completed a full tour with Coastal

In 1941 the Whitley was replaced by the Halifax. Here, Chris Cheshire's MP-L of 76 Sqn is being serviced.

Command and was on his sixth bomber operation, while the front gunner, Sergeant Gordon (Jock) Niven, was on his very first mission.

In 1938 Christopher Cheshire had followed his older brother, Leonard, into the Oxford University Air Squadron. Had he had enough time to amass ten hours solo flying before the war started, he would have received an immediate commission before entering into full time RAF training. As it was, Christopher had only seven hours solo to his name by 3rd September and thus spent the first year of war as a sergeant undergoing 'square bashing' for the first four months and then full service flying training at Cranwell. He was commissioned as a Pilot Officer on gaining his 'wings' in September 1940. The rest of that year was spent on an Operational Training Unit and he was posted to his first operational unit, 78 Squadron at Dishforth, in January 1941.

After making himself 'au fait' with the squadron aircraft, the Armstrong Whitworth Whitley Mk.V. and undertaking local area familiarisation training, Pilot Officer Christopher Cheshire undertook his first operation, as a second pilot, on the night of Tuesday the 11th February 1941. `Chesh' was assigned to the crew of Sergeant H. A. Davis, who was down to fly Whitley Z6470. The target was Bremen, in northwest Germany and they were one of four of the squadron's Whitleys that joined Hampden, Wellington and other Whitley aircraft despatched this night. Although the aircraft's intercom system failed prior to take-off, Sergeant Davis elected to continue with the briefed sortie, but this failure contributed to the fact that Z6470 was one of the fifty-two aircraft whose captains had to report, on their return, that they had been unable to identify the primary target. They did at least manage to find their way home, despite the appearance of on unexpected fog over a lot of bases that led to twenty-two aircraft crashing their return.

Christopher's major emotion on this, his first operation, was one of bemusement rather than apprehension, particularly on seeing Flak for the first time But he was well aware that Bremen was not such a deep penetration target (the whole flight took a little over six hours) and was grateful for a reasonably gentle introduction to operations.

It was almost a complete month before he made his second trip, on Monday 10th March, when 78 Squadron detailed three aircraft to join an attack on the docks and shipping in Brest Harbour. On this occasion his captain was Sergeant R. J. (Bob) Fraas and the aircraft was T4236. Bob Fraas took the Whitley over the target at 11,000 feet and the observer, Sergeant F. M. Unwin, released the bombs. Immediately after their release a small patch of cloud drifted across the target, obscuring it completely and preventing them from observing the results of their endeavours, although the crew did see several orange and red fighter flares in the target area. Just over six hours after take-off Whitley T4236 was on the final approach to Dishforth, where it overshot the flarepath in bad visibility and ended up in a heap on the Great North Road (the Al) right on the airfield's perimeter. Fortunately no-one was injured and the crew scrambled safely out of the damaged aircraft. (This was the night of the first Halifax operation).

One week later, on Tuesday 18th March, Chesh was briefed to fly, again as second pilot, with Pilot Officer D. F. McKenzie in Z6470, the aircraft in which he undertook his first operation. The target this time was Kiel, about seventy miles south of the Danish German border, which was to be attacked by ninety-nine aircraft. It should have been attacked by one hundred aircraft but Z6470 got bogged down in soft ground on its way to the flarepath and could not proceed, leaving Chris Cheshire with an immense feeling of anti-climax.

Cheshire's third operation took place on Sunday 23rd March and was his first trip to the 'Big City', Berlin. He was detailed as 'second dickie' to Flight Lieutenant G. K. Lawrence and his crew. Guy Lawrence was a very experienced pilot and one of the Squadron's senior captains and his aircraft for this raid was Z6466. Only two Whitleys from 78 Squadron took off, just after 8pm, to join another twenty-six Whitleys and thirty-five

F/L Christopher Cheshire of 76 Sqn in L9530. Note the 'Cheshire Crest'.

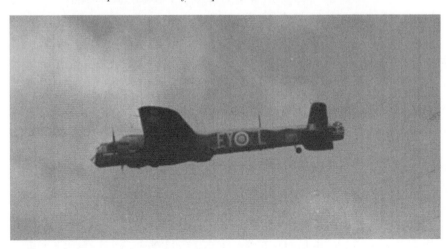

Christopher Cheshire's Whitley Z6625, EY-L. (Eddie Gurmin).

Wellingtons on the long haul to the German capital. The city's Diplomatic Quarters were Guy Lawrence's primary target and, having positively identified it through 2/10ths cloud, he attacked from 14,000 feet and returned safely to base, just after 5am, without any untoward experiences. Looking back on his first trip to the 'Big City' as he lay in his bed after debrief and breakfast, Christopher realised how really tired he was from his exertions of the nine-hour flight, but he was also surprised (and very grateful) when it suddenly occurred to him that he'd been bored for most of what had been a very uneventful flight.

A return to Brest on Sunday 30th March, with his Flight Commander - Squadron Leader Wilding - in Z6492 was to be Chesh's fourth trip. The squadron despatched nine Whitleys as part of a 109 aircraft attack on the Scharnhorst and Gneisenau. Squadron Leader Wilding released the bomb load on the cruisers' reported position from 14,000 feet through 5/10ths cloud. His fifth operation took place a week after this, on 7th April, and it was to be his second with Bob Fraas. This trip, however, would take a little longer than their first trip together, the target was Kiel. Ten aircraft from 78 Squadron joined another 39 Whitleys, 117 Wellingtons, 61 Hampdens and two Stirlings on this, the largest attack of the war so far. Visibility over the target was perfect and bright moonlight had the effect of dimming the intensity of the enemy searchlights. The crew observed a large fire in a naval armament depot (which was to burn for two days) and Sergeant Fraas took Whitley Z6492 over the target at 11,000 feet as Sergeant Unwin released the bombs. Turning away from the target the aircraft was caught in searchlights, but rapid avoiding action got them away with only one minor hit from Flak. All 78 Squadron's aircraft returned safely but the Command lost two Whitleys and two Wellingtons this night.

Having operated only once a week at most since undertaking his first operation, it must have come as a bit of a shock when Christopher was informed, on the morning after this Kiel operation, that he and Bob Fraas and crew were on again that night. They had been detailed to take Z6492 back to Kiel again that night as part of a 160 aircraft attack. Bob, Chris and crew made two glide bombing attacks on the shipyards, observing an outbreak of fire after releasing their bombs amid many searchlights and heavy Flak. Although the Command lost another four aircraft this night, all of 78 Squadron's crews once again returned safely.

78 Sqn. Slim Smalley (2nd from left) shows the crew where they're going – or where they've been. Sid Lang is far right, kneeling. (Eddie Gurmin)

The following day, Wednesday the 9th April, the new Aerodrome of Middleton St. George officially opened as a bomber station, although some of 78's ground crew had moved in there two days earlier. The Squadron's aircrew and aircraft arrived on the 10th and on the 15th, Group Captain T.C.Traill, OBE, DFC, assumed command of the station.

When 78 Squadron arrived at Middleton the station was still in the process of being built and there were many piles of four-inch clay drain pipes lying around. It was not long before some wag discovered that they made an even better whistling noise than an empty beer bottle when dropped over Germany. The Squadron ultimately delivered many of these unorthodox missiles to the enemy under the firm belief that the whistling noise they emitted as they descended would put the German sound locators off tracking their aircraft.

Having operated two nights on the trot, Christopher was not on the Operations Order again until 29th April. His seventh operation (and last as a second pilot) was with Sergeant L. Thorpe and Whitley T4147 was to be their aircraft for an attack on Mannheim in south-east Germany. This raid was carried out by seventy-one aircraft, thirteen of them from 78 Squadron. This was to be a round trip of over 1,000 miles from Middleton St. George, a long nine-hour slog mostly over enemy territory. One of the other Squadron aircraft on this raid was Z6625, a brand new machine on its first operation. Coded 'EY-L for London' (in official parlance), it was being flown on this occasion by Squadron Leader Walter (Willie) Williams, the 'A' Flight Commander. His wireless operator for this raid was Sergeant Eddie (Taff) Gurmin, who was on his second operation since having returned from taking part in Operation Colossus (see Chapter 3). The Mannheim raid would bring his total up to eleven. Also in Squadron Leader Williams' new aircraft was observer Sergeant Gordon (Slim) Smalley, who was on his first operation, on the eve of his 21st birthday. About half-an-hour from the target, with Slim frantically ensuring that his navigational calculations were correct and that he had the aircraft's exact position charted, midnight arrived and Slim was amazed to hear, over the intercom, his Flight Commander lead the whole crew in a rousing chorus of 'Happy Birthday to you...'

Pilot Officer Cheshire's big day (or rather night) arrived on Saturday 3rd May. He was now a fully-fledged bomber captain and allocated the basis of a crew. Chesh went into the crew room to look for them. The first one he saw was Taff Gurmin. 'You are Sgt. Gurmin, aren't you?' 'Yes Sir.' came the reply, 'Well I'm afraid I've got some bad news for you.' Said Chesh. 'What's that sir?' asked Taff. 'You've been selected as my first wireless operator.'[24] 'That's not bad news sir,'[25] said Taff and they went off to find the rest of Cheshire's new crew. They had been allocated the new Whitley, Z6625 and full crew for this auspicious occasion comprised Slim Smalley as Observer, Taff as Wireless Operator, Sgt Lissett as second Wireless Operator in the rear turret and the second pilot was Sgt Ken Hudgell.

Although officially known as 'L for London', it was not long before Slim and Taff began calling her 'Ell for Leather' (Taff even used that when transmitting radio messages), something that Chris Cheshire did not discover until 1991. Once again the Squadron despatched thirteen aircraft, this time as part of a 102-strong attack on Cologne, an 8 hour trip from Middleton. Nightfighters were observed in the target area but Chesh and his crew dropped their bombs unhindered from 18,000 feet, despite 9/10ths cloud. On

---

[24] *At this period of the war, with dual-trained WOp/AGs it was the practice to put two of these tradesmen in each crew, a first and a second WOp/AG. Initially the second WOp/AG did two or three trips in the rear turret to get used to operations, this was followed by several trips on the radio set while the first W/Op occupied the rear turret to give advice and assistance as required. After three or four satisfactory trips on the set the second W/Op became a first W/Op and the circle began again.*

[25] *Taff Gurmin was later to admit that his initial feeling on being approached by Chris Cheshire was one of concern. He felt that Mr. Cheshire was too 'posh' for a little Welshman like him, but was then to state that Chesh turned out to be a wonderful pilot and a great guy in every way. He considered himself very fortunate to have 'Chesh' as his skipper.*

return they were diverted to Linton-on-Ouse, where they landed at 04.35 hours to complete Chris Cheshire's eighth operation.

The Cologne trip was to signal the start of a close crew relationship between Chesh, Slim and Taff that was to last for many months. Sgts Hudgell and Lissett were to fly with them for a further five operations, thus forming, as near as possible for this period of the war, a semi-permanent crew. Their target on the 5th May was Mannheim again and, despite seeing several nightfighters, Z6625 returned without any trouble. Two nights later Chesh and the chaps were one of fifteen crews from 78 Squadron having another go at Salmon and Gluckstein[26] in Brest Harbour and the following night they once again attacked the docks at Bremen, although they had an interesting diversion en route. As they were approaching the enemy coast in bright moonlight, they spotted a small fleet or about ten German destroyers sailing north. A short discussion took place amongst the crew while they decided whether or not to attack this SEMO (Self Evident Military Objective) or carry on to their primary. Working on the very sound principle that if their attack on the destroyers was successful they'd all be heroes but that should their bombs miss this very tempting target they were in for a right rollocking, they wisely decided that discretion was the better part of valour, radioed base with the position and course of the enemy destroyers and continued on to Bremen.

Cheshire's twelfth operation, on Saturday the 10th May, was to Hamburg. As they were flying over Flamborough Head on their way out, one of the Whitley's engines packed in. Cheshire gave his crew the option, either to turn back or carry out the mission on one engine. To a man the crew opted to continue the operation. Thus they continued on their way to Hamburg where Slim Smalley released their bombload in a single stick from 17,000 feet. They then turned round and returned to base, flying all the way on one Merlin engine. This must have given Taff Gurmin quite some time to think about his biggest fear. Although he kept most of it to himself, Taff could not swim and was terrified of water. Ditching in the North Sea was his biggest nightmare, so much so that he was the only member of his crew who actually welcomed the traditional greeting from the German Flak gunners as the

---

[26] *The battlecruisers Scharnhorst and Gneisenau were nicknamed Salmon and Gluckstein by the RAF. This was the name of a well-known national chain of tobacconist shops, although some sources say they were chemists. They were far more likely to be tobacconists, knowing RAF aircrew!*

aircraft reached the enemy coast, at least he knew he would soon be over dry land again. On every trip the first thing Taff did on entering the aircraft was to check that the rope attaching the dinghy to the kite was secure and undamaged and that he had a good sharp knife about his person with which to cut the same before the aircraft sank while still attached. Over the months he had been on operations he had also collected quite a good store of emergency rations that he carried in a little bag and religiously placed just outside the rear turret doors or under the radio table depending on which position he was flying. We shall learn more of Taff's Tuck later.

On the 12th May, the target was Mannheim again but a safe landing at one minute before 5am meant that Chris Cheshire had returned from his thirteenth operation and he went off on a few days well-earned leave.

Chesh's second pilot of the last six operations, Sgt Ken Hudgell, was now appointed an aircraft captain and on Thursday 15th May he borrowed Z6625 plus Slim and Taff for a short trip to Boulogne, but Chesh returned from leave to reclaim his aircraft, observer and wireless operator for another attack on Cologne on the 16th. Taff Gurmin was in the rear turret on this trip, with second wireless operator Sergeant Lissett on the set. All went well until they were approaching Dunkirk on the French coast on their way home and Cheshire had started to lose height ready for the Channel crossing. The aircraft descended to 10,000 feet and the crew found themselves slap-bang over the centre of Dunkirk instead of skirting it as planned. Searchlights started probing the sky in their search for the Whitley, with their numbers increasing every second. Taff reported this fact to Chris and then started to give a running commentary as the lights finally fastened on to the aircraft. Then the Flak opened up and `L for Leather' was getting well and truly plastered. Taff sat in his turret with one hand on the turret controls and the other trying to shade his eyes from the blinding lights. Taff was not much amused with the situation and began to vent his anger at his protagonists in very loud, extremely unprintable epithets, not least of which was to doubt the married status of the parents of the Luftwaffe gunners.

Whilst Taff was still in full flood, Chesh's unflappable voice came over the intercom, 'Who on earth is that swearing?' he asked. Somewhat stunned, Taff admitted his guilt. Well if you must swear, please ensure that your microphone is switched off.' said Chesh. 'Sorry Skipper.' from a slightly chastened Taff who switched his microphone off and continued his tirade.

Suddenly there was an almighty bang and the rear turret went dead in Taff's hand. He reported this fact to Chesh who replied 'You have the best view Taff, how can we get out of this lot?' Dive to port Skipper.' answered Taff, 'But that will take us back into France.' said Chesh, 'That's alright Skipper, then we can find a quieter place to cross the coast.' Cheshire dived the Whitley to port and they lost the Flak and the searchlights – but not a moment too soon, the rear turret was immobile and one engine was shot to bits. As they crossed the French coast again Taff spotted a nightfighter flare and reported it to Chesh. 'Keep your eyes peeled Taff,' came the reply, 'What can you do with the damaged turret?' `It looks as though the hydraulic power has gone completely, Skipper.' said Taff, 'I can turn it manually but only very slowly. I can only fire one gun and I can't elevate or depress them. If we hit trouble I'll tell you to dive if I need them raised or climb if I need them depressed. "Right, Taff.' replied Cheshire, I'll see what I can do on one engine, keep your fingers crossed.' Shortly afterwards Taff spotted the enemy nightfighter as it flew right over the top of them, fortunately without seeing them. The damaged Whitley would have been no match for a Bf110.

They droned on across the Channel on one engine with 10/10ths cloud cover below them. Taff broke the tense silence with the announcement that they were over the English coast. `How do you know that?' asked Cheshire, 'I can see the searchlights on the clouds Skipper.' came the reply. Thank God for that.' said Chesh, somewhat prematurely, as the British anti-aircraft gunners took their turn at knocking seven bells out of the damaged Whitley. 'I bloody give up!' was heard to come from the rear turret, but Slim Smalley had other ideas. Uttering similar doubts about the parentage of his own side's gunners as his friend in the rear turret had earlier voiced about their German equivalent, Slim grabbed the Very pistol and fired off the colours of the day. The shooting stopped and 'L for Leather' limped back to Middleton St. George where Chris Cheshire made another of his perfect landings. Taff opened the doors of his turret to find the rear fuselage awash with hydraulic oil – as was his little bag full of Taff's Tuck. Very forlornly, he picked up his carefully saved bag of goodies, carried it - still dripping oil - out of the kite to the side of the runway and drop-kicked it into the long grass.

The aircraft was in a dreadful mess with holes everywhere. Two members of the Durham Light Infantry (DLI), who were doing a stint of guard duty on the camp, came by the Whitley on their way to breakfast. They stood for some time, just looking at `L for Leather' with their mouths agape, then one said to the other 'Well mate, Ah divent mind sayin' they'll niver get me up in one of them bloody things!'

After debriefing, the crew had breakfast and then went off to bed. Later that afternoon Taff had a wander down to the hangar where the ground crew had already started to patch up Z6625, One of the ground crew approached Taff, 'Who was in the rear turret last night Sarge?' he asked, 'I was,' replied Taff, `Why?' thought it might have been' came the answer, 'Hold your hand out.' Taff did as he was bid and the airman dropped into it a small lump of shrapnel. 'Where did you find this?' asked Taff, `In the bit of horse hair under your arse.' came the reply. The shrapnel had travelled through the bottom of the fuselage, severed the hydraulic pipe that supplied power to the turret, then through the armour plating under the rear gunner's seat and finally come to rest in the thin cushion on which Taff had been sitting. Not surprisingly Taff went a little white at this news, 'What's the matter, Sarge?' asked the kindly Erk, 'I've just realised,' said Taff, 'How close that came to a part of my anatomy that I've grown very attached to over the years!'

Ken Hudgell's replacement as second dickie on this trip was Sergeant R. G. Chandos who would fly with Chesh only once, his place then being taken by a Canadian ex-mounted policeman, Sergeant Sid Lang, for Chesh's fifteenth operation on Tuesday 27th May, when once again the target was Cologne. Sid Lang was reputed to be as mad as a hatter, one of his regular tricks when being shot at by German Flak was to slide open his co-pilot's side window, stick his head outside and then remark 'Aint close, I can't smell the goddam cordite.' Chesh also had a new rear gunner on this trip, with Sergeant T. Lissett being replaced by Sergeant D. A. Wilson. 'Ell for Leather' made two runs across Cologne on this night, releasing their incendiaries on the first and seeing fires start as a result, then dropping their H.E. bombs on the second run, when, unfortunately, cloud obscured their view just after they'd been released.

As already mentioned, the Station Commander at Middleton St. George at this time was Group Captain T. C. Traill, a man who was highly respected by all his officers and men. He was particularly keen on inter-service co-operation and did all he could to encourage his subordinates to learn about the activities and capabilities of the other services. To this end he arranged a programme of exchange visits with and to the neighbouring Army and Royal Navy establishments.

The first of such visits was to the Royal Navy's submarine training base at Lythe, just north of Whitby on the north-east coast. This visit was scheduled to take place on Wednesday 28th May, a day when no operations were planned for that night.

National attention at this time was focused on the Navy's hunt for the Bismarck which, a few days earlier, had sunk the brand new pride of the British fleet, HMS Hood, which had gone down very quickly with an enormous loss of life. So it was in the hope of hearing the latest news of the hunt straight from the `horse's mouth', that the Middleton party of aircrew, including Pilot Officer Christopher Cheshire, left their home base early on a cold and misty May morning.

Upon their arrival and after the customary exchange of greetings, the visitors received an easily assimilated lecture on the intricacies of operating a submarine. They were then driven a few miles to the small harbour at Lythe and taken aboard a somewhat antiquated, but fully serviceable submarine where they were met by the Captain of the vessel. They were not, however, to have their planned short sea voyage for, just as they were being introduced to the old naval tradition of ship's cocoa, a signal was received ordering the aircrew back to Middleton to prepare for unexpected operations that night.

They returned to the wardroom to partake of the Navy's usual tipple, a pink gin, when shortly after being issued with same, the Duty Officer called for silence for the radio news bulletin. The familiar 'pips' of the BBC News were followed by the voice of a well-known newsreader, *'This is Alvar Liddell reading the one o'clock news. The Bismarck has been sunk....'* Anything else that Mr. Liddell had to say was lost in the cheers of everyone in the wardroom, more gin bottles were opened and the ensuing spontaneous party caused the delay of lunch. This in turn meant that the visitors' planned early return was not quite as early as it should have been.

It was around 6pm when the party arrived back at Middleton St. George where the pilots and observers amongst them learned that their target for the night was to be Kiel and that the briefing would be at 7.30. The Squadron was putting up eight aircraft that were to join another six Whitleys in yet another attack on the Tirpitz. Christopher Cheshire's crew were resting so, for the first time ever, he found himself carrying out the airtest alone, a task which, thanks to his trusty groundcrew, went without a hitch.

At the briefing the Squadron's aircrew were led to believe that, following on from the sinking of the Bismark, Churchill wanted to try for the 'double' by destroying the Tirpitz too. The Met Officer, a civilian, informed that them that there was currently plenty of cover over the target, but that this was expected to break up by their estimated time of arrival at Keil and that they could anticipate reasonable weather with but scattered showers en-route. Making there way out to their usual aircraft, Z6625, 'L for London/Leather', the two wireless operator/gunners, Sergeants T. Hall (as second W/Op) and Taff Gurmin, agreed that Taff would occupy the rear turret on this occasion. Chesh's second pilot would once again be Canadian ex-Mountie Sid Lang and his Observer, as was now usual, was Slim Smalley. By 22.00hrs they were lined up on the flarepath ready to go and at 22.03hrs 'Ell for Leather' was logged as airborne.

Chris Cheshire eased the Whitley off the runway and set course for the target, getting an accurate pin-point of their position as they crossed the English coast, despite the misty conditions. Their present course would mean crossing the Enemy coast north of the Elbe estuary, approximately half way between Brunsbuttel and the island of Sylt. The first two-and-a-half hours or so were dogged by cu-nim cloud from 6,000 to 20,000 feet and although Cheshire tried to climb above it severe icing prevented this. Apart from this, everything was going to plan when, in the distance, they saw large flashes of light ahead. The collective experience of the crew allowed to them to rule out flak, but the flashes didn't look like lightning either. With his brief naval experience of that morning still fresh in his mind, Chesh voiced the possibility of this unusual phenomenon being due to a major naval engagement, but as there had been no mention at briefing of naval activity in the vicinity of their flight path they dismissed this possibility.

As Z6625 flew closer to the source of the flashes, the interior of the aircraft filled with intermittent sparks and the needles of the flying instruments, with the exception of the air speed indicator and the altimeter[27], began to flicker and jump all over the place, making Chesh's task of maintaining an accurate, steady course almost impossible. Sid Lang, in the front turret, treated those who could see it, to an impromptu display of vivid sparks jumping between

[27] *The airspeed indicator is operated by the pressure of air in the pitot tube, while the altimeter is worked by a sealed barostat. Neither would be affected by rapidly varying barometric pressure whereas the other instruments (compass, turn &bank indicator, rate ofclimb/descent indicator, artificial horizon, etc.) were all worked by air-driven gyros.*

his gloves and the guns. It was Taff Gurmin in the rear turret who suggested that all the sparks and flashes could be due to the Whitley flying through an electrical storm and, despite none of the crew having any previous experience of this, the total absence of any other rational reason for their predicament led them all to agree with him. Taff was, in fact, sat in the rear turret with his arms folded, keeping them well away from his guns that had flashes of lightning over twenty feet long trailing back from each barrel. Tommy Hall, the second W.Op/A.G. who was on the radio set was getting so much static that he called Taff on the intercom to say he was going to wind out the trailing aerial. Taff shouted back 'Don't you dare, that will really bugger things up!' so the trailing aerial stayed in its housing.

Despite the Met man's promise, cloud was still virtually 10/10ths as their ETA for the enemy coast arrived, an event that was made obvious to them by the usual 'warm welcome' from the Luftwaffe's Flak gunners, although even this seemed to have much less accuracy than normal. Slim Smalley managed to gets a dubious pin-point through a small gap in the clouds that indicated that they were further north than intended, but they did eventually manage to find the Ostsee Kanal and set course for Kiel as the clouds closed in around them once more. Their ETA at Kiel coincided with intensive Flak, thankfully still inaccurate, leading Chesh and Slim to the conclusion that they were at least in the vicinity of the target. After circling around and having lost height, still without a sensible compass reading, they had a fleeting glimpse of water surrounded by buildings that encouraged Chesh to spend some time trying to find the target area. The complete cloud cover persisted, however, and they never had even the tiniest glimmer of the ground, be it land or water. Reluctantly, Chesh decided that the time had come to set course for base, despite the fact that he was still trying to cope with erratic instrumentation that refused to settle down until after they had recrossed the enemy coast on their way back.

About an hour's flying time from base Tommy Hall received a radio message ordering all 78 Squadron aircraft still airborne to divert to RAF Abingdon, near Oxford, because of bad weather at base. At 07.00 hours, during a reasonably clear spot in the bad weather, Chesh gently eased Whitley EY-L, complete with full bomb load, on to the runway at this Oxfordshire aerodrome. Debriefing was over fairly quickly as the Station Intelligence Officers had already listened to almost identical stories from two other crews that had landed slightly ahead of Z6625.

By eight-o-clock the weather had clamped in again, the crews were enjoying a hearty breakfast in their respective messes and Christopher was listening to the BBC news. The bulletin was along the lines of 'a small but determined force from Bomber Command attacked Kiel harbour and despite poor weather conditions they were able to hit their main target...'. To say that Pilot Officer Cheshire was amazed at the inaccuracy of this statement does not do justice to the range of emotions he experienced. His amazement rapidly turned to concern as, being young and fairly naive, he had - up to this time - firmly believed that the Air Ministry's communiques always reflected an accurate and truthful account of operational activities. As Christopher's naivety was shattered, the concern turned, quite understandably, to disillusionment.

Despite this there was however, a consolation to being stuck miles from base on a strange airfield, at least as far as Chris Cheshire was concerned. In fact he was not in the least put out by this diversion, nor by the fact that it would be almost forty-eight hours before the weather would clear sufficiently to allow them to return to Middleton. Christopher Cheshire's parents lived within three miles of Abingdon!

On arrival back at Middleton St. George two days later, they had the opportunity of discussing their experiences over Kiel with the other Squadron crews who had taken part. They were amazed to learn that, despite the exceptionally bad weather conditions, the Squadron (and in fact the whole Command) had only lost one aircraft. it seemed that only one crew, that captained by the very experienced Flight Lieutenant Guy Lawrence (who was knighted for his civil activities some twenty-five years later) claimed any success. Guy Lawrence was the captain who had taken Christopher on his third trip a second pilot and, being some ten years older than the average squadron pilot, had acquired a lot of experience and guile that he had put to good use. He decided to ignore the route recommended at the briefing and had approached Kiel from the Baltic, to the north of the target. So doing, he managed to avoid all the Flak, get under the 'clag' and at least got a good sight of Kiel harbour and the Tirpitz[28], even if he and his crew couldn't be sure of having done any serious damage.

---

[28] *Tirpitz was finally sunk in Tromso Fjord on 12th November 1944 by Lancasters of Nos. 9 and 617 Sqns, led by Wing Commander J.B. 'Willie' Tait.*

On his return to Middleton, Chris Cheshire's observer Sergeant Slim Smalley, made a bee-line for the Met office. His objective was to have a 'few words' with the civilian met.man. Why, he wanted to know, did the 'scattered, isolated showers', not to mention 10/10ths cloud complete with icing, stretch all the way from Yorkshire to Kiel and back? Slim was assured that the trouble was caused by a depression off the Azores that had unexpectedly moved rapidly north into the North Sea. Being a little dubious of this explanation, Slim asked the met.man to calculate the speed of movement of this depression and was not in the least surprised to learn that it must have travelled at something between 1,500 and 2,000 mph. Slim was not surprised at all, he was by now well used to all sorts of strange 'reasons' why the weather had not materialised as forecast. But that didn't mean that he believed any of them!

Chris Cheshire's next and seventeenth operation took place on Sunday 8th June and the target was Dortmund. Taff Gurmin was on leave so his place in the rear turret was taken by Sergeant D. A. (Tug) Wilson. Otherwise the crew was the same as for the last Kiel trip. No.78 Squadron supplied ten aircraft, including Chesh's Z6625, to a total force of thirty-seven Whitleys that were the only Bomber Command aircraft operating this night. Dortmund, situated on the north-east fringe of the Ruhr, was only a comparatively short distance from the RAF's bomber bases and was thus considered by most aircrew to be preferable to many other targets in Germany's heartland. At the early evening briefing the crews were told that the Ruhr's existing cloud cover was likely to disperse in the early hours of the morning so departure was scheduled for circa 22.45 hours onwards.

At about 22.00 hours, Chesh and his crew made their way to `Ell for Leather' and prepared for take-off. Despite the heavy cloud cover over the eastern districts of the UK they were airborne at 22.55 hours and climbed to 14,000 feet before reaching the cloud base. They maintained this height until approaching the Dutch coast where they managed to get a fix on their position through a gap in the clouds.

Whilst discussing their course for Dortmund as a result of this fix, Chris Cheshire began to get the impression that all was not well with his normally unperturbable observer (navigator). Slim Smalley was decidedly euphoric and most disinclined to alter course, or provide his Skipper with a new compass heading. Something made Chesh turn on his oxygen (the use of oxygen over 10,000 feet was, at this stage of the war, a piece of advice rather than the instruction it would become later) and he soon realised that there was no supply of the life-supporting gas. Chesh ordered Slim, who was by now suffering badly from anoxia[29] to check the flow indicator on his oxygen regulator and had his suspicions confirmed. Slim was also without oxygen. Chesh reduced height in order to reduce the effects of his observer's annoxia and once Slim was aware of what had happened to him he made every effort to gather his wits and gave his Skipper the course for the target. Fortunately the met. man was right this time and as the cloud dispersed they were virtually able to map read their way to Dortmund.

Despite the usual Ruhr industrial haze they were able to pick out Dortmund where two fires were already burning. They released their bombs without meeting too much Flak and set course for base, with Slim now almost back to his normal self. Chesh, however, was not taking any chances with his trusty observer's health and, as soon as practicable, put the Whitley's nose down and then levelled out at 5,000 feet. Just as Chesh was beginning to think that the night's little adventures were almost over, Sergeant Hall, on the radio set, received a signal instructing them to divert to Prestwick (approximately forty miles south of Glasgow) because of thick fog at Middleton St. George. Slim Smalley rapidly worked out the new course and passed it to his skipper, by which time the aircraft was once again in thick cloud. This diversion added considerable mileage to the trip and none of the crew were particularly enamoured at the prospect of landing away from base for the second operation running.

Some time later, while still flying in 10/10ths cloud, Chesh and Slim agreed that a radio fix of their position would not come amiss and the Skipper asked Sergeant Hall to obtain one for them. Despite several attempts they received no reply, other than one informing them that they could return to base where the fog had now cleared. Slim was now in the unenviable position of having to work out a new course for Middleton with very little idea of where Z6625 was at that precise moment. Being the 'warrior' that he was, he soon produced a course which, under the circumstances, seemed appropiate and Chesh set the new heading on the compass and turned the aircraft to follow it. After continuing on this course for about thirty minutes, Chesh was

---

[29] *Anoxia is the name given to lack of oxygen. It should be noted that anoxia affects different people in different ways and in different timescales, thus it is quite possible for two members of the same crew to display totally differing reactions.*

getting very concerned about their very low fuel state and decided that it would be prudent to send out an SOS asking for an urgent radio fix on their position. Again there was no reply. Cheshire's experience was that a 'no reply' could usually be taken to mean that they were on course but one could not rely on this assumption.

 It was now about 05.30 hours, they had been airborne for just over six-and-a-half hours and their fuel state was by now causing Chesh extreme concern. As it was so close to the shortest night of the year and dawn could not be long in breaking, he decided that he would reduce height in the hope of finding a break in the clouds. Knowing that they could well be in the vicinity of the Pennines, Chesh started his slow descent through the clag with great trepidation. At 3,000 feet they were still in thick cloud but, with all fuel gauges reading almost zero, Cheshire had no option but to continue to lose height despite the very possible risk of flying into a hillside (otherwise known as a 'solid cloud'). Just as they were passing through 2,500 feet Chesh spotted a small break in the clouds through which he could see green fields. He did not waste a second, reefing the Whitley around in a tight turn and sticking her nose down straight at the ever diminishing chink in the clouds.

They emerged from the swirling mists at a height of about 500 feet above the ground and found themselves flying in a wide valley in the centre of which was a small village containing a church with a high steeple. With the needles on the fuel gauges now below the 'empty' position Chesh desperately searched the valley for a suitable landing place. All the fields seemed incredibly small, with a more than generous sprinkling of tall trees and surrounded by hedges or stone walls. Pilot Officer Cheshire finally spotted a field that contained no cattle and appeared to be clear of obstructions. Checking that his crew were all securely strapped in, Chesh lowered his flaps and undercarriage and commenced his approach, instructing Sid Lang in the second pilot's seat to keep his hand on the undercarriage lever ready to pull it up and retract the wheels should his Skipper tell him to - an order he would give if it looked like they were going to run into the stone wall at the far end of the field. Just as their wheels touched the ground the port engine cut out from lack of petrol and they were greeted by a field full of mole hills that caused much bumping but, fortunately, also acted as a form of brake, slowing the Whitley down much faster than normal and enabling Chesh to bring the aircraft to a stop some ten yards short of the stone wall. While Sid Lang thankfully removed his hand from the undercarriage lever the intercom was filled with loud exhalations of breath and there was much relief all round. Chris Cheshire looked at his watch, it was 6.15am.

Within three minutes of coming to rest and just as the crew were climbing out of the aircraft, they were approached by the local policeman who asked them whether they were German or British. They pointed to the large RAF roundels on the side of the Whitley and then gave the village bobby a few moments to recover his aplomb. After learning that they had landed at Clapham, a small village between Settle and Ingleton, some twelve miles west of Skipton in West Yorkshire, Christopher Cheshire told the policeman that it was imperative that he telephoned his base to let them know that the aircraft and crew were all safe and asked where, at six-thirty in the morning, he could find a telephone. The constable recommended he tried the village pub, which would be open, so, asking the policeman to ensure that no unauthorised persons were allowed to enter the aircraft, the aircraft's Captain set off in the direction indicated by the bobby, leaving his crew to relax and assist the policeman to guard Z6625.

As they watched their skipper trudging across the field in his flying boots the crew casually asked the village policeman what he, the single representative of Law and Order in the area, would have done if they had been Germans. The bobby put two fingers in his mouth and let out a loud whistle. Immediately four of the local men stood up behind the nearest stone wall that had been sheltering them. They were all armed with shotguns.

The proprietors of the local pub were most welcoming and insisted that Christopher had a large brandy before using the telephone. He allowed himself to be persuaded. Making long distance telephone calls in war-time Britain was frustrating at the best of times and the first crack of dawn was not the most propitious of moments. Thirty minutes elapsed before Christopher finally got through to Middleton St. George and was able to speak to his Flight Commander, Squadron Leader Walter Williams. During the conversation Chesh got the distinct impression that while 'Willie' Williams was happy to learn that the crew were all safe, he was not overly amused at the prospect of recovering the Whitley. Christopher was instructed to ensure that no-one was allowed to enter the aircraft (an order he'd already given to his crew and the local bobby) and to ring back in two hours for further instructions.

The Pendulum and the Scythe

The pub landlord and his wife insisted that all the crew received a good Yorkshire breakfast, so Christopher Cheshire trudged back to 'his' field, gathered Slim, Sid, Tug Wilson and Tommy Hall and, leaving the policeman and his armed associates to guard the Whitley, returned to the pub. After a much needed and well appreciated breakfast they returned to `L for London' and took stock of the situation. The field in which Chesh had landed the Whitley was less than 400 yards long by no more than 150 yards wide. It was enclosed by stone walls or hedges and there was an electricity pylon not too far away in the next field. Getting Z6625 airborne again was not going to be easy, in fact it looked impossible without removing a large section of wall. Their deliberations were interrupted at this point by the arrival of some of the local inhabitants, the majority of whom had never seen an aircraft of any description. The opportunity to view a fully operational bomber at close quarters was not to be missed and they were eager to learn what had happened, where they had been and what they were doing at Clapham. For security reasons Cheshire's reply had to be confined to generalities, so he informed his audience that they had returned from a bombing mission and, due to unforseen circumstances, they had been obliged to make a forced landing, counting themselves fortunate to have landed in such pleasant Yorkshire surroundings. He was just apologising for having circled low over the village so early in the morning and disturbing their sleep when the local headmaster, his staff and hordes of excited schoolboys descended upon their field. For the next twenty minutes or so all the adults present had their work cut out trying to prevent the eager young boys from climbing into and onto the aircraft, not to mention keeping an eagle eye open for would-be souvenir hunters. It was a great relief to everyone present when the headmaster decided that enough was enough and ordered his young charges back to their classroom.

Returning once again to the local pub, Cheshire made his second telephone call to Middleton St. George and learned that Willie Williams and the Squadron's Commanding Officer, Wing Commander Vernon Robinson, accompanied by the unit's Engineering Officer, would arrive after lunch. It was the Wing Commander's intention to fly the Whitley out of the field and land it at Liverpool for refuelling. Chris was just about to remind his Flight Commander that they didn't have enough fuel left to start the engines, never mind get airborne, when Willie Williams advised him that a petrol bowser and a truck with some ground staff would arrive in the next two to three hours.

The Pendulum and the Scythe

Pilot Officer Cheshire returned once again to his aircraft where it was immediately obvious that they would have to widen the gate opening to allow the bowser into the field and he was pleasantly surprised at how many willing hands appeared to help with this task. In due course the truck and bowser arrived as expected and enough AVGAS to get the Whitley to Liverpool, plus a small safety margin, was pumped into the tanks. Once the refuelling was completed, all the Whitley's surplus equipment, including just about everything that could be removed - especially the guns (which were probably the heaviest removable items in the aircraft) were all removed and loaded into the truck that had accompanied the AVGAS bowser.

It was well into the afternoon when the senior party arrived from Middleton St. George. Wing Commander Robinson, an experienced and extremely skilful pilot, walked up and down the field and weighed up the situation. He asked if the assembled villagers could assist by flattening the mole hills along his planned take-off path and once again many willing hands set to work. There was still much apprehension amongst the RAF personnel present as the Wingco climbed aboard Z6625. The length of field available just didn't seem long enough to allow a successful take-off, even without the molehills.

By this time, word had got around the village that 'things' were about to happen and even more of the local inhabitants arrived to watch the proceedings. Both of the Whitley's engines started without difficulty and Wing Commander Robinson taxied slowly to the point from which he intended to start his take-off run. Chris Cheshire, his crew and the other RAF men present were fully aware that what their Wingco was about to attempt was fraught with difficulties and they waited with bated breath as he revved both engines up to maximum power, holding the aircraft on its brakes much longer than was normal, until it appeared to those watching that the Whitley's tailplane was virtually airborne from the backdraught of the propellers alone. After what seemed an age the Wingco released the brakes and Z6625 surged forward, moving just like its unofficial identity name, 'Ell for Leather'. All the aircrew watched in silence, inwardly fearing that a terrible disaster was about to befall their CO and no doubt several silent prayers were offered. With only fifty yards of field remaining the Whitley still seemed to be firmly attached to Mother Earth and the hearts of Chesh and his crew sank. At the last possible moment the Wingco eased back on the stick and the Whitley left the ground, clearing the the stone wall by inches. The ensuing cheer from the spectators was loud enough to temporarily drown out the roar from the

229

two Merlin engines as 'Ell for Leather' gradually gained height and headed towards Liverpool.

As the local villagers dispersed and went about their business, Chesh and his crew decided to have something to eat at the local pub before setting off back to base, which they reached at about midnight and headed straight for bed, where they offered up a heartfelt prayer of thanks for the chink in the cloud. Christopher Cheshire never again set out on an operation without first making sure that all the oxygen cylinders in the aircraft were full.

The next operation for Chesh and Slim, once again re-united with Taff Gurmin, took place two days after their return to Middleton, although Chris had been awakened at 8am on the morning of their return and told to report to the 'flights' as an operation was planned. Fortunately this was cancelled and by the time they next appeared on the Operations Order, on Wednesday 11th June, Z6625 had been returned to Middleton St. George and the crew were all suitably rested. The target for that night's operation was to be another Ruhr town, Duisburg, which was situated in the eastern section of the Ruhr, just where the Dortmund Ems Canal joins the Rhine. There was, at this time, a shortage of second pilots and Christopher Cheshire had obviously drawn the short straw for he was to take only Slim, Taff and a new rear gunner, Sergeant Jones, on the six-and-a-half hour trip to Duisburg.

Twelve aircraft from 78 Squadron joined another twenty-four Whitleys and nine Halifaxes from 4 Group and thirty-five Hampdens from 5 Group on this attack and Chesh was airborne at 23.45 hours. Slim Smalley spent some time in the second pilot's seat for the sake of a bit of company, before going down into the nose to get ready to release the bomb load. He identified the target easily in the bright moonlight (10/10ths cloud having cleared just before reaching the target) and, regardless of the Flak that was both heavy and fairly accurate, dropped the bombs from 14,000 feet, observing fires starting as a result. The trip home was uneventful, with Slim once again spending some time in the second pilot's seat. A very tired Christopher Cheshire eased the Whitley onto the ground back at Middleton St. George just before 6am and then he and Taff went on a well-earned week's leave.

The following night, 12th June, Slim Smalley found himself detailed to fly with Wing Commander Robinson who was taking Z6625 to attack the marshalling yards at Schwerte, just south of Dortmund. The weather over the target was lousy, with 10/10ths cloud down to 2,000 feet, but the Wingco had not flown all that way just to bring his bombs back. He dived down under the cloud, Slim let the bombs go on the first bit of railway track he saw and they scuttled back up into the cloud cover and headed for home, crossing the English Channel in almost full daylight before landing at Middleton St. George just before 6am, after six-and-a-half hours in the air. After a four day break Slim had an uneventful trip to Cologne with Sergeant Jepson on the 16th and was then re-united with Chesh and Taff two days later.

The target on Wednesday the 18th June was Bremen and 78 Squadron put up thirteen Whitleys as part of this one-hundred aircraft raid. Pilot Officer Cheshire was once again to fly Z6625 and his crew comprised Slim, Taff and Sid Lang plus yet another new rear gunner, Sergeant Burgess. 'L for London' was logged as airborne at 22.45 hours and the trip to the target was uneventful. Unfortunately all the attacking aircraft were hindered by thick industrial haze and although Slim could identify the target area the haze made it impossible to identify the exact aiming point, despite a prolonged search that resulted in Z6625 receiving Flak damage to one wing. They dropped their bombs and headed home, touching down at 05.30 hours.

Chris Cheshire did not appear on the Operations List for quite a while, but poor Slim seemed to spend the next ten days being sent out with every new captain on his first trip as skipper - and having some close calls. His new pilot on the 20th June was Pilot Officer Bob Cant whom Slim had known in training. They took off in T6490 at 10.45pm and headed for Kiel as one of 115 aircraft sent to bomb the Tirpitz (yet again!). As usual the German warship was saved by cloud cover so the bulk of the attacking force donated their bombs to the city instead. The heavy Flak over Kiel was extremely thick and T6490 was quite badly hit, losing the port engine with the cowling shot completely away and the undercarriage and wheel damaged. Slim released the bombs at the first opportunity and Bob Cant worked wonders in getting the badly damaged Whitley home again. They touched down at 05.15 hours, but as soon as the port undercarraige started to take the aircraft's weight, it collapsed and T6490 slewed across the airfield. Fortunately no-one was hurt but, with the danger of fire ever present in their minds, the crew evacuated the aircraft at a great rate of knots. The rear gunner won first prize for the most magnificent sprint back to the hangar!

After this, Slim did two trips with Pilot Officer Wright, to Cologne on Tuesday the 26th when once again electrical storms played havoc with the attack, while on Sunday the 29th they went to Bremen, a much more successful raid, although on return they had to divert to Linton-on-Ouse, where they landed safely after almost seven hours in the air.

During June 1941 the newly reformed 76 Squadron moved, with their Halifaxes, from Linton-on-Ouse to Middleton St. George and from then on was constantly recruiting crews from 78 Squadron. Also at about this time Chris Cheshire, although only a substantive Pilot Officer, was carrying out the function of a Flight Commander on 78 Squadron, with the acting rank of Flight Lieutenant. One of his many duties was to allocate crews for transfer to the new Halifax squadron across the airfield. Taff Gurmin had heard many horrendous stories about the Halifax and was totally convinced that flying in them would be the death of him. He swore that he would finish his first tour on his faithful old Whitley and was determined to do everything in his power to assure this. To this end he would casually appear in Chris Cheshire's office every morning, on the pretext of helping his Skipper with the paperwork, thus ensuring that he was around when Chesh received the next call for a new crew for 76 Squadron. Sure enough, the call would come, Chris would look at the flight's crew listing on the wall of his office and say 'Well Taff, it looks like our turn this time.' To which Taff would reply 'No Skipper, it can't be us yet, what about X and his crew, they've been here longer than us.' Chris would ponder for a moment and then say 'Alright Taff, we'll send them this time, but it's definitely us next time.' This went on for several days and Taff thought he'd resolved his little problem.

On Wednesday the 2nd July Slim again flew with Chesh and Sid Lang, although without Taff who was resting, Sergeant Boucher taking his place at the radio set and Sergeant Forster in the rear turret. Their aircraft was once again Z6625 'L for London/Leather' and the target was Cologne, Cheshire's fourth trip to this city. Take-off was at 22.45 hours and the bombs were dropped from 12,000 feet through haze and low, wispy cloud and a building resembling a warehouse was seen to go up in flames. They landed at 05.14 hours after an uneventful trip that was to be Christopher Cheshire's last Whitley operation.

On Monday the 7th July, Flight Lieutenant Cheshire met Sergeant Gurmin outside his office and stopped Taff before he had time to get off his bike. 'Don't get off that bike, Taff,' said he, 'We are going straight over to 76.' 'Oh God, no.' said Taff, 'Oh God, yes.' came the reply, Taff's Skipper had tumbled his little ploy and off they went to 76 Squadron just across the airfield. They reported to the squadron CO, Wing Commander G. T. Jarman,

DFC. Slamming to attention in front of the Wingco's desk, Chris threw up a crisp salute and said 'Flight Lieutenant Cheshire reporting for duty, sir.' Jarman looked up at the six feet three inches of Chris and then looked at all five feet six inches of Taff and asked 'Who is this?' My wireless operator, sir, Sergeant Gurmin.' Jarman looked more closely at Taff, 'He's not very big, is he?' `You can't get big blokes in rear turrets, sir.' said Taff.

Cheshire's new unit was the second to be equipped with the Handley Page Halifax. It had been formed from 'C' Flight of 35 Squadron on 1st May at Linton-on-Ouse, moving to Middleton St. George the following month and carrying out its first Halifax operation on the night of 12th/13th June. For some strange reason Slim was still on the strength of 78 Squadron and still giving the benefit of his experience and support to new captains, although with Chesh posted, he did have the opportunity to stay with just the one, Sergeant Bob Turnbull. On the 5th July, flying Z6490, they went to Munster, northeast of the Ruhr, as part of a ninety-four aircraft raid on this target, which had not been attacked for five months. With good visibility and only light defences all crews reported a successful attack. Two nights later they took P5005 to the railway yards at Osnabruck, slightly south of the Mittelland Canal, dropped their bombs on target without any problem and headed for home. Flying in clear weather with a bright moon shining, they had just crossed the enemy coast on their way back when they were suddenly attacked by a Messerschmitt Bf110 nightfighter. Several times the '110 bored in with all guns blazing and each time Bob Turnbull turned the Whitley into the fighter's attack, with the rear gunner getting in short bursts at every opportunity. Slim Smalley scrambled from his observers desk into the nose turret, loaded an ammunition drum onto the single Vickers machine gun and cocked it, ready to win fame and the undying gratitude of the rest of the crew. The blasted thing jammed! Fortunately the rear gunner got in an extremely accurate burst as the nightfighter came in for yet another attack and the Whitley crew watched it break off, belching smoke and flames and then dive down until it hit the sea. When reporting the night's events at debriefing they got the impression that the unit's Intelligence Officers didn't really believe their claim of one Bf110 destroyed. Bob Turnbull left them in no doubt as to the veracity of his gunner's claim and stormed off to breakfast. On the 10th July they took off in Z6490 to attack Oldenburg but the operation was cancelled over the radio shortly after take-off. On Tuesday the 29th July Slim Smalley followed Chesh and Taff to 76 Squadron.

A crew climbs aboard a Halifax B. Mk.I of 35 Sqn at Linton-on-Ouse.

Meanwhile, on 76 Squadron, Chris Cheshire had completed a short Halifax conversion course and already carried out his first Halifax operation on the night of 14th/15th July. The target was a rubber factory in Hannover. Chesh had once again crewed up with Taff Gurmin and had acquired a new rear gunner, Flight Sergeant 'Timber' Woods, who had completed a full tour on Coastal Command and was just starting on his first bomber operation. Compared to the Whitley, the Halifax carried an extra crew member who was one of a new breed of aircrew category, namely a Flight Engineer. For his first Halifax operation, Cheshire was actually to have two of them, Sergeant Spriggs, who was one of the more experienced flight engineers on the Squadron, and Sergeant Reggie Wash, fresh out of training[30] and about to undertake his first operation. The rest of the crew comprised Sergeant Jimmy Butler as observer (Slim was still on 78 Squadron), Sergeant Pierce as front gunner and the second pilot was Sergeant Paul Horrox.

The Squadron despatched seven Halifaxes to Hannover, as did 35 Squadron, forming part of an eighty-five aircraft strong force. Chris Cheshire and crew flew in Halifax B.Mk.I, serial no. L9464 and took off just after half-past-ten at night. Over the target they were flying at 9,000 feet and Chesh sent Reggie (Washy) Wash and Paul Horrox down the fuselage to man the beam guns. Paul Horrox, who was also on his first trip, saw several twin engined aircraft below them and, at first thinking they were Messerschmitt Bf110s, cocked his two Vickers Gas Operated machine guns ready to fire. Watching the other aircraft intently he soon realised that he was actually observing Hampdens and he relaxed slightly and had just managed to calm some of the butterflies in his stomach when Washy, who was just to his left but facing the other way, let off a long burst from his twin machine guns. Not surprisingly, Paul nearly had kittens and Chris Cheshire must also have been alarmed because he was straight on the intercom demanding to know who was shooting and at what. Washy did not answer – his intercom plug had come out of its socket - so Paul advised Chesh that it was Washy who was firing but he was damned if he could see what he was shooting at. At this point the flight engineer came back on the intercom. He'd realised that his plug had come out and had replaced it in time to catch the tail-end of the conversation so he informed his Skipper that he'd been shooting at searchlights. Flight Lieutenant Cheshire was not amused and a few gentle hints about the inadvisablity of shooting at searchlights from 9,000 feet were dropped along with the information that unnecessary shooting gave the bomber's position away to any enemy nightfighter that may be lurking in the vicinity. Jimmy Butler released the bombs from 9,000 feet and they were seen to explode slightly northwest of the aiming point.

---

[30] *RAF training courses for flight engineers did not start until May 1942 (at RAF St.Athan). Prior to this date, most FEs were selected from ground engineering trades, given an aircraft manufacturer's course, then a gunnery course at an Air Gunnery School before being awarded an 'Air - Gunner' brevet, which some FEs amended to read 'FE'. The official `E' brevet did not appear until September 1942.*

On return to base at about 04.15 hours they were instructed to join the circuit and await their turn to land and were advised that they were third in the stack but that they may have to wait a while because a strong cross-wind on the runway was causing some problems. While carrying out their circuits the crew observed first one and then the other aircraft in front of them come to grief on landing, both coming off the runway and coming to rest on their bellies, having wiped off their undercarriage in the rough, fortunately with no serious casualties. As a precautionary measure Chris Cheshire ordered his crew to their crash positions behind the main spar, where Taff Gurmin found himself seated next to Jimmy Butler who had quite a few Halifax operations in his Log Book already. As they were on the final approach Jimmy asked Taff how good a pilot Chesh was. Taff, who was now on his twelfth trip with his Skipper replied that Chesh was 'bloody good'. Jimmy then asked how many operations Chesh had done. 'About twenty or so.' came the response.'How many trips on Halifaxes?' came the next question. This is his first.' said Taff. 'Oh hell!' said Jimmy, closing his eyes and bracing himself even tighter against the main spar. A minute or so later he re-opened his eyes - the loud bang and crash he'd been anticipating had not occurred and he was convinced that Chesh must be overshooting to go round again and that he might yet have a few more minutes to live. He then noticed a faint but familiar rumbling noise and stood up to look out of the fuselage window. With a grin from ear to ear he turned back to Taff. 'Bloody hell Taff, we're down!' As usual, Chris Cheshire had landed his aircraft as smoothly as ever, greatly impressing his watching ground crew to whom he had been an unknown quantity up to that point.

Flight Lieutenant Cheshire then went on leave for a fortnight and therefore was not on the Operations List again until Thursday the 30th July, although three members of his new crew did fly during this period. On the night of 21st/22nd July, Paul Horrox went to Mannheim as second pilot to Sergeant Dunlop in L9529. This was only a small raid by eight Halifaxes and thirty-six Wellingtons with the town centre as the aiming point.

On Friday the 24th July Taff Gurmin looked death in the face and got away with it, but got in to trouble with Chesh later. Some bright spark 'upstairs' decided that it would be a good idea to send unescorted Halifaxes, in daylight, to bomb the Scharnhorst, which had just arrived in the French harbour of La Pallice, about 200 miles north of the Franco-Spanish border and overlooking the Bay of Biscay. The grand total of fifteen aircraft from

35 and 76 Squadrons were selected as the force to battle its way unprotected into what was effectively a 'Valley of Death'.

It had originally been planned to launch a surprise attack on both the Scharnhorst and Gneisenau in Brest Harbour on 24th July. The attacking force was to be a mixed one of 150 heavy and medium bombers, escorted by three squadrons of Spitfires. Unfortunately the Scharnhorst cleared off to La Pallice unexpectedly so that put the kibosh on that scheme. Then some prize twit with his head in the clouds and his finger far removed from the pulse decided to allow the medium bombers, complete with Spitfire escort, to carry on with the Brest attack on the Gneisenau, whilst the heavies (Stirlings and Halifaxes) went unescorted to La Pallice. Then someone else had their twopennyworth, withdrawing the Stirlings from the daylight attack and sending them in the night before, just to let the enemy know that the RAF still knew where the Scharnhorst was and that they would be back again soon. In fact the whole thing was such an absolute 'pigs-ear' that the Admiralty must have had a major role in the (mis)-planning.

Just prior to the La Pallice operation nine Halifaxes from 35 Squadron and another six from 76 Squadron were temporarily detached to Stanton Harcourt in Oxfordshire in order to reduce the distance to the target by about 200 miles and thus allow an increase in bomb load. On the 24th, as the medium bombers and their escort headed for Brest, the aircraft of 35 Squadron took off, followed at around 10.30 hours by three of the six Halifaxes of 76 Squadron. The raid was to be led by 76's Commanding Officer, New Zealander Wing Commander G. T. Jarman, flying B.Mk.I L9496, who, with Chris Cheshire on leave, had nabbed Taff Gurmin as his wireless operator and Timber Woods as his rear gunner.

The plan was for all six of 76's aircraft to fly in two vics of three, the first to be led by Wg.Cdr. Jarrnan and the other by Flight Lieutenant Williams. Unfortunately, Flight Lieutenant Williams' aircraft went unserviceable just before take-off and with the other two aircraft of his vic waiting for him, he had to carry out a rapid change to the spare aircraft. Because of this they were late getting airborne and never managed to catch up with the main formation.

Flying at only 1,000 feet the CO formed his three remaining aircraft into a vic formation whilst heading for the rendezvous with the nine Halifaxes of 35 Squadron that was to take place over Exeter. The other two aircraft in

The Pendulum and the Scythe

Wingco Jarman's vic of three were flown by Flight Lieutenant Walter Hilary and Sergeant Harry Drummond. The three aircraft from 76 Squadron arrived over Exeter at about 11.30 hours where the nine aircraft from 35 dropped into formation behind them. The Wingco then set course for the Lizard, which they crossed just before noon, dropping down to 100 feet as they did so. Flying in glorious sunshine above a calm sea, it took the force only fifty-seven minutes to reach their turning point fifty miles west of the Isle of Ushant off the coast of Brittany. Having turned onto their final 258 mile leg to the target, the formation began the climb to their intended bombing height of 19,000 feet. After about 120 miles of this last leg, as they were passing and getting a good pin-point from the Isle de Yeu, they passed a German destroyer that immediately began to take evasive action, the destroyer Captain assuming that he was to be their target. As the Halifax formation sailed serenely on, it became obvious to the Captain that they had bigger fish to fry and he radioed the force's size and course to his shore base. One quick look at a map and it would be quite obvious that a formation of heavy bombers observed off the Isle de Yeu and heading along that course could have only one destination and, linked with the previous night's Stirling attack on the Scharnhorst, the force's intended target had to be the Battlecruiser in La Pallice. Taking no chances the Luftwaffe scrambled about twenty-five Messerschmitt Bf 109Fs from the three airfields around the target.

On approaching La Pallice all the Halifax flight engineers and radio operators took up their briefed positions manning the beam guns: all the wireless operators, that is, except one. As the wireless operator in the attack leader's aircraft, Taff Gurmin had been ordered to stay on the radio set come hell or high water, in case of any urgent messages that may be sent or need sending, and that is exactly what he did. Unfortunately this dedication to duty was a total waste of time as regards sending or receiving messages for the T1082/1083 radio set in L9496, unlike that in MP-L, which was in tip-top condition, had ceased to function just after take off and Taff had spent the whole trip so far with the useless thing in bits, trying hard to get it working again.

Just short of the target heavy Flak from the shore and the Scharnhorst herself started to make itself felt and Flight Lieutenant Hilary's aircraft lost an engine. Unable to continue the climb to bombing height, he had no alternative but to abort, turn away and head for home, leaving Wing Commander Jarman and Sergeant Drummond to continue. Hilary had only just turned away when eighteen Bf109Fs came in to the attack, shooting down all three Halifaxes in the vic to starboard of the leading three aircraft. Jarman, realising that his and Sergeant Drummond's aircraft were now fully exposed to the attacking fighters, called on Harry Drummond to formate even closer to his own Halifax. Drummond needed no second bidding and tucked his aircraft right in behind and beneath his leader's tail.

Meanwhile the Flak was continuing to engage the bombing force, with several aircraft being hit and L9527 of 35 Squadron, flown by Flight Sergeant Goodwin, was seen to go down trailing smoke from two engines. In trying to avoid the worst of the Flak the Halifaxes' formation keeping lost some of its cohesion and again the Bf109Fs bore in, continuing their attacks throughout the bombing run. As they started their bombing run, Taff looked up through his window and received a severe shock. The 35 Squadron aircraft were immediately above them, bomb doors open, and as he watched, Taff saw their bombs cascading all around their aircraft. It was a miracle that they all missed L9496.

Jarman and Drummond, still nose to tail, swept over the Scharnhorst and dropped their loads of 250 pounders on the Wingco's order (Reconnaisance photographs later showed what looked like a single stick of thirty bombs in a dead straight line, unfortunately they were ten yards to starboard of the Scharnhorst). As they turned away Drummond's rear gunner was wounded in the shoulder and while another crew member got him out of the turret and another took his place in it, the enemy fighters took advantage of the lull in defensive fire. One '109, approaching from the rear, flew straight over the top of both aircraft, stall-turned in front of the Wingco's aircraft and flew back over both of them, raking both Halifaxes as he did so. Wing Commander Jarman had his automatic pilot shot to pieces and Harry Drummond had a large hole blown in his windscreen, amazingly without any of the crew receiving serious wounds, only Drummond himself receiving Perspex splinters in his knuckles.

Wing Commander Jarman was not carrying a second pilot on this operation. Instead he had brought along the Squadron's Gunnery Officer, Flying Officer McLeod, whose function was to stand with his head in the astrodome and direct the formation's defensive fire against the attacking fighters. As they were leaving the target area this officer spotted another Halifax, about half a mile to port, which was in serious trouble with at least one engine on fire and several Bf109s continuing to harry it. McLoed pointed this out to his CO who suggested that they and Sergeant Drummond should go to the assistance of the unfortunate crew in this 35 Squadron aircraft. Hearing this suggestion over the intercom, Taff Gurmin detached himself from the bits of his radio set, which still stubbornly refused to work and looked out of the fuselage window at the seriously stricken Halifax to port. He flicked the microphone switch on his face mask and said 'Wireless operator to Captain. With all due respect, Sir, it looks like that poor blighter's had it already. All we'll be doing over there is asking for some of the same treatment that he's already had.' There was a brief silence. 'You may have a valid point there, Gurmin.' came the reply, and no sooner had the words left the Wingco's lips than the doomed Halifax burst into flames and started to dive towards the ground. Taff went back to trying to repair the recalcitrant radio set.

The enemy fighters continued to harass the departing Halifaxes well after they had left the target area, although Sergeant Drummond's rear gunner, Flight Sergeant Begbie shot down one before he was wounded and Timber Woods in Wing Commander Jarman's aircraft accounted for another. All together three of 76 Squadron's aircraft (including two of Flight Lieutenant Williams late vic of three - the third had had engine trouble and turned back) and another two of 35 Squadron's were shot down. A further five aircraft returned to Stanton Harcourt with serious damage that took three weeks to repair and two others had slightly less serious damage. Only three aircraft returned with what was classed as relatively slight damage. All crews except one (whose bombs had hung up) succeeded in delivering their attacks and although only one crew claimed a direct hit, there were in fact five of them and as already stated (Chapter 3) the Scharnhorst sailed back to the relative security of the built-in smoke screens of Brest that night, with at least 3,000 gallons of water in her hull.

Having finally left the '109s behind, the surviving ten Halifaxes headed back to England in ones and twos. Sergeant Drummond was still formating on the CO's aircraft, but about a third of the way home his port inner engine packed in as a result of damage received over La Pallice. He carried on watching his leader's Halifax gradually pulling away from him. Drummond's observer got a good pin-point over Fowey, five miles east of St.Austell in Cornwall, but the crew's jubilation at being once more over terra-firma was exceedingly short lived as the port outer engine packed in as they crossed the coast. Nevertheless they made it safely back to Stanton Harcourt just as Wing Commander Jarman touched down on the runway. Taff Gurmin finally managed to get the recalcitrant T1082/1083 radio set to work and was at last able to transmit the 'Mission completed' signal - just as they were circling

Stanton Harcourt Prior to landing! Wing Commander Jarman was awarded the DSO for this operation.

After landing Taff was standing talking over their recent experiences with some of the crew. Turning to their front gunner, Sergeant Pat Patterson, Taff asked what he had thought of all those '109s. 'I never could see much with my eyes closed, Taff.' came the relieved response. Chris Cheshire had a lucky charm (as did most aircrew throughout the war). He was the proud owner of a toy Cheshire cat and it flew with him on every raid. Taff received a mild rollicking when Chris Cheshire returned from leave. Talking to Taff about the La Pallice raid, Chris remarked that, from what he'd heard, Taff had been lucky to get back from the raid. 'We only got back because I took your lucky cat, Skipper.' Flight Lieutenant Cheshire was outwardly not amused.

Slim Smalley joined 76 Squadron on 29th July, just as Christopher Cheshire, now promoted to substantive Flying Officer, returned from his leave to ensure that Slim was once again a member of his crew in nice time for Chesh's second Halifax operation. It was also at this time that Christopher acquired his second 'L for London'. Halifax B.Mk.I, Serial No. L9530 and coded 'MP-L' had initially been issued to 35 Squadron on 3rd June 1941, but did not carry out any operations with this unit. It was then transferred to 76 Squadron and carried out its first operation, to Hannover on the night of 19th/20th July at the hands of Pilot Officer Ireton. It was to carry out its second operation with Flight Lieutenant Christopher Cheshire at the controls and was to be his aircraft from then on.

Chesh's 22nd operation took place on the night of Wednesday 30th July and was his fifth trip to Cologne. The frequency of his visits to this city, just south of the Ruhr, was due to the combination of a then current Air Ministry directive and the vagaries of the weather. The Directive, issued to Sir Richard Peirse (Bomber Command's C-in-C at this time) instructed him to attack the enemy's synthetic oil production plants whenever the weather was good enough. On the not infrequent occasions when it was not, Peirse chose to direct his force at the suitable alternative of Cologne for three very sound reasons: it was a relatively short range target, it was outside the main Ruhr Flak defences and, because of its readily identifiable position on the Rhine, it could be attacked in marginal weather conditions.

So L9530 and Flight Lieutenant Cheshire undertook their second operation with 76 Squadron, joining a further six Halifaxes and one-hundred-and-nine other aircraft in yet another attack on Cologne in 'marginal weather conditions'. Chesh's crew now had the nucleus of Taff Gurmin, Slim Smalley, Reggie Wash and Timber Woods and on this occasion they had a Sergeant Evans in the front turret. Paul Horrox was on leave at this time and was replaced for this trip by a Sergeant Williams. They took off at 23.20 hours and the trip was uneventful except for thunderstorms and severe icing. Slim released the bomb load from 7,500 feet and a not inconsiderable explosion was observed immediately afterwards. They landed safely back at Middleton St. George at 05.10 hours after five-and-a-half hours in the air. It was after this raid that the famous 'Cheshire Crest' was painted below the cockpit of 'L for Leather'. This generated a real buzz amongst the Squadron's ground crews because it was the first time such an unofficial marking had been painted on a 76 Squadron aircraft.

Two nights later the Command attacked two targets, with eighty aircraft going to Hamburg and fifty-five to Berlin. On this night 76 Squadron put up its largest effort to date with ten aircraft despatched to join forty Wellingtons and five Stirlings on the Berlin raid. Once again Chesh flew L9530 with Paul Horrox, Slim Smalley, Taff Gurmin, Reggie Wash and Timber Woods plus, on his second trip with Chesh, Sergeant Evans in the front turret. This was Chesh's second long haul to the 'Big City' and everything went as planned, with Slim releasing the bombs onto the primary target from 15,000 feet despite a slight haze over Berlin. They returned to base and landed at 05.12 hours after seven hours in the air. Chesh had successfully completed his 23rd operation.

Shortly after this operation, L9530 was chosen to be the `model' for a series of official Halifax photographs. Chesh took the Unit Medical Officer in the second pilot's seat on the flight during which the airborne shots were taken, it was the Doc's first flight. Many photographs were taken, both in the air and on the ground, which is why most published books that deal with the Halifax feature at least one photograph of MP-L.

By the time he undertook his 24th operation on the night of Wednesday 6th August, Christopher Cheshire's acting rank had been confirmed, so it was a substantive Flight Lieutenant C.C.Cheshire and crew who appeared on the Operations Order against `L for London' for a raid on Karlsruhe. Once again the usual six crew members were the nucleus with the seventh, on this occasion, being a second wireless operator, Sergeant Barrett, so Taff Gurmin spent this trip in the front turret for a change.

There were four simultaneous minor raids on this night, with thirty-four Whitleys and nineteen Wellingtons going to Frankfurt, thirty-eight Wellingtons to railway workshops in Mannheim, thirty-eight Hampdens, Whitleys and Wellingtons to Calais and thirty-eight Hampdens and six Halifaxes to attack the railway workshops in Karlsruhe. Karlsruhe, about seventy miles west-northwest of Stuttgart and fifty miles south-southwest of Mannheim, was the most southerly German target that Cheshire had attacked and the six Halifaxes, all from 76 Squadron, took off from Middleton St. George at around 10.30 pm. The trip out was fairly normal (as normal as flying' a heavy bomber over enemy occupied territory can be) and Chesh' settled onto the bombing run at 9,000 feet. Slim had advised `Bombs gone' and his Skipper was just closing the bomb doors when Taff, in the front turret, shouted 'Turn port Skip, hard port!' Cheshire reacted immediately, turning the wheel on the control column hard left and pushing his left foot forward on the rudder pedal. This prompt evasive action allowed them to miss, but only by inches, a Wellington that had been coming at them head-on. It was almost certainly from the Mannheim raid and badly off course, and not, as some aircrew speculated at the time, a captured aircraft repaired and flown by Luftwaffe aircrew. The crew of 'Ell for Leather' breathed a loud sigh of relief and headed back to base. En route to Middleton, Taff had the urgent need to visit, the loo. For some strange reason the Mk.I Halifax was not equipped with an Elsan toilet, they just had 'Pee' tubes. Taff warned Chesh that he was leaving his turret for a short while and set off to the nearest Pee tube. It was full. So was the next one, and the one after that. In desperation, Taff opened one of the beam gun windows and tried to empty the Pee tube. Unfortunately, as it emptied, the slipstream caught it and blew the lot back all over poor Taff. They landed at 05.37 hours, another long seven hour and some odd minutes slog, but nobody wanted to sit next to Taff Gurmin at debriefing.

One of the friendships that Christopher Cheshire made when he first arrived on 78 Squadron in January 1941 was with a jovial army officer who had been seconded to the unit as an adviser on air defence matters. In the mess one evening, he was talking about his love of game shooting and invited Christopher up to his shoot in Scotland on the 'Glorious Twelfth'. Chesh had, however, already booked his annual leave for earlier in the summer and, realising that it would be very difficult to arrange for more so soon afterwards, he thanked his would-be benefactor but had to decline his generous offer. The army officer replied that he quite understood but added that he was sure it would be far more enjoyable taking pot-shots at grouse than being potted at by German Flak, a sentiment with which Christopher wholeheartedly agreed.

At Middleton St. George Tuesday the 12th August dawned with mist and early morning showers. There were variable amounts of cloud all day and westerly winds in the region of ten to twenty mph. The showers returned briefly during the early evening but, by half-past-eight, as 'Chesh' and his crew walked across the tarmac to 'L for London', it was a lovely evening. At the briefing earlier that evening the crew had learned that they were to fly L9530 as one of six Halifaxes from 76 Squadron that were to form part of a seventy aircraft force detailed to attack the German Air Ministry buildings in Berlin. The crew comprised all six of the 'regulars', Chris Cheshire - 1st pilot and aircraft Captain on his 25th operation, Paul Horrox - 2nd pilot on his fifth operation, Slim Smalley - observer on his 26th, Taff Gurmin - wireless operator on his 29th, Reggie Wash –flight engineer on his sixth and rear gunner Timber Woods on his sixth with Bomber Command. The seventh crew member for this trip was a new WOp/gunner about to undertake his very first operation. Sergeant Geoff (Jock) Niven would occupy the front turret.

As the crew walked to L9530 Christopher Cheshire's thoughts were far removed from shooting grouse in Scotland. Having just been reminded that he was due to be screened from operations shortly[31], he was in fact, thinking more about where he was likely to be posted at the end of his tour. Having reached the Halifax however, all such thoughts vanished as the crew began to carry out their pre-flight checks. Chesh and Slim checked out the enormous 4,000 lbs cookie that had been winched up into the aircraft's belly. Unfortunately the Halifax bomb bay had not been designed to accommodate such a large bomb and the only way it could be fitted in was to leave the bomb doors partly open with the bomb protruding into the slipstream, adding a considerable amount of drag to the airframe.

---

[31] *The Command's policy was to screen aircrew after 25 to 30 operations and post them to non-operational duties such as instructing at an OTU, a job that most experienced aircrew believed - and not without justification - to be more dangerous than flying on operations.*

Loading a 4,000 lb 'cookie' onto a Halifax.

The crew climbed into 'MP-L', started the four Merlin engines, completed their internal pre-flight checks. Then, with the usual 'thumbs up' from their ground crew chief, Flight Sergeant Brown and his lads, they taxied out in line to the end of the runway. As usual when carrying a 4,000-pounder Chesh found the take-off a very tense time, but he felt much more at ease once he had lifted the Halifax off the runway and cleared the hedge on the airfield boundary. The Duty Officer logged L9530 as airborne at 21.35 hours. Having set course on the briefed route for Berlin they climbed slowly but steadily to an altitude of 12,000 feet and settled down for the long haul to the 'Big City'. It was not until 1986, when Christopher and his brother Leonard were talking 'old times' that he learned that Leonard had tried to telephone him several times prior to take-off, to warn him against following the briefed route to Berlin as he was convinced that it would be disastrous. Leonard Cheshire was at that time a Squadron Leader on his second tour (he'd somehow managed to stretch his first to fifty operations) and a Flight Commander with 35 Squadron stationed at Linton-on-Ouse. Had the call reached Christopher, he would certainly have followed his brother's advice.

Squadron Leader G. L. Cheshire followed his own hunch and took a more southerly route to that briefed. He and his crew had a trouble-free trip while watching aircraft to the north of them getting hammered by Flak[32]. As it was `L for London' was steadily cruising along the official route, heading for the enemy coast that they were to cross roughly mid-way between Bremen and Hamburg, both of which had been offered as secondary targets.

When 'MP-L' was about thirty minutes flying time from the German coast, Reggie Wash, the flight engineer, who by his very nature was unflappable, informed Chesh that their fuel consumption was all to hell and they'd already used so much that they couldn't possibly make it to Berlin and have enough to be able to return to base. Neither Washy nor Chesh could think of any reason why the consumption should have been so high, so, in case it was just the fuel gauges messing about they agreed to continue on their present course for another fifteen minutes and check again. A quarter of an hour later, the Skipper handed control over to Paul Horrox and joined Washy at the flight engineer's panel behind the pilot's seat. Sure enough, the gauges showed that a little over half their fuel load was already gone. Chesh realised that Washy's dismal forecast was right and asked Slim to work out a course for the nearest alternative target. He returned to his seat and took control back from Paul. Seconds later, Slim came back with a course for Hamburg, which was marginally closer than Bremen, so on a cloudless night with good visibility, Chesh turned the Halifax to port and headed for Germany's second largest city.

They met very little Flak until they were on the outskirts of Hamburg itself and then all hell broke loose around them. Being the only RAF bomber over the City, every Luftwaffe anti-aircraft gun crew in Hamburg was able to give 'MP-L' its undivided attention. Lying on his belly in the nose of the aircraft, Slim Smalley released the bombs over the centre of the city and Chesh then held the Halifax straight and level for the sixty seconds required to take their aiming point photograph. Miraculously the enemy Flak gunners missed this heaven-sent opportunity to blast them out of the sky. Hearing Slim say 'Bombs gone', Taff got on the radio to transmit back to base the 'Operation completed' signal. Chesh operated the lever to close the bomb doors and was waiting to feel them clunk shut when the first Flak shells hit them. Initially,

[32] See Cheshire VC by Russell Braddon.

The Pendulum and the Scythe

Chesh still had control of the bucking Halifax but then there was an almighty crash at the rear of the aircraft and both his and Paul's control columns went totally limp in their hands. Neither control column had any effect whatsoever on the aircraft's behaviour, nor did either of the trim wheels. The Halifax went into a gentle nose down position and Christopher Cheshire had little option but to order his crew to abandon ship. Taff Gurmin had just received Base's acknowledgement of his signal and Plugged back into the intercom as Chesh said 'Jump for it boys.' Taff couldn't believe his ears, 'Do you mean bale out Skipper?' he asked. 'Yes' said Chesh, 'and make it quick!'

Although the Halifax was at 11,000 feet when it was so badly hit, time was still of the essence. Slim Smalley's seat was directly over the nose compartment escape hatch, so he folded the seat away in preparation to open the hatch. Taff tried to get to the hatch as quickly as possible, but in his rush he'd forgotten to disconnect his oxygen tube from the economiser. He lunged forward only to be almost catapulted back to his radio set as the oxygen tube reached its limit of elasticity and then recoiled. He ripped his mask and helmet off, threw it onto the radio table and then dived forward and opened the escape hatch while Slim shook the legs of Geoff Niven in the nose turret.

As the hatch was opened a blast of icy cold air shot in through the aperture and the interior of the Halifax was filled with swirling papers and dust. Taff clipped on his parachute and stood by the open hatch thinking that he should be second last out, just before his Skipper. He was about to try to move aside but then realised that all he would achieve would be to get in everybody else's way. He stepped forward over the hole, turned around, sat on the edge and taking his ripcord in his right hand, launched himself into space. He was closely followed by Paul Horrox and Slim Smalley who shook hands before jumping. Thinking that all of his crew who could do so had now left the aircraft, Cheshire found himself with a small problem – he couldn't locate his parachute. After two minutes frantic searching he found the missing item close to the escape hatch and clipped it to his harness.

He was sitting on the edge of the hatch with his legs dangling out of the aircraft, just about to jump, when he noticed a movement in the centre fuselage. Pulling his legs back inside the Halifax he saw Reggie Wash coming towards him, clipping on his 'chute as he made his way forward. Washy, who had dropped the photo flash flare down the flare chute for the bombing photograph, had been knocked end over end by the big Flak explosion and just managed to pick himself up and find his parachute.

247

Having wished Reggie 'Bon voyage' and seen him off the premises, Chesh once again sat on the edge of the escape hatch before launching himself out into the cold night sky.

As soon as his parachute had opened Chesh looked up and saw that L9530 had got itself into a slow spiral descent and was circling around him. The Halifax had taken on the sinister appearance of a large and ugly vampire and the German Flak was still banging away at it - and consequently at Christopher too. In true British fashion, Chesh considered this to be very unsporting of his enemy and was greatly relieved when 'MP-L' finally gathered speed and took itself off in an almost westerly direction, finally crashing at Parnewinkel near the small town of Wenzendorf some twenty-five miles northeast of Bremen. It was not until 1992 that Christopher discovered why his Halifax had suddenly appeared like a vampire as it circled around him. As Paul Horrox, who was second to leave the aircraft, was floating down on his parachute, he looked up to see the Halifax sailing on quite serenely - but with no tail! The complete tail unit, from in front of the leading edge of the tailplane had been blown off by the last direct Flak hit, killing Timber Woods outright and explaining why neither pilot had any control over the aircraft after the loud explosion. Sergeant Geoff Niven's body was found by the Germans the following morning.

Having watched his aircraft heading off to the west, Cheshire then had time to look downwards and see the type of terrain on which he was going to land. Directly below him was what looked like a large village. Remembering his classroom instruction on parachute descent, he pulled on one of the 'chute straps and side-slipped, changing his direction towards open fields. By luck rather than judgement, he found himself in a field, in the middle of a herd of Friesian cows who paid not the slightest attention to the interloper.

Lying where he had landed for a few moments, Chesh took stock of his position. He felt very much alone and wondered what had happened to his crew. He thought about shouting out their names but realised that they were more likely to be separated by miles rather than yards and decided that all his shouting would achieve would be to bring German soldiers to his location. He suddenly felt very hungry and reached into his flying suit pocket for the small food parcel with which he'd been issued before take off. It wasn't there. It must have fallen out either in the aircraft or during his parachute descent. Sadly it dawned on him that the whole course of his war career had changed in a very short space of time and he wondered how his parents and brother would take the news that he was 'missing', that his aircraft had 'failed to return'. In short, Flight Lieutenant Christopher Cheshire and his crew had become just another statistic. The prospect of becoming a prisoner-of-war for the duration was not one that particularly appealed and thoughts of escape were at the forefront of his mind. Still in the field in which he had landed, Christopher estimated that he was somewhere west of Hamburg and decided that his best chance of escape lay in heading west towards Holland where he might be able to make contact with the Dutch Resistance Movement. His attention was suddenly drawn to the night sky above him where a Wellington was receiving the same treatment that he and his crew had experienced such a short while ago. The searchlights stuck to the Wimpy like a leech, Flak was exploding all around it and within seconds the Wellington was nose diving towards the earth. Chesh had not seen anyone baleout of the stricken aircraft. Feeling very downhearted, he gathered himself together, took off his flying suit and hid it and his parachute in the ditch that separated his field from its neighbour.

Despite being a few minutes ahead of Chesh, Taff was also in the line of fire as the Germans continued to shoot at MP-L and each near miss made his chute flap and sway. Nearing the ground Taff realised that the wind was blowing him backwards. He also remembered the advice given by 'Parachute Pete', his instructor at Yatesbury. The theory was to side-slip the chute by pulling hard on one of the straps. Taff was about to do this when he remembered the subsequent warning, 'Pull too hard and spill too much air from the chute, it will collapse and you'll end up seriously dead!' Taff decided that he would be quite happy to land backwards. Other advice came back to him as he noticed a line of trees in his probable landing area. 'When you land by parachute, it's like jumping off a twelve foot wall, lad. So brace yerself! Working on an average tree height of forty feet, Taff decided to brace himself when level with the tree tops. The next thing he knew, he was lying in a heap on the ground. The trees were actually bushes, no higher than six feet.

Taff lay still for a minute, listening. All he could hear was his heart, beating more loudly and faster than usual. He stood up, released his parachute harness and took a step forward, only to sink up to his knees in a bog (76 Squadron lost another aircraft in this same area later this night. This was L9531 flown by Sergeant C.E.Whitfield. Whitfield and four of his crew also landed in this same bog and tragically all were drowned. Taff Gurmin's guardian angel was certainly working overtime this night). Using the branches to pull himself out of the mire, he climbed up onto the roots of the bushes and took a look around in the moonlight. He thought he could see a pathway about thirty feet away so, taking a deep breath, he ran like the wind towards it. The second man to walk on water reached the pathway and started to walk along it, whistling softly 'There'll always be an England' and hoping to meet up with one of the crew. No such luck. He walked straight into the arms of a Luftwaffe officer and ten men who had watched him descend on his parachute and had come hunting for him.

Flight Lieutenant Cheshire started walking in a westerly direction. He was using the stars as a guide and progress across country was slow. At about 2 am he found himself on a main road with an amazing amount of traffic on it for that time in the morning. In particular there seemed to be a lot of cyclists, which gave Chesh the idea of trying to 'borrow' a bicycle to help speed him on his way, supposing, of course, he could find one unattended. He decided to follow the road, hoping to find a bike standing outside a house or a garage. At the first house he came to, a dog started to bark ferociously the minute Chesh approached, so he moved on rapidly. Five minutes further down the road he came to another house with a garage attached. He crept up the path and tried the garage door but it was securely locked so he quietly retraced his steps and carried on down the road. At the third house it looked as if his luck was in. There, leaning against an outhouse, was exactly what he was looking for. Overjoyed, he moved towards his prize when, totally out of the blue, a gun was pushed against his ribs and a husky voice said 'For you the war is over.'

Christopher found himself face to face with a German Gefreiter (Corporal) who promptly handcuffed him and marched him a hundred yards or so to a Kubelwagen containing two more German soldiers. He had been caught by a patrol specifically sent out to round up RAF airmen who had been unfortunate to be shot down, but fortunate to have survived. Flight Lieutenant Cheshire was driven in the direction of Hamburg where he was deposited at the local Luftwaffe Headquarters approximately thirty minutes later. Chris was placed in a large room which, to his surprise contained a large map showing all the Flak gun emplacements from the Elbe Estuary to a point north of Hamburg. Each gun position had a number written inside a red circle and, not having much else to do for the moment, Chesh started to count all the emplacements. Having reached 247, he was trying to assess, by means of the numbers in the red circles, what this meant in terms of individual guns when one of the doors into his room was opened and a familiar figure was led into the room.

Having been picked up by the search party, Taff Gurmin was taken to the Flak post that had been responsible (so they said) for shooting down L9530. The Luftwaffe officer started to question the wireless operator, but Taff was not feeling particularly co-operative and the only answer he would give was 'I don't know'. The 88mm Flak guns outside the building were still banging away and Taff could hardly hear himself think. Suddenly a German soldier ran into the office in which the Welshman was being questioned, gabbled something in an excited manner and everyone rushed outside. One of the soldiers had the presence of mind to grab Taff and pulled him along behind them. As he was being hustled outside, Taff grabbed a German steel helmet from a table and put it on his head. He'd had enough excitement for one night and didn't fancy being brained by falling shrapnel.

When he got outside everybody was looking skywards. The guns were shooting at the Wellington that Cheshire was also watching from his landing field. One of the German soldiers took a sideways glance at Taff, just to make sure he was behaving himself, saw the coal-scuttle helmet and drawing his comrades' attention to this strange sight they all fell about laughing. Even Taff managed to raise a tired smile.

Sometime later, Taff, now carrying his inner and outer Sidcot suits, was taken down a pathway to a road. After a minute or so a car drew up and Taff was ordered to sit next to the driver. As he walked around the car, someone in the darkness of the back seat put two fingers up to him against the rear side window. Being too tired to even wonder who it might be who was being so impolite to such a likeable chap as himself, Taff simply returned the reversed Churchillian sign, saying as he did so 'And you mate!' He opened the front passenger door and and was wondering where to put his Sidcot suits when a pair of hands emerged from the darkness of the back seat and took Taff's flying clothing from him. Taff climbed in and the car moved off, stopping some ten minutes later at a Luftwaffe camp. Taff was ordered out of the car and taken into the building. Seeing Chesh sitting there alive and well, Taff was so overjoyed that he momentarily forgot they were supposed to ignore each other in enemy company and almost rushed up to him to shake his hand. He remembered just in time and he and Chesh just winked at each other.

At this point the door opened again and in limped 'Washy' Wash (he had banged his leg on landing), carrying not only his own flying gear but Taff's Sidcot suit too. It had been Washy in the back of the car that had delivered Taff. Poor Reggie Wash! By this time both Chesh and Taff had regained their composure and both studiously ignored their flight engineer. They were all questioned individually and then Taff and Washy were taken to separate cells in the guardroom.

Cheshire's ensuing interrogation was most civilised and basically conformed to the standards laid down in the Geneva Convention. Christopher was asked for his name and rank, information which he readily gave. After a pause, the Hauptmann (Captain) conducting the interrogation asked for Chesh's Squadron number and aircraft type. He refused point-blank to supply these details and his interrogation was terminated. He was then taken down a long corridor to a small room containing only a single bunk bed and was informed that he would shortly be going by train to an unspecified town in Germany.

It seemed that he had only just dropped off to sleep when he was awoken by a shout of '*Heraus!*'[33] Having received a slice of black bread and a cup of ersatz coffee (made from acorns), Cheshire was handcuffed to a Feldwebel (Sergeant) and they were taken by car to Hamburg's main railway station where they met up with Taff, Washy and their guards and boarded a train for the Dulag Luft near Frankfurt- am-Main.

The journey was a long and tedious one, with the train seeming to stop at every station it came to, no matter how small it was. The Luftwaffe guards were pleasant enough, considering the circumstances, and at midday they produced black bread and wurst (sausage) for each prisoner. These were gratefully received and soon devoured as it was some considerable time since any of them had had anything substantial to eat.

At one point during the journey, a Luftwaffe pilot passed the prisoners' reserved compartment, probably on his way to the toilet. On his return he opened the compartment door and spoke to the guards, obviously checking with them that it was alright to speak to their charges. In pretty fair. English he told them that he had been shot up over England and only just managed

---

[33] *The literal translation of 'Heraus' is 'Out' or 'Outside' though colloquially it can be used as the German equivalent of 'Rise and shine!'*

to nurse his damaged aircraft back across the Channel to crash-land in France. The burn scars on his face and hands bore testimony to this event and that he'd been lucky to survive his ordeal. He then looked at Taff, smiled and said 'Are you still going to hang out the washing on the Siegfried Line?' There's still plenty of time for that, mate,' replied Taff, 'You wait and see.'[34]

A little later, Cheshire apologised to Taff and Washy for landing them in their current predicament. Taff replied for both of them when he said 'No apologies necessary, Skipper. If we'd been with anyone else we'd have bought it ages ago.'

Arriving at Frankfurt in the late afternoon, his guard bundled Cheshire into a taxi and they were driven the six miles to the Frankfurt Dulag Luft, a clearing centre to which all RAF and allied airmen prisoners were taken and processed before being sent to an Oflag (Officer's camp) or a Stalag Luft (primarily for captured aircrew), both of which were fully fledged PoW camps. Chesh was not taken into the Dulag itself, but was locked in a small room in a nearby building. He was given a plate of totally unpalatable food that he tried to eat sitting on the iron bedstead that was the only item of furniture in the room. Christopher was very tired and, despite his surroundings, he slept until daylight. All that day he was kept in his small room, having no communication with anyone other than a somewhat taciturn guard who twice accompanied him to the nearest lavatory.

When Taff and Washy arrived at Dulag Luft, they were put into solitary confinement while their clothes were taken away to be searched. As was the practice at this time, they both had silk maps of Germany hidden in one shoulder of their battledress jackets, another of France in the other and a small compass was sewn into the waistband of Taff's jacket. Only the compass remained when their clothes were returned. A Luftwaffe Feldwebel entered Taff's cell, opened a packet of English 'Gold Flake' cigarettes and offered one to the prisoner. 'No thanks,' said Taff smugly, 'I don't smoke.' The Feldwebel then gave Taff a pencil and a form bearing the International Red Cross symbol on the top and asked him to fill it in. Taff looked at the form, seeing questions about his squadron, aircraft type, bases, etc. and he said "This isn't a Red Cross form, it's one of yours and I'm not putting

---

[34] *Taff often wondered if this Luftwaffe officer survived the war.*

anything on it!' Taff got very annoyed at the attempted trickery and told his inquisitor exactly what he could do with his form. A blazing row ensued and Taff refused to even write his name, rank and number on the bogus form. The Feldwebel about turned and marched to the door of Taff's cell. He opened the door and faced the prisoner once more. 'You know what this means, don't you?' he asked. 'No' said Taff, `What does it mean?' 'Without your details on this form we cannot inform the Red Cross of your

35 Sqn, September 1941. Front row 8th from left is F/L Leonard Cheshire, 10th from left W/C Robinson (CO), also in the photograph are S/L Willie Tait, S/L Jimmy Marks and S/L George Holden. (RAF Linton-on-Ouse Archives)

whereabouts,' he said with a sadistic smile, 'Your parents will think that you are dead!' Taff Gurmin was only twenty years old and the thought of his Mum and Dad not knowing what had happened to him was not a pleasant one. Alright,' he said, 'Give me the bloody form.' The German closed the cell door and returned to the table, putting the form upon it and handing Taff the pencil, rubbing his hands with glee. Taff sat down at the table, wrote his number, rank and name and then put the pencil down. 'Go on,' said the Feldwebel, 'Keep writing!' Taff looked him straight in the eye and with as much feeling as he could muster said 'Get stuffed, mate.' The Feldwebel realised he was beaten, picked up the form and stamped out of the cell.

Cheshire's second morning at Frankfurt was however, completely different. He was given a more generous breakfast and, shortly after he had finished this repast, his door was opened by a distinguished looking grey-haired Oberst (Colonel) who took Chesh along to his office for further interrogation. Offering him a cigarette and coffee, the Oberst opened the proceedings by telling Cheshire of the great advances made at Leningrad by the victorious Wehrmacht, how this Russian city was already surrounded and that its surrender was imminent. He then, in a roundabout manner, attempted to find out where Flight Lieutenant Cheshire had been stationed and which type of aeroplane he had been flying when he was shot down. Christopher repeated at least three times that, under the terms of the Geneva Convention, he had no obligation to supply such information. After an hour of similar questions and answers the Oberst had Cheshire returned to his room, informing him, as he did so, that he would shortly be taken to a camp where he would find somewhat better accommodation than he'd had during the past thirty-six hours. And so it was.

The next morning Taff and Washy were taken into the main camp and shown into a small room containing three two-tier bunks. They still did not know if any of the other crew members had survived and their non-appearance seemed ominous. Taff was particularly concerned about his best friend Slim Smalley. He asked another prisoner if he had seen a chap called Smalley and to his great joy the answer was 'Yes, he's in the mess room.' Taff ran into the room looking for his six feet two inch friend but couldn't see him anywhere. 'Smalley!' he shouted and a total stranger walked up to him and asked him what he wanted. 'You're not Smalley.' said Taff, 'Yes I am,' he said 'I'm Geoff Smalley.' and a friendship was started that was to last for the duration. Much to Taff's great relief, Slim and Paul Horrox arrived the next day, although their pleasure at being reunited was saddened by the final realisation that Timber Woods and Jock Niven would not now be joining them.

Paul Horrox was captured shortly after landing and was taken to a farm house where he was reunited with Slim Smalley. They were then both taken to a Hitler Youth Barracks where they spent their first night in captivity. The following day they were taken to the same Luftwaffe base where Chris Cheshire and Taff Gurmin had spent the previous night. Paul was also left alone with the Flak positions map and was studying it when a Luftwaffe Officer entered the room. 'Ah. So you find that map of interest, yes? Well come over here and look at this one, it's much more interesting.' It was a map of the Eastern Front and Paul, like Cheshire before him, was treated to a German overview of how well the Russian campaign was progressing. From this base they were taken to a Police Station in Hamburg and then by train to the Dulag Luft at Frankfurt.

The Oflag seemed to be efficiently serviced by orderlies and the accommodation and food was, to Cheshire's mind, more than adequate for those of PoW status. The Senior British Officer (SBO) was a Squadron

Leader and appeared to be there in permanency. He interviewed every new arrival at the camp and Cheshire was no exception. Chris was aware that most PoW camps had managed to establish clandestine communications with London, so he wasted no time in telling the SBO about the map showing all the Hamburg gun positions and told him about the total figure of 247. The SBO responded by saying that this information was of very little importance because the number and position of these emplacements would probably change from day to day and therefore not worth passing on to London! Christopher Cheshire is still convinced to this day that even if this information had saved only one RAF bomber from being shot down in the Hamburg area, then it would have been worth transmitting.

With the interview with the SBO at an end, Christopher got up to leave. 'Oh, Cheshire,' said the SBO, 'I don't seem to have written down the date of your last sortie. What was it?' 'The twelfth of August, sir.' said Christopher. 'Bad luck old chap' came the reponse 'not to have been shooting grouse instead.'

Additional Notes to Chapter Six.

1)   The four non-commissioned members of the crew found themselves in Stalag IIIF (Kerchain), which was probably one of the worst, if not the worst PoW camp in occupied territory. Paul Horrox and Reggie Wash were two of fifty-two out of a planned one-hundred prisoners who managed to escape from a tunnel that they, with Taff and Slim, had helped to dig (Taff gave Wash his compass). Of the fifty-two escapers, fifty-one were recaptured and one was shot dead 'while escaping'. Paul was on the 'loose' for three weeks, managing to reach Czechoslovakia before being caught by the Hitler Youth. Shortly after this, in May 1942, they were all moved to Sagan. In August 1943 they were moved again, this time to Stalag Luft VI, near Konigsberg in East Prussia. Twelve months later they were transferred to Thorn in Poland and then, only a few weeks afterwards to Fallingbostel in Germany. These rapid moves were a direct result of the Russian's advance on the eastern front. Taff was liberated from Fallingbostel by the British Eighth Army (The Desert Rats) in late April 1945. Paul escaped again just before the end of the war. He was in a large party of prisoners, including Slim and Washy, being marched away from the advancing Allied armies when, on the night of 17th April 1945, they were told by their guards that because they were behind schedule they must walk all the next day. Sergeant

Horrox and three of his friends thought, 'Bugger this for a game of soldiers' and ducked out of the column as it was forming up and hid under some hay. When the column had marched off (shuffled off is probably a more apt description) Paul and his friends got out of their hiding place and set off in the opposite direction. It was not too long before they met up with the spearhead of the Eleventh Armoured Division who whipped them off to their rear lines and gave them a good feed. Paul was then taken to the RAF base at Celle where he scrounged a lift in a Dakota, arriving in the UK on 21st April. He got home even before his parents had been informed that he'd been released.

2)   While carrying out additional research for this chapter, the author was fortunate enough to make contact with one of Christopher Cheshire's ground crew. Norman Frankish had been a Leading Aircraftman (LAC) flight mechanic-engines in 1941 and had been one of the team who had waved L9530 off on that fateful August night. Norman was delighted to find out, at long last, what had happened to their aircraft and the aircrew to whom they'd lent it. He well remembered the great sense of devastation experienced by the whole ground crew team when MP-L failed to return. Because of his unassuming, gentlemanly manner, Chris Cheshire had become a great favourite with his ground crew and when he had made his successful landing after his first operation on 76 Squadron he had also impressed them with his flying abilities. When Leonard Cheshire took command of 76 Squadron in August 1942, he made a point of seeking out his brother's ground crew and having them service and look after his aircraft while he was on the Squadron. A nice vote of confidence from a great leader and true gentleman.

3)   In April 1992, Christopher Cheshire was showing his brother Leonard the three write-ups he had done to assist me with this chapter. At this point it is perhaps apt to remind the reader that when Chris Cheshire was shot down, Leonard had already completed a first tour of fifty operations and was then engaged on his second tour, as a Flight Commander on 35 Squadron. It is also worth remembering that at the time of reading Christopher's manuscript, Leonard had his full incredible war service behind him and almost fifty years of peacetime caring for others less fortunate than himself. His experience far outweighed that of his younger brother, even in August 1941, so any comments made would obviously be based on that experience. The first two write-ups, 'Sparks and Flashes' (28th May 1941) and 'The Chink in the Cloud' (8th June 1941) passed without much comment other than to have a mutual chuckle over old times. The third was different, however. 'Grouse shooting' the story of Christopher's last operation, was

Leonard Cheshire as CO of 76 Squadron.

read through in complete silence. Finally, Leonard looked up from the typewritten pages and said `Christopher, I must admire the courage and determination you and your crew showed under such adverse conditions, but do you know what I would have done in your place? "What?" said Christopher. 'I'd have dropped the bomb in the North Sea and come straight home.' said Leonard. 'Thus saving a fully trained crew and an expensive aircraft.'

Chapter Seven

1942: The Battle of Edghill

Just as the Battle of Britain was beginning, in June 1940, Ray Edghill joined the Royal Air Force. He took his 'Oath of allegiance' at Cardington where he was allocated the Service number 1173753, or '753 for short and was then posted to Blackpool for 'square bashing'. Once this was completed he found himself, with two hundred other new recruits, detached to Jurby on the Isle of Man to help defend the airfield (with pikes!) while they awaited available spaces at the Initial Training Wing at Aberystwyth. From there he went to Prestwick Elementary Flying Training School, in January 1941, to train as a pilot. Ray was not destined to become a 'driver, airframes' however and the following month he remustered to observer, moving across to Prestwick's Navigation School in early March. By August 1941, Ray had completed his aircrew category training and was awarded his Observer's brevet and three chevrons. In October 1941, '753 Sergeant Edghill, C.M. arrived at 19 OTU at Kinloss to join No.29 Course on Whitleys and training proceeded smoothly for the rest of the year.

The New Year of 1942 was, however, to see a serious change in Ray Edghill's fortunes. During the evening of Thursday 6th January he was undertaking a routine night-flying cross-country exercise in Whitley Mk.V, ZV-B, Serial No.N1498, as one of a crew of seven: Pilot Officers J. G. Irvine and J. G. Castling, both New Zealander pilots, an English pilot (and the aircraft captain) Sergeant Derek Pike, Ray Edghill as Observer and three Wireless Operator/Air Gunners, C. S. George, C. W. Green and E. F. Kane, all Sergeants. They were returning to Kinloss on the final leg of the exercise, the first night cross country that 19 OTU had been able to dispatch for some time because of constant gales, severe frosts and considerable snow falls.

Whitley ZV-B had been out of radio contact with its base for some time and with worsening weather conditions and no radio fixes to guide it, the seven men on board were now getting increasingly concerned about their chances of a safe return to Kinloss. They were only about thirty miles from base when, at approximately 20.30 hours, the Whitley's wing tip touched the top of Carn a Choire Mhoir and 'B-Bertie' crashed into the snow covered hills at Tomatin, about fifteen miles southeast of Inverness, killing Pilot Officer

Castling, Pilot Officer Irvine, Sergeant George and Sergeant Green on impact.

Ray Edghill (bottom left) in October 1941.

Ray Edghill recovered consciousness about twenty minutes after the crash. He had been thrown into the front well of the aircraft and was covered with debris. As he came round he was aware of something burning. Frantically trying to remember where he was and what had happened to him, Ray's brain cleared and he realised that the unthinkable had occurred - they had flown into a hill. Despite the fact that he had known that flying around Scotland in 10/10ths cloud without wireless or sextant made the likelihood of such an event almost a certainty, the actuality still came as a shock to the system. The burning smell that was assailing his nostrils reinforced the trauma. He glanced around; there was no-one about, only the crackle of fire and the acrid smell coming from beyond the smoke-filled cockpit. Curiously the flames seemed to stretch out to him, beckoning him to come closer. He was fascinated by them as only the concussed or half-dazed can be. He tried to move but found that he was pretty well pinned down. So, piece by piece he started to remove the wreckage and debris that was covering his lower body. Once that was achieved he tried to raise his right leg, only to realise, from the ensuing pain, that it was obviously badly injured. Gritting his teeth and making a special effort, he managed to drag himself upright and clambered up to the remains of the flight-deck. He stood there for a moment. No pilot, no wireless operator, no instructor. Where was everyone? Looking aft he again saw the beckoning fingers of flame, this time accompanied by a hissing sound. Even in his befuddled state of mind he realised that he must somehow get out of the burning aircraft, but to force his way out he needed a fire axe. To reach the nearest fire axe, which was positioned behind the wireless operator's position, he must brave the flames for a short period.

The Pendulum and the Scythe

Fixing his mind on one thing at a time seemed to be helping, so he struggled towards the fire. Three times he dragged himself towards the fire-axe and three times he was beaten back by the heat. His face felt sore and the vague idea that he was burning, but that he must not allow himself be roasted alive, took shape in his mind. What he couldn't quite grasp for the moment was how to avoid it. The Very Pistol - that should do it, thought Ray. He turned quickly to the starboard side of the cockpit and looked for the pistol. The holder was there, but no, there was no sign of the bloody pistol. Facing aft once more, he decided to have one more go at reaching the axe. Just then there was a small explosion in the fire and out came a small black puff of smoke - it hovered for a while and then began to move towards him. Fascinated, he focussed his eyes on the little ball of smoke as it gently eased itself over the throttle console, hovered over the pilot's seat and then swiftly moved upwards and out!

Just then a voice from outside the aircraft said 'Get out of there quickly you silly bugger, she's going to blow up at any minute!' Of course, thought Ray, the skipper must have got out the same way the ball of smoke had - through the pilot's escape hatch in the roof of the cockpit. But what of the others? Coming to his senses, he had a quick look around inside the front part of the aircraft. Both New Zealand trainee pilots had been crushed and the Instructor and the Wireless operator were also dead. `Come on you dozy sod. Get out of there!' Again his skipper called him from outside the aircraft. Ray responded more by instinct than in fear of his life. God, but his right leg hurt - that's it, hold on with both hands and hop - that's a bit better, onto the pilot's seat, now, one big heave and a one-legged jump - hey presto, fresh air! Now slide down onto the port wing – gently does it, ouch! That hurt. Hell, now to reach the ground. It's no good, I'm going to have to jump. Jumping Jehovah!! The pain is bloody awful, but must get away from the kite, it's going to blow up.... Ray got himself up on his outstretched arms and the good leg, looking like a semi-collapsed member of a leapfrog team. He was just about to stand upright when the firm hands of his skipper, Derek Price, and the Canadian Rear Gunner Sergeant Kane, gently took hold of both his upper arms and half dragged, half carried the still dazed observer well away from the burning aircraft.

The crashed 'plane was now burning fiercely but Derek Pike once again approached it in a last attempt to look for any other signs of life. There was none. He returned to Ray and Sergeant Kane and the three survivors took stock. 'I pulled out of our descent at 3,000 feet.' said Derek. 'Heaven only knows where we are then,' said Ray,'There shouldn't have been any mountains over 2,500 feet on our track.' Can you walk?' asked the rear gunner. 'Well I can try.' replied Ray and off they set. 'That's no bloody good,' said Kane, 'You're like a one-legged kangaroo! Come on, put your arms around our shoulders and we'll see you through.' Ray did as he was bidden and the going was easier for a little while. Unfortunately the terrain they were struggling across was not only uneven, it was also sloping and covered in snow. Progress was slow - painfully so for Ray and much too difficult for his companions. 'Let's all try to keep in step,' suggested Derek. 'Left, right, left, right.' Slip, slide, recover and then try again. They had hardly gone a hundred yards before the physical effort started to tell. 'I think you two should leave me here and go on and get help.' said Ray. 'And what will you do?' asked the rear gunner. 'That's a good idea.' said Derek, 'You stay here - don't move - and we'll come back with a rescue party.' He put his flying jacket on the ground and helped Ray to lie down on it. The Canadian gunner then took off his flying jacket and carefully placed it over the injured observer's body. `Whatever you do, don't bloody move. We'll be back as soon as we can.' said the pilot. 'OK, skipper' said Ray, 'Good Luck.'

With that, the pilot and the gunner set off down the mountain. Ray watched them until they were out of sight, but he could still hear the crunch of their footsteps on the ice crystals. Then that too disappeared and all Ray could hear was the howl of the wind. Ray Edghill had never felt so alone. He wished he had kept his mouth shut and let them all struggle on, slipping and sliding their way down the mountain. He knew he'd been right to suggest that they leave him behind and crack on at their faster pace, but it wasn't much consolation in his loneliness. Some tufts of low cloud scudded by as if they were in a funeral procession and every now and then an eerie, weak moonbeam would light up a patch of snow as if picking out minature gravestones. Ray shuddered, suddenly the wind seemed to get colder. He imagined that the clouds were talking to each other as if uncertain what to do next. Ray was sharing that uncertainty. What a place to die, he thought, with only the clouds to administer the last rites. 'Oh, to hell with it' said Ray, to no-one but himself and the scudding clouds, 'I'm not going to lie here and die. If I'm going to die at least I'll go down bloody fighting.'

He pushed off the gunner's flying jacket, tucked his good left leg under his body and stood up. He overbalanced, tried to steady himself with his right leg and fell flat on his face. Try again. This time Ray got on to his knees first, took a deep breath and then slowly stood up. Now what, smarty? Hop, skip, jump? Try hopping you dope - oh hell, the slope's getting steeper - he fell in a heap in the snow. Blast it. Perhaps I can roll down a little way, he thought, no that's no good. Get onto your knees again, Ray told himself. Right, now stand up. OK so far. Right, now hop steadily, no, not too fast, try to get some rhythm into it, that's better... Oh bloody hell! Not on the deck again! Come on pick yourself up and stare again, come on, get going... What's this? A barbed wire fence. What in heaven's name is a barbed wire fence doing over half way up a bloody mountain? Take it easy and investigate. Ray Edghill hopped over to the fence - something to do with the Army? Who knows, anyway it looked like an effective aid to navigation, not to mention giving something to hang onto as he hopped his way further down that bloody mountain. Progress became much easier and considerably faster, despite the increasing pain in his injured right leg. He began to wonder about the others, had they reached a source of help? He hoped they hadn't yet started back up the mountain to look for him or his name was going to be mud with a capital `M'. He imagined the feelings of the members of a search party dragged out of their cosy warm homes and made to trek half way up the side of a mountain, only to discover that the objective of their efforts had not waited for them. He decided that he wouldn't be able to look them in the face and made a big effort to speed up his progress. Suddenly he found himself on very squelchy ground. His next step took him up to his calf in freezing cold water. Now what? Surely not a lake. Even the Army wouldn't run, a barbed wire fence through a lake, surely. Another step, the water came up to his knees. Should he try to swim? Don't be stupid, Edgehill, keep hold of the fence, turn sideways and keep both hands on the wire. Move one hand at a time and then pull yourself along, hand over hand, That's better, but hope the water doesn't get any deeper - don't want me whatnots in this icy stuff - talk about 'brass monkeys'. Thank God for that, the water's getting shallower- hurray, no iced balls for starters, Gordon Bennett, how bloody tired can you get? Absolutely knackered, got to keep going, my Momma done say don't go to sleep in wet clothing. Wonder what she'll say when she hears about the crash. I know, she'll say serve you right, for joining up against her wishes. How will my father find out? Can the cable service to Trinidad still be used? Oh well, write and hope it gets through.'

Ray continued to talk to himself as he continued his weary way down the mountain, he had no idea whether or not he spoke out loud or just in his mind as one does when concentrating one's efforts to the exclusion of all else. 'Easier going now, clear of the bog and the wind has dropped. Oh shit, the bloody fence has ended. Still the hopping's much improved and things are going fairly well. Let's try some kangaroo leaps -one leap, two leaps, three leaps and rest. Almost level ground now, but look out for stones - quite a few big ones around here. Hope to get some leave after this lot. If things get too unpleasant at home I can always go up to Brecon, might get a game of rugby. Must write to Nora and warn her some leave possible. One, two, three, rest. What's that over there on the left? It can't be, it is, it's a cottage! The chimneys are smoking, a warm fire, boy is that going to be good. Now, one two three and rest. Now, just keep hopping.' Ray raised his voice, 'Help! Help! Help!' Then once again to himself, 'Why doesn't anyone come? Are they all deaf? Oh no, this can't be, just a bloody big boulder. How on earth did you think that was a cottage you bloody, bloody fool. Heard of hearts of stone, but never a cottage turned to stone.

This is the end. Must sit down and rest. What's this? Tears? Yes, tears of disappointment, frustration and resignation to death. At least it's fairly comfortable here, but I wish I'd brought the flying jackets. Crying! You bloody great baby! What are you crying for, baby! Come on, buck up, pull yourself together and make the effort. What have you got to lose – just your life. Anyway, it's the will that counts. That reminds me, I haven't made one, but maybe 'next-of-kin' is good enough. Come on, one more effort, one more prayer. Please, dear God, let me keep going a little bit longer. Here goes, onto left knee – getting expert at that now - right hand on the boulder, cottage! Huh, what a twit. Now, straighten up. Hop, hop, hop, rest. That rest was good, the rhythm's better now - and the hops are getting longer - take some deep breaths, that's better. Funny, I can hear a chapel bell, a single bell ringing out clearly in a monotone, go on, go on, go on. There's the Brecon Beacons[35], all covered in snow, couldn't have been that much off track. Wouldn't it be a turn up for the books if the rescue party was drawn from the school! Steady now, must be hallucinating again, this bloody tiredness is getting me down. Hang on, is that a light over there on the left? Now steady on, you've already imagined a cottage, take it easy.

But it does look like a storm lantern. No, yes, there's another one and another. There's three of them, surely can't imagine three lights - and they're moving!

---

[35]*Ray had spent his early teenage years in the Brecon area. The obvious similarity of terrain between them and his current surroundings led to mild hallucinations at this point. Note that the description of Ray's descent down the mountain is almost verbatim from his story to the author. I wouldn't attempt to improve on such an excellent description.*

The Pendulum and the Scythe

I can hear voices! It must be the rescue party, thank heavens I found them before they climbed the mountain. 'Help! Help! I'm over here!' Hop, hop, hoppity, hop. 'I'm here!' The lanterns have changed direction, they must have heard me, yes, someone just shouted 'Hello!' back. Come on, meet them half way, hop, hop, hoppity, hop. `Help! I'm over here!' Splash. Oh no, where are they? I can't see them anymore, what has happened? Damn it, I've fallen into a ditch. Why do they have to make them so bloody deep? I can't see over the top. Hell, I can't even reach the -top with my hands. Certainly can't climb out of the bloody thing with this gammy leg, shout man, shout. 'I'm over here, help, over here, in this bloody ditch!' At last, a reply, 'We're coming, hold on!' Over here!' shouted Ray. Look at all those outstretched hands trying to grab my wrists. With one united pull, Ray Edghill's rescuers extricated him from the ditch. A reassuring but broad Scots voice seemed to be in charge, 'Jimmy, run and tell Mother, light a fire and have lots of hot water ready. Ian, Ross, put his arms around your necks and take him to the house.' And to Ray, `You'll be alright, Laddie, We'll see to that.' Then once more to his fellow rescuers, 'No, that's not good enough. Harold, Jack, make a chair with your arms and change with Ian and Ross when you're tired.'

It was too dark for Ray to distinguish the features of his rescuers although he immediately recognised the voice of his skipper and the Canadian drawl of Sergeant Kane. However the spirit of friendliness created a sense of good will that gave off its own warmth. It was so comforting that not even the Scottish mist could dampen Ray's pleasure at being safe. Once inside the house 'Mother' gave directions as to where Ray should be placed and he found himself resting comfortably on some cushions in front of a blazing fire. The man who had led his rescuers, now identified as the local schoolmaster, asked for hot water, a sponge and scissors. 'No need to worry now, Laddie. We'll soon have this cleaned up.' he said as he set to work removing the lower right leg of Ray's trousers with the scissors. Ray raised himself up on his elbows and watched the schoolmaster as he gently slid the detached portion of trouser leg down over his foot. The schoolmaster suddenly changed colour and rushed out of the room. Ray could hear the poor man being sick. At the time Ray put this down to exhaustion, it never occured to him that it was the state of his leg that was the cause of the schoolmaster's nausea.

The schoolmaster returned to the room, 'When is that bloody doctor coming?' he demanded. 'He's got to come from Inverness,' said Ian, 'He'll be at least another half-hour yet.' Gradually, as the warmth penetrated Ray's body, the pain from his injured leg grew stronger and stronger and he finally realised why the schoolmaster had been sick. It must be bad to have such an effect on a burly big Scotsman like him, thought Ray. He started to shiver as delayed shock set in and more hot water bottles were brought and placed on all parts of the airman's body. `Mother' reappeared and knelt down at Ray's side, she took his hand in hers but quickly realised, as he grimaced, that it was not just his face that was burned. She gently put it back down on a cushion and looked into his eyes `Och, but what will your Mother say?' she asked, 'I've a boy of my own in the Merchant Navy and he's already been torpedoed twice. I've a special bottle of whisky here that we've been keeping for him, but I'm sure he'd be proud of us if we gave you a wee drop. Would you like that now?'

Ray was not a whisky drinker, in fact, just at the moment he didn't want a drink of any kind, but how could he possibly refuse such an offer without hurting the sailor's mother or giving offence? After all, these people had left the comfort of their warm homes on a wild night to effect a mountain rescue. They had opened their home to an unknown airman and were now making this heart-warming gesture. He looked up at the smiling face and said 'Yes please, but not too much.' The bottle was produced and the schoolmaster opened it with not a little ceremony. He poured a 'wee dram' into a small glass while the lady of the house cradled Ray's head in her right arm and then soon put the glass to his lips. It tasted vile and he was glad it had gone. Perhaps it will help me to sleep, thought he.

It was not long however, before he felt very ill indeed. He as he looked around, seeking something in which to deposit the vomit that he could feel welling up in his throat. He desperately wanted to avoid being sick all over the cushions and carpet on which he was lying. That damned whisky. He tried to sit up, but gentle hands pushed him down again, finally he could hold it no longer and he was sick where he lay. What a way to repay all their kindness, he thought. But the mess was quickly mopped up and not long after that an ambulance arrived, complete with an RAF doctor. The MO took one look at Ray's leg, checked his pulse rate and said `OK Sergeant, I'll give you a shot of morphine; that will help you to sleep.

The ambulance had arrived at Raigmore Hospital before Ray woke up again. He was soon being wheeled into a ward where the stretcher was surrounded by all levels of nursing staff. 'Sign here please, if you find it difficult, just put a cross.' said one authoritarian sister. Very quickly but gently, his clothes were removed and Ray found himself tucked up in bed. A very fragile looking young girl appeared at his bedside, examined his eyes and his leg and then said 'Don't be surprised if you wake up without your leg.' before turning abruptly away and leaving the ward. 'What on earth does she mean?' thought Ray, and anyhow, who the hell does she think she is to say such things?' Before he could clarify any of his unspoken thoughts with the nursing staff, a couple of porters arrived and whisked him off to the operating theatre.

Sometime later, Ray recovered consciousness to find himself back in the ward. He looked around him and then carefully checked to see if he was still 'all there'. It was with much relief that he discovered he was, although all he could see of his right leg was a large plaster cast (yes, it was definitely the right length for a complete leg) and he could see some rather scabby skin had been sprayed onto his burnt hands. His thoughts returned to the 'fragile young girl' who had prepared him for the worst, just who the hell was she? Suddenly she was at his bedside, but this time she had a definite air of authority. It's alright,' she said, 'As there were no broken bones I decided to take a chance. I've sewn up the cuts and we'll have to see how it goes.' Ray then realised that this 'fragile girl' had saved his leg and possibly his life. Because of traditional work roles in 1942, it had never occurred to him that a young girl could be a qualified orthopaedic surgeon - and a bloody good one at that!

It wasn't until May 1942, almost five months after the crash, that Ray Edghill was finally declared fit for duty and returned to Kinloss. With typical service efficiency, he was promptly sent on two weeks' leave. On his return in mid-May, was detailed to carry out some bombing exercises to 'see how he felt' about flying again following his somewhat harrowing experience. For these exercises he was crewed with Sergeant Jock Gillies whose usual bomb aimer had gone sick (as an observer, Ray was dual trade, navigator and bomb aimer). Despite the weather confining their bombing height to no more than 3,000 feet, the bombing results were considered good. While perhaps not ecstatic at being in the air again, Ray was not as apprehensive as he had feared he might be and was quite happy to continue as aircrew. He continued to fly with Jock Gillies pending the return of their regular bomb aimer. During the evening of Monday 22nd June, Sergeant Edghill was surprised to find himself summoned to the CFI's office and, after a somewhat unusual interview, ordered to report to the newly promoted Flight Sergeant Gillies as his bomb aimer (temporary) for a forthcoming 'maximum effort'.

The Pendulum and the Scythe

As the OTU aircraft and trainee crews had been used in the Thousand Bomber raid on Cologne at the end of May and again for Essen on 1st June, it did not really require the brainpower of a genius to work out that any maximum effort utilising OTU aircraft and crews had to be another 'Thousand' raid or similar. Early next morning, the 23rd June, Jock Gillies lifted Whitley Mk.V, BD381, off the grass at Kinloss and headed south for Abingdon, from where the aircraft of 19 OTU were to be despatched with those of the resident OTU, No.10. Jock Gillies' crew for this forthcoming operation comprised Ray Edghill as bomb aimer, Sergeant A. Collins as navigator, Sergeant S. Downing as wireless operator and Sergeant C. Lee, a Canadian, in the rear turret. BD381 was to be one of twelve aircraft despatched by 19 OTU as their contribution to the third Thousand Bomber' raid.

Having spent a couple of nights at Abingdon, they were finally briefed for an attack on Bremen that was to take place that night, Thursday the 25th June. A Bomber Command force of 472 Wellingtons, 124 Halifaxes, 96 Lancasters, 69 Stirlings, 51 Blenheims, 50 Hampdens, 50 Whitleys, 24 Bostons, 20 Manchesters and 4 Mosquitoes was detailed to bomb various targets in and around Bremen in a space of only sixty-five minutes. This force of 960 aircraft was reinforced by a further five from Army Co-operation Command (probably Whitleys) and a total of 1,067 aircraft was made up by the inclusion of 102 Hudsons and Wellingtons of Coastal Command. This latter force was not, however, operating under Bomber Command orders (their Royal Naval Lordships were being bloody-minded again) but were separately targeting the Deschimag Shipyards.

On arrival over Bremen, the crew of BD381 found 4/10ths cloud, unfortunately right over the aiming point, so they had to stooge around for a while until they could see enough of the ground to identify some docks and shipbuilding sheds on the left bank of the Weser as they flew down river. Ray spotted some dockyard cranes and guided Jock in over this target and they released their bombs before setting course back to Abingdon. Bomber Command lost forty-eight aircraft on this raid (5%), but by far the heaviest casualties were suffered by the OTU's of 91Group. They lost 23 of the 198 Whitleys and Wellingtons despatched (11.6%). 19 OTU however, lost only one of their twelve Whitleys. UO-Z (P5062), flown by Sergeant J.Makerewiez, failed to return.

The Pendulum and the Scythe

After some sleep during the morning of 26th June, Jock Gillies and his crew took off from Abingdon to return to Kinloss. Just south of Edinburgh the aircraft developed a serious glycol leak in one engine and Ray Edghill identified the Fleet Air Arm base of Crail as the nearest emergency landing ground. Despite Crail being only a very small airfield, Jock made a good job of dropping the Whitley onto it and they spent the night there. Ray Edghill was pleasantly surprised to discover that, although the Royal Navy were downright unwelcoming and trigger-happy over the North Sea, they couldn't be more hospitable when on dry land and he was put to bed in a very 'merry' condition. Next morning he was somewhat perturbed to be vigorously shaken awake by a Chief Petty Officer who had some difficulty in making the hung-over airman understand that his fully-attired presence was required at the Flying Control building where an Anson aircraft awaited him. Hastily pulling his clothes on and feeling like 'death warmed up', Ray made his way to the Anson where the pilot informed him that he was wanted back at Kinloss urgently because, he believed, Sergeant Edghill had been posted to a squadron!

On arrival back at Kinloss, Ray was ushered into the Adjutant's office. He was then informed that 76 Squadron had been scouring the country for an unattached replacement observer and, as Ray had not been re-crewed, he was it! With a promise that his 'heavy' kit would be sent on after him (he never did see it again) he was bundled back into the Anson and flown straight down to Middleton St. George. As only the Armed Forces can, Ray's immediate, super-urgent, Anson-flown posting was a complete and utter 'Balls-up'. Upon his rapid arrival at Middleton to join 76 Squadron as the only un-crewed observer in the country - if not the whole RAF - Sergeant Edghill discovered that the vast majority of 76 Squadron were in the Middle East on detachment and what was left (roughly three men, a dog and two-thirds of an aircraft) were not operational! He was put in Dinsdale Hall, a nearby country house that had commandeered for aircrew accommodation, to await the Squadron's return. He was advised that, in the meantime and if required, he was to fly with their sister unit, 78 Squadron. In the end, Ray's posting was changed to 78 Squadron and, by the end of July, he was crewed up with an Irish Sergeant pilot called Tait (as was the Squadron Commander - Wing Commander 'Willie' Tait). Sergeant Tait already had an observer, one Flight Sergeant Stan Hauxwell, so Ray was detailed to fly as bomb aimer. In point of fact, Stan and Ray shared the navigation, with Stan (hopefully) getting them to the target and Ray (just as hopefully) getting them all home again.

Ray's first operation in a Halifax B.Mk.II, with which 78 Squadron was equipped at this time, took place on the night of Friday 31st July 1942. The target was Dusseldorf, in the Ruhr and their bomb load comprised two 4,000 pounder cookies. This necessitated leaving the bomb doors partially open and removing the bulb from the 'Bomb doors open' warning light. The Command despatched 630 aircraft this night, including 70 Halifaxes and 113 Lancasters, the first time that the number of Lancasters exceeded the one hundred figure. Between them, the aircraft dropped over 900 tons of bombs on or around Dusseldorf. On their way in to the target, Sergeant Tait's Halifax was caught in a box barrage and had a very tough time getting to the aiming point. They eventually weaved their way through the Flak, Ray Edghill dropped his bombs on the target and they got out of the Dusseldorf area as fast as their four Merlins would carry them. As they left the target area, Ray visually checked the bomb bay to make sure his 4,000 pounders had gone and, seeing that the front one was no longer there, happily assumed that they'd both left.

It was not until Tait was on the final approach to Middleton St. George that he complained of the aircraft's poor performance and the sluggish response he'd been getting from the controls all the way home. Tait's first attempt to land was abortive and he bitched at the engines for being so unresponsive as he opened them up to go round again. His second attempt fared no better than the first, the aircraft was handling like a soggy sponge and Tait just couldn't get the Halifax on the right line. It was third time lucky and he managed to get the extremely reluctant aircraft down onto the ground and taxied her around to their dispersal where they were greeted by frantic waving from the ground crew. Thinking that it was nice to have such friendly chaps on the ground to welcome them home, the whole crew was all the more shocked to learn, when they'd descended from the kite, that they still had one of the cookies in the bomb bay! This, rather than an overwhelming desire to welcome them home, had been the reason for the frantic waving of the ground crew. At least Tait now knew why the Halifax had been such a pig to fly home.

Five nights later Sergeant J. Tait and his crew were on the Operations Order again. On the night of Wednesday the 5th August, Bomber Command despatched only twenty-five aircraft, seventeen to Essen and eight to Bochum, to carry out a GEE bombing trial. 78 Squadron detailed six aircraft for the Bochum attack, although in the event, one of them failed to take off. Sgt. Tait and crew were airborne in R9454 at 22.00 hours and Stan Hauxwell navigated them very carefully around the more heavily defended areas of the Ruhr. But despite his best efforts, the Halifax was coned by searchlights. Tait threw the aircraft all over the night sky in desperation and, after some ten minutes, they finally escaped into blessed darkness by a steep dive from which they almost didn't recover. They continued on to Bochum, climbing to regain their lost height as they did so, and attacked the primary target by using GEE, releasing their bomb load from 14,000 feet at 00.51 hours.

As agreed, Ray Edghill took over the navigation on the way home and, being determined not to be coned again on their return flight, he deliberately took a more northerly route home. They landed safely at Middleton at 03.46 hours and learned that of the five squadron aircraft that had taken off, one had returned early, a second had crashed on return to the UK and two were missing. Only Tait and crew in R9454 had completed the mission and made it back to base. Ray felt fully justified in his deviation from the briefed route home.

It was then quite a while before Ray undertook his next operation, although this wasn't for want of trying; a series of problems quite outside their control prevented Tait's crew from actually completing a mission. On Thursday 6th August they were detailed to attack Duisburg but, due to trouble starting a recalcitrant engine, they were late at the take-off point and their part in the raid was scrubbed. Three nights later, on 9th August, they were scheduled to take part in a 216 aircraft attack on Osnabruck. Allocated Halifax W1115, they climbed on board, started the engines, taxied out to the end of the runway and lined up on the flarepath. Sgt.Tait opened up the throttles and all four engines responded sweetly, he closed the throttles again, did his last pre-take off checks, released the brakes and gradually opened up the throttles once more. The Halifax gathered speed, slowly at first and then faster and faster. About half down the take off run an engine cut dead and, by superb control and careful application of the brakes, Sergeant Tait managed to keep the big bomber in a straight line and bring it to a halt before just before they ran out of airfield. What could have been a very serious accident prevented two other Squadron aircraft from taking off and joining the Osnabruck attack.

On Tuesday the 11th August, flying R9454 with Mainz as their destination, the crew actually got airborne at 22.00 hours. They had not been in the air for long however and were still over the UK when they were attacked by a

Luftwaffe intruder nightfighter[36]. Fortunately, Sergeant Butler in the rear turret was wide awake and, under his direction, Sergeant Tait commenced a series of violent manoeuvres that caused the nightfighter to miss its intended target on several occasions and, after twenty minutes of being unable to make a 'kill' it went off to find a less alert victim. When they were sure that they'd finally lost the intruder they were approximately over Cassel, about fifteen miles due south of Dunkirk in northern France. A fuel state check revealed that they had insufficient petrol left to get them to Mainz and back home again, so they did the only sensible thing in the circumstances and about-turned for base, jettisoning their bombs in the North Sea on their way back. A welcome spot of leave followed this latest escape.

Jock Gillies and crew, with whom Ray had gone to Bremen on 25th June, had arrived on 78 Squadron in late July/early August. His Canadian rear gunner, Sergeant Lee, shared a room with Ray Edghill. Jock saw many advantages to having an observer and a navigator and started to negotiate the transfer of Ray to his own crew. Ray went off to London on leave and was recalled in late August. He arrived back at Dinsdale Hall to find that Jock Gillies and crew had been killed in a flying accident. The 'official' line was 'low flying' but Ray knew Jock to be a good, cautious pilot and Ray now believes the crash was probably caused by rudder overbalance (see Chapter 4).

It was not until Friday 4th September that Sergeants Tait, Edghill, et al, found themselves once again on the Operations Order. They were detailed to take W1250 to Bremen, but the aircraft wasn't ready in time for take off and they were scrubbed. This was the night that saw the Pathfinders introduce the technique of splitting their force into three sections; illuminators, visual markers and backers-up. The new idea worked well; the target was well bombed and the new technique became standard practice. The day after this raid, Sergeant Tait[37] went down with a severe case of chicken pox and most

---

[36] *The Luftwaffe had discontinued intruder operations over Britain in late 1941 on Hitler's express orders. While it is possible that a German crew made an unofficial sortie across the North Sea, it is more likely that the Halifax was intercepted by a Beaufighter. Nos. 25, 68 and 409 Squadrons all reported engagements against bombers attacking targets along the northeast coast.*

[37] *# Flight Sergeant J. M .Tait was killed on the night of 26/27th March 1943 in an attack on Duisburg during the Battle of the Ruhr. His aircraft, W7931, EY-J, crashed at Gaanderen,*

of his crew, including Ray Edghill were transferred to the new Flight Commander, Squadron Leader J. B. Brough, a second tour man. Two nights later, on Thursday 13th August and again in W1250, the target was once more to be Duisburg but, despite their new skipper, their very own personal Gremlins would not leave them alone. They got airborne at 00.35 hours, but on reaching point 51.56N 02.35E over the North Sea, serious mechanical trouble broke out and the bomb load was again jettisoned prior to an early return.

They finally got to carry out a complete operation on the night of Tuesday 8th September when the target was Frankfurt. Again in W1250, they were airborne at 19.56 hours and headed for the target area at which they arrived without any serious trouble - either mechanical or enemy initiated. They identified their aiming point by reference to the river and woods to the south of the city and attacked from 13,000 feet at 23.30 hours. Hits were observed just north of the Aiming Point (AP) and good fires were seen in the city centre. The PFF had trouble in locating Frankfurt with any degree of accuracy on this night and most of the bombs of the 249 aircraft strong force fell southwest of the city and onto the town of Russelsheim where the Opel tank factory and the Michelin tyre factory were damaged. Only seven aircraft (2.8%) failed to return from this raid.

The Gremlins returned on 10th September when their target was again Diisseldorf. Once more flying W1250 with Squadron Leader Brough as skipper, they had a Sergeant J. Mills along on his 'second dickie' trip but, just as they were flying parallel with the Norfolk coast, the port inner engine developed a severe glycol leak. Squadron Leader Brough told Ray to jettison the bombload yet again and they returned to Middleton St. George where they landed after only one hour and fifty minutes in the air.

Three nights later, on Sunday 13th September, the same crew - but without Sergeant Mills - were airborne in W1036, EY-K at 23.46 hours, bound for Bremen as part of a 446 aircraft strong force. Unfortunately, Squadron Leader Brough developed a severe case of eye strain and, without a second pilot, felt that were he to continue with the mission he would be putting the lives of his crew at undue risk so, at 01.00 hours, when they were halfway

---

Holland, with the death of three and four (including Ray Edghill's friend, Stan Hauxwell) taken prisoner.

across the North Sea and he was almost blind, Brough again instructed Ray Edghill to jettison the bombload and they once more returned to base without completing the operation for which they'd been briefed.

Towards the end of August, a Canadian pilot (Sergeant R. J. Mills) and his crew had joined the Squadron. Because of illness, Mills' Navigator had not completed the OTU course and, towards the end of September 1942 (by which time the Squadron had moved from Middleton to Linton-on-Ouse), Ray Edghill was asked to join Jackie Mills' crew as a 'senior man' to help them complete their early trips. After flying several cross-country exercises as an eight man crew, they were finally called for their first operation on Thursday 8th October. As was the practice from 1942 onwards, squadrons would - if at all possible - send novice crews on a mining (or Gardening) operation for their first trip. So it was with Sergeant Mills' crew, with Ray Edghill along to keep a watchful eye on the navigation. Their 'garden' for this trip (codenamed Xeranthemums) was situated off the Frisian Island of Ameland and they were allocated Halifax W1250, Squadron Leader Brough's old aircraft. Mills eased the aircraft off the runway at Linton-on-Ouse at 21.32 hours, only to discover that the air speed indicator was not working.

Looking straight down from the bomb aimer's clear vision panel, Doc' Dockendorf, the wireless operator, could see the reason why - someone had left the pitot-head cover on! While the skipper commenced a slow circling climb, Doc radioed base and the Station Engineering Officer suggested that they switch the pitot head heater on, which would start to disintegrate the rubber cover and then try to remove it as best they could. Jackie Mills switched on the heater and Doc and Ray opened the emergency hatch in the nose undersurface. With the aid of Ray's penknife tied to a set of parallel rules, they managed to push the cover off the pitot-head, thus restoring the machinations of the ASI. Unfortunately, the struggle to remove the cover against the slipstream, resulted in the loss of the penknife and the rule. It is to be hoped that no-one was in the immediate vicinity when they terminated their inevitable obedience to the laws of gravity. Doc and Ray closed the emergency hatch and the Halifax proceeded on its way to the target area. They got a good fix from a lighthouse on the island of Schiermonnikoog and made a timed run at 500 feet, releasing their mines at two minutes after midnight. They were fairly certain that at least one of the mines' retardation parachutes had failed to open, but as there was absolutely nothing they could do about it they headed back to base, where they landed at just before 3 am on the Friday.

The following Tuesday, 13th October, Jackie, Ray and the crew were once more detailed for operations. As one of 288 crews briefed, they were again allocated Halifax W1250 and their target was to be Kiel. They were routed to cross the Danish coast north of Esbjerg and, having crossed Denmark, to head south down to the east of Kiel and bomb the city port on a westerly heading. They didn't get there. After taking off at 18.37 hours, they flew across the North Sea but managed to get themselves south of their intended track, partially due to the navigator's difficulty in keeping track of Jackie Mills' weaving manoeuvres. Unintentionally arriving over Flensburg, not, far from Schleswig, and being the only RAF bomber in the area, they received an exceedingly warm welcome from the Luftwaffe Flak gunners. Coned by searchlights, the Halifax took a real pounding, the intercom was put out of action, the ammunition feed to the rear turret was severed and the turret put out of action, not to mention the aircraft being made to resemble a flying colander. By means of hand signals, Jackie Mills ordered Ray to jettison the bombload and this had just been completed when a Flak shell burst right beneath them, turning the Halifax on its back. The gyro compass toppled, loose equipment was sent flying all over the inside of the fuselage and the Halifax went into a spin. Ray Edghill could see that Jackie Mills was not having much joy in his attempts to regain control of the spinning aircraft and was obviously considering telling his crew to bale out. Ray remembered a similar experience over Bochum with Sergeant Tait and shouted to his skipper to put the Halifax into a dive, keep it there until the old bitch was flying in a straight line with her wings level and then gently ease her back into level flight.

Ray Edghill's advice and the ensuing dive saved W1250 for two reasons: it allowed the overbalanced and locked-over rudders to return to the neutral position and thus restore control to the pilot (see Chapters 3 and 4) and it also took the Halifax out of the searchlight cone and into the blessed darkness away from the Flak. Having jettisoned their bombs, there was no earthly point in continuing on to Kiel, so they very gingerly returned to Linton-on-Ouse and made a safe landing at 00.27 hours, only to find themselves in hot water on two counts. The CO was displeased because they'd jettisoned their bombs and the Squadron Engineering Officer was hopping mad when he saw what they had 'allowed' to be done to 'his' aeroplane!

On Sunday 1st November, Wing Commander Willie Tait relinquished command of 78 Squadron on his posting to Bomber Command HQ. His replacement was Wing Commander G. B. Warner DFC. The following Friday, 6th November, Bomber Command's main target for the night was Genoa, which was attacked by 92 Lancasters. Sixty-five further aircraft were sent Gardening in various minefields from Lorient in the south, to the Frisians in the north and Halifax DT525, flown by Sergeant Jackie Mills, was one of them. Jackie had three new crew members for this trip. The Squadron Gunnery Leader, Flight Lieutenant G. T. Turner, volunteered to occupy the rear turret, while Sergeants Masterson and Grey replaced Sergeants Pinard and Doc' Dockendorf. Jackie's crew was completed by Pilot Officer H. L. Humphries (the navigator he'd had since September 6th and Sergeant Ray Edghill as bomb aimer. Their specific 'garden' for the night, codenamed Nectarine, was just to the north of the Frisians, not far from Wilhelmshaven.

They were airborne at 18.20 hours and flew to the target area without any problems. They dropped their mines on a timed run from an identified fixed point and then headed back across the North Sea for home. Crossing the water they got a bit south of their intended track (again - once could be accidental, twice in the same aircraft was probably due to an undetected compass deviation) and found themselves approaching the Hull balloon barrage. Jackie Mills did a quick turn to starboard, made sure their IFF was operating properly and then turned port to head west again. Recognising the York to Darlington railway line, they commenced their descent for Linton-on-Ouse and had just reached circuit height at about fifteen miles from base when the Halifax B.Mk.II developed the infamous rudder overbalance (see Chapter 4). Despite all Jackie Mills attempts to regain control DT525 crashed at Wass, near Ampleforth, ten miles due east of Topcliffe at 22.50 hours and caught fire. Three of the crew were killed outright, Flight Lieutenant Turner, Pilot Officer Humphries and Sergeant Clark, while the remainder were injured to some degree. Ray Edghill was thrown clear of the aircraft and into some trees where his right leg (again) was severely broken exactly half way between the scars of the same leg's damage in his first crash. He then fell to the ground, badly lacerating his face and hands on various twigs and branches as he fell. He and the three other survivors were soon picked up and admitted to hospital. This was Ray Edghill's second crash and both had taken place on the sixth of the month.

Ray spent the next eight months in York Military Hospital and RAF Sleaford Hospital, followed by the Convalescence Unit (The Lees) at Hoylake. He was finally declared fit for duty and returned to 78 Squadron (now at RAF Breighton), as a Flight Sergeant, on Saturday 18th June, 1943. One of the first people Ray met on his return to the Squadron was his old skipper, Jackie Mills, who was now a Flight Lieutenant approaching the last operation of his first tour. Jackie had been fortunate to escape the 6th November crash with only minor injuries and had returned to operations with a new crew very quickly. Jackie greeted Ray warmly and, after asking him how he was, told him that he was shortly to finish his tour. 'I'll tell you what,' he said, 'you saw me through my first trips, now, if you'd like, I'll take you on my thirtieth.'

Flight Lieutenant Jackie Mills' thirtieth operation eventually took place on Tuesday 13th July 1943 and his usual bomb aimer, an exceptionally tall Texan, agreed to stand down and let Ray take his place. This was all approved by the Flight and Squadron Commanders and was looked upon as giving Ray a chance to see how he felt about flying on operations again. At the same time it gave him a skipper he knew and trusted and one that stood as good a chance as any of coming back again. The Command despatched 374 aircraft this night, including 214 Halifaxes, and the target was Aachen. This attack was a little unusual in that 5 Group did not take part. A strong tail wind brought the first waves of the main force into the target area before Zero Hour and, when the first PFF markers went down, an unusually large number of aircraft bombed within the first few minutes of the raid. Visibility was very good and large areas of Aachen appeared to burst into flames almost at once. Eight large industrial buildings were severely damaged, including an aero-engine factory, a rubber factory, a tyre factory and a wagon works. Additionally, almost 3,000 other individual buildings were destroyed. In the space of half-an-hour before reaching the target area, Ray Edghill saw at least nine four-engined bombers shot down. Not exactly guaranteed to inspire confidence on a return to operations after eight months! Total Command losses for the night amounted to twenty aircraft (5.3%), including fifteen Halifaxes, two Lancasters, two Wellingtons and a single Stirling. Flight Lieutenant Jackie Mills had finished his first tour and brought Flight Sergeant Edghill safely home again.

Almost immediately after undertaking this operation Ray Edghill was detached to 1652 HCU, at Marston Moor, to be re-crewed. He returned to 78 Squadron on 31st August 1943 as the observer/navigator in the crew of Pilot Officer A. G. Beasleigh. Beasleigh carried out his 'second dickie' trip with

Warrant Officer Kitchen and his crew on the night of Sunday 5th September when they took Halifax JD173 to Mannheim. Pilot Officer Beasleigh's crew was an unusual mix of ranks. The were four commissioned officers, Beasleigh himself and the second tour rear gunner H. Scarcliffe DFM, were Pilot Officers, the bomb aimer, W. Cameron, was a Flying Officer, while the flight engineer, W. Perriment (another second tour man) was a Flight Lieutenant, - a fairly exalted rank for an FE. The wireless operator, M. Emmerson and the mid-upper gunner, W. Anderson, were both Sergeants and the navigator, Ray Edghill, was now a Flight Sergeant. They were briefed for their first operation as a crew on the 6th September. They were allocated Halifax B.Mk.II Serial No. JD454 and their target was to be Munich.

Halifax JD454 was to be one of 147 Halifaxes and 257 Lancasters despatched to Munich on this Monday night and Beasleigh lifted the bomber off the Breighton runway at 19.02 hours. The weather was clear over the UK and they were routed to fly over London at 4,000 feet, en-route to leave the country via Beachy Head. They climbed to 12,000 feet while crossing the Channel and continued on until, at exactly the anticipated time and place, they identified the PFF route markers and set course direct for Munich, continuing their climb to 16,000 feet as they did so.

Ever mindful of his reponsibilities as the navigator, Ray was keeping a sure eye on the route and their timing. At the appropriate time he flicked the intercom switch on his face, mask, 'ETA target five minutes Skipper.' he said. 'Thanks Ray' replied Beasleigh, then to the bomb aimer 'Can you see the AP yet, Bill?' `Yes Skipper, PFF marker flares ahead.' Are you sure they're not dummies, Bill?' asked the skipper, 'Look good to me Skipper. What do you think Perry?' The second tour flight engineer looked through the right hand windscreen, 'Yes Skipper, they're real enough.' he said. 'OK Skipper, starting the bomb run now.' said the bomb aimer, 'Right a bit... Steady, steady, left-left, steady....' The crew listened to his instructions, waiting for the sudden lift of the aircraft that signalled the release of their bomb load. Just as the waiting was becoming unbearable the bomb aimer said 'Sorry Skipper, dummy run. We'll have to go round again.' The crew remained silent as the skipper gently turned the aircraft around and headed back the way they had come. 'Everyone keep a sharp eye out for fighters and other bombers.' he said. The gunners needed no extra bidding and the flight engineer stationed himself in the astrodome to give another pair of eyes.

Once again the pilot brought the Halifax round onto the right heading for the bomb run and again the crew listened with bated breath while the bomb aimer issued his instructions to he pilot. 'Dummy run Skipper, take us round again please.' Ray swore aloud under his oxygen mask and noticed Perry duck his head under the instrument panel to peer into the nose at the bomb aimer lying prone at his bomb-sight. Only Perry's eyes were visible above his oxygen mask, but if looks could kill, their bomb aimer would be dead now. They both fully realised that their young Bomb Aimer was only doing what he'd been trained to do - press home his attack with determination and as much accuracy as possible - but there were times when discretion was the better part of valour, and now was definitely one of them! Ray got the distinct impression that Perry was sharing his own thoughts, you don't do two bloody dummy runs over the target.

Without a word being said, Beasleigh again turned the aircraft onto a reciprocal course and repositioned it for the third run into the target. Just as the bomb aimer started his guiding instructions again, the crew's blood turned to ice in their veins, the rear gunner broke into the running commentary from the bomb aimer with 'Enemy fighter astern, corkscrew port, Go! Go! Go!' Beasleigh immediately threw the Halifax into a diving turn to the left, but already it was too late. A strangled cry came over the intercom from the rear gunner, 'They've got me...' and all hell broke loose inside the heavy bomber.

The nightfighter attack took place at 23.40 hours Double British Summer Time (00.40 hours German time) and only Perry Perriment and Ray Edghill survived the onslaught to spend the rest of the war as PoWs. The rest of the crew perished in a hail of cannon shells or in the ensuing crash. Ray Edghill had had his third unpleasant end to a flight and again, it was the sixth of the month...[38]

 Ray Edghill came down at Solln, on the southern outskirts of Munich where his parachute caught on the chimney pot of a two-storey house. There was no-one about and he managed to release his harness, drop gently to the ground and take refuge at the bottom of the house's external cellar steps. He looked at his watch, it was ten minutes past midnight. He was wondering

---

[38] *It is possible that their attacker had been Oberleutnant Eckehardt-Wilhelm von Bonin, a Bf110 'ace' from II Gruppe /NJG1, who claimed two Halifaxes in the target area at this time.*

what to do next and the stories he had heard about German civilians lynching downed airmen did nothing to comfort him. He was between the devil and the deep blue sea - try to walk out of Munich and risk ending up swinging from a lamp post or stay where he was, hope to give himself up to a member of the German forces and hope to escape at some time in the future. Within ten minutes the problem was taken out of his hands as the householder, who had come to investigate the slight noises he'd heard, came down the cellar steps. Ray did the sensible thing in the circumstances and surrendered to this civilian who had so far shown him no malice.

It was difficult to know who was more concerned at their current predicament, Ray Edghill who had just surrendered, or the German civilian now confronting the young Terrorflieger. When he finally realised that Ray was not going to attack him, he relaxed a little and, by means of sign language, instructed the airman to follow him. They mounted the cellar steps and walked to the back door of the house. The German knocked on the door that was opened by the man's wife. He went to usher Ray into the house but found his way barred by the woman. A brief but vehement argument ensued, which Ray could not understand, but he got the general drift of the conversation when the woman slammed the door in their faces.

The German smiled weakly at Ray and led him back into the garden where he fidgeted nervously, obviously waiting for someone to come and take the young airman off his hands. Ray looked at his watch, it was a quarter-to-one in the morning, no, make that quarter-to-two German time, no wonder his captor didn't look too bright. The thought of thumping him and making a run for it crossed Ray's mind but, for the same reason that he'd discounted escape earlier, he again decided that it was just too dangerous. Out in the country it would certainly be worth a try, but not here in Munich itself.

Ray checked his wrist watch again, it was now five-to-two. His captor took out a packet of cigarettes, opened it and offered one to the airman. Ray took one gratefully and the light that followed. He filled his lungs with smoke and then exhaled slowly, savouring the taste of his first cigarette since just before take-off five long hours ago. He looked again at the German standing beside him - he was looking expectantly down the road - and as Ray watched he saw the man's features lighten in relief.

Ray followed his gaze down the road and saw three figures cycling towards them, one slightly ahead of the other two. As the three got closer Ray's heart sank. Unless he was very much mistaken, they were wearing the dark uniforms of the SS. As the obviously more senior of the three dismounted and approached him, Ray Edghill stood his ground and took another long drag on his cigarette. In common with most RAF aircrew, Ray was not too hot on SS rank insignia but he thought the strutting example of the Tutonic Master Race in front of him was probably a Sergeant[39] and every inch a Nazi. The SS man marched up to the airman, obviously displeased with Ray's casual attitude (Ray felt afraid but was damned if he was going to show it). Ray once again put his cigarette to his mouth and inhaled. The SS sergeant knocked the burning cigarette from Ray's left hand. Ray looked straight into the eyes of the Nazi and, as casually as he could, bent down to retrieve his cigarette. As he did so, his peripheral vision revealed the SS man take a step back and swing his right foot straight at the airman's head. Ray deftly swung his head and body out of the way and stood up in time to see an off-balance and very red faced Nazi wobbling in front of him, trying to retain his balance. The airman once again looked down at his cigarette, wondering if another attempt to pick it up might be pushing his luck too far. Looking back at the Nazi's face he decided it just might be, for the SS man was already removing his Walther pistol from its highly polished holster.

Very slowly, he raised the Walther until the tip of its barrel was pointed at and about three inches away from the centre of the airman's forehead. 'I will shoot you!' The Nazi's English was good although the German accent was still there. I am a member of the Royal Air Force,' said Ray, 'and I demand to be handed over to the Luftwaffe.' Might as well be shot for a sheep as a lamb thought he, although he certainly didn't feel as brave as he was acting. 'DEE-MAND?' shouted the Nazi, 'DEE-MAND? You are in no position to dee-mand anything! You are a murderer! Killing children and destroying hospitals - I WILL shoot you!'

The other two SS men, obviously just young minions, hung back, not quite sure what to do in the current situation. Their NCO's pistol was unsteadily waving around, pointing at everything and everyone in the vicinity while his left arm gesticulated in such an energetic fashion that the swastika arm band slipped down over his elbow and restrained its movements. As if realising

---

[39] *Ray later worked out that the SNCO was actually an Oberscharführer, roughly equivalent to a Flight or Staff Sergeant.*

that he was making a fool of himself, he once again steadied his pistol in front of the airman's face and Ray heard the German civilian at his side mutter 'C'est la guerre.' He decided to give it one more try. 'I am a member of the Royal Air Force and I DEE-MAND to be handed over to the Luftwaffe.' he said, mimicking the Nazi's pronunciation and intonation. A moment's stunned silence followed. The Nazi underlings shuffled their feet and stared at the ground. Pulling himself up to his full five feet and seven inches and getting very red faced, the SS NCO became very animated. DEE-MAND! DEE-MAND!' he repeated, I haff told you that you are in no position to demand anything. You are a murderer and ve Germans haff had enough of your cowardly attacks on our vimmen und children.' His loss of composure showed itself in a much more obvious German accent. He paused, took a step back from the downed airman and steadied himself. Once again he raised his pistol to the airman's forehead. 'I VILL SHOOT YOU!' he shouted.

The onlookers remained silent and motionless. Ray and the Nazi stood glaring at each other and although Ray was convinced that his last moment had come, he refused to lower his eyes or appear in any way contrite. The Nazi recovered his composure. Lowering his pistol he said 'You are too young to shoot. If his Britannic Majesty has to use such young boys to fly in his Royal Air Force, then England will lose the war.' He turned to the other SS men, 'Gerhard, Kurt.' he snapped, 'Chain him to your bicycles and take him to the Police Station.' With that he about turned and took a step towards his own bicycle but then turned back to Ray who was quietly thanking God for his lucky escape. 'Be careful.' grunted the Nazi and then continued to his bicycle, mounted and rode off. Ray was escorted to the nearest Police Station where he was searched and then put in a cell. It was 01.45 hours by his watch and, with the adrenalin caused by his encounter with the SS now subsiding, he realised he was dog-tired and lay down on the cell bunk. He was asleep almost immediately.

It seemed he'd just dropped off to sleep when he was roughly shaken awake and found himself confronted by four members of the Hitler Youth. That's all I need now,' thought Ray, 'a beating up from these cocky little swine.' But all they did was question him. All he'd give was his number, rank and name and after ten minutes they left him alone again. It was 02.25 hours as he lay down to go back to sleep. Half an hour later the Hitler Youth woke him up again and again questioned him. After a further ten minutes of '1173753, Flight Sergeant Edghill, C.M.' they left him alone once more. This occurred every half hour throughout what was left of the night until he was finally woken by a policeman at 05.55 hours (German time) and escorted to the toilet and a wash basin before being returned to his cell. Ray was by now very tired and he could no longer be bothered with the mental effort of keeping track of German time and, as it was pretty obvious that it was going to be some while before he needed to know what the time was in England, he wound his watch forward one hour. At 06.30 hours two policeman entered his cell and asked him for his personal details. Once again Ray trotted out '1173753, Flight Sergeant Edghill, C.M.' and he was once again left alone. He lay back down on the bunk and drifted off into a dead sleep.

He was woken at 09.10 hours, taken out of his cell and escorted to an office at the rear of the building. Here he was handed over to three different policemen who marched him outside and bundled him into the back of a parked van. Two of the policemen climbed into the back with him while the third got into the driver's seat, started the engine and drove off.

Forty-five minutes later they arrived at a rather impressively large building that Ray assumed to be the Civil Police Headquarters. He was soon proved correct and was bundled out of the van and up several flights of stairs before finding himself stood in front of a closed door bearing a plaque with the wording Politzeipreisident on it. He was closely flanked by two of his guards while the third one knocked on the door and waited. Two or three minutes passed in absolute silence before a voice on the other side of the door shouted 'Komm!'

Ray Edghill was half pushed and half marched into the office, still closely flanked by the two armed policemen. The Chief of Police was sitting behind his desk, studiously ignoring the Flight Sergeant's presence as he appeared to study a file on his desk. Ray surreptitiously looked around the room. On the wall behind the senior policeman were three large framed photographs, Goering to the right, Hitler in the centre and Himmler immediately below Hitler. Ray also noticed a fourth nail in the wall, to the left of Hitler's photograph, and the tell-tale marks showing that a fourth frame had been hung there until recently. While he wondered about the identity of the person in the missing frame, his eyes continued to look around the room. There was an empty chair placed about two yards in front of and facing the police chief's desk. He also noted a third chair, placed a little behind and to the right of that on which the senior policeman was sitting. On the desk, apart from the usual paraphernalia, was a small glass containing several cigarettes and

283

Ray noticed that not only did the police chief have a cigarette between the first and second fingers of his left hand, but that there was another cigarette end burning itself out in the ashtray. Right now, Ray could kill for a cigarette. Eventually, the Polizeipreisident took another lung full of smoke from his cigarette, put down the file he'd been studying so intently and looked up at Flight Sergeant Edghill. He motioned to the armed guards to leave the office and, when they'd gone, ordered Ray to sit in the chair facing his desk.

His English was excellent, 'Are you wounded?' he asked. 'No' replied the airman curtly. He was tired, very hungry and gasping for a cigarette, but he was not wounded. Their eyes met across the desk and, almost as if he could mind-read, the policeman deliberately took in another lungful of cigarette smoke and smiled with great satisfaction as he exhaled.

`Details - Name?'

`Edghill.'

`Rank?'

`Flight Sergeant.'

`Have you any proof?'

`My identity discs.' said Ray, unbuttoning his battledress top to expose the discs as he did so.

`I mean real proof,' said the Police Chief laconically, 'Not just any old number that anyone could stamp on a disc.' Just then the door behind Ray opened and the policeman looked up.

'Ah! Komm, Ernst.' he said, indicating the chair on his left. As the newcomer walked past the airman and around the right hand side of the desk, Ray observed that the man was very short and wore a scruffy-looking raincoat. As he sat down and faced the airman their eyes made contact. It was obvious to Ray that this was no ordinary policeman, in fact, the more he looked into the man's weasel eyes, the more convinced he became that the Gestapo had just entered his own personal equation. 'Ernst' got up from his chair and had a whispered conversation with the policeman, after which he went and stood erect in front of the window so as to be in silhouette. His small stature made the raincoat appear to be several sizes too large and, had

284

it not been for the menacing look in the man's eyes, Ray might have laughed at him.

`You must realise,' continued the police chief, 'that we Germans have a duty to protect our state from spies. You understand, Flight Sergeant Edghill, we do not expect you to betray your comrades, but we do expect you to come up with some positive proof of your identity.' The airman remained silent, his eyes focusing on something at infinity, almost as if his inquisitors were not there. 'Gestapo Ernst' once again moved to the police chiefs side and whispered in his ear before returning to his strategic position in front of the window. The policeman opened the top left hand drawer of his desk and took out some strips of aluminium foil that were painted black on one side. He dropped them on his desk. We will give you another chance to prove yourself, Flight Sergeant,' he said, 'our countryside is scattered with these,' he indicated the foil strips that Ray had immediately recognised as Window. 'And dairy cows have eaten some and become very sick. We believe that our children will also find these strips and will also eat them and then die.' he continued. 'But while we believe that the Royal Air Force may wish to poison our cows, we don't really believe that they wish to poison our children also. Prove it, tell us what these strips are for.'

Ray well knew what the strips were for, he was equally sure that the Germans also knew what they were for, Bomber Command had been dropping the stuff since Hamburg, five weeks ago and he was damned if he was going to tell them. 'I was navigating the aircraft and have nothing to do with that stuff.' he replied.

'Come on,' said the police chief, 'it's all over the countryside, you must know about it.'

'According to the Geneva Convention,' said Ray, 'you only need to know my name, rank and number, and I have already given them.'

'This isn't Geneva,' countered the policeman 'and I am not bound by any convention.' Then more gently he said, 'Come now, for humanitarian reasons, tell us what it is.' Ray remained silent, mainly because he couldn't think of anything suitable to say. 'Ernst' once again crossed the room to whisper in the police chief's ear and then left the room. The policeman helped himself to another cigarette from the small glass on his desk. He made a great play of lighting it before leaning back in his chair. He looked at Ray and, almost confidentially, said 'You know, Flight Sergeant Edghill, it is difficult for us to know who is a genuine member of the RAF. We do not want to ask anyone to betray their country, so we always ask for some small humanitarian act to demonstrate goodwill. This seems very reasonable to me and, I hope, to you too. We will give you another chance, so please co-operate this time.' The airman remained sullenly silent, wondering what else these Nazi bastards were going to dream up. He was feeling very vulnerable, fearful, tired and hungry. It was now 11.15 hours and he'd had very little useful sleep for almost thirty hours, nothing to eat or drink for eighteen hours and now, not even a smoke since his meeting with the SS.

The police chief ignored the airman and started to look at his files again. It was almost 11.45 when the telephone rang. After a short conversation in German, the policeman put down the handset, got up from his desk and walked over to the door that he opened to call in an armed guard. He issued orders to the guard and then turned to Ray.

`Flight Sergeant Edghill,' he said, 'this guard has orders to shoot you if you move. Don't do anything silly, I won't be long.' With that, he went out, leaving the office door open.

True to his word, the police chief returned within five minutes, '*Komm!*' he shouted. Ray got up and turned around, noticing as he did so his guard standing by the door with his Schmeisser at the ready. Ray walked quietly to the door and followed the senior policeman to the top of the stairs where two more guards held him back until the police chief had reached the bottom. He was then pushed and jostled down the staircase as his guards tried to stay either side of him on a staircase barely wide enough for two people. Ray Edghill had just about had enough. He deliberately walked with his left foot as far left and his right foot as far right as he possibly could, quite happily putting up with the knocks and shouts of 'Raus!' that he received. Finally they came to a courtyard where the police chief was waiting for them. They walked through an archway into the street and Ray was ushered into a waiting Mercedes car with the police chief. There was a truck load of armed policemen immediately behind the car and two armed motorcyclists at the front and rear of the small convoy. Ray was just thinking how spacious and comfortable the back of the Mercedes was when the rear door nearest him opened and `Gestapo Ernst' climbed in, sandwiching Ray between him and the senior policeman.

The Pendulum and the Scythe

The convoy moved off and Ray, wondering where he was being taken now, kept a look out for bomb damage but he saw none. He came to the conclusion that the route had been specifically selected to avoid him seeing any of the RAF's handiwork. They eventually stopped by a block of flats adjacent to a small field and the airman was ordered out of the car. The armed guards never relaxed their vigilance for a moment as Ray was led into the field. Wondering whether or not he'd been brought here to be shot, although he'd heard that sort of thing usually happened out in deserted countryside, he was very concerned at how deathly quiet the whole area was and, apart from his guards, there wasn't a soul to be seen. Then he noticed a cigar shaped object sticking out of the ground in the centre of the field and the penny dropped. The Nazis obviously expected him to do something about this unexploded bomb!

The police chief lit another cigarette and, blowing the smoke in Ray's direction, said 'We have had to evacuate these buildings because of that bomb. The occupants are either very young or very old and have nothing to do with the war. So you see, Flight Sergeant Edghill, we are not asking you to save a factory or a gun position, but we ask you to defuse that bomb for humanitarian reasons and let the people return to their homes.' Ray's heart sank, he knew as much about defusing unexploded bombs as he did about tap-dancing. The police chief continued, 'For humanitarian reasons, Flight Sergeant Edghill, we asked to identify some strips of material and you refused. Now, for humanitarian reasons, you are ordered to defuse that bomb.' Ray knew exactly what he'd like to do to these Nazis with their 'humanitarian reasons', but this was neither the time nor the place. He took a deep breath, 'I was navigating my aircraft.' He said, 'I am not an armourer.' Gestapo Ernst made his presence felt. 'You vill defuze der bomb!' he said.

The police chief took a packet of cigarettes out of his pocket and offered one to Ray, 'Have a cigarette, Flight Sergeant Edghill.'

'No.' said Ray taking a few steps towards the bomb. Then he realised that all he was doing was cutting off his nose to spite his face. There was nothing he wanted more at that moment than a cigarette and, the way things were looking, it could well be his last. He retraced his steps, 'Yes I will.' he said, taking one out of the proffered packet. The senior policeman gave him a light and, despite his predicament, Ray really savoured that first taste of a cigarette for almost twelve hours. He inhaled deeply and deliberately blew the smoke into the weasel face of 'Gestapo Ernst'. He turned about and sauntered as casually as he could towards the bomb, stopping briefly a few yards from it before walking all around it very warily, viewing it from all sides, he wondered if it was a delayed action bomb or just a dud and then tried to work out the odds of it exploding within the next half hour or so if it was a delayed action type. This mental exercise was more in the way of a means to contain his fear than any real interest in the actual odds involved. He did not possess sufficient knowledge of the subject on which to base his calculations accurately. He took another long taste of his cigarette and decided his chances of survival were probably something like 15,000 to 1 and considerably less if the bloody bomb was fitted with an anti-handling trembler type fuse. Concluding that death was not too far away, Ray decided that if he was going, he'd at least be comfortable before he went. He sat down on the ground with his back to the bomb, making sure that his back wasn't actually in contact with it, just in case the fuse was a little too sensitive. He tried to look as casual as possible and continued to smoke his cigarette, observing as he did so that the hedgerows around the field seemed to be full of armed guards intently watching his every move.

Because of his uniform, the police chief was clearly visible but 'Gestapo Ernst's' mackintosh blended well with the hedgerows and it took Ray a minute or so to locate him. The irony of his situation did not escape him, but the thought of an RAF Flight Sergeant being blown into thousands of tiny pieces by an RAF bomb was one that he kept pushing to the back of his mind. Ray finished his cigarette and was wondering how long his captors intended to have him sit by this bomb, when he noticed some movement at the edge of the field. He saw the police chief cup his hands around his mouth as if to shout but no sound reached his ears. He continued to watch the senior policeman and saw him make an indication with his arm that looked to Ray as if he was being beckoned. Ray did not hang about. He got to his feet and ran towards the police chief but, after covering a few yards, he decided that a reasonably fast walk might be better. He didn't wish to show his captors the relief he felt at being allowed out of the immediate vicinity of that bloody bomb.

As he approached the police chief, the man once again took out his cigarettes and Ray hoped he might be the recipient of another one. It was not to be, all that was offered was a sharp, 'You follow,' he said, pointing to where 'Gestapo Ernst had started to walk slowly towards the block of flats. Ray followed the uniform and the mackintosh past the flats and back to the roadway. The senior policeman and the Gestapo agent stood to one side, allowing the armed guards to push the airman into the road and force him to turn right towards the Mercedes. Ray was surprised to see that in between him and the black saloon car, the left hand side of the road was now lined with people two and three deep in places, waiting, he thought, to be allowed to re-occupy their flats. Any concern he may have felt for these unfortunates suddenly turned to fear as they started to stone him. He walked slowly and deliberately in the middle of the road, taking most of the missiles on his fairly well padded torso, but one stone found a more sensitive mark - his face. He put his hand up to his left cheek bone and felt a trickle of blood. Angrily he turned to look directly at the stone throwers and made eye-to-eye contact with a short German man blatantly too old for military service. They stared at one another for a moment and then the German bowed his head in obvious shame. The stone throwing ceased.

Ray squared his shoulders and, looking straight ahead, marched smartly to the Mercedes. Looking back he saw that his guards were still following him but that Gestapo Ernst and the police chief were still by the flats. Ray rapped on the driver's window of the Mercedes and, to his great surprise, the guard leapt out of the car and saluted before opening the rear door for Ray to climb in. The driver returned to his seat, spoke briefly to the second guard in the front passenger seat, before driving off, accompanied by the motorcycle escort and returning to Police HQ where he was again bundled into the police chief's office.

Flight Sergeant Edghill was tired, painfully tired. He was also hungry, thirsty and very brassed off. His legs ached, his feet ached, his cheek was sore and his mind was dulled, so when the police chief asked him to sit down he readily complied. 'Are you tired?' asked the policeman. 'I'm alright,' Ray replied tersely.

'We Germans' continued the policeman, 'have had a long and tiring time. We don't like the war but we have our duty to do. We are a proud race and mean to stay so.' Ray did not respond, mainly because he couldn't think of anything appropriate to say. The captor and prisoner sat in silence for several minutes before a knock on the door disturbed their reverie. Before the policeman could say Komm; a uniformed figure, complete with steel helmet, entered the office. The man was unshaven and grimy and, while he conversed easily with the police chief, Ray came to the conclusion that the smoke stained German was probably the Fire Chief. At least he discovered that the police chief's Christian name was 'Hans'. Having finished their conversation, Ray's supposition was confirmed when the newcomer turned to the Flight Sergeant and said in halting English,

'Ve haff all fires under control now.' His eyes were tired but surprisingly cheerful. He had the look of a man who was pleased at having completed a hard task satisfactorily. He nodded to the police chief and then, as he turned to leave, said to Ray 'Vell, I am going to have something to eat and then off to bed.' He nodded to the prisoner and left the office.

The thought of something to eat renewed Ray Edghill's hunger pangs. He'd had nothing to eat or drink for 24 hours now. As if Hans could read his mind, he asked 'Would you like some soup?' Ray replied quickly and decisively, 'Yes' he said. The policeman walked to the hatch in the office wall and opened it. He spoke rapidly in German but Ray thought he recognised the word 'Suppe.' Hans returned to his desk and started to speak as if confiding to a close friend. 'For you the war is over but for me and the fire brigade there will be more work than ever. We have to put up with almost nightly raids but we have fewer and fewer men. There will be people to be re-housed, repairs to be made and lists of missing persons to be compiled, all in addition to our normal work. Ray looked at him blankly, he couldn't think of anything but the soup. Again they lapsed into silence and it was a relief when the door opened and a uniformed policeman brought in a steaming hot bowl of soup and a spoon. Ray took the offered bowl and proceeded to shovel spoonful after spoonful into his dry mouth and empty stomach. He knew the police chief was watching him but he couldn't care less. Gradually, as the hunger pangs began to subside, Ray slowed the rate at which his spoon was moving. 'Good?' enquired Hans, 'Very good,' came the reply.

Hans opened one of his desk drawers and extracted a key. He got up, walked over to the door, opened it and looked out along the corridor. He closed and locked the door as quietly as possible and then moved across to the hatch in the wall. He opened this and looked through it and then closed it and placed a small beam across it so it could not possibly be opened from the outside. He returned to his seat, threw the keys on the desk and sat down.

'We have other masters you know' he said conspiratorially. Ray was puzzled, 'That soup was the best I've ever tasted,' he replied. 'I'm glad you liked it,' said Hans. He leaned forward over his desk and continued in a whisper. 'Many senior German officials know that we cannot win this war. In September 1940 we had subdued all of Europe. Three years later we have difficulties with Italy, the Russians are getting closer to the Reich and the RAF attacks get more severe.' He paused and looked intently at the Flight Sergeant. 'The trouble is, we do not know how to stop this war.' He paused again. 'You realise' he hissed, 'that if you breathe a word of this to anyone I shall deny ever having this conversation? And what is more, I'll hand you over to our other masters as a spy!'

Ray remained silent. He was shocked by the police chief's revelations. He'd been shot down, threatened three times with shooting by the SS, made to sit next to an unexploded bomb and then stoned. Now what the hell was happening?

`Well?' he said.

`Well,' replied the chief, 'I want you to do me a favour.'

`What sort of a favour?' asked Ray, frantically trying to think what sort of favour he could possibly do for Munich's senior police officer. Hans leaned forward again. 'I want you, after the war, to tell the British Authorities that I treated you well' he whispered. Ray couldn't believe that his ears had actually heard what his brain was registering but, thinking quickly he said, 'I think there should be some very positive action for me to report to the authorities.'

`Such as?' queried the policeman.

`Well,' suggested Ray, 'You could find some reason for taking me out into the country and there I could escape.'

`No' replied Hans. 'If the civilian population caught you they would kill you, before I could get there to protect you,' he added with a grin, 'and if the Gestapo found you, you would tell them about me.'

`No I wouldn't,' countered Ray.

`Oh yes you would. You certainly would,' he continued. Their methods are out of this world. Forget we have had this conversation. Forget it.' Hans got up, walked to the door key in hand and unlocked it. He turned back to the hatch but paused beside Ray before he got there.

Ray Edghill visiting the graves of his crew at Durnbach Cemetery, Bavaria, in 1993.

'Remember,' said Hans[40], 'if you breathe a word of this to anyone.......' The sentence remained unfinished as he drew the index finger of his right hand quickly across his throat. Hans continued to the hatch, removed the beam, opened the hatch and shouted through the aperture to someone on the other side. Ray had no idea what was said but heard the word 'Luftwaffe'. A voice from the other room answered `Jawohl' and Ray was quickly bundled out of the police chief's office, down the stairs, right out of the building and into the custody of the Luftwaffe.

His two new guards ordered him into the sidecar of a motorcycle combination and thankfully Ray Edghill complied. He slouched down into the sidecar and tried to make himself comfortable and then looked at his watch. It was 15.30 hours, more than 14 hours since he'd first snagged his parachute on that chimney. The motorbike and sidecar moved off, Flight Sergeant Edghill laid his head back into the corner of the seat back and closed his eyes. At least now he was a prisoner of the Luftwaffe, he might live to see the end of the war.

---

[40] *The names of Ray Edghill's German captors, as they appear in the latter pages of this chapter have been changed.*

Chapter Eight

1943: Not Dim...

Louis Wooldridge[41] was born in June 1921 in the small town of Stalybridge, seven miles east of Manchester. He became 'air-minded' in the early thirties when Winifred Brown (a contemporary of Amy Johnson) landed in a field near his home as a promotional stunt for the film What Price Glory?, a story of First World War aviators. After leaving school, Louis became an apprentice engineer with the firm of Henry Simon & Sons in Stockport but, in July 1939 and one month after his eighteenth birthday, he joined the Royal Air Force as a flight rigger/ part-time air gunner. In company with other new recruits from the Manchester area, he travelled by train to RAF West Drayton where he received his service number - 649746 -and his full kit. After a few days at West Drayton he, along with approximately another two hundred recruits, were posted to RAF Finningley for initial recruit training.

Upon the outbreak of war all the recruits were hastily posted to their respective trade training camps. All, that is, except for 649746 AC2 Wooldridge L.P. and his small group of U/T (Under Training) flight riggers who were temporarily retained at Finningley to await the commencement of their course. While still at Finningley they were put to work helping the ground personnel of 7 Squadron (Ansons) and 76 Squadron (Hampdens), both of which were part of the 13 Group Pool (Training) Squadrons belonging to 6 Group (See Chapter 1). Their duties included general assistance with refuelling, loading bombs and carrying out guard duties on the airfield. After a week of this Louis and his fellow trainees were finally

---

[41] No known relation to Squadron Leader John 'Dim' Wooldridge who was 'B' Flight Commander on 106 Squadron (5 Group at Syerston) whilst Wing Commander Guy Gibson was CO in 1942, prior to Gibson being appointed to form 617 Squadron, just as he completed his tour with 106. John Wooldridge then went to the Tri-Service Petroleum Warfare Dept as a Wing Commander where he helped to develop FIDO and PLUTO (PipeLine Under The Ocean). An accomplished pianist and composer (he had been a pupil of Sibelius), he also wrote the script and musical score for the Dirk Bogarde / Dinah Sheridan film Appointment in London. Louis Wooldridge does, however, play the piano.

posted to No.5 School of Technical Training (5S of TT) at RAF Locking, near Weston-Super-Mare, Somerset.

At Locking they learned that the peace-time course duration of nine months had been cut to six months. The syllabus hadn't been reduced, just the time in which the recruits had to assimilate the knowledge. The course's final exam, in March 1940 saw Louis gain a mark of 62% and promotion to the dizzy height of AC1 (had he managed another 18%, he would have been promoted to Leading Aircraftman - LAC) and a posting along with another six of his fellow course members (all 'Hostilities Only' recruits), to No.15 FTS at RAF Lossiemouth, Scotland.

After thirty-six hours of travelling, Louis and his course mates arrived at Lossiemouth to find that 15 FTS had moved down south a week before they'd arrived. Not having a clue what to do with the new arrivals, someone in Station Headquarters (SHQ) finally got up the nerve to ring RAF Records Office at Gloucester. Instructions were duly received that the seven men were to remain at Lossiemouth to await the arrival of 46 M.U. (Maintenance Unit) in a few weeks time. It did not take long for the Station Warrant Officer (SWO) to learn that amongst this merry band of new arrivals there was a 'regular' airman of no fixed employ who was obviously too good to waste on such mundane things as guard duties and fire pickets, which was what Louis' six friends found themselves well and truly lumbered with.

It must have warmed the cockles of the old SWO's heart to find a real, responsible 'regular' airman with nothing in particular to do, and he had just the very job for the lad! AC1 Wooldridge soon found himself seconded to airfield duties as assistant to the Duty Pilot, a Sergeant Brown, who was based at the Airfield Watch Office (forerunner of Flying Control). Louis was detailed as 'Airman of the Watch' on a twenty-four hours on/twenty-four hours off shift rota with one other airman. The Watch Office comprised two wooden huts situated on the edge of the grass airfield immediately in front of the middle of three 'C' type hangars. The huts were enclosed by two rows of timber posts, one foot apart, in between which earth had been piled and packed down. This barrier was three feet high in front of the Watch Office window on the airfield side, but six feet high everywhere else. In front of the Watch Office were three sandbagged gun emplacements, each containing one 1916-vintage Vickers machine-gun with 600 rounds of ammunition.

Thus eighteen year old Louis Wooldridge found himself in charge of RAF Lossiemouth's flying duties between the hours of 17.00 hours and 09.00 hours every other night. His night duties consisted mainly of answering two telephones, one internal and the other for calls from other RAF stations. He had frequent calls from operational bomber squadrons, asking if any of their overdue aircraft had landed there.

Sometime in late May/early June, No.20 OTU arrived at Lossiemouth under the temporary command of New Zealander Squadron Leader G. T. Jarman[42] This was followed a few weeks later by Louis' new unit, 46 MU and he joined them as soon as they'd settled in. Lossiemouth was bombed by Heinkel He 111s on 26th October and shortly after this there appeared in Station Routine Orders (SROs) a request for ground crew volunteers for aircrew. Louis Wooldridge and several other tradesmen applied forthwith, but after undergoing various aptitude tests, interviews and medicals, they were informed, by the Unit Test Pilot, that all their applications had been turned down because the MU considered them to be too valuable in their current trades. In December 1940 Louis Wooldridge was promoted to Leading Aircraftsman and the next set of SROs after this contained a request for volunteers for service in the Middle East where, so the grapevine said, there was a severe shortage of aircrew and all applications were looked upon favourably. '746 Leading Aircraftsman Wooldridge again volunteered, this time with more success and, in March 1941, he found himself on embarkation leave, at which time he received first-hand experience of the Blitzes on Manchester, Liverpool and Glasgow.

In due course, Louis embarked on HMT Cape Town Castle bound for Singapore (so much for volunteering for the Middle East!) and after avoiding the Bismarck versus Hood encounter, he arrived there in early August 1941 after a two-month journey. From Singapore harbour he was transported to RAF Kallang (part of Singapore civil airport) to join 243 Squadron operating Brewster Buffalo fighter aircraft, where he was detailed to help service the aircraft (WP-B) of the 'A' Flight Commander, Flight Lieutenant Tim Vigors, an ex-Battle of Britain Spitfire 'ace'.

---

[42] *This officer keeps appearing! See Chapters 3, 5 and 6.*

Not too long after his arrival at Kallang there appeared in SROs yet another invitation for ground crew to apply for transfer to aircrew. Once again, Louis Wooldridge applied. Things went much better this time and after the usual medicals, aptitude tests, etc., he ended up at an interview with the AOC Malaya, Air Vice-Marshal Pulford. Young Leading Aircraftsman Wooldridge obviously made a favourable impression, for two weeks later he was advised of an impending posting to Southern Rhodesia for aircrew training. This posting finally took place in early December 1941, when he boarded a 1920-vintage, former Holland-to-Dutch East Indies liner called the SS Johan De Witt, which took him non-stop to Durban in South Africa where he arrived in late December 1941. The Japanese captured Singapore on 15th February.

The SS Johan De Witt was forced to anchor off Durban for a week - the South Africans weren't expecting them - before she was finally allowed into harbour to disembark her passengers. The following day Louis and his fellow aircrew trainees boarded a train and, three days later, arrived at Bulawayo, Southern Rhodesia. From here they were taken by transport to the Initial Training Wing (ITW) at RAF Hillside. 649746 Leading Air-craftsman Wooldridge L.P. was at long last to commence training for aircrew, as an air gunner.

The air gunners' ground course lasted four months, after which they moved to RAF Moffat, near Gwelo, for flying training. At the beginning of May 1942, on his successful completion of this course, Louis Wooldridge was awarded his `AG' brevet and sergeant's chevrons. This was followed by another three-day train journey to Cape Town where Louis and the other new air gunners boarded the Bergensfjord (previously a Norwegian trans-Atlantic liner), which arrived at the King George V dock in Glasgow on 7th June 1942. From here they went by train to the Aircrew Reception Centre in Bournemouth where, after tests for night vision, they were sent on seven days disembarkation leave.

On his return from leave, Louis was posted to RAF Castle Kennedy near Stranraer where he flew in Blackburn Bothas with Polish pilots until August 1942. From Castle Kennedy he was posted to 20 OTU at Lossiemouth, the station he had left almost 18 months previously. Here he renewed acquaintances with many of his old friends and was even taken for a trip in a Beaufighter by the Unit Test Pilot who had refused his initial application for aircrew.

The Pendulum and the Scythe

The crewing-up procedure took place on the main parade ground. The gathered aircrew were lined up, given a welcoming `chat' by the CO and left to sort themselves into crews. Louis' first crew lasted just one week, for while his pilot could fly a Wellington without any problems, he had some trouble landing it. Carrying out circuits and bumps one day, Louis was getting a real jolting in the rear turret on every heavy landing. After about the fifth landing, a particularly heavy one, Louis noted that he seemed nearer the ground than normal and that the rear underside of the tail was ploughing up the grass - the tail wheel and its yoke had given up and parted company with the airframe. Louis promptly appraised his skipper and instructor of this disconcerting fact and the rest of the exercise was cancelled. The pilot was posted to fighters and the crew was disbanded.

A few days later, one of the rear gunners became very ill and looked like being hospitalised for quite a while, so Sergeant Wooldridge was 'invited' to join this man's crew as a replacement. The pilot, Sergeant Johnston, was a Glaswegian; Yorkshireman James 'Ginger' Watson was the bomb aimer; Edwards, the navigator came from London and Baron, the wireless operator was from Lancashire. All were sergeants. The crew completed the OTU course and went on leave but Louis and five other gunners were held back because they had not completed a final round of air-to-sea firing. They were not happy! They'd actually cleared the station and had been given their leave passes but they still had to stay to complete this exercise. After three days of hanging around waiting for a pilot and a serviceable aircraft, the six gunners decided enough was enough and cleared off on leave regardless. They got as far as Aberdeen station where they were met by an army of RAF policemen who politely, but firmly, escorted them back from whence they'd come.

The next morning the six wayward air gunners were on the carpet in front of the CFI's desk. As usual, it was the 'regular airman' Sergeant Wooldridge, at whom the Squadron Leader's steely gaze and questions were directed. 'What,' he demanded to know, 'do you think you were playing at?' Proceeding on leave, Sir.' replied Louis. 'Leave?' said the Squadron Leader, 'Leave?! Leave is a privilege and is countermanded by direct orders. You are personnel of this OTU and are subject to the orders issued by me.' Summing up all he'd learned from the various 'barrack room lawyers' he'd met in his 3 years in the service, Louis very politely pointed out that they were no longer personnel of 20 OTU, having cleared the station and collected their leave passes before being ordered to remain behind for the air-to-sea firing exercise and that he himself now belonged to 1658 HCU to

Louis Wooldridge by the rear turret of HR838, 51 Sqn. Note the 'Monica' aerial below the turret. (Louis Wooldridge)

which he was to report with his crew after his leave. The Squadron Leader seemed to see Louis' point and appeared to calm down somewhat, so the sergeant took full advantage. 'Sir, we did not complain when we were held back for this exercise, but we've been kept hanging around for three days now without any opportunity to carry it out.' The CFI pondered Louis's statement for a short while and then said 'Very well, I can see that you've been messed about. An aircraft will be made available immediately and you will carry out your firing exercise and then you can proceed on leave - but don't take the law into your own hands again. Dismissed!' The six sergeants were marched out of the CFI's office. True to his word, a Wellington (and a pilot) were made available within the hour, the sextet of sergeants completed their final firing exercise and scuttled off on leave straight after lunch.

After enjoying only three days leave instead of the seven he should have had, Louis Wooldridge reported to 1658 HCU at Riccall where the crew successfully converted onto the Halifax. On the night of 17/18th November, Louis' pilot, Sergeant Johnston undertook a 'second dickie' experience trip to drop leaflets over Strasbourg. The Halifax in which he was flying was the only aircraft lost on this night. Once again, Louis found himself as part of a disbanded crew but not many days had passed before he joined the crew of Sergeant Claude Wilson as a mid-upper gunner. Wilson's crew comprised Peter Finnett (navigator); Raymond (Rube) Airey (bomb aimer); another regular airman 'Ginger' Anger (flight engineer) and Don Hall (wireless operator). Louis was in the mid-upper turret and Les Sharp in the rear turret. Once again, all the crew were sergeants. Raymond (Rube) Airey, like Louis, came from the Manchester area; their skipper originated in Dover and the rest of the crew were all Londoners. They completed their HCU course on New Year's Day 1943 and were posted to 51 Squadron at Snaith where they arrived on 4th January.

The first operation as a crew took place on Sunday, 7th February 1943. They were detailed to fly Halifax B.Mk.II Serial No DT513, MH-N and their target was Lorient. They were one of nine aircraft from 51 Squadron as part of a total force of 323 aircraft despatched to bomb the U-boat bases in this unfortunate French port. PFF's marking went well and the two main force waves produced a devastating attack. Claude Wilson took `N-Nuts' over the port at 22,000 feet and Rube Airey released their eight 500 lbs GP bombs on target, despite a smoke haze. While in the target area they observed a Wellington shot down and saw three parachutes open. This was quite a gentle introduction to operations, marked only by a slight but understandable miscalculation on landing. Snaith and Burn are only five miles apart, as the crow (or the Halifax) flies, and their circuits overlap. It was therefore not difficult for an inexperienced crew returning from their very first operational sortie to find that they had accidentally landed at Burn. They did a quick taxi around the perimeter track, took off and landed five miles further south-southeast. It was a very red faced crew who faced the Intelligence Officer for debrief.

Exactly one week later, on Sunday, 14th February (Valentine's Day!), they attended briefing to learn that their second trip was also to be their first to Germany. The target was Cologne. The crew was allocated Halifax MH-U, known on the squadron as the 'Cops' kite' because its serial number W1212 was interpreted as an abbreviation of Whitehall 1212, at the time the well-known telephone number for Scotland Yard. `U-Uncle' was one of nine Halifaxes of 51 Squadron that helped to make up a total force of 243 aircraft and Claude Wilson lifted the Halifax into the air at 18.19 hours. Arriving over Cologne to find 10/10ths cloud, Rube Airey aligned his sights with the PFF's sky markers that had been dropped using H2S and released their 6x1000lbs GP bombs from 18,000 feet. They returned safely to Snaith at 23.09 hours. Total force losses were 9 aircraft (3.7%).

It was back to Lorient on Tuesday, 16th February with an early evening take off, again in the 'Cops kite'. The squadron contributed 12 Halifaxes to the night's total force of 377 aircraft that were to carry out the last major raid of the series against these U-boat pens. At least 363 aircraft including 51 Squadron's `U-Uncle' dropped mainly incendiary loads in clear visibility, The Command had flown 1,853 sorties in eight raids in response to direct instructions from Air Ministry (but at the specific request of the Royal Navy), despite Butch Harris pointing out the futility of bombing U-boat pens covered by 20 odd feet of reinforced concrete. During these eight raids, 1,675 aircraft claimed to have bombed the target, dropping almost 4,000 tons of bombs. Only 24 aircraft (1.3%) failed to return from these attacks but Lorient was now almost completely ruined and deserted - apart from the U-boats and their crews still lying safely in their reinforced funk-holes.

Claude Wilson and crew in W1212 landed back at Snaith at one minute after midnight to find that sixty 4lbs incendiaries had hung up in their bomb bay. Two nights later (18th February), the crew were allocated DT580 `MH-Z' for a trip to Wilhelmshaven as one of 195 aircraft. 'Z-Zebra' was a B. Mk II Series 1 (special) with the Tollerton nose fairing and no mid-upper turret, so Louis Wooldridge spent the trip as 'spare bod,' helping out around the nose section. Rube Airey was sick for this trip, his place being taken by Flight Sergeant Richards, who released their three 1,000lbs GP bombs, 810 x 4lbs and 24 x 30lbs incendiaries from 19,000 feet onto the PFF markers. Louis clearly remembers standing next to Flight Sergeant Richards, drinking coffee as they returned over the North Sea, with the moonlight making the sea below look silvery and cold.

The following night, Wilhelmshaven was again the target and again they had 'Z-Zebra'. This time Les Sharpe was 'spare bod' and Louis occupied the rear turret. As on the previous night, the PFF flares went down in the wrong place and the main force unleashed its load to the north of the town. After the raid it was discovered that the Pathfinders had been issued with out of date maps that did not show recent town developments and this caused a general updating of all maps.

It was almost a week before Claude and his crew were next on the ops list on Thursday 25th February. The target was Nuremberg and they were to fly in DT526, 'V-Victor' as part of a 337 aircraft strong force despatched in poor weather conditions. 'V-Victor' was airborne at 18.25 hours but about thirty-five miles north-west of Ramsgate severe icing caused their airspeed indicator to cease functioning and they jettisoned their bomb-load into the North Sea and returned to base. They were allocated 'V-Victor' again the following night, when the squadron was to send eleven Halifaxes as part of a 427 aircraft attack on Cologne. They took off at 19.00 hours and had as uneventful a trip as one could hope for, with Rube Airey releasing their bombload on to the PFF markers from 17,000 feet.

Having destroyed Lorient but not its U-boat pens, and still against the advice of Butch Harris, Bomber Command was now instructed to start attacking the second French U-boat base on the Navy's list. So, on Sunday 28th February, the Command despatched 437 aircraft, of which fifteen were from 51 Squadron, to attack St. Nazaire. Claude Wilson and his crew were once again flying 'V-Victor' and, without the severe icing problems encountered on their last trip, had no trouble in carrying out the briefed operation. Rube Airey released their bomb load through haze onto the PFF markers from 14,500 feet after having checked their position with a pinpoint on the river. As they left the target many fires were raging and these could be seen for at least fifty miles of the journey home. Widespread destruction was caused and 60% of St Nazaire was flattened.

Checking the Operations List on the morning of Wednesday 3rd March, Claude Wilson was annoyed to find that his crew was on operations but that Louis Wooldridge was not included, his place having been taken by a Sergeant Tucker. Claude went to see his Flight Commander and the Squadron Gunnery Leader, but was unable to get Louis reinstated. They had decided to give one of the squadron's spare gunners the chance of an operation and that was the end of the discussion. Louis had the night off while the rest of his crew went to Hamburg; fortunately they returned safely.

On Friday 5th March, in DT614, MH-H, they took part in the opening raid of the Battle of the Ruhr, being one of 442 aircraft despatched to Essen. This was also the night on which the Command flew its 100,000 sortie of the war. The only setback to this raid was that 56 aircraft (almost 13%) turned back early because of technical defects and other causes. Three of these early returns were from the eight Oboe Mosquitoes upon which the success of this raid depended. The five remaining Mosquitoes did, however, open the attack on time and marked the centre of Essen perfectly. All the PFF's marking was 'blind' so the industrial haze that normally protected Essen from accurate bombing did not interfere with the accuracy of this attack. The main force bombed in three waves, with Halifaxes in the first, Wellingtons and Stirlings in the second and Lancasters in the third. Two-thirds of the bomb tonnage was incendiary and one third of the HE bombs had long delay fuses. The attack lasted for forty minutes and 362 aircraft claimed to have bombed the main target. Later reconnaissance photographs showed 160 acres of destruction, with 53 separate buildings within the Krupps works hit by bombs.

The Pendulum and the Scythe

It was back to Nuremberg on Monday 8th March. During the afternoon, Claude Wilson and his crew carried out an air test on BB240, MH-X, because their regular aircraft, 'V-Victor' had a ropey engine. Like 'Z-Zebra', (DT580) flown previously, 'X-X-ray' was a B.MKII Series I (Special) with a Tollerton nose fairing and no mid-upper turret[43]. Because of this, Louis Wooldridge occupied the second pilot's seat. Just before 8 pm he followed Claude's right hand on the throttles with his left as, with the engines at 2,650 rpm and the propellers in fine pitch, the Halifax moved off down the runway.

At 120 mph Claude eased the heavily laden aircraft into the air and commenced his climb. When they were safely airborne and climbing gradually, Claude brought the flaps up and retracted the undercarriage and then told Louis he could let go of the throttles. Wilson changed the props to coarse pitch and, adjusting the throttles to climbing power, circled Snaith while they gained height, before setting off for the target.

On reaching the English coast at 10,000 feet, they switched on their oxygen, while the aircraft's navigation lights and IFF were switched off. The French coast was crossed to the usual welcome from the coastal Flak batteries before they entered the dark sky above the totally blacked out 'Fortress Europe' in front of them. Not long after crossing the French coast, the protective mantle of darkness was suddenly stolen from them as the moon broke through the clouds above. Looking around from his right hand seat, Louis was astonished to see many other aircraft around them in the night sky. Shortly after the moon revealed the bomber force in all its naked glory, 'Ginger' Anger – the Flight Engineer - told his skipper that he was going aft to the rest position to transfer the fuel supply to the engines from the main fuel tanks in the wings to the two hundred gallons in the auxiliary tank in the bomb bay, so as to empty this vulnerable tank before reaching the target.

About two minutes later just as Ginger switched the fuel feed, all four engines started to race and roar, whereupon the flight engineer immediately switched back to the wing tanks. Keeping his skipper advised of his actions, Ginger checked all the fuel pipes before again switching to the auxiliary fuel tank. Again the engines raced and roared and again Ginger quickly switched back to the main tanks. Checking first with Claude, Louis left the cockpit and went down the fuselage to see if he could help Ginger. The FE showed the mid-upper gunner how to switch the fuel tank feed and then returned to

---

[43] *Known on the squadron as a B.Mk.II-Z.*

his monitoring panel, just behind the pilot. When he was in position, Ginger told Louis to switch tanks. This Louis did and, yet again the engines started to race, Louis immediately switched back to the main tanks but Ginger had had time to note that while the auxiliary tank was switched on, the fuel gauge was reading empty. Despite the Form 700 (aircraft's servicing record book) showing that the auxiliary tank had been filled with 200 gallons of Avgas the bloody thing was empty! Ginger advised his skipper of this unpleasant fact as Louis made his way back to the cockpit. Claude Wilson's immediate concern was exactly how much fuel did they have? Was there enough to get them to Nuremberg and home again or should they abort the mission and turn for home? None of them wanted to abort the mission - Nuremberg was their intended target when they'd 'boomeranged' with an unserviceable airspeed indicator in February.

Ginger got down to some serious mathematics. Within a few minutes he advised Claude that, if they reduced speed to their most economic cruise, they would just have enough to reach the target and get back to a base in the southeast of England with a very small reserve. Snaith was out of the question unless they about-turned now. Claude Wilson put the alternatives to his crew, pointing out that they would be within their rights to abandon the sortie without any recriminations. He also told them that continuing at a reduced speed would certainly mean a late run over the target and probably a solo run at that. All six members of Claude Wilson's crew voted to continue the operation.

They arrived over the target just as the last of the main force were leaving the area but managed to evade the probing searchlights and their accompanying Flak barrage. Claude Wilson held the Halifax steady at 17,000 feet while Rube Airey released their single 1000lbs GP bomb and all their 4lb and 30lb incendiaries onto what remained of the PFF markers. The slow journey home was nerve-racking, especially for Louis Wool-dridge who was sorely missing the reassurance of the two Brownings in his mid-upper turret. All he could do was to keep his eyes peeled from the second pilot's seat, which had nothing like the all-round view he was used to. Their guardian angel was working overtime however and, despite lagging well behind the main force, they eventually reached the Kent coast in safety, switching on their IFF and navigation lights as they approached.

The first airfield they came to was West Malling, a nightfighter base, and Claude transmitted a Darkie call to advise Flying Control that they had a problem. West Mailing replied immediately with 'Pancake X-Xray' and Claude Wilson eased the Halifax into the circuit. He carried out a perfect three-point landing at 03.45 hours, after which he taxied around the perimeter track and parked the aircraft near Flying Control. It turned out that they were not the only heavy bomber at West Malling. Almost a whole squadron of Halifaxes had already landed, having been diverted from their base because of bad weather. They were debriefed by the Station Intelligence Officer who promised to let Snaith know that they'd landed safely and then proceeded to the mess for an early breakfast, followed by a couple of hours sleep in borrowed beds. At about 10.30 hours Claude Wilson rounded up his crew and they made their way back to X-Xray', where the ground crew informed them that they had had less than thirty minutes petrol left in their tanks when they landed. They certainly would not have made it back to Yorkshire. After some of 29 Squadron's nightfighter crews had had a good look at the Halifax, Claude and the lads climbed aboard, started the engines and taxied out to the end of the runway. With a final wave of thanks to all at West Mailing, they took off to fly back to Snaith.

Some sixty-five minutes later, as they over flew their home airfield prior to landing, they could see all the other squadron aircraft parked in their respective dispersals and that their own dispersal lay empty awaiting their return. Claude called for permission to land and, after some delay, this was given, although Flying Control sounded as if it was in some turmoil. As they circled the airfield prior to landing, the crew gradually became aware of great activity on the ground below. Numerous faces were gazing skywards at `X-Xray' and their Flight Commander's car was racing around the perimeter track towards their dispersal. They landed and taxied to their dispersal, wondering what all the fuss was about. As they switched off the engines and did their post-flight checks, they were somewhat perturbed to see many faces staring at them as if they were ghosts or some other strange phenomena. They unstrapped and made their way down the fuselage to the door in the port side. The ground crew had already opened it and as they climbed down from the kite, they could not help but laugh at the strange looks on the faces of the ground crew as they stood around with their mouths agape.

`Where the bloody hell have you lot been?' asked Squadron Leader 'Dinty' Moore, their Flight Commander. 'What happened to you? You've all been listed as missing!' He was almost shouting at them but the relief on his face was obvious. Claude Wilson explained where they'd been and why and that West Malling's Intelligence Officer had promised to let Snaith know that they were safely down. 'Dinty' Moore promised an investigation into the empty auxiliary tank (an airman was later charged with neglect of duty) and Bomber Command was asked to find out from Fighter Command why West Malling had not advised Snaith that BB240 was safe.

They took BB240 to Stuttgart on Thursday 11th March and, apart from 'fairly heavy' Flak over the target, it was an, unremarkable trip. The following evening, however, contained lots of excitement the squadron could well have done without. Claude Wilson and his crew had been allocated DT526, MH-V for a trip to Essen, the briefing had taken place and the crews had been taken out to their aircraft at the dispersals. The aircraft in the next dispersal to 'V-Victor' was 'M-Mother', captained by Sergeant Rawcliffe. As on every other dispersal, Rawcliffe and crew were standing around the aircraft having a last cigarette or carrying out last minute checks. Rawcliffe's bomb aimer, Flight Sergeant John Richards (known as David Niven because of his remarkable resemblance to the actor) decided to have a final check of the bomb selection gear in the Halifax nose compartment. He returned a very short while later, remarking that everything was in order. About five minutes after his return, the crew noticed black smoke coming from the bomb bay. Niven immediately re-entered the aircraft to discover that the floor above the bomb bay was on fire. He grabbed a fire extinguisher and emptied it into the flames. They did not decrease one iota. He picked up a second fire extinguisher and repeated the procedure, still no decrease in the size of fire, but by now the fuselage was starting to fill with dense black smoke. Niven sensibly decided that he'd done all he could and, grabbing the two metal boxes containing the carrier pigeons, made a hasty exit, and not a minute too soon.

As 'Niven's feet touched the ground a large sheet of flame erupted from the aircraft's centre section and the Halifax slowly folded in the middle as the flames took hold. 'Niven' quickly followed the example set by his skipper, crew-mates and the ground crew and cleared the immediate area at a great rate of knots. Within minutes the 1,000 lbs high explosive bombs exploded, depositing little bits of 'M-Mother' over half the airfield. Several other aircraft were damaged in the process although fortunately, no one was injured.

After the explosion, as all personnel emerged from their various hiding places, the airfield fire tender arrived on the scene and began to fight what was left of the fire. Within minutes of starting to cover the burning remnants of 'M-Mother' with foam, there was another almighty explosion on the other side of the airfield. Packing up their hoses as quickly as they could, they raced across the airfield to find that Halifax 'H-Harry' had also caught fire and blown up[44]. The more superstitious members of the squadron took this as an omen; the squadron codes were 'MH' and the two aircraft that had blown up were 'M' and then 'H'. The Squadron's participation in the Essen trip was 'scrubbed.' All Halifaxes were grounded for two weeks after this incident, while investigations were carried out to determine the cause of the fires. This was eventually traced to an electrical short circuit and once the aircraft were modified, operations were once more underway.

On Friday 26th March, flying DT526, V-Victor' again, the target was Duisburg - another Ruhr target. The squadron despatched eleven Halifaxes as part of a 455-aircraft attack and Rube Airey released their two 1,000 lbs GP bombs and 3,840 lbs of assorted incendiaries from 19,000 feet onto the PFF markers over 10/10ths cloud at 21.56 hours. Back at Snaith for debrief, Claude Wilson informed the Intelligence Officer that he did not consider the attack to be too accurate and that it looked like a wasted effort with bombs too widespread. He was right. This raid was one of the few failures of the Battle of the Ruhr. The 10/10ths cloud completely prevented visual marking and five out the nine Oboe Mosquitoes despatched were forced to return early with technical failures. A further Mosquito was shot down, the first loss of an Oboe Mosquito, leaving only three to sustain the blind marking throughout the raid. The result was a widely scattered attack.

The Operations Order was up the next day and Claude Wilson and his crew were again on it. Still allocated V-Victor', the crew attended briefing to find that the target was to be Berlin, their first trip to the 'Big City'. Louis Wooldridge was occupying the rear turret, with Les Sharp acting as spare bod and it was really cold that night. The temperature was down to minus 32 degrees Fahrenheit and the only way Louis could keep the turret mechanism from freezing up was to sit on one hand (to keep it warm) and keep the turret moving with the other, before changing hands and repeating the procedure.

Unfortunately, when over Brandenburg and less than 30 miles from the target, Flak damage resulted in the shutting down of the starboard outer

---

[44] *Group Captain Tom Sawyer, who was Snaith's Station Commander at this time, gives a good account of this incident in his book "Only Owls and Bloody Fools Fly at Night".*

engine and, estimating that they'd be down to about 10,000 feet by the time they reached Berlin (the Merlin engined Halifax would not maintain height on 3 engines with a full bombload) and realising that they would be well below the rest of the Main Force and in great danger from the bombs of higher aircraft, they made the very sensible decision to jettison their bombs live and head for base. The whole crew were really 'brassed off' at having to abandon the sortie after getting so close to the target that everyone wanted to have in their Log Book, but they all knew that to continue under the circumstances was just asking for trouble. They landed back at Snaith just after 03.00 hours on Sunday morning. Later that day the Squadron Gunnery Officer, Flight Lieutenant Parnham, collared Louis Wooldridge and asked why his was the only aircraft on the unit which did not report trouble with the rear turret freezing up. Louis informed the Gunnery Officer of his 'change hands' technique.

This Berlin raid was basically a failure, but a stroke of good luck caused severe damage to a secret military installation outside the city. The bombing force approached the city from the southwest and PFF established two separate marking areas. Unfortunately, both were well short of Berlin. No bombing photographs were plotted within five miles of the aiming point in the city centre and most bombs fell from seven to seventeen miles short. Approximately 25% of all bombs actually dropped on the city turned out to be duds so, all in all, the raid was almost a non-event. This lack of accuracy did, however, provide an undreamed of bonus. Hidden in the woods at Teltow, eleven miles south west of Berlin, was a secret Luftwaffe stores depot.

By pure unmitigated chance, this depot happened to be right in the middle of the main concentration of bombing and a large quantity of valuable radio, radar and other technical stores was destroyed. With true Teutonic thoroughness, the Luftwaffe hierarchy decided that the Teltow depot had been the true target for Bomber Command this night and were full of admiration for the 'special unit' that had found and bombed it so accurately. "C'est La Guerre!"

Another of 51 Squadron's Halifaxes was involved in an unusual incident en-route to Berlin this night. DT670, skippered by Sergeant B.T.Brett, had three of its four machine-guns in the rear turret go unserviceable so Brett wisely elected to jettison his bomb load and return to base. Just after turning back, the Halifax was approached by two aircraft, one of which was showing its navigation lights. The second of the two aircraft closed in to the rear of DT670 and opened fire with a cannon mounted on the nose. The Halifax's rear gunner, Sergeant Alexander Barrie, BEM, held the fire of his one remaining serviceable Browning until the attacking aircraft was only 150 yards out before giving it all he'd got. Strikes were seen on the starboard wing of the attacker and its starboard engine burst into flames before it dived steeply through the clouds. Its disappearance was shortly followed by a bright flash on the undersurface of the clouds. Both Alexander Barrie[45] and Sergeant C. Vandy in the mid-upper turret were totally convinced that the aircraft that attacked them was a Wellington. Sergeant Brett and crew failed to return from Stettin just over three weeks after this event (20th April 1943).

On Sunday 3rd April, Claude and crew with Sergeant Anderson from 15 AFU along as second pilot, were again allocated DT526, V-Victor' for yet another Ruhr target - Essen. This was the crew's second trip to the heart of 'Happy Valley' as part of an attack that saw the number of Lancasters despatched reach the 200 figure for the first time, as part of a total force of 348 aircraft. The weather forecast was not entirely favourable so PFF prepared themselves for both ground and sky marking. In the event, Essen was cloud-free and the main force was somewhat confused to find two kinds of marking being carried out. Confused they may have been, but they were certainly not deterred - the resulting bombing was devastatingly accurate and a higher proportion of aircraft produced good bombing photographs than on any previous successful attack on Essen. A total of 635 buildings were destroyed and a further 526 seriously damaged. Fifteen Halifaxes were despatched by 51 Squadron and Claude Wilson was glad to find the target area clear of cloud. Rube Airey released their bomb load from 16,000 feet at 21.50 hours, smack on the PFF markers.

Back at Snaith, Claude reported that, early in the attack, flares and bombing appeared to be scattered, but Louis Wooldridge stated that when 'V-Victor' was about twenty miles along its homeward trip the fires seemed to taking a good hold. Twelve Halifaxes and nine Lancasters failed to return from this attack and a further two Halifaxes crashed on their return to the UK. One of the missing bombers belonged to 51 Squadron. `M-Mother', DT738 was a replacement for the aircraft destroyed in the 12th March double explosion and was still captained by Sergeant J Rawcliffe. He and his whole crew perished, including the rear gunner, Sergeant Tubby' Howarth, whom Louis Wooldridge had been with ever since they had first joined up together in Manchester in July 1939. They are all buried in the Reichswald War Cemetery at Cleve.

The following day (Monday 4th April) Claude Wilson and crew were once more on the squadron's Battle Order and again they were allocated 'V-Victor'. An early afternoon air test found this aircraft to be unserviceable and not repairable before the scheduled take-off time so they were allocated DT580, 'Z-Zebra' instead. `Z-Zebra' had just been fitted with a new, low-profile, four gun turret and there was no time to carry out an air test so the crew just had to trust to luck and the efficiency and thoroughness of 'Zebra's' ground crew that she would be alright on the night. Briefing revealed the night's target to be Kiel and, after the usual drive out to the dispersals and pre-flight checks, Claude, Rube, Peter, Ginger, Don, Les and Louis climbed aboard the aircraft ready to go. A green flare from the tower signalled `start engines' and it was not long before it was `Z-Zebra's' turn to move onto the perimeter track and join the queue at the end of the runway. Louis Wooldridge, back in a mid-upper turret for the first time since early March, was enjoying the view from his eagle's perch and was looking forward to testing his four Browning machine-guns over the North Sea. As the skipper turned onto the runway and lined up for take-off, Louis centred his turret facing aft and returned the waves of the various station personnel who had gathered to wave the aircraft off. The Halifax vibrated and shook as Claude opened up each of the throttles in turn to check for mag-drop and again as he opened up all four Merlin XVII engines to start the aircraft moving down the runway. As the tail came up, Louis couldn't fail to notice a faint stream of white smoke trailing back from each engine nacelle, a stream that was getting thicker every second. Just then he heard his skipper telling the flight engineer that all four engines were losing power. Louis quickly switched on the microphone in his oxygen mask and informed them of the white smoke. Ginger Anger took a confirmatory look out of the cockpit and correctly diagnosed the problem, the built-in Gravener fire extinguishers had set themselves off and the engine-smothering foam would be shorting out the electrics.

The Pendulum and the Scythe

Claude Wilson and crew pose alongside DT580 'M' of 51 Sqn shortly before the incident on 4th April 1943.

The skipper immediately closed all four throttles, dropped the flaps fully down and pulled the control column hard back into his stomach to force the tail back down onto the runway before applying the brakes as hard as he dared. 'Z-Zebra' was well over halfway down the runway at this point, so Claude warned the crew to brace themselves as the aircraft bucked and bounced as he tried to keep the tail on the ground and reduce their speed. The Halifax, complete with full fuel and bombload, continued its mad dash down the runway, seemingly impervious to all the pilot's attempts to slow it down. Looking forward over his shoulder, Louis could see the airfield perimeter fence approaching at an alarming speed and knew that the LNER Edinburgh to London main rail line was in a shallow cutting on just the other side of that fence! Just to complete the picture of impending doom, Louis could also make out the billowing black smoke of an approaching express train. Looking back aft, he could see Wing Commander 'Tom' Sawyer's Hillman car, followed by the fire tender and the 'Blood wagon' careering across the grass chasing them as fast as possible.

Claude Wilson must also have seen the approaching express train for in a last-ditch attempt to avoid a major catastrophe he swung the Halifax to port, off the runway and onto the grass where the soft ground helped to finally bring the aircraft to a stop with the best part of the starboard wing overhanging the railway line. Less than a minute later the express train of about thirteen coaches, packed with civilians and servicemen and women on their way to London, thundered underneath the still windmilling propellers of the Halifax's wing.

Once Flying Control was satisfied that 'Z-Zebra' was no longer obstructing the runway, the rest of the Squadron received the `green light' and proceeded on their way to Kiel. A quick inspection of 'Z-Zebra' revealed an overstrained undercarriage (hardly surprising) and, with no further spare aircraft being available, Claude and the crew were stood down for the night. The following day they went off on seven days well earned leave.

They returned to Snaith to find that the Squadron was enjoying a brief stand-down from operations, but that training exercises were being undertaken. They carried out a Fighter Affiliation exercise on the 18th April, but were not called for operations again until Tuesday 20th April, when briefing revealed the target to be Stettin. They were detailed to fly Halifax HR750, MH-W, an aircraft that should have been known as 'W-William' but the Squadron had given her another name. A veteran aircraft, with many bomb symbols painted on her nose, she had been named Wanchor's Castle' and proudly bore this name, together with an illustration of a 'W' above an anchor and a small castle, on her nose above her 'Ops score'.

'Wanchor's Castle' was one of twelve Halifaxes contributed by 51 Squadron to a total force of 339 aircraft. Because Stettin was over six hundred miles from the UK, HR750 was fitted with an additional fuel tank in the forward part of the bomb bay, thus reducing its bomb load to one 1,000lbs GP bomb, forty-eight 30 lbs incendiaries and four-hundred-and-fifty 4lbs incendiaries. Take-off, for Wilson and crew, was at 21.16 hours and, as they climbed away from Snaith, the weather was clear and the sky virtually cloudless with bright moonlight. They did not need to climb very high however, because, as briefed, once over the North Sea they dropped down to only 100 feet for most of the outward flight.

Crossing the North Sea Louis Wooldridge, up in the mid- upper turret, had time to observe the calm water, silvery in the moonlight, as they skimmed low across the waves. He rotated the turret to face forwards and briefly admired the moonlight reflected on the four whirling propellers as they pulled the loaded Halifax through the air, before focusing his eyes to the horizon to watch for the approaching coast of occupied Denmark. Suddenly, Louis spotted a large ocean-going U-boat on the surface, about four miles ahead and to port of the Speeding Halifax. He quickly reported his observation to his skipper who took its bearing and passed this to the navigator, Peter Finnett, with the instruction to note its position from his log and get Don Hall, the wireless operator, to send a coded signal back to base. As the Halifax drew closer to the U-boat, Louis watched it crash-dive as the German crew finally spotted the oncoming aircraft and decided to make a hasty exit.

Minutes later the Danish coastline came into view and Claude Wilson eased the Halifax up slightly to clear the cliffs before getting right down on the deck again and speeding across the darkened countryside. Despite being arduous for the pilot, low level flying has many attractions for young men, the fantastic sensation of speed being not the least of them. Louis Wooldridge was thoroughly enjoying this sensation as trees, small buildings, bridges and such like sped by at an amazing rate. About half way across Denmark, the Halifax came upon a small 'L' shaped cluster of farm buildings and Louis watched as a door opened, allowing a shaft of light to penetrate the farm yard. Four figures emerged from the farmhouse, all frantically waving large white cloths to wish the aircraft and its crew well. Louis appreciated this gesture from an oppressed family in a Nazi-occupied country and he raised and lowered his four Browning machine-guns in acknowledgement of their greeting. The four white cloths were waving even more furiously as the Halifax sped on into the night.

The trip to Stettin was going to be a long one and, with only 600 rounds of ammunition for each gun, Louis decided to use only two guns at any one time. He chose to use them in a diagonal manner (e.g. port upper with starboard lower), so as to maintain the benefits of gun harmonisation (cone of fire). Having crossed the Danish east coast, Claude Wilson started to climb the Halifax to the briefed bombing height of 12,000 feet. When Wanchor's Castle' reached a position about three miles north of the German north coast in the vicinity of Lubeck, the skipper and mid-upper gunner spotted three clusters of yellow marker flares that had just been dropped by PFF Lancasters to mark the turning point for Stettin. When Claude Wilson advised his navigator of the markers appearance, Peter Finnett remarked that they were 'dead on time.' He had no sooner said this when two of the three Pathfinder Lancasters were enveloped in smoke and flames before starting to fall from the moonlit night sky. No parachutes were seen to emerge from either aircraft but Peter Finnett's casual remark on the Pathfinder's punctuality took on an entirely new meaning. No one on board Wanchor's Castle' had seen any Flak or tracer prior to the destruction of the Lancasters and this gave rise to some conjecture as to the cause of their sudden demise. (It is now known that some of the Luftwaffe nightfighter Experten preferred not to use tracer shells in their guns because it momentarily affected their night vision). Needless to say, both gunners were exceptionally alert after this.

Leaving Lubeck and Rostock behind them, they reached the bombing height of 12,000 feet as they crossed the German coast and then turned onto the final approach leg for the target. As they were crossing the coast the enemy Flak batteries opened up and, although they weren't hit, they were certainly jolted about. As Claude Wilson later reported at debrief, it was definitely 'Not pleasant!' Approaching Stettin as part of the first wave of the main force, there was as yet no sign of the target indicators (TIs). In the moonlight Louis Wooldridge surveyed the surrounding countryside from his vantage point on top of the fuselage. The whole area looked so calm and peaceful that it was, for a split second of time, difficult to remember that there was a war on.

Right on time and dead ahead of Wanchor's Castle', the first red and green TIs suddenly cascaded into view. This was all the defenders were waiting for and all hell let loose. The sky was filled with exploding Flak shells and probing searchlights but, miraculously, 'Wanchor's Castle' proceeded on its bomb run unscathed. Rube Airey released their bombload right onto the TIs at 01.09 hours, then Claude Wilson put the Halifax into a diving turn out of the target area and back down to low level for the return flight. Shortly after leaving Stettin, Louis was alarmed to see the ditching hatch, immediately in front of his turret, open. A gloved hand appeared and waved at the mid-upper gunner -and then gave him a 'V' sign, before disappearing back inside the fuselage. The next minute, Louis's turret was momentarily covered in paper and then he remembered that Ginger Anger had been tasked with throwing out their load of propaganda leaflets on the return through German airspace. As Ginger continued to throw bundle after bundle out through the open hatch, Louis trained his turret to the rear of the Halifax and he and Les Sharp in the tail briefly watched the leaflets trailing out behind the aircraft before fluttering gently down to the ground.

The Pendulum and the Scythe

While Ginger was still unloading the leaflets, the aircraft passed over a reasonably large town. Spotting a big, light-coloured building surmounted by a tall spire containing a four-faced clock, Louis guessed it was probably the Town Hall. Illuminated as it was by the bright moonlight, Louis could see quite clearly that the clock was reading half-past-one. Telling himself that he needed to test his diagonal two gun selection for accuracy, Louis let rip at the two clock faces he could see. As they disintegrated into very small pieces, he felt a tug at his leg and, looking round to the open ditching hatch, saw a worried look on the face of Ginger Anger who obviously had visions of the aircraft being attacked by nightfighters. Louis removed his oxygen mask and gave Ginger a broad grin and a 'thumbs-up' sign and, thus reassured, the flight engineer returned to his laborious task.

Ginger had just finished throwing out the leaflets, closed the hatch and returned to his normal position in the cockpit when the Halifax approached a German aerodrome. Having asked his skipper for permission to open fire as they flew past, both he and Les Sharp turned their turrets to starboard, while Claude Wilson lowered the starboard wing to give them both a better view. Both gunners let fly at the glass roof panels of the hangars as each in turn came into their sights. They then turned their attention to a row of parked aircraft and created as much havoc as possible there too. While this was continuing, the door of a long wooden hut, adjacent to the parked aircraft, opened up to let a long shaft of light shine across the airfield as various figures hurried out of the but and towards some sand-bagged gun emplacements. This was all the justification the two young gunners needed and their guns were quickly trained on the scurrying figures and finally, the hut itself, before the speeding Halifax left the aerodrome behind.

Briefly relaxing for a few moments after all their excitement, they were suddenly brought to instant alertness by the criss-crossing of red, green and white balls of fire, above and below their aircraft. Obviously the aerodrome had phoned ahead and this was the Luftwaffe's attempt to give them their comeuppance. The light Flak hosed all about them, initially appearing to rise into the sky ever so slowly and then, as it neared the aircraft, screaming past it at a hell of a speed. One burst of this fire removed the external wireless aerial completely. This had been suspended between the twin tail fins and the upper fuselage just aft of the cockpit and it passed only two feet above the mid-upper turret. Louis was not pleased; pinpointing one source of the enemy gunfire at the edge of a wood, he trained his turret in its direction and, allowing sufficient deflection, he let off a long burst that temporarily

314

silenced the enemy fire. It did not start up again until the Halifax was just about out of range and another quick burst from Louis silenced the position until they had left the area.

About fifteen minutes later, as they were nearing the Baltic Sea, Louis Wooldridge spotted some light Flak off the port bow of the aircraft. He could not determine from whence it came but decided to keep his eyes in that direction as they drew nearer. As the Halifax approached the coast, Louis learned that the Flak he'd been watching was not from a coastal battery as he had expected, but from a source on the sea itself. By this time they were approaching the area off Kiel when Louis finally spotted the source of the light Flak. It was another surfaced U-boat and Louis could just make out its silhouette about three-quarters of a mile off the Halifax's port beam. Breathing a sigh of relief that their opponent was not a Flak-ship, Louis waited until the U-boat came within range and then opened fire, observing his tracer hit the submarine's conning tower before shooting off in all directions.

Claude Wilson was not pleased at his mid-upper gunner loosing off. He had seen Louis's U-boat, but he had also seen the large U-boat depot ship with a further six or seven surfaced submarines alongside it, which was about a mile further on. It had been his intention to try to sneak past the whole lot without being observed. There was now very little chance of that, so Claude put the Halifax right down on the deck and hoped to get by as quickly as possible. By now Louis had spotted the depot ship in the moonlight and could see figures running all over it. He let rip at them too as the Halifax sped by. Somehow, they got past without a shot being fired at them. They had stirred up a hornet's nest and got away with it!

A slight navigational error resulted in Wanchor's Castle', suddenly finding itself over Esbjerg on the North Sea coast of Denmark. The Halifax's lone arrival over the port resulted in every light Flak and machine-gun in the neighbourhood opening up on one solitary target. Flying along a sandy riverside, steady machine-gun fire was being directed at the aircraft's starboard side. Louis Wooldridge turned his turret to face the enemy but found that he could not depress his guns low enough to return fire. Advising the skipper of his problem, Claude obligingly dropped the starboard wing to an almost vertical position and allowed Louis and Les to silence the enemy fire with a long burst from their guns. Having sorted out that problem, they next found themselves coned by several searchlights. Claude Wilson was blinded and asked his gunners to shoot them out. Les and Louis had a good go at this and were successful in extinguishing enough of them to let Claude manoeuvre his way over the roof tops and out over the North Sea to comparative safety.

At least Peter Finnett was now sure of their position and quietly worked out a new course for base onto which the Halifax settled down for the last leg of its journey. But the night's excitement was not yet over. Claude Wilson decided he needed to pay a visit to the Elsan so, handing over control to the second pilot, he set off down the fuselage, past the mid-upper turret to the 'thunder box.' Shortly after Claude had left his seat and unbeknown to him, Peter Finnett had passed a slight course alteration to the second pilot who set this new course on the compass and merrily continued to fly on, while Claude had a wander around the aircraft to see how his crew were faring after the events of the night.

After thirty or so minutes, Peter Finnett came on the intercom to advise the pilot that Snaith's beacon should be visible in about ten minutes. Ten minutes later there were none of the usual landmarks visible. The navigator was beginning to think he must be 'losing his marbles' and quickly rechecked all his calculations. Suddenly the intercom was filled with squeaks, signifying that the aircraft was approaching a balloon barrage and the whole crew knew that there were none near Snaith. Then they could hear anti-aircraft shells exploding in the low cloud below them and Louis Wooldridge was so astonished to see a Heinkel He111 fly across the nose of the Halifax that he didn't have time to open fire at it. As Claude hurriedly returned to the cockpit, Peter Finnett asked the second pilot what course he was flying and learned the reason why they were flying over the London balloon barrage during a raid by the Luftwaffe – the second pilot had inadvertently been flying a reciprocal course. (An easy mistake to make, especially on a first operation).

Claude Wilson resumed control and headed north to base, where they were advised of intruders in the vicinity by the receipt of the codeword 'Bandits.' They finally landed at Snaith just before 06.00 hours after eight and a half hours in the air, the last of the squadron to do so. At debrief, Claude and the crew recounted their various escapades of the night and when they got to the Esbjerg incident, the Station Intelligence Officer chuckled. 'So it was you lot was it? Practically the whole squadron reported some poor bugger getting shot to hell over Esbjerg. From what we've heard you're all bloody lucky to be home.' With that it was off to breakfast and then bed. Later that day Louis Wooldridge was informed by Sergeant Wheeler (from Louis's home town of Stalybridge),the NCO i/c ground crew for MH-W, that he had just forty rounds of ammunition left in the mid-upper turret's storage boxes, out of the 2,400 rounds he had started the trip with.

This Stettin raid was the most successful attack carried out beyond the range of Oboe during the whole 'Battle of the Ruhr' period. As already stated, visibility was good and the PFF marking was perfect. Twenty-four fires were still burning when a photo-reconnaissance aircraft flew over the town over thirty-six hours later. Approximately one hundred acres in the centre of Stettin were claimed as devastated, much of this area comprised industrial buildings. The cost was fairly high though with twenty-one aircraft (6.2%) failing to return.

The crew operated next on Monday 26th April, taking Sergeant A. Siriel along as second pilot in W1212 the `Cop's Kite' (MR-U), to Duisburg as part of the squadron's fourteen-Halifax contribution to a total force of 561 aircraft. They returned to Snaith at 04.41 hours after an uneventful four hour and twenty minute trip. Unfortunately the squadron lost two aircraft on this attack, HR787 (MII-J) captained by Flight Sergeant C. M. Brigden and HR778 (MH-D) skippered by Sergeant G. Fisher. All seven crew members in both aircraft died. Seven had certainly not been their lucky number.

Two days later, on Wednesday 28th April, Wing Commander Tom Sawyer was promoted to acting Group Captain. That night the crew were allocated Halifax HR789, `Z-Zebra,' loaded with two C.708 (1,500 lbs) mines and briefed to go Gardening. The squadron despatched nine Halifaxes as part of the second successive large-scale mining operation in the Kattegat. The total force for the night comprised 68 Lancasters, 60 Halifaxes, 47 Wellingtons and 32 Stirlings, which laid the largest number of mines (593) ever laid during a single night. This record was, however, only achieved at the cost of 22 aircraft - the highest loss of aircraft whilst mine-laying during the whole war.

Claude Wilson and crew were briefed to drop their mines in the Kattegat, east of Copenhagen, Denmark, an area codenamed Verbena. They were airborne at 20.25 hours and headed out across the North Sea at 1,500 feet. At about midnight they entered the Skagerrak and then altered course to starboard to overfly the extreme northern tip of Denmark, entering the

Kattegat just north of Frederikshaven. Climbing to 2,000 feet, Claude followed Peter Finnett's instructions and once again turned to starboard to fly down the Kattegat towards their briefed release point just east of the Danish capital. This was always a dangerous place to drop mines because it was a favourite haunt of German nightfighters, based at Aalborg, lurking in the hope of intercepting the Mosquito courier aircraft that regularly flew between Sweden and England.

As usual, the weather decided not to co-operate with the met forecast and `Z-Zebra' met 10/10ths cloud in the target area, Claude Wilson had to drop down to 800 feet, below the cloud, to give Rube Airey and Peter Finnett a chance of spotting the right area in which to plant their 'vegetables'. Having identified Verbena, they were just settling into their release run-in when two streams of light Flak suddenly appeared on either side of Louis Wooldridge's mid-upper turret. He couldn't see the source of this fire so blindly fired in the direction of the enemy fire in the hope of at least putting his opponents[46] off their aim. After a few bursts, the enemy fire ceased and Rube Airey released the mines at 00.31 hours. Claude Wilson then headed the Halifax back to base. They arrived over Snaith at about 03.30 hours to find the runway fogbound, but the enthusiastic use of gooseneck paraffin flares helped to increase visibility sufficiently for Z-Zebra to land at 03.45 hours. (The flares not only lit the runway quite well but the heat emitted by them caused the fog to lift slightly - a smaller forerunner of FIDO).

They had the next night off, but were back on the Operations Order on Friday 30th April, in the 'Cops Kite' W1212, 'U' and again the target was Essen. The squadron despatched nine Halifaxes as part of a total force of 305 aircraft which, despite full cloud cover over the target, created new damage in areas all over the city, although there was no major concentration. 'U-Uncle' returned to Snaith with Flak damage to the leading edge of the starboard wing and, at debriefing, Claude Wilson was heard to remark 'It was the usual Essen trip - 10/10ths cloud and Flak.' One of the squadron's aircraft was among the twelve that failed to return. HR733, flown by Sergeant D. R. Wilson, was shot down with the loss of five lives. Only the two gunners survived.

---

[46] *It has since been established that the Halifax's opponents were based on Zealand and fired 229 rounds of 20mm and 320 rounds of machine-gun ammunition.*

Five days later, on Wednesday 4th May, Claude and the crew were briefed to take Halifax HR789, 'Z-Zebra' to Dortmund in yet another attack during the Battle of the Ruhr. 51 Squadron contributed ten of the 141 Halifaxes that formed part of a total force of 596 aircraft on the largest 'non-one-thousand' raid of the war to date and the first major attack on Dortmund. The initial PFF marking was accurate but some of the backing-up fell short and a decoy site also attracted a fair proportion of the bombing. Nevertheless, half of the force did bomb within three miles of the aiming point and the city's report reveals that 1,218 buildings were destroyed and 2,141 seriously damaged. These included the Hoesch and the Dortmunder Union Steel Works and many facilities in the dock area. Z-Zebra's bombload, two 1,000 lbs GP bombs and 3,960 lbs of mixed incendiaries, was released at 00.59 hours from 19,000 feet onto a concentration of red markers. A large fire - believed to be oil tanks – was observed to start up as the bombs struck home. Thirty-one aircraft (5.2%) failed to return from this raid and a further seven crashed on their return to the UK in bad weather. Louis Wooldridge awoke later that morning to find that he had been promoted to Flight Sergeant.

The Battle of the Ruhr continued apace, with Duisburg being the designated target for the night of 12/13th May. This was to be the fourth attack on this city and inland port during the Battle and the Command despatched 572 aircraft of which eighteen were contributed by 51 Squadron. The PFF marking was almost perfect and the Main Force bombing was particularly well concentrated. The centre of Duisburg and the port area, just off the Rhine, suffered severe damage. 1,596 buildings were totally destroyed and four of August Thyssen's steel plants were damaged. In the port area, the largest inland port in Germany, twenty-one barges and thirteen other ships totalling 18,291 tons were sunk, while a further sixty vessels, totalling 41,000 tons, were damaged. This attack was deemed to be so successful that, other than for nuisance raids by Mosquitoes, the Command found it unnecessary to re-visit Duisburg again until 21st May 1944. Thirty-four aircraft (5.9%) failed to return.

For Claude Wilson and crew, this attack saw the operational baptism of the new Halifax that they would fly for the rest of their tour. 'Q-Queenie'; Serial No. HR838 was a B.Mk.II Series la with the perspex nose (as used on the B.Mk.III) and low profile, four-gun mid-upper turret, but still retaining the triangular fins. It had been built by Handley Page themselves and had just arrived on 51 Squadron.

The Pendulum and the Scythe

Louis Woolridge of 51 Sqn in the four-gun mid-upper turret of Halifax HR838.

They took off from Snaith at 23.04 hours and climbed to join the invisible bomber stream in the dark night sky. They crossed the enemy coast to the usual welcome from the Flak and continued on across Holland, heading for their target that was situated about twenty-five miles inside Germany. Shortly before reaching Duisburg, the long bluish finger of a radar controlled 'master' searchlight appeared in the sky about half-a-mile ahead and to starboard of 'Q-Queenie'. Almost immediately it fastened onto another Halifax and was quickly joined by other, white, searchlights. From his mid-upper turret, Louis Wooldridge could see from its identification letters 'MH-J' that this Halifax belonged to 51 Squadron and that it was being flown by Pilot Officer G. W. Locksmith. Within seconds of the aircraft being coned, the heavy Flak opened up and, despite all Locksmith's efforts to escape, the Halifax was hit, went into a steep dive and was soon lost to view. Pilot Officer Locksmith's aircraft (HR786) did not return to base[47].

On reaching Duisburg, Claude Wilson settled 'Q-Queenie' onto her bombing run at 19,000 feet, with Rube Airey giving his skipper the usual 'left, left - right - steady' instructions and with both gunners sweeping the night sky on the lookout for nightfighters. Some sixth sense made Louis Wooldridge look above him and what he saw scared him witless. Right above them was a Lancaster with its bomb doors wide open and Louis got a very close-up view

---

[47] *It is now known that, although unseen by Louis Wooldridge, MH-J was claimed shot down by a German nightfighter and crashed at Jisp, Kanaaldijk, approximately 13 miles northwest of Amsterdam.*

of a 4,000 lbs Cookie and more incendiary canisters than he had time to count as the Lancaster move from their port quarter to starboard nose position. 'Jink starboard Skipper, jink starboard.' Louis almost shouted down the intercom. Claude Wilson did not hesitate and the Halifax quickly lost one thousand feet as he side-slipped 'Q-Queenie' to the right as the Lancaster's bomb load missed the Halifax by inches. Louis quickly explained the reason for his instruction and informed his bomb aimer, who was complaining vehemently about the ruination of his bomb run, just how close they had all come to accompanying the Lancaster's load - and their own - onto the city below. They continued their run at 18,000 feet and Rube Airey released the Halifax's bomb load onto the PFF markers at 02.12 hours before they headed back to base to land exactly two hours later.

While Claude Wilson and crew in 'Q-Queenie' had had a lucky escape, other squadron crews had not been so fortunate. The Squadron lost four aircraft from the eighteen despatched; DT645 captained by Sergeant D. C. Smith (all seven crew members killed), HR786 - Pilot Officer G. W. Locksmith (all killed), JB806 -Sergeant B. Brown, RAAF (pilot plus one other killed, five taken prisoner) and DT684 - Flight Sergeant N. E. Jones (six killed, one PoW). The rear gunner in Pilot Officer Locksmith's aircraft, Pilot Officer G. O. M. Massip-de-Turnville, was the deputy Squadron Gunnery Officer. Thus 51 Squadron lost twenty-two members killed and seven taken prisoner of war in one night.

The next night, Thursday, 13th May, the squadron contributed twelve Halifaxes to the Command's total of 442 aircraft despatched to attack Bochum, another town in the Ruhr but a little further east than Duisburg. There were no 5 Group aircraft involved in this raid because they had their own 168-aircraft attack on Pilsen. The Bochum attack started well but, fifteen minutes into the attack, German decoy fires drew much of the bombing away from the target. 'Q-Queenie' dropped her seven 1,000 lbs GP bombs onto PFF markers from 17,750 feet at 02.12 hours but no aiming point photograph was taken because, earlier in the flight, Claude Wilson had had to take violent evasive action to avoid another aircraft and the photoflash jumped out of its chute, damaging its fuse. Claude had another narrow escape when over Solingen on the return trip. His windscreen was pierced by a piece of Flak that caused Perspex splinters to lodge in his face. Despite this incident, they made a safe return to Snaith and landed at 04.44 hours after five hours in the air. 51 Squadron lost another two aircraft, HR790 (MH-A) flown by Pilot Officer G. W. H. Byres and DT526 flown by Flight

Lieutenant R. D. Johnstone. In both cases three crew members were killed and four taken prisoner. The Command lost a total of 24 aircraft (5.4%) on this attack.

There was only one major raid during the next nine days and 51 Squadron were not involved. In the early evening of Sunday 16th May, Wing Commander Guy Gibson led 19 Lancasters of 617 Squadron off from RAF Scampton bound for the Ruhr Dams. Only 11 aircraft returned.

Dortmund, on the night of Sunday 23rd May, was the target for Bomber Command's next major raid of the Battle of the Ruhr. 51 Squadron made its best effort yet to contribute nineteen Halifaxes, including `Q-Queenie; to the total force of 826 aircraft - the largest 'non-thousand' raid to date. Newly commissioned Claude Wilson, now a Pilot Officer, as was Peter Finnett, and crew had Warrant Officer R. E. Leeper along on his `second dickie' trip and `Q-Queenie' was airborne at 22.45 hours. As they approached the Ruhr it was Louis Wooldridge's turn for the narrow escape. A Flak shell exploded slightly above and forward of Q-Queenie's mid-upper turret and two pieces of shrapnel pierced the perspex dome around Louis' head and shoulders. One piece penetrated the perspex behind the gunner's head, creating a hole about two inches across. The second entered the turret just in front of Louis' face, struck the port upper Browning machine-gun and rattled off into the fuselage below. Somehow both bits missed the gunner completely, leaving Louis to complain, for the rest of the trip, about the howling gale entering his turret from the two inch hole behind his head.

Later, as `Q-Queenie' made her bombing run over Dortmund at 17,000 feet, Rube Airey released their load onto the PFF flares at 01.07 hours and then discovered that one of their 1,000 lbs GP bombs had hung up. Calling for Ginger Anger, the flight engineer, to help him, Rube Airey made his way back along the fuselage to the floor above the bomb bay and he and Ginger removed an eight-inch diameter inspection panel directly beneath the mid-upper turret. Rube and Ginger took turns to try to lever open the bomb release hook with a screwdriver, while Louis kept a lookout for nightfighters, interspersed with quick glances down to see how his bomb aimer and flight engineer were doing. As Dortmund is at the eastern end of the Ruhr, as long as they could release the hang-up in the next twenty to thirty minutes, it was still guaranteed to land somewhere in the Ruhr, so they kept up their poking and prodding until, finally, the 1,000 pounder left the aircraft. Louis Wooldridge felt the aircraft lift slightly as the bomb was released and he craned his neck over to look downwards in an effort to see where it was likely to hit. He was astounded to see a Focke Wulf FW190 about 2,000 feet directly below them, which was as unaware of their presence as Louis had been of the enemy aircraft. The newly released 1,000 pounder whistled past the '190's port wing, rocking the fighter as it did so. Louis watched in great amusement as the enemy fighter dropped his starboard wing and dived out of harm's way. He was not seen again.

This attack on Dortmund, after a nine-day break in major operations, was very successful. The Pathfinders marked the target accurately in clear weather conditions and the following attack went to plan, with large areas in the centre, north and east of Dortmund devastated. Nearly 2,000 buildings were completely destroyed and many industrial premises were hit, particularly the large Hoesch steelworks, which ceased production. It was deemed unnecessary to attack Dortmund in strength again for another twelve months. Thirty-eight aircraft (4.6%), including eighteen Halifaxes failed to return. Four of the missing Halifaxes belonged to 51 Squadron, HR 836 – Flying Officer J. E. Rigby (all seven crew members killed), HR 844 - Sergeant R R Masscassll (all seven taken PoW), HR 835 - Sergeant L. A. Wright (six killed, one PoW) and HR 842 -Sergeant J. W. G. Park (Skipper killed, six PoW). Once again the Squadron had had a bad night. The last three operational nights had cost 51 Squadron ten aircraft lost with forty-two aircrew killed and a further twenty-nine taken prisoner.

Four nights later (Thursday 27th May), it was back to Essen and once again the crew of 'Q-Queenie' had another pilot on board for his 'second dickie' trip. The 'new man' this time was Flight Sergeant J. J. Anderson and they were airborne at 23.13 hours. Twelve Halifaxes from 51 Squadron were detailed to form part of a 518-aircraft strong force. This was to be the fourth trip to Essen for Pilot Officer Wilson and his crew and their sixth on the trot to the Ruhr. Wilson had been asked to make a 'running commentary' recording of the operation and, for once, the whole trip proceeded without any problems – apart from the usual 'Flak and 10/10ths cloud' over the target. The latter necessitated sky-marking from the Pathfinders and, as usual, this resulted in scattered bombing with many aircraft undershooting. The limited damage in Essen was mainly confined to the central and northern areas but nevertheless, 488 buildings were destroyed. Twenty-three aircraft (4.4%) failed to return, a slightly lower than normal loss for a Ruhr raid.

'Q-Queenie' landed back at Snaith at 03.18 hours and the crew were 'officially' photographed as they climbed down from the aircraft and made their way onto the crew bus. On arrival at the debriefing room, they were met by Group Captain Tom Sawyer, the Squadron CO and Air Vice-Marshal Sir Roderick Carr, AOC of 4 Group, both of whom wished to know how 'things had gone'. For the first time in their tour the skipper could truthfully say, 'A piece of cake, Sir!' The same could not be said for two of the Squadron's aircraft. HR750 - Pilot Officer R. Beaston (all seven made PoW) and NE789 - Sergeant F. J. Prothero (five killed and two PoW), failed to return.

Claude and crew were next on the Operations List on Saturday 29th May and again they had someone along as second pilot. Sergeant T. J. Bishop joined the crew of 'Q-Queenie' for a 719-aircraft attack on Wuppertal in the southeastern corner of the Ruhr. 51 Squadron contributed thirteen Halifaxes and HR838 took off at 22.47 hours. This attack was aimed at the Barmen half of the long and narrow town of Wuppertal and was the outstanding success of the Battle of the Ruhr. Both PFF marking and Main Force bombing were particularly accurate and a large fire area developed in the narrow streets of the old town centre. Although there is no mention of it in the town's records, it is probable that this fire was so intense as to develop into the first, albeit smaller version of the 'firestorm' that was to envelop Hamburg two months later. Approximately 1,000 acres (almost 80%) of Barmen's built-up area was destroyed by this fire and five out of the town's six largest factories, 211 other industrial premises and almost 4,000 houses were completely destroyed. The number of buildings classed as 'seriously damaged,' at 71 industrial and 1,800 domestic, also indicates the high proportion of destruction. Thirty-three aircraft (4.6%) failed to return.

En route to the target, Louis Wooldridge noticed an unusual rumbling noise within the aircraft's fuselage. He looked down between his legs and caught a brief glimpse of something rolling around on the floor of the fuselage beneath his turret. He averted his gaze to the outside of the aircraft and carried out a quick scan all around his field of fire before once again peering down into the belly of the aircraft. Yes, there was definitely something rolling around the fuselage floor - Ye Gods, it was the million candle power photoflash and its nose vanes (that activated it during its descent from the aircraft) were revolving!

Pausing only to advise his skipper of his discovery, Louis quickly vacated his turret and grabbed the pyrotechnic. He was joined by Ginger Anger and together they gently replaced it in its chute. They could only assume that it had jumped out of its housing when the aircraft, hitting an air pocket an hour or so before, had dropped like a descending lift for about 1,500 feet. On reaching Wuppertal, Rube Airey guided `Q-Queenie' onto the PFF markers at 17,000 feet and released their bomb load at 01.52 hours. Seconds after their bombs and incendiaries had left the aircraft, the photoflash was automatically released but because the nose vanes had rotated whilst it was rolling about the fuselage, the time delay had been considerably reduced. It went off less than 500 feet beneath the Halifax. Had Louis Wooldridge not spotted the photoflash rolling about loose, `Q-Queenie' would have been another statistic. As it was all thirteen 51 Squadron aircraft returned safely to the UK for the first time since 4th May. `Q-Queenie' landed at Waterbeach at 04.15 hours on the Sunday morning. They had diverted there because Don Hall, their wireless operator, had inadvertently misinterpreted a diversion instruction for another squadron. They returned to Snaith later that day.

One morning in early June, Pilot Officer Claude Wilson was summoned to an interview with his Flight Commander and Group Captain Tom' Sawyer. The rest of the crew remained at the flight office wondering what sort of trouble they were in and frantically trying to remember if they'd put up any 'blacks' that had just been discovered. After what seemed an age, Claude returned to the flight office to enlighten his crew as to how serious their trouble was. He had been asked if the crew would be prepared to volunteer for Pathfinder duties. This meant continuing on operations to a total of fifty or sixty operations instead of the Main Force quota of thirty. They had already carried out twenty-four and were not that far off being screened at the end of their tour. Les Sharp, the rear gunner, had only been married for three weeks so he declined the `invitation' immediately. Rube Airey also decided that the Pathfinders were not for him and as they had to volunteer as a complete crew or not at all, Claude had the unenviable task of informing his Flight Commander of the crew's decision.

Meanwhile 'Q-Queenie' had disappeared into a hangar and was being worked on under strict security. The ground crew didn't seem to know what was happening and even the skipper could not discover what was going on. Finally, on Wednesday 9th June, the crew was detailed to air test `Q-Queenie' and then carry out a special fighter affiliation exercise. As they descended from the crew bus at Queenie's dispersal, Les Sharp was the first to notice a strange double arrow head shaped aerial sticking out backwards from the rear fuselage, immediately under his rear turret. The crew quickly gathered around the rear of the Halifax, poking and prodding the strange aerial and wondering what the hell it was and what, if anything, it did. Their ponderings were interrupted by the arrival of Group Captain Sawyer and a 'boffin' who proceeded to explain that the aerial was the external part of a new warning device called Monica.

On Sunday 9th May, a Junkers Ju88C6/R-1 nightfighter[48], Werke Nummer 360043 wearing the identification codes 'D5+EV' of 10 Staffel, Nachtjagdgeschwader 3, took off from its base at Aalborg, Denmark. Its mission, with another similar aircraft, was to patrol the airspace around Denmark in an attempt to try to intercept a Mosquito courier aircraft that the Luftwaffe believed was due to fly from Sweden to the UK. The pilot, Oberleutnant Heinrich Schmitt, and Wireless/Radar Operator, Oberfeldwebel Paul Rosenberger, had no intention of carrying out this patrol. Because of friction with and surveillance by the unit's resident Gestapo 'spy', they had long planned to defect to England and at last the opportunity had arisen. Their gunner, Oberfeldwebel Erich Kantvill, was not party to the plans of Schmitt and Rosenberger but by the time they were airborne was not in a position to do anything about them.

Once airborne, Schmitt turned the aircraft westwards and set up his patrol line as normal. After a short while, however, he dived the Ju88 down to sea level and sped for Scotland, transmitting an SOS to the effect that an engine was on fire and he was having to ditch in the North Sea. As soon as this message was transmitted, Rosenberger jettisoned the aircraft's dinghies and they continued for Scotland at low level. At 17.50 hours, Blue Section of 165 (Ceylon) Squadron - Flight Lieutenant A. F. Roscoe and Sergeant B. R. Scaman in Spitfire Vb's BM515 (SK-T) and AB921 (SK-X) respectively, were scrambled from RAF Dyce to intercept a 'plot'. They were vectored onto the incoming Ju88 by the Peterhead Sector Controller, Flight Lieutenant G. S. Crimp, and intercepted the enemy aircraft a few miles northeast of Dyce. As the Spitfires approached, Oberleutnant Schmitt lowered the Junkers' undercarriage in the international sign of surrender and fired off red Very lights and waggled his aircraft's wings for good measure.

---

[48] *This Ju88 is now exhibited at the RAF Museum, Hendon.*

Flight Lieutenant Roscoe in Blue 1 then lowered his undercarriage in reply and, instructing Sergeant Scaman to take position behind the Junkers 'just in case', he flew in front of the enemy nightfighter and led all three aircraft back to Dyce where they landed safely.

The following day, Professors R. V. Jones and E. M. Wright of British Scientific Intelligence were advised of the Junkers arrival and immediately caught the overnight sleeper to Aberdeen. On Tuesday, 11th May they visited the enemy nightfighter to investigate its electronic equipment. Professor Jones was satisfied that he could trust Oberleutnant Schmitt to fly the Ju88 for the test programme he envisaged but he needed to have a British observer to operate the radar equipment. Jones was delighted to find that the selected observer was an old colleague called Derek Jackson who had earned a Doctorate of Science and was now a Squadron Leader Observer/Radar Operator with a DFC. Jones told Jackson that Schmitt had volunteered to fly the aircraft for these tests but Jackson told him quite bluntly 'I'm not flying with any bloody German!' Jones asked him if his own regular pilot was safe and walked right into 'Do you bloody well think that I would go up with him if he wasn't?' So the trials were carried out by Squadron Leaders Christopher Hartley and Derek Jackson. It took Professor Jones and his team just one month to uncover the secrets of the Ju88's Lichtenstein BC Radar (FuG 202), design and build a warning device for fitment into Halifax HR838, `Q-Queenie' ready for testing on the 9th June.

This warning device was code named Monica and worked by transmitting radio signals to the rear of the aircraft and then receiving any signals 'bounced' back by following aircraft. It issued its warning to the crew of the equipped bomber by sounding a series of bleeps over the intercom. Claude Wilson and his crew completed their trials and the new equipment went into operational service on the night of 19/20th June. An incredibly fast introduction for a new piece of electronic equipment.

Shortly after taking part in the development of Monica and probably because of it, Claude Wilson and crew were informed that they were screened. They had finished their first tour of operations. Claude Wilson and Peter Finnett received the DFC and Rube Airey the DFM.

Additional Notes to Chapter Eight

i) Louis Wooldridge finished his first tour as a Flight Sergeant and then went to RAF Abingdon for Instructor Training before being posted to 22 OTU, Wellesbourne Mountford as an instructor. It was not long before he managed to get himself returned to ops and was posted to 15 OTU at RAF Harwell for crewing up for a second tour. Here he crewed up, again as mid-upper gunner, with pilot Sergeant Jim Allen. From 15 OTU they went to 1663 HCU at Rufforth where Jim Allen was taught to fly the Halifax by Flying Officer Claude Wilson DFC, Louis' first skipper. At the end of their Halifax conversion course Jim Allen and crew were posted to 578 Squadron at Burn in late April 1944. The crew completed their tour with 578 Squadron in September 1944 and Louis Wooldridge, now a Warrant Officer with a DFC, resumed the role of instructor, with yet another posting to Lossiemouth. (20 OTU). Louis Wooldridge, as part of Jim Allen's crew, had another lucky escape on 21st January 1944. On a night flight from Harwell in Wellington UK-K, they were flying at 15,000 feet when both engines failed. The aircraft dropped like a stone and three minutes later, after skimming an Army camp, it ground looped and broke its back in three places in a crash landing at Askham Bryan, three miles from York. Louis was thrown out of the rear turret but escaped with cuts and bruises.

ii) Claude Wilson and Peter Finnett were killed after the war whilst flying a Stirling in Transport Command. They took off from Castel Benito, climbed to 800feet and then the Stirling nose dived into the deck. Amongst the RAF personnel watching this tragic crash was Flying Officer Jim Allen DFC.

iii) Halifax HR838 (MH-Q, Queenie), the aircraft that flew the Monica trials, was taken over by Warrant Officer Leeper, RCAF, and crew when Claude Wilson and his crew were screened. This aircraft failed to return from Nuremberg on the night of 10/11th August 1943. Warrant Officer Leeper and crew are buried in a Munich cemetery.

Chapter Nine

1944: Just do your best lad!

"Ops On"

I dreamed last night I was back again, with the chaps once again I stood;
There was Trev and Jimmy and Gordie - and Dick in serious mood
Geoff and Jack in a huddle, checking the course and the height,
Making a note of the weather, 'Buttoning the job up tight.'
The Winco giving his 'Pep' talk, Intelligence giving the 'Gen',
The Met bloke with the usual Bull, 'Good cover chaps - bout Ten-Ten',
But clearing up at the target, giving a spot-on view. '
'OK chaps' says the Wingco, 'Best of luck now it's up to you.'
Out we stream to the crew truck, around the perimeter track,
Off at the kite and start checking, Where's that b-- trolley-acc?'
Give the old engines a warm up, check, them to see they're OK,
Ground crew busy around us, 'Right chaps -Chocks away!'
Taxi her round to the runway, 'There goes the green, this is it.'
Roll her on for the take off, check her for maximum power,
Check skipper's safety belt fastened; take one last look at the Tower.
Geoff puts the power on slowly, the 'Old girl' responds with a will,
We swiftly climb into the darkness, 'a Night hawk out for the kill'.

- written by Ken 'Watson Marshall DFC (1949)

In the far northeast of Scotland, on a grey October morning in 1943, one-hundred men were assembled in a large empty hangar. A new course was about to start at 20 OTU, Lossiemouth and twenty members of five aircrew categories had been gathered from basic and advanced training schools around the world and told to sort themselves into crews.

After about thirty minutes of much milling around, Dick Elliott, a Pilot Officer bomb aimer from Woodford Green, Essex, was approached by an acquaintance from his Bomb Airners course.

'Have you crewed up yet, Dick?'

'No, not yet.' came the reply.

'Well, there's a pilot called Sanders over there, they reckon he's OK.' Dick took the hint and wandered across to speak to the tall, slim Sergeant pilot.

'Looking for a Bomb Aimer?' enquired Dick.

'Why not?' came the calm, laconic reply, 'We've got to start somewhere.' Dick and his pilot, one Geoff Sanders from Shirley, Birmingham, wandered around the hangar together, finding themselves a navigator and then meeting up with two sergeant gunners, Gordon Heard from Exeter and Trev (E.J.) Trevallion who, although of Welsh stock, was as perfect an 'English' gentleman as one could hope to meet. They then met up with a Sergeant wireless operator by the name of Jimmy Quaggin who came from the Isle of Man. Having got all the three legged jokes out of their systems, Geoff suggested that, having now formed themselves into an embryo crew, they should get to know one another better in less draughty circumstances and led them over to the canteen at the Station cinema where he treated them all to a cup of char and a wad. Bomber Command had a new crew.

Their first flight together was at 10.00 hours on 12th October 1943 in one of the OTU's clapped-out Wellingtons. Their instructor for this trip was Flying Officer Berney and they spent almost three hours carrying out circuits and bumps. Berney, a New Zealander, was obviously satisfied with Geoff Sanders ability to handle the aged Wimpy, for on the following day – at the same time -they were sent off on their own to repeat the exercise. This led to cross-country flights involving map reading, navigation and landing away from base. After a couple of these exercises it became obvious to the OTU's Navigation Leader, not to mention Geoff and his crew, that their navigator appeared to have one minor problem - he couldn't navigate, so he was packed off back to Nav' school and was replaced by a Canadian Pilot Officer called Jack Munn, who very quickly settled in as one the lads. Training continued with more cross countries (now without getting lost), practice bombing on the Rose Valley range and some fighter affiliation exercises.

The Pendulum and the Scythe

At one stage during their sojourn at Lossiemouth, Gordon Heard was acting as rear ballast on a circuits and bumps exercise with an instructor and another crew whose regular rear gunner was sick. After three or four 'touch' landings, they were just getting airborne again when the starboard mainwheel struck a fence and ripped the tyre to shreds. Flying control informed them of their predicament over the radio and the instructor took control of the Wellington for the tricky landing ahead. Completing their final circuit, the instructor gently landed the aircraft on the port wheel only, then slowly lowered the tail wheel onto the grass, keeping the starboard wing slightly high. Only as the Wimpy lost forward speed did the instructor allow the damaged wheel to touch the ground, at which point it promptly dug into the earth, whipping the aircraft around in a ground loop and leaving it to finish its careerings on its nose, with the tail pointing skywards. Gordon Heard found himself over ten feet above the ground and, in his haste to vacate his elevated perch in the pranged Wimpy, very nearly strangled himself. He forgot to unplug his intercom lead!

After forty-five hours, five minutes day and fifty hours, forty-five minutes night flying from Lossiemouth, the Powers' decreed that Sergeant G. E. Sanders and crew were ready to move on to the next phase of bomber training. The skipper was commissioned, joining his bomb aimer and navigator in the Officers Mess and the crew were posted to 1663 HCU at Rufforth, Yorkshire, in March 1944. Here they acquired a `Geordie' flight engineer, Sergeant Ken Marshall and the now seven-strong crew began conversion to the Handley Page Halifax. Despite now being a full crew, the hierarchy still frowned upon officer aircrew mixing with their non-commissioned crew members, so the only way they could socialise was off camp in the local pubs. Geoff, Dick and Jack always found this attitude of senior training officers most strange and were greatly relieved to find that this ruling was not enforced once they reached their operational squadron. The HCU was equipped with the Merlin engined Halifax Marks II and V which, having survived operational squadron service, were almost as clapped out as the OTU's Wellingtons. Nevertheless, having amassed a grand total of thirty hours flying, including four and a half hours at night, Pilot Officer Sanders and crew were posted to Elvington for a week's attachment to 77 Squadron. Until their dying days, none of the crew could figure out why they had this short stay on 77 Squadron, but, while they were there, they carried out two further cross country exercises, one by day and the other by night, before being posted to 578 Squadron, based at Burn, where they arrived on 27th April 1944.

RAF Burn, just south of Selby on the A19 trunk road, was at that time under the command of Group Captain James Warburton who had only just taken over the Station - on 29th March - exactly one week after his predecessor, Group Captain N. W. D. Marwood-Elton, DFC, had failed to return from an attack on Frankfurt on the night of 22/23rd March. Marwood-Elton had gone on this raid as second pilot to Pilot Officer J. R. Atkins in Halifax B.Mk.III LW794, LK-Q, which had been shot down by a Junkers Ju88 nightfighter. Fortunately the whole crew, including the Station Commander, survived this traumatic ordeal although they were all invited to spend the rest of the war as the guests of Herr Hitler and his cohorts.

For the week between Marwood-Elton's unfortunate one way trip to Frankfurt and the arrival of James Warburton, the Station was temporarily commanded by the Officer Commanding[49] 578 Squadron, Wing Commander David S. S. (Wilkie) Wilkerson, DFC. Wilkie had just been promoted from Squadron Leader Flight Commander to Wing Commander in charge of 51 Squadron when 578 Squadron was formed from 'C' Flight of 51 on 14th January 1944 and he was instructed to take over the new unit on the orders of the AOC (Air Vice-Marshal 'Roddy' Carr) himself. Wingco Wilkerson was a born leader, yet he retained the common touch found in so many of our great leaders. He was very approachable and much liked and well respected by all on the squadron.

The day after arriving at Burn, Geoff and the lads went off on a seventy-minute day conversion exercise in Halifax 'F-Fox' (LW473), after which the flight engineer, Ken Marshall, went down with a severe bout of 'Flu that completely blocked his sinus and was to keep him off flying for two weeks. On the 29th April the crew took off at 17.30 hours for a cross country exercise in 'D-Dog', with a stand-in engineer called Brian Fawcett - an exceptionally tall man. After about two hours flying, Geoff just had to do 'what a man's gotta do', so putting 'D-Dog' onto 'George' - the automatic pilot - he got up to make his way back to the Elsan. He had just passed Brian Fawcett at the engineer's position immediately behind the pilot's seat when 'George' decided to try his robotic hand at aerobatics, starting with a flick roll to

---

[49] *OC - Although generally referred to as the CO (Commanding Officer), the correct term is Officer Commanding. As this ties in with usual service terminology, ie. 'Socks, Airmen' (otherwise known as 'Socks, Airmen for the use of) this makes perfect sense.*

David Wilkerson in the pilot's seat while on 35 Squadron earlier in the war.

starboard. Having rolled the aircraft through 90 degrees and positioned the wings in a perfect vertical position, 'George' then decided to test his skill at stall and spin recovery. The nose of the Halifax lurched sickeningly downwards and the aircraft began to spin, with the resulting G-forces preventing Geoff from returning to his controls.

It was at this point that the long arms of Fawcett came to the rescue. Holding on to the edge of his engineer's panel with one hand, Brian Fawcett was able to reach and grab Geoff Sanders with the other. Using all his considerable strength, Brian swung Geoff back into his seat in the cockpit, where the skipper rapidly disconnected the auto-pilot and started to take corrective action. Quickly correcting the spin and enabling the crew to move about once more - albeit only with considerable effort - Geoff pulled back on the control column in an effort to bring the Halifax out of its screaming dive. Seeing his skipper struggling with the controls, Brian Fawcett moved forward, reached over Geoff's shoulder and helped him pull back on the control column. Jack Munn, the navigator, also came to his assistance, pushing on the back of the column from the lower, forward compartment in the nose. Gradually, their combined efforts started to have the desired effect and the nose of the aircraft started to move up from the vertical.

Dick Elliott, watching the action in and about the cockpit, decided that he couldn't get near enough to help. Realising that there was absolutely nothing he could contribute to the struggle for all their lives, he was suddenly struck by the comic aspects of the almost pantomime antics of his skipper, navigator and stand-in engineer and burst out laughing. Not having quite the same viewpoint as Dick, Geoff was not in the least amused at the time, but he eventually managed to get 'D-Dog' back on the straight and level and gingerly returned to base where, on taxying into dispersal, they were met by Wingco Wilkerson.

`Are you alright Sandy? Is your crew OK?' asked a concerned Wilkie.

'Y-Yessir,' stuttered an astounded Geoff Sanders, 'But the aircraft isn't!'

`Never mind the aircraft,' said the Wingco, 'It's you and your crew I'm concerned about.'

The Pendulum and the Scythe

After they had climbed out of the aircraft, the Wingco drove Geoff back to the Mess for a chat. Having discussed the events of the recent flight, Wilkie suddenly said 'Do you know Jim Talbot?' Geoff had to confess that the name didn't ring any bells. `Well, he's Handley Page's Chief Test Pilot and he slow rolls all the Hallies!' Geoff thought 'He's bloody welcome to it.' but just said 'Oh!' The Wingco got up from his chair, patted Geoff on the shoulder and went about his duties, leaving an astounded but very grateful young pilot sitting the Mess. The crew were later informed that their involuntary manoeuvres had overstressed `D-Dog's' airframe and that she was a write-off. Geoff Sanders' tour had very nearly ended before it had begun and, had the five feet five inches tall Ken Marshall not been on the sick list, it probably would have done - Ken's arms were nowhere near as long as those of Brian Fawcett. The crew had had a lucky start and luck was something a crew needed plenty of if they hoped to complete a tour in Bomber Command.

On the morning of 30th April Geoff Sanders went down to the Flights and was informed that he was to carry out his first op as `second dickey' that night and that he was to fly with Flight Lieutenant Harold Brown and his crew. Geoff returned to the Mess, sought out his bomb aimer and told Dick 'Tonight's the night.' Full of goodwill and bonhomie, Dick wished Geoff a good trip and suggested that he leave his keys with him - just in case.

`That's not such a good idea.' said Geoff.

`Why not?' queried Dick.

`Because Harold Brown's bomb aimer is sick,' came the reply,

`You're coming with us!'

Dick managed to exchange a few pleasantries before beating a hasty retreat to the nearest toilet in order to relieve the imminent involuntary loosing of the bowels that had been brought on by his skipper's 'subtle' and unexpected announcement.

Dick quickly recovered his aplomb, composure and control of his nether regions and, after an early tea, he joined Geoff and Harold Brown's crew for briefing. The squadron was to send 23 Halifaxes as part of an attack by 4 and 8 Groups on the railway yards at Acheres in the northwest suburbs of Paris. Geoff and his crew were starting their tour of operations during the pre-'D-Day' build-up period, when Bomber Command was temporarily under the control of General Eisenhower at Supreme Headquarters Allied Expeditionary Force (SHAEF). Raids during this period were invariably aimed at communications targets and German military installations in Occupied France. The Acheres raid was part of Tedder's 'Communications Plan', the objective of which was to isolate enemy reinforcements from the planned Allied landing areas.

Flight Lieutenant Brown was to fly the same aircraft he'd used for his last seven trips. This was a Halifax B.Mk.III, serial no. LK809, coded LK-H (How). It had been built by Fairey Aviation as one of 200 aircraft produced to Contract No.ACFT/891 and had arrived on 578 Squadron in early April 1944. LK809 carried out her first operation on the 9th April when Harold Brown, then a Flying Officer, took her on a 4 hour 25 minute trip to Lille.

The first squadron aircraft took off for Acheres at 21.00 hours and H-How, with Geoff Sanders and Dick Elliott on board, was airborne ten minutes later. Bombing of the railway yards was carried out from a comparatively low level at around midnight and the Master Bomber was heard to say 'Good show' as the aircraft left the target area. The Mayor of Acheres .later reported that the bombing had completely destroyed the railway yards and that there had been no civilian casualties. All 128 aircraft involved in this attack returned safely, with the last 578 Squadron Halifax landing at just after a quarter-to-three in the morning of May Day.Despite all their training, Geoff and Dick felt totally unprepared for their first operational sortie. The amount

In front of LK809, H-How, left to right standing are: Trev, Ken, Geoff, Dick, groundcrewman, Jimmy, Jack and Gordon. Among the groundcrew kneeling front is Joe Raby (centre row, far left). (Geoff Sanders)

of 'Gen' fed to them at briefing regarding the target, route, defences, bomb load, met. and pressures, etc., left Dick completely bemused. Once over enemy territory, the initial impression of tracer was one of lovely coloured balls of light crawling ever so slowly up towards them, their speed gradually increasing as they got nearer, until suddenly they whistled past the aircraft at incredible speed. The sparkle, crack and the resultant buffeting of the Flak was another major impression, as was the magnificence of the large flares in the sky and the complementary brilliance of TIs on the ground among exploding bombs and burning buildings. All this combined into a dream-like first impression that never ever left Dick and compared to which, even the most magnificent firework display paled into insignificance.

Having returned unscathed from their first foray into the unknown, Geoff was later that day informed that he and his own crew would be operating that night and that they had been allocated LK809, LK-H. There were to be six separate attacks this night (1st/2nd May 1944), 139 aircraft went to an aircraft assembly plant at Toulouse, 137 to the St.Ghislain railway yards and 120 to the railway repair depot and stores at Chambly. Another 75 went to the Berliet Motor Works at Lyons, a further 46 to aircraft repair workshops at Tours and 132 aircraft were despatched to the marshalling yards at Malines in Belgium.

It was to the last of these attacks that 578 Squadron contributed sixteen of their Halifax B.Mk.IIIs, the first of which took off at 21.52 hours. Geoff Sanders, with stand-in flight engineer Sergeant W.W.Broughton, lifted 'H-How' off the Burn runway at 22.00 hours and set course for the target. Initially they flew through 10/10ths cloud, but this cleared at the English coast leaving them in good visibility and they arrived over the target at 23.45 hours. Some of the squadron crews were later to report that they had been unable to see the PFF markers and it was noted that the Master Bomber appeared to be having some difficulty in telling the main force to bomb the widely scattered reds and greens that were quickly swallowed up in the smoke and haze from the burning target, The Master Bomber kept repeating Press on, press on.', which was greeted with derisive replies from some crews. The 578 Squadron aircraft were forced to orbit the target while more markers were laid, something that greatly displeased the crews because of the additional danger of mid-air collisions. Ground defences were negligible but the enemy's nightfighters were fairly active. Fortunately, LK809 was not troubled.

Because of the marking confusion, bombing was badly scattered and, while the locomotive sheds were hit, there was also much damage to civilian property. All of 578 Squadron's aircraft returned safely to Burn, with 'H-How' the second to last down at 02.22 hours. Geoff Sanders and his crew had completed their first operation as a team and were most surprised to learn that they were all off on a week's leave - already! All, that is, except the Flight Engineer. Ken Marshall with the 'Flu still raging, was still confined to bed in the Station Medical Centre. The rest of the crew returned from leave on May 8th to find the whole squadron celebrating the immediate award of a DSO to the CO, Wing Commander D.S.S.Wilkerson.

Ken was still unfit for duty so Geoff required another stand-in FE for their next operation on May 11th. This was Sergeant L. G. T. Stevens and he joined Geoff, Dick, Jack, Jimmy, Gordon and Trev for an early evening briefing. The squadron was sending seventeen aircraft which, with thirty-six other Halifaxes from 4 Group and six Pathfinder Mosquitoes, were to attack a large gun battery at Trouville, opposite Le Havre on the mouth of the Seine. This was one of six separate raids this night and it turned out to be the only one that was totally successful.

All 578 Squadron aircraft reached the target area and fourteen of them dropped their bomb loads on the PFF markers despite a thick haze. Dick Elliott released H-How's eighteen 500 lb MC bombs and shortly afterwards a large explosion was observed, throwing debris up to 1,000 feet. The squadron's three remaining aircraft arrived over the target after the TIs had burned out and so, for fear of causing French civilian casualties, did not release their bombs. Later reports showed the bombing to have been extremely accurate. All aircraft returned safely and at 02.49 hours, LK-H was the last of 578 Squadron's aircraft to land.

At long last the MO released Ken Marshall from the sick list and he was able to rejoin Geoff and the lads for some local flying on 14th May. This was followed, next day, by a fifty-minute fighter affiliation exercise and, on the 18th, by a bombing exercise that was not completed because of a deterioration in the weather. A Bullseye exercise to Bristol followed on the 20th and the oldest and youngest gunners on the squadron[50] got in some air-to-sea firing

---

[50] *With Gordon Heard only just 18 years old and Trey Trevallion over 36, Geoff Sanders believes that his crew contained the oldest and youngest gunners on the squadron.*

on the 21st. On Monday 22nd May they were once again on the Operations Order.

The target for the night was the Les Aubrais railway complex at Orleans and 578 Squadron contributed 21 aircraft to a total force of 108 Halifaxes from 4 Group and twelve Lancasters and Mosquitoes from the PFF. This trip took LK809 and her crew five-and-a-half-hours and was uneventful. While the squadron operated again on the 24th May (twice in fact, to Aachen and Colline Beaumont, near Bologne) Geoff Sanders and his crew were not detailed for operations again until the 27th May, when, at the briefing for a raid on Bourg Leopold in Belgium, Group Captain Warburton announced the immediate award of a DFC to the squadron Bombing Leader, Flight Lieutenant Hart.

Bourg Leopold is positioned east of Antwerp and about twenty miles west-southwest of Eindhoven, Holland. At this time it was the location of a large Wehrmacht camp and stores depot and Allied Intelligence rightly believed that it was housing a full Panzer Division. Bomber Command was ordered to attack the camp in some strength and Harris detailed 331 aircraft for the raid - 267 of them Halifaxes - of which twenty-one were supplied by 578 Squadron, whose first aircraft took off at 23.49 hours.

The Pathfinders played their part superbly on this raid, with one of their Oboe-aimed markers falling right slap-bang on the aiming point. The main force's bombing was extremely accurate and caused severe damage. As 'H-How' was on the run-up to the target, Dick Elliott in the nose, could see precisely where he had to release his bombs. The release point was right in the middle of the thickest concentration of Flak Dick had ever seen (or was ever to see throughout the whole tour). There appeared to be little Flak elsewhere but Dick found himself in the unenviable position of having to guide his skipper and crew right into the centre of this large box of Flak. The run-up only lasted a few minutes, but to Dick Elliott it felt like weeks. Amazingly, 'H-How' emerged unscathed. The crew's luck seemed to be holding well.

On the return flight all 578 Squadron aircraft were diverted because of bad weather at Burn. Thirteen of them, including 'H-How' landed at Silverstone, a Training Unit where the Flying Controllers were not used to landing an operational squadron. They maintained all the normal Flying Training safety margins and the elapsed time from an individual aircraft arriving in the stack, to actual touchdown was in the region of thirty minutes. Burn could land the complete squadron in about twenty minutes. A further six Halifaxes landed at Catfoss – one of which (LW474, LK-Z) had been attacked by nightfighters en-route to the target and had had its port-inner engine set on fire. 'Z-Zebra's' pilot, Pilot Officer Malvern, jettisoned his bombs and landed at Catfoss an hour ahead of the other squadron aircraft. The two remaining Halifaxes landed at Crouton (LW469, LK-A) and Carnaby (LW496, LK-O), the latter also having had a run-in with enemy fighters, during which the wireless operator was wounded. The following day, 30th May, the squadron was placed on stand-by to carry out an attack on the railway yards at Trappes, in the western suburbs of Paris. However, this operation was cancelled before briefing, so it was not until the 31st May (Ken Marshall's 21st birthday) that Geoff, the 'birthday-boy' and the rest of the crew were once again called for operations. They were to take LK809 to Trappes as part of the squadron's 23 Halifax contribution to a 219-aircraft strong attack on the same target that had been cancelled the previous day. All twenty-three squadron aircraft returned safely, despite flying through storms both ways. This meant that 578 Squadron had achieved the most unusual feat of operating throughout a full calendar month without losing a single aircraft.

On 1st June, operations were ordered and then cancelled, so the squadron's next raid took place on Saturday 2nd when sixteen Halifaxes were despatched to join another 255 aircraft in attacks on four enemy coastal gun positions in the Cap Gris Nez area. Bombing was really accurate at only one of these sites but this was of no great importance as the raids were part of the invasion deception plans and were not in the immediate vicinity of the planned landings. Despite 10/10ths cloud from 2,000 to 9,000 feet, 578 Squadron took off from Burn from 23.29 hours onwards and reached their allotted target at Haringzelles just after 1 am. Geoff held 'H-How' steady on the bomb run as Dick watched the Aiming Point creeping up the cross wires of the bombsight. Just as he was about to 'press the tit' to release their bombs, cloud totally obscured his view of the target and so, because of repeated warnings to all crews about French civilian casualties, Dick aborted the run. The Standing Instruction a this time was 'If you can't see the target - don't bomb!' so Dick jettisoned six of their 500 lb. GP bombs off the French coast and Geoff landed 'H-How' back at Burn with another two 500 pounders and seven 1,000 pounders still on board.

At this time the whole unit was confined to camp, 'something' was very obviously 'on' and whatever it was it could not be far away. Operations were ordered on the 3rd June and then cancelled at 22.00 hours. Operations were ordered again on Sunday 4th June when the squadron sent twenty-four Halifaxes as part of a 259 aircraft attack on four more gun positions, three in the Pas de Calais area and one at Maisy in Normandy. This last target was situated between what would shortly be Omaha and Utah beaches where US troops would land in less than thirty-six hours. The 578 Squadron aircraft were detailed to attack gun positions at Boulogne, but 'H-How', the first aircraft airborne, arrived over the target to find it completedly covered by cloud and so added their bombload to those of 6 Group on a clear Calais. Squadron Leader A. Harte-Lovelace, the 'A' Flight Commander was next over Boulogne and dropped his bombs through the cloud onto the Flak positions. The cloud had cleared somewhat by the time the rest of the squadron's aircraft reached the target and the remaining twenty-two bombed Boulogne successfully.

The squadron was detailed for operations again on Monday 5th, but once again these were later cancelled and the unit was stood down. By this time, the crew of 'H-How' were getting somewhat fatigued with the current intense level of operational activity, not to mention being a bit 'brassed-off' with all this 'Ops on, Ops off' stuff and they asked their skipper to see if the CO would allow them a short stand-down. Fully expecting to receive a 'flea in his ear' Geoff asked Wing Commander Wilkerson the question. 'Yes, Sandy.' came the most unexpected reply, 'But you may well be sorry you asked.' On Tuesday 6th June, 578 Squadron operated twice within twenty-four hours. The first attack, by twenty-two Halifaxes with first off at 02.28 hours, was on the Normandy coastal batteries as part of a 1,012 aircraft raid from which three failed to return. One of these was MZ513; LK-K from 578 Squadron. `K-King', flown by the 'B' Flight Commander, Squadron Leader W. G. Watson, was hit by bombs from higher flying aircraft and, despite the best efforts of this experienced pilot who tried to nurse his badly damaged Halifax home, the crew finally had to abandon MZ513 over the North Sea. The bomb aimer (Flying Officer W. O. Hefferman), flight engineer (Flight Sergeant W. L. Middleton) and wireless operator (Flying Officer E. Onions) were picked up by Allied shipping, including American Landing Craft No. LCT708, but no trace was ever found of Squadron Leader Watson, his navigator (Flying Officer J. A. Hall), mid-upper gunner (Sergeant C. A. Goode) or rear gunner (Flying Officer S. G. Turner). Because of their twenty-four hour stand-down, 'H-How's crew did not take part in this historic raid and 'whinged' like mad. Geoff Sanders gave them no sympathy, but took great delight in pointing out that the Wingco had been right, they were sorry they had requested some time off and unofficial stand-downs were never mentioned again.

Nevertheless they were back on the Operations Order for the second raid of D-Day. With first take-off scheduled for 23.14 hours, 578 Squadron detailed twenty-five of their Halifaxes to join a total force of 1,065 aircraft despatched to attack road and railway centres on the lines of communication behind the Normandy landing areas. All targets were in, or very near to French towns and 3,488 tons of bombs were dropped on targets in Acheres, Argentan, Caen, Chateaudun, Conde-sur-Noireau, Coutances, Lisieux, St.Lo and Vire and, while every effort was made to bomb accurately, casualties to French civilians were inevitable. Cloud once again affected accuracy at many of the targets and at Acheres, the Master Bomber called off the raid because of it. The Halifaxes of 578 Squadron took part in the attack on Chateaudun, twelve miles northwest of Orleans, where the railway was bombed between 02.03 and 02.16 hours from heights of 6,600 feet and above. Weather in the target area was good, while opposition was negligible and an enormous fire was observed by many crews as they turned for home. LK809, H-How sailed through this operation without any trouble at all, but MZ619; 'H-bar' (the letter with a straight line over the top of it) failed to return. Nothing was heard from this crew after they took off and the aircraft was later found to have crashed at Jallans in France with the death of all on board.

The whole squadron was stood-down on Wednesday 7th June, but were back on the Group's Operations Board on Thursday when once again communications targets were the order of the day. Five major railway targets were selected in order to prevent German re-enforcements reaching Normandy from the south and east and 578 Squadron sent twenty-six crews, including that of Geoff Sanders in LK809, to attack the marshalling yards at Alencon, approximately 100 miles west-southwest of Paris and north of Le Mans. Take-off from Burn was circa 22.45 hours and the squadron dropped their 500 lbs GP bombs on the target between 01.14 and 01.26 hours from heights of 6,500 feet and above. With negligible opposition the target was left burning and the solitary nightfighter sighted did not prevent any of the unit's aircraft from making a safe return.

Bad weather over Burn caused a two day stand-down on the 9th and 10th so it was not until 22.05 hours on Sunday 11th June that Geoff Sanders lifted 'H-How' into the air to commence his tenth operation. Again, railways were the targets and 578 Squadron sent twenty-six Halifaxes to bomb a road-rail bridge at Massey-Palaiseau in the south-southwest suburbs of Paris just after midnight. The Master Bomber instructed the crews to bomb from between 2,000 and 3,000 feet, below the cloud base, so Geoff took H-How' down to 2,000 feet but cloud still obscured the target. They jettisoned ten of their 500lb.GP bombs off the French coast and took the other eight back to Burn.

Two more operations against communications targets followed in quick succession, the railway yards at Amiens on the night of 12/13th June, when two of the squadron's aircraft failed to return, and a locomotive depot at Douai on the night of 14/15th. It was on this latter trip that Geoff required the services of a replacement rear gunner, it was Gordon Heard's turn to be sick, with a bad attack of hay fever. As they were returning home at 9,500 feet, they received a warning of an approaching nightfighter from their Monica equipment. Ken Marshall, with his head in the astrodome, spotted a Ju88 flying over the top of LK809 from port to starboard. Ken warned Geoff and both gunners but, fortunately, the nightfighter crew was not as alert as that of the Halifax and it continued on its way without attacking. The crew's luck was still working and they returned safely to base from where they went off on a week's leave.

They returned to Burn to learn that, in their absence, the squadron had carried out its first daylight operation – to Siracourt - on the 22nd June. Geoff Sanders, remembering the heavy losses of the early war daylight raids, was somewhat shaken at the Command's return to day attacks and he didn't fancy them one little bit. At least their first operation on return from their leave was to take place at night. Following the arrival of the first 'Doodlebug' (V-1) that exploded at Swanscombe, near Gravesend in Kent on 13th June, Bomber Command despatched 412 aircraft to attack four V-1 sites. The gunners' first job before every trip, long before briefing, was to check out their turret, guns and ammunition. The morning of Friday 23rd June started off no differently and, while Trev was checking out the mid-upper turret, Gordon was giving his rear turret an even more thorough than usual going over because somebody else had flown 'H-How' the previous day. The turret itself was OK, the ammunition was fine, but on checking the Browning machine guns he found that all four had bad indents in the barrels. Although he was already convinced that he was probably going to have to remove them and cart them over to the Armoury, Gordon set to work to try and clean them out. As he was rubbing away at the indent of the third barrel he was dimly aware of the arrival of a motor vehicle of some description but was so intent on his work that he didn't bother to look up. He was therefore somewhat surprised when a voice that he immediately recognised as that of the squadron's CO said,

`Having a spot of trouble Sar'nt Heard?'

'Yes sir.' replied Gordon, 'There are indents in all four barrels and I can't shift them. I'm just about to remove them and take them to the Armoury.'

`Come on then Sar'nt, I'll give you a hand and then I'll run you across there in the Tilly.' said Wing Commander Wilkerson. The Browning's barrels were removed in double-quick time and loaded into the back of the Tilly and off they went.

Unfortunately, even the armourers couldn't shift the indents and there were no spare barrels on the station. `H-How' could not fly that night without guns in the rear turret. 'Come on, Heard' said Wilkie, 'load 'em back in the Tilly, we're going to Snaith.' True to his word, the Wingco took Gordon and his guns over to the parent unit where new barrels were available. Then Wilkie drove them back to Burn and dropped them off at 'H-How's' dispersal, where Gordon re-fitted them in the turret. The Wingco then took the rear gunner to the Mess and ensured that he was provided with a late 'pre-op' meal before he went into the briefing to let Geoff know what had transpired and that Gordon would join the crew as soon as he'd finished eating.

The rear turret of LK809 was fully armed and ready for duty long before twenty-three Halifaxes from 578 Squadron were sent to bomb the V-1 storage site at Oisement/Neuville au Bois, northwest of St.Omer. Several V-1s were seen on their way to southeast England while the aircraft were en-route to the target, thus adding to the desire to make a good job of this operation. All crews reported the best concentration of markers and bombing they had ever seen, but more to the point for the crew of 'H-How', Geoff Sanders brought them all home safely from his thirteenth operational sortie.

Operations were now coming fast and furious, with the squadron attacking another V-1 site, at Le Grand Rossingnol near Boulogne, in the early hours of Sunday 25th June. Gordon Heard was once again down with hay fever so Geoff again obtained the services of the same Pilot Officer rear gunner who had stood in last time. Having successfully bombed the target, Geoff was flying 'H-How' home when Trev Trevallion in the mid-upper turret came on the intercom.

'Trev to Skipper, I can smell smoke.'

`Well don't just sit there Trev,' replied Geoff, 'Go and see what it is.' Doing as he was bidden, Trev extracated himself from the turret, thinking that the lower he got into the fuselage, the more the smoke smelt familiar. Getting his feet firmly on the fuselage floor, he looked around and was amazed to see the stand-in rear Gunner standing by the Elsan with his back towards Trev, smoking a cigarette. Unable to believe his eyes, Trev scrambled back into his turret and appraised Geoff of the situation. The skipper thanked Trev for the information and said nothing further regarding the incident until they were safely back on the ground at Burn. As the crew got out of the Halifax, Geoff took the Pilot Officer gunner to one side and informed him in no uncertain terms that no rear gunner in his aircraft ever left the turret without the skipper's express permission. He most certainly did not leave the turret for a crafty fag while still within range of the enemy and anyone who was stupid enough to light a cigarette in the immediate vicinity of a tin bucket half-full of semi-volatile chemicals needed to pay a very rapid visit to the nearest 'trick cyclist[51]. In short, Geoff didn't give him the lickings of a dog and, quite rightly, flatly refused to fly with him ever again.

Just over 53 hours after landing back from Le Grand Rossingnol, Geoff and crew were off on their first daylight sortie. Five Mosquitoes and two Lancasters from PFF led 104 Halifaxes from 4 Group (including twenty-five from 578 Squadron) in a 27th June attack on the V-weapon base at Marquise Mimoyecques, half way between Calais and Boulogne. Initially associated with flying bombs, it was not until Allied troops over-ran this site that it was discovered that this was the home of the V-3, an underground, six-inch multi-barrelled set of long range guns with muzzle velocities of 5,000 feet per second. Because of its huge reinforced concrete protection, this site was never seriously damaged until 617 Squadron dropped several of its Tallboys on it on July 6th. The 1,000 lb. MC and 500 lb GP bombs dropped by 578 Squadron this day didn't stand a chance against this target.

On return to base, Geoff Sanders had `H-How' nicety lined up on finals and was just about to set her down when Dick Elliott warned him that some prize twit had just landed downwind and was now heading straight at them. Geoff

---

[51] 'Trick Cyclist' - service slang for psychiatrist.

let out a few choice words as he opened all four throttles and lifted the aircraft's nose to go around again. Climbing away at 100 mph indicated air speed, Dick - standing at Geoff's side - raised the flaps to 40 degrees down and then retracted the undercarriage as Geoff slowly increased speed to 145 mph and completed another circuit. The other pilot, a Flight Lieutenant, got very short shrift from the Wingco. He send the offender back to an HCU the same day. Dick's timely warning had allowed Geoff to avoid a very nasty head-on crash. The crew's luck, not to mention teamwork and experience, was working well.

Ten hours later, at 05.35 hours on Wednesday 28th June, Geoff and crew were off again. This time their objective was a V-weapon site at Wizernes, south of St.Omer. This site is now known to have been intended for launching V-2 (A4) rockets armed with nuclear and biological warheads and also for the long range V-2 (A9/A10), with sufficient range to reach America. At this time the Germans already had stocks of Tabun and Sabin nerve gas and were working hard on the development of a nuclear warhead. Fortunately, the 103 Halifaxes of 4 Group, led by five Mosquitoes and two Lancasters of PFF, so damaged this target that its construction was never completed by the Todt Organisation. Of the twenty-four Halifaxes despatched by 578 Squadron on this daylight raid one, MZ560, LK-J flown by Flight Sergeant G. Heuston, returned early because of an engine failure and two others landed away from base with wounded crewmen aboard. LL548, LK-C (Flight Sergeant J. D. Matthews - RAAF) landed at Manston with a wounded navigator, while MZ583, LK-Y (Flight Lieutenant R. M. Bleakley, RCAF) landed at Carnaby with a wounded bomb aimer. The remaining twenty-one aircraft returned safely to base, although quite a few had damaged airframes due to the heavy Flak encountered over Calais, St.Omer and Gravelines.

On Thursday 29th June, the squadron detailed twenty-four aircraft and crews to standby for operations that were later cancelled, so Geoff Sanders' eighteenth operation began on 30th June at 17.35 hours as he lifted 'H-How' into the air for his third daylight raid on the trot. He, along with another 265 crews were heading for a road junction close to the small town of Villers Bocage, approximately 20 kilometres southwest of Caen, through which the tanks of two German armoured divisions (2nd and 9th Panzer) would have to pass in order to carry out an attack on the point at which the British and American armies flanked each other. Thanks to Enigma intercepts, Allied

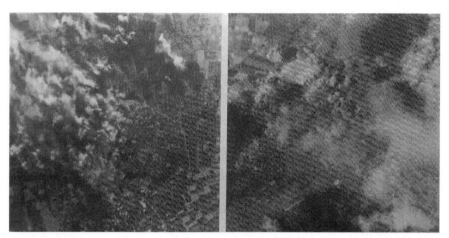

Aiming Point photographs from H How. (Left) Wizernes 28th June 1944 (Right) Somain 11th August 1944.

Intelligence had learned that this attack was to take place this night, so 'Butch' Harris despatched 151 Lancasters, 105 Halifaxes and 10 Mosquitoes from 3, 4 and 8 Groups with instructions to make the road junction impassable.

En-route to the target at low level, `H-How' had just crossed the front line when Gordon Heard in the rear turret advised his skipper that a Lancaster was overhauling them at a great pace. Geoff had just acknowledged this information when Dick Elliott in the nose warned Geoff that there was an enemy Flak position on a small hillock dead ahead. As Dick was reporting this fact, the Lancaster came barrelling past `H-How', going flat out and waggling its wings in salute as it overtook. 'Bloody show-off said Geoff as he altered course slightly to avoid the Flak guns ahead. Suddenly there was an almighty explosion that shook `H-How', there were red and green T.I.s in the sky and flaming wreckage on the ground. The Lancaster had been a Pathfinder hurrying to reach the target at its allotted time, but unfortunately its bomb aimer had not been as observant as Dick Elliott. It had flown directly at the Flak position and had been blown out of the sky with their first salvo. Once again, an alert Dick Elliott had helped the crew avoid a nasty end... and their luck still held.

When they reached the target the Master Bomber, Squadron Leader B. W. McMillan, was controlling the attack with great care, ordering the main force to bomb from no higher than 4,000 feet so that they could all be sure of seeing the markers in the smoke and dust of exploding bombs. While holding steady on the bombing run Geoff had to swerve 'H-How' rapidly 40 degrees to port to avoid another aircraft, but he quickly turned back towards the target so that Dick could continue the run, bringing back a superb Aiming Point photograph. The force dropped 1,100 tons of bombs with extreme accuracy and totally prevented the Panzers proposed attack. A Pathfinder Mosquito pilot, Flying Officer D. Tidy of 105 Squadron, waited in the target area until the dust and smoke had settled and on his return to base reported that while the five roads leading to the junction were clearly visible and almost undamaged, the actual junction itself looked as if an enormous excavation had taken place. Only two aircraft were lost on this important daylight raid, one Halifax and the Lancaster that the crew of H-How' had seen blown up.

The next day, Saturday 1st July, they attacked the V-1 storage site at Oisement/Neuville au Bois again, while on Sunday the squadron was stood down. On Monday operations were ordered but later cancelled and on Tuesday the squadron sent twenty aircraft on an attack on a V-1 storage site at St.Martin-l'Hortier, slightly east of a line between Dieppe and Rouen. Geoff and the boys were not on the Operations Order for this daylight but, at 01.55 hours on Thursday morning they were on their way to that same target by night.

Less than fourteen hours after their return from St.Martin-l'Hortier, they were off again to another V-weapon site, this time at Croixdalle, east of Dieppe. Again in their old faithful, LK809, H-How, they were one of twenty-two Halifaxes from 578 on this attack. Shortly after take-off, while climbing through 10/10ths cloud to reach operational height, the moisture content of the cloud was so high that it caused the immersion switch (fitted to automatically release the aircraft's dinghy in the event of ditching in the sea) to trigger, releasing the covering panel and the dinghy that only narrowly missed the Halifax's tailplane as they flew up, over and down to land in the vicinity of Nottingham, although the crew did not realise they had lost them until they returned to base. Carrying on to the target, they found it marked with red TIs that appeared to be a little west of the Aiming Point and despite moderately heavy Flak on the run-up, 'H-How' once again sailed through undamaged. One of the squadron's crews was not so lucky however, Flight Lieutenant D. McGowan, a Canadian pilot flying LW678; LK-L, was accosted by heavy Flak in the area of Dieppe but brought his damaged aircraft back to Burn with his bomb aimer, Flying Officer E. J. McConky - another Canadian - slightly wounded.

Nearing Burn on their return, Geoff and the crew observed a mid-air explosion just south of Nottingham. This turned out to be a 578 Squadron aircraft, MZ519, LK-U, flown by Pilot Officer R. Parfitt and crew, there were no survivors[52]. In all, 551 aircraft, comprising 314 Halifaxes, 210 Lancasters, 26 Mosquitoes and one Mustang attacked five V-weapons targets on Thursday 6th July. The Mustang was flown by Wing Commander Leonard Cheshire, CO of 617 Squadron, on the attack on Marquise-Mimoyecques (578 Squadron had been there on 27th June), where their Tallboy bombs finished Hitler's V-3 long- range guns for good. On 617 Squadron's return from this operation, Leonard Cheshire was ordered off operations for the rest of the war. He had carried out 102 operations. He would carry out his 103rd as an observer over Nagasaki on 9th August 1945. Also ordered to rest after this attack were his three Flight Commanders, Squadron Leaders J. C. (Joe) McCarthy, K. L. (Les) Munro and D. J. (Dave) Shannon[53]. All three were original members of the squadron and survivors of the Dams Raid.

On both Friday 7th and Saturday 8th July, operations were ordered and later cancelled because of bad weather over the intended target areas. Just before lunch on the Sunday however, 578 Squadron despatched twenty-six of its Halifaxes, including Geoff and crew in LK809, to bomb yet another V-weapon site at Les Catelliers, in cloudy conditions. In fact the weather over continental Europe was to be no friend of Bomber Command or the Allied ground forces for the next eight days. Operations were ordered again on the morning of Monday 10th and then cancelled at 18.00 hours. Exactly the same thing happened on Tuesday. On Wednesday 12th the squadron at last managed to get the better of the weather when it despatched twenty-two aircraft to bomb the V-1 supply dump at Thiverney, although Geoff and the

---

[52] *Although this aircraft, with its crew, was 'lost' to the RAF, it was classified as Category E, a 'write-off', rather than 'missing. Indeed, aircraft that ditched and from which the crew were rescued, were classified 'Cat.E'.*

[53] *Geoff Sander's flight engineer, Ken Marshall, flew a 'Captain's Night Check' with Squadron Leader D.J. Shannon, DSO*, DFC* in an Avro York of 246 Squadron on 18th October 1945. Dave Shannon was at this time Flying Officer Ken Marshall's Flight Commander.*

boys were not called for this operation. On Thursday operations were ordered and then cancelled yet again, this time at 15.00 hours. They were ordered again on Friday and then cancelled at 18.00 hours. Finally, just before midnight on Saturday 15th July, Geoff and crew took off to bomb the V-1 site at Nucourt, NNW of Paris, to carry out their 23rd operational sortie.

The crew's seventh daylight attack took place on Tuesday 18th July, when twenty-one aircraft from 578 Squadron formed part of a 942-aircraft strong force sent to bomb five fortified villages in the area east of Caen, through which the British Second Army was about to make an armoured thrust (Operation Goodwood). These raids took place at dawn in clear conditions and four of the targets (Colombelles, Mondeville, Sannerville and Cagey) were satisfactorily marked by Oboe. At the fifth target, Manneville, however, the Master Bomber, Squadron Leader E. K. Cresswell, realising that there had been an Oboe failure, ordered his deputy, Squadron Leader E. J. Chidgey, to mark the target visually. Chidgey put down accurate yellow TIs that were efficiently backed up and, under Cresswell's guidance, the main force bombing was highly concentrated. All aircraft bombed from between 5 and 9,000 feet and, despite the previous best efforts of army and naval gunfire to silence the enemy Flak batteries, five Halifaxes and one Lancaster were lost. Bomber Command dropped in excess of 5,000 tons of high explosive and 349 USAAF medium bombers of the AEAF dropped sufficient fragmentation bombs to bring the total tonnage up to 6,800 tons. Elements of two German divisions - the 21st Panzer and 16th Luftwaffe Field Divisions - were badly affected by the accurate bombing. This raid has since been deemed to be one of the best, if not the best operation in direct support of Allied ground troops ever carried out by Bomber Command. Total Allied air superiority over the battlefield area by day prevented any German fighters from putting in an appearance and all six bomber aircraft lost were as a result of Flak.

The first of 578 Squadron's Halifaxes to take off for Caen was airborne at 03.57 hours and LK-H, flown as usual by Geoff Sanders - now a Flying Officer - was second in line. While still over the UK en-route to the target, 'H-How' was flying behind another one of their squadron's aircraft - 'Q-Queenie' (LK794) when they observed one of 'Queenie's' engines burst into flames. Geoff knew 'Queenie's' Australian skipper, Vic Starkoff, quite well and was alarmed to see the aircraft suddenly dive towards the ground. Only the rear gunner, Flight Sergeant H. C. Sloan, had time to bale out and the rest of the crew were killed when LK794 hit the ground at Bisham, near

Maidenhead[54]. All other squadron aircraft carried out the raid as briefed and then returned to Burn, although several were damaged by Flak. Halifax serial no. NA510; LK-Z flown by Flying Officer M. C. Day, in particular, was found to have over twenty Flak holes in its airframe.

Later the same day 578 Squadron despatched nine aircraft on a second raid (to Vaires railway yards) but Geoff and his crew were stood down after their early morning raid. On Wednesday 19th July operations were ordered again and at 11.00 hours Geoff took the crew up for a forty-five minute air test. At three in the afternoon the operation was cancelled yet again. A night raid was ordered for Thursday 20th, with take-off planned for around 11pm. As the map curtains were drawn back at briefing the crew of 'H-How' learned that their 25th trip was to be their first one to Germany. Twenty-six aircraft of 578 Squadron were to join another 123 Halifaxes, 13 Mosquitoes and four Lancasters, drawn from 4 and 8 Groups, in an attack on the synthetic oil refinery at Bottrop in the Ruhr. Whilst obviously somewhat apprehensive about a trip to 'Happy Valley' and all that this implied, Geoff and the lads were nevertheless quite excited at the prospect of their first operation to the Fatherland.

The squadron's first aircraft took off for Bottrop at 22.56 hours, with 'H-How' third in line. Twenty minutes into the trip Flying Officer M. H. Clark - in 'Z-Zebra' (LW346) had his airspeed indicator go unserviceable and he was forced to abandon the mission. He jettisoned his bombs in the North Sea and headed for a tricky landing at Carnaby emergency strip. On reaching the target the other crews met barrage Flak from 16,000 to 20,000 feet (although those crews with previous Ruhr Valley experience felt that there was nothing unusual in this) plus rocket projectiles with glowing orange tails that were exploding at about 19,000 feet. Searchlights were very active and, as was his normal custom in such situations, Geoff Sanders dropped his seat to its lowest position and flew on instruments and the directions given by his bomb aimer. Dick was, as usual, lying in the nose of the Halifax, resting on his parachute pack with a tin helmet strategically placed under a certain prized part of his anatomy - no sense in taking unnecessary risks with one's

---

[54] *A crater, fifty feet wide and some twenty feet deep, left by LK794, can still be seen beside a small crossroads, The fact that, apart from the lone survivor, nothing of the rest of the crew was ever found, gives an indication of the awesome force of the explosion. The crew are listed on the Runnymede Register of aircrew with no known graves.*

equipment! Decoy markers were dropped by the enemy and although they cascaded just like the PFF markers they were meant to imitate, their colours were not so intense. Several 578 Squadron aircraft were damaged by Flak while over the target, including 'T-Tare' (MZ515), which had a starboard engine burst into flames. This was successfully extinguished and the pilot, Warrant Officer J. W. Driver, brought his aircraft and crew safely back to base on the remaining three engines.

Going into the target Gordon Heard, in the rear turret of LK809, was extra-specially alert. Apart from the Flak and searchlights below him, he could see many enemy nightfighters, both twin and single engined, flying above the bomber stream. Fortunately 'H-How' sailed through this operation without a scratch and the crew noticed nothing of any further consequence until they were almost back at Burn when a mid-air collision was observed in the vicinity of Hull. They were all the more astounded therefore, to learn after debriefing, that the squadron had suffered its biggest 'chop' night of the war. Six aircraft were missing, two of them (LK834, E and MZ696, K) being the mid-air collision near Hull. The total force had lost only one Lancaster and seven Halifaxes and it was almost unbelievable that six of them should belong to 578 Squadron. All fourteen crew members in 'E-Easy' and 'K-King' were killed, while 'M-Mother' (MZ511) crashed at Heerde in Holland with only two survivors and 'P-Peter' (MZ556) crashed at Vluynbusch with four survivors. 'D-Dog' (MZ617) crashed at Herpen, Holland, with the loss of all on board but `C-Charlie' (MZ572) just went missing and no trace of her or her crew has ever been found.

Fortunately, because of the relative isolation of individual crews from other squadron crews at this stage of the war (it was really only the officers meeting in the mess who got to know other aircrew officers and, unless someone else from the same training course was on the unit, most non-commissioned aircrew did not intermingle outside of their own tight-knit crew) losses of this magnitude had little, if any, effect on the crews who returned. The usual, if somewhat cynical, reaction was 'Oh well, at least we've moved a bit further up the leave roster.' Most, if not all, aircrew developed the introspective attitude that was centred upon the well-being of their own crew. This, linked to the 'It can't happen to us.' syndrome, was the only way in which these very young and extremely brave (although they would all strenuously deny the latter) men could close their eyes to the fact that their chances of completing their contract of thirty or more operations over enemy occupied territory were very, very slim indeed.

The Pendulum and the Scythe

On Friday 21st July operations were ordered but once again cancelled, this time at 14.00 hours and the squadron was stood down on the Saturday. Back on the Operations Order for a night raid on Sunday, the crews learned that they were to have another go at Germany, the target this time being Kiel. Nineteen Halifaxes from 578 Squadron were to join a total force of 629 aircraft on this, the first major raid on a German city for two months. Geoff Sanders, now a Flight Lieutenant, and his crew took off at 22.45 hours and headed out across the North Sea, reaching and attacking the target at around 01.15 hours. The defences consisted of a heavy Flak barrage from 12,000 to 20,000 feet, plus rocket projectiles and, having bombed successfully, Geoff turned H-How' around and started the journey back to Burn. Just as they were crossing the enemy coast in the Arnum Bank area, the skipper, who had observed a Lancaster approximately five miles to the north of them, asked the navigator, Jack Munn, if they were on track.

`No Skipper,' came the immediate response, 'We're a bit south of track, but we'll pick it up again OK at the next course change.' Seconds after this brief exchange, Ken Marshall, the flight engineer who was in the astrodome - helping to keep watch for nightfighters - saw a Flak-ship off the coast open up on the aircraft to the north of them. The first shot exploded just in front of the hapless Lancaster, the second shot went off right behind her. The third one hit the Lancaster in the centre of its fuselage and started a raging fire. Slowly at first, the Lane' started to lose height, but gradually its nose dipped at a steeper angle and the aircraft dropped lower and lower until it hit the sea below. Once again the crew's luck had seen them through and they landed back at base at 03.50 hours, with another operation under their belts.

The rest of Monday (24th July) morning was taken up with sleeping, but they were woken shortly after midday to be told that operations were 'on' again that night. Because 'H-How' was not fitted with long-range fuel tanks Geoff and the lads were allocated MZ560, `J-Jig', which was usually flown by Flight Lieutenant Ross Hutchinson, RAAF (later Sir Ross), but none of the crew were particularly enamoured at carrying out their first trip without their own trusty steed 'H-How' - particularly when the serial number of the aircraft they'd been ordered to fly had the same prefix (MZ) as that of five of the six aircraft lost on the Bottrop raid. The target for the night was to be Stuttgart, a long eight-hour trip from Burn. Because of its situation in a series of narrow valleys, Stuttgart's central areas had eluded the best efforts of Bomber Command for many years. Now, thanks to `Oboe', the city's relative immunity would come to an abrupt end. 'This attack was to be the first of three heavy and accurate raids that would cause Stuttgart its worst damage of the war, with most of the city centre being devastated. The Command despatched 614 aircraft, of which seven were Halifaxes from 578 Squadron. On this occasion all the squadron's aircraft were flown by experienced crews, with the first off at 21.35 hours. Geoff Sanders lifted `J-Jig' off the deck at 21.40 hours and set course for the target, some 800 miles away. Arriving over Stuttgart at about 01.40 hours, Dick Elliott guided his skipper to the aiming point and released their nine 500 lb MC bombs smack on the target as usual. Geoff closed the bomb doors after Dick gave the word and was just turning away from the target area when Dick shouted 'Nose up Skipper!' Geoff acted immediately, pulling back on the control column for all he was worth. Dick had just seen a complete topside view of a Lancaster that had turned straight across `J-Jig's' nose. Dick saw a very surprised and horrified look on the face of the Lanc's pilot as Geoff pulled the Halifax up into an almost vertical climb and, despite the speed and violence of his skipper's reaction, he was convinced that poor Gordon Heard in the rear turret was about to catch the Lancaster's wing tip around his lower anatomy. Somehow Geoff's response to Dick's timely warning enabled them to miss the Lancaster but the sudden nose-up attitude caused `J-Jig' to stall and go into a steep dive.

Only Dick and Ken knew or could see what was going on in the cockpit but not even these two stalwarts could do anything to help their skipper because of the G-forces pressing them down in their respective positions. All their lives were once again in Geoff's hands; only he could save them as the Halifax's dive got steeper and faster. Geoff was heaving back on the control column with his feet on the instrument panel to give himself more leverage - but still the Halifax continued its downward path. Geoff was remembering another nose dive, the one before they'd started operations, Ken was thinking 'We're going to be walking home from here tonight.' Not for a second did the thought of actually dying ever enter the young man's head.

`What's happening Skipper?' asked Jack Munn, voicing the question that was on everyone's lips.

`All OK chaps,' came Geoff's calm reply, 'Everything's under control.' Using all his strength and a bit of nose-up trim, Geoff gradually eased `J-Jig' out of its dive at about 5,500 feet - they'd lost about 15,000 feet in less time than it takes to tell the story. Geoff slowly coaxed the aircraft back up to 7,000 feet, although the whole airframe was vibrating terribly and all the controls were very sluggish. Nursing the unresponsive Halifax home meant making all course changes very gently and the whole trip back was a seemingly endless watch all around for nightfighters and ahead for nasty looking clouds and potential Flak positions. All along their route home Gordon Heard, in the rear turret, kept seeing bombers going down in flames. At one point he could see so many burning on the ground that it reminded him of an airfield flarepath. Although the Command lost only seventeen Lancasters and four Halifaxes on this attack, it seemed to Gordon at the time that losses were much heavier.

Finally Geoff gently eased the badly crippled 'J-Jig' onto the Burn runway at 05.40 hours in the morning of Tuesday 25th July and every member of the crew breathed a sigh of relief at getting their feet back onto 'terra firma'. Later that day, at about lunchtime, the ground crew Chiefy informed them that `J-Jig' was a complete write-off, apart from the engines. The whole airframe had been overstressed (not to mention the overstressing of the poor bloody crew who'd been flying her!) and a vast amount of rivets had been pulled out of the aircraft's skin. They were, in fact, extremely lucky to have made it back. Geoff Sanders and the boys certainly seemed to be leading a charmed life. Or was it just that the more you practice at something, the more experience you acquire and the more proficient you get, you just appear to be lucky? Ross Hutchinson was not overly impressed at losing his favourite aircraft, but as Geoff pointed out to him in the Mess later, 'You shouldn't have joined if you can't take a joke.'

The squadron was stood down for the rest of Tuesday, but on Wednesday operations were ordered and then cancelled at 14.00 hours. The Operations Order went up again on Thursday and was once again cancelled, this time at 13.30 hours. This ops on/ops off' routine was considered by most crews to be more wearing on the nerves than the actuality of operations themselves and certainly did not help the composure of anyone, be they experienced 'Old Lags' or 'Fresher' tyro crews recently arrived on a squadron. On Friday 28th July, Geoff and his crew undertook another daylight attack, to a V-1 launching site at Foret de Nieppe, south-east of Calais, for which they were, thankfully, back in `H-How' and on Saturday the squadron made two more attacks on the same target, although Geoff and the boys did not participate in either. On Sunday they went to Tilly (Villers) Bocage, twenty kilometres south-west of Caen, in `E-Easy' (LK843), to bomb German positions in front of American troops. The port-outer engine kept giving trouble all the way to the target, backfiring viciously and frequently. It cleared briefly but started to misbehave again so Geoff told Ken to 'Shut the bloody thing down.' and they returned on three engines. On Monday 31st July the squadron stood by for operations that were again cancelled at 15.00 hours, at which point Geoff, Dick, Jack, Ken, Jimmy, Trev and Gordon cleared the vicinity of Burn as fast as their legs would carry them and headed off on ten days leave.

Throughout the month of July 1944, 578 Squadron had carried out 303 sorties to seventeen targets, during which they had dropped 1,162 tons of bombs and lost eight aircraft (six of them on the Bottrop raid) with twenty crew members killed and thirty-six missing. Flight Lieutenant D. W. McGowan and Pilot Officer J. B. Malvern were both awarded the DFC, while Flight Sergeant Maurice Trousdale (flight engineer to Pilot Officer Cy Barton, VC – see Chapter Three) received the DFM for his actions on the night of 31st March.

While Geoff Sanders and his crew were on their well-earned leave, the squadron carried out 160 sorties by day and night to targets in the Normandy area. Geoff and the boys returned to Burn to take 'H-How' on another daylight raid, this time to the marshalling yards at Somain, south-southeast of Lille on Friday 11th August. This was Geoff's and Dick's thirtieth sortie and only four months earlier would have constituted a full tour. At this point of the war however, there was, for some reason or other, a bottleneck in the flow of newly trained crews to the squadrons. This was not explained to the operational crews at the time, nor, in fact, were they officially informed that the tour length had been extended, they just kept plodding on at the job in hand. Geoff's crew accepted the extended tour without demur. Dick Elliott summed it up nicely when he said that as far as he was concerned he'd much rather do forty operations over mainly French targets than only thirty over the Ruhr and Berlin. Ken Marshall remembers thinking 'This bloody tour's dragging out.' but then thought no more about it.

On Saturday 12th August 1944, the squadron was 'stood-to' for operations that night. Briefing revealed that the target was to be the Opel motor factory in Russelsheim, east of Mainz. This attack, by a fairly small force of 297 aircraft, was to see the Pathfinder Force trying out a new type of Newhaven marking. Visual identification of the aiming point was always difficult at night and anything burning on the ground, even TIs, tended to dazzle bomb aimers and so the PFF Blind Marker force was to split. First in were the Blind Illuminators who dropped hooded flares. They were closely followed by the Visual Markers who were to identify and mark the target. Next came the Blind Markers who would only drop their yellow TIs if the Visual Markers had failed. The idea behind these changes was to assist the Backers-up and, indeed, the Main Force, as it was deemed easier to bomb small, compact groups of markers than one large conflagration.

This time however, haze prevented the Visual Markers from identifying the Aiming Point and, because of 5 to 10/10ths cloud, bombing was scattered. Neither was accuracy assisted by heavy Flak and the persistent attentions of enemy nightfighters that appeared in large numbers towards the end of the attack. The local damage report later stated that the tyre and despatch departments, plus the power house were hit, but most of the bombs fell in open country to the south of the target. Only nine people were killed and thirty-one injured, compared to the loss of thirteen Lancasters and seven Halifaxes (6.7% of the force), a very high loss rate for this stage of the bombing offensive.

The twenty-four aircraft from 578 Squadron started to line up on the perimeter track at Burn at about a quarter-past-nine in the evening. Geoff and his crew, once again flying their trusty 'H-How', took their place at the end of the runway where Geoff applied the brakes and carried out his pre-take-off checks. Elevator trimming tabs to two divisions tail heavy, rudder and aileron trim both to neutral. Mixture control down, propeller speed control fully up. On the checkword 'fuel', Ken Marshall checked the fuel cock settings and then Dick Elliott, sitting in his usual take-off position in the fold-up seat beside his skipper, set the flaps to 35 degrees down. Geoff himself set the superchargers to 'M' ratio, cooling gills one-third open and the air intake to 'cold air'. At a nod from Geoff, Dick gently opened all four throttles to -2 lbs per square inch boost while Geoff held LK809 on the brakes. All four engines responded evenly and steadily and Dick closed the throttles again. Geoff released the brakes and nodded to Dick who again opened the throttles, slowly at first -until the Halifax began to accelerate - and then opening them more fully, leading slightly with the starboard engines to counter the Halifax's gentle tendency to swing in that direction. Once Geoff had got the aircraft's tail up and could control the swing with the rudders, Dick pushed the throttles fully open and held them hard against the stops. At an indicated airspeed of 100 mph, Geoff gently eased H-How off the runway and into the air at 21.25 hours.

As LK809's speed increased to 130 mph Geoff began the initial climb, easing up the flaps and retracting the undercarriage as he did so. Ken then closed the flap isolating cock and engaged the undercarriage mechanical up-locks before returning to his flight engineer's panel. As the boost gauges on the Skipper's instrument panel reached +3 psi, Geoff changed to `S' gear while Dick increased the engine rpm to 2,500 revs. Passing through 15,000 feet, Geoff closed the engine cooling gills and continued the climb to their operational height of 20,000 feet.

In the twenty or so minutes it had taken them to climb to height, 'H-How' had flown over Lincoln and was approaching the Wash. From here they overflew Norfolk and headed out over the English Channel. Crossing the Belgian coast, slightly over half way to the target, they were buffeted by heavy Flak and, although they appeared to have escaped any damage, it was only a short time before Ken noticed that the cylinder head temperatures on the starboard inner engine were starting to rise as the oil pressure was dropping. He let Geoff know the situation and they agreed to watch the starboard inner very closely. Just over an hour later, Ken advised Geoff that, with the engine's oil pressure well below the 70 psi minimum and the cylinder head temperatures now above the maximum of 230 degrees Centigrade, they were going to have to shut the starboard inner down and feather the propeller. The aircraft was then about 130 miles (half-an-hour's flying time) from the target. As with most skippers, Geoff gave his crew the option, abort the sortie and go home, or continue on only three engines. It didn't take them long to arrive at the concensus of opinion that it would be much safer to carry on to the target than to risk the attempt to turn across the bomber stream and go home - and apart from this consideration, they hadn't 'boomeranged' in thirty ops and no-one wanted to start now. With the loss of one Hercules engine, the fully-laden Halifax lost a little forward speed and very gradually started to lose height as they continued on their way to Russelsheim where they arrived fifteen minutes after their 'Time on Target' (TOT) and found themselves alone over the enemy town. Their skill and determination had got them thus far, now Lady Luck took a hand.

The enemy nightfighters, which had arrived over the target area during the latter stages of the main attack, were busily following the Main Force on their way home. The Russelsheim Flak gunners thought they'd finished for the night and were so surprised to see a lone Terrorflieger over their town that it took them a little time to get their 'eye' back in and start loosing off at the solitary Halifax. Despite their late arrival and although now down to only 12,500 feet, Dick saw that there were still a few TIs and several fires indicating the aiming point, so he guided Geoff in onto the bombing run, with both gunners – plus Ken with his head in the astrodome - keeping six very sharp eyes open for nightfighters. Many times during their tour Gordon Heard had spotted nightfighters in their vicinity, but, unless they were posing an actual threat to his aircraft and crew, he rarely said much. On this occasion he was grateful to find that they had the night sky to themselves.

Letting one of the remaining TIs drift into the cross-wires of his bomb sight, Dick gave his skipper the 'Steady, steady.' instructions before pressing the tit that released their 2,000 lbs HC bomb and 1,170 four pound incendiaries and announcing `Bombs gone.' Geoff held 'H-How' straight and level for the AP photograph while Flak burst all around them. When, after what seemed like hours, the photoflash finally went off, the aircraft was, quite amazingly, still unscathed so Geoff put the nose down and banked away, hurrying out of the target area and onto the new course that Jack Munn had supplied. They were on their way home.

This was where the flight engineer really had to earn his aircrew breakfast. The shot-up starboard engine was the only one that supplied hydraulic power for the bomb doors, flaps and undercarriage. The bomb doors had been opened by reserve hydraulic power stored in an hydraulic accumulator, but they now needed to be hand-pumped back up into the closed position to reduce drag and fuel consumption. The hand-pump was situated in the mid-fuselage, adjacent to the crew rest position, so Ken set off down the fuselage. Reaching the rest position (in which the last thing he was going to have time for was a rest), Ken connected up his oxygen tube and plugged in his intercom lead before starting the laborious task of closing the bomb doors. Geordies are famous the world over for their engineering expertise. It's got something to do with knowing how to talk sweetly to inanimate, technical objects with just the right words, in just the right tone of voice. Ken Marshall was no exception to this fine Tyneside tradition. Obeying his skipper's instruction to leave his intercom switched on so that Geoff would know he was alright, Ken was about to give away some of his 'hard won' trade secrets.

`Come on you damn thing, puff-pant, puff-pant-gasp, close, damn you, puff-pant-grunt.' (In common with most young aircrew of the period, Ken did not really swear in 1944; he never really swore right up until he died) 'Gordon bleedin' Bennett, but this is flippin' hard work, puff-pant, puff-pant-grunt. Close, you ruddy-bomb-flamin'-doors, flippin' close!' At this point Geoff tactfully enquired

`How's it going Ken?'

`Getting there, puff-pant, Skipper, puff-pant.' came the gasped reply.

`Hard work, is it Engineer?' asked the Skipper.

`Yes Skipper, puff-pant-gasp. Flippin', puff-pant hard work!' grunted Ken.

`Well, never mind,' said Geoff nonchalantly, 'Just do your best lad.'

Having closed the bomb doors, Ken rushed back to his engineer's panel to check his gauges and switch fuel tanks. They continued on their way home without further incident, arriving over Burn about half-an-hour after the rest of the squadron aircraft had landed. Ken had to once more 'retire' to the rest position and the hydraulic pump in order to pump down the flaps and undercarriage. Geoff called up Burn's control tower on the radio.

'H-How calling Roundshot, over.'

`Go ahead H-How, Roundshot receiving you loud and clear. Do have any injured onboard? Over.'

'H-How to Roundshot, no casualties, repeat no casualties, but am on three engines only. Request permission to land. Over.'

'Roundshot to H-How, clear to land. Over.'

`Roger, Roundshot and thank you. Will commence landing from this circuit. Over and listening, out.'

From the circuit, Geoff turned onto the downwind leg and Ken pumped the flaps down to 35 degrees. Geoff turned onto the cross-wind leg and Ken pumped the undercart down and locked (at least the weight of the Messier undercarriage legs helped here) and as Geoff banked 'H-How' onto the final approach and he was certain he could comfortably make the runway on a straight approach, he started to wind off the rudder trim and told Ken to pump the flaps fully down. As usual, Geoff set LK809 down on the tarmac first time, as gently as a bird and gradually slowed down as they went along the runway. As H-How reached the turn-off point, they were met by Wing Commander Wilkerson in his Austin van. Having again checked that the crew were all uninjured, Wilkie sped off back to the debriefing room where he welcomed the crew with the usual rum-laced- mugs of tea[55].

After debriefing they learnt that two of the squadron's aircraft, K-King' (Flying Officer O. S. McPhillamy) and T-bar (Sergeant J. J. Pearson) had failed to return. K-King' (LW383) crashed at Chapelle a Oie, killing four of the crew, while 'T-bar' (NA604) crashed at Monchbruch in Germany with total loss of life. It is likely that both of these aircraft fell to nightfighters. Additionally, LW473, LK-B (Flight Sergeant Jim Allen) landed at Woodbridge Emergency Landing Ground after a spot of bother.

While returning over Belgium both port engines temporarily cut out, then, having managed to restart them, predicted Flak had a go at them, causing the port outer to burst into flames. Jim Allen immediately feathered the prop and shut down the engine and, miraculously, the fire went straight out without using the fire extinguisher. The crew later found out that the Flak had severed an oil line, which then dropped oil onto the exhaust pipe and burst into flames. Jim Allen's[56] initial remedial actions had been all that were required.

Returning to the 'Flights' later in the day after some well earned sleep, the crew of H-How' was informed that, as Ken had suspected, the Flak over the Belgian coast had nicked an oil feed pipe and gradual loss of oil had caused the overheating and lack of oil pressure. Their remedial action had however, saved the engine. They were then told that Flight Lieutenant Sanders had been recommended for an immediate award of the DFC. (The rest of the crew all received DFCs or DFMs – as appropriate - sometime after the completion of their tour).

---

[55] *Talking to Geoff in 1992, Ken remarked that he couldn't remember ever being offered rum in his post-op tea. Geoff reminded him that, in those days, his engineer didn't drink. 'Oh! That's right,' said Ken, 'Did you have rum in yours then?' he asked. 'Of course,' came the reply, 'I had yours too!' Having read this in November 1992, Dick Elliott also confided that he was another member of Geoff's crew who never received rum in his post-op tea. Until he died, Geoff swore that he has absolutely no knowledge of the whereabouts of a third ration of rum.*

[56] *Jim Allen's mid-upper gunner was Louis Wooldridge. See Chapter 8.*

The rest of Sunday was a stand down, but on Monday 14th August the crew were on again. The squadron despatched ten Halifaxes to take part in an 805-aircraft daylight attack (Operation Tractable) on seven German troop positions facing the Third Canadian Division that was advancing on Falaise.

'H-How' was still undergoing repairs so Geoff and the boys flew LL548, 'C-Charlie', on this three hour forty minute trip, Geoff's 32nd. 'H-How' was still being repaired on Tuesday so they took LL585, 'S-bar', to bomb a Luftwaffe base at Tirlemont (now Tienen) about twenty miles due east of Brussels, Belgium. This was one of nine Luftwaffe bases in Belgium and Holland that were attacked by a total force of 1,004 aircraft. Only three failed to return. Geoff and the crew were stood down on Wednesday 16th and Thursday 17th, although the squadron sent twenty aircraft to Kiel on the night of the 16th August.

They were back in their old faithful 'H-How' on the night of Friday 18th August for a 234-aircraft raid on the synthetic oil plant at Sterkrade, almost next door to Bottrop. Three of the squadron's twenty Halifaxes were damaged by Flak and there were many sightings of nightfighters, but all returned safely to base. 'H-How's' bomb sight went unserviceable as they started the bomb run so Dick released their twelve 500 lbs MC bombs and four 500 lbs GP bombs on an estimated but pre-calculated bombing angle. They landed back at Burn at 03.25 hours on Saturday. The squadron was stood down for the rest of Saturday, Sunday and Monday and on the Tuesday the crew went off on another spell of leave. On Wednesday 23rd August, Wing Commander D. S. S. Wilkerson, DSO, DFC, handed over command of 578 Squadron to Wing Commander A. G. T. (Jimmy) James and went off to an HCU for a 'rest'.

Geoff, Dick, Jack, Ken, Jimmy, Trev and Gordon returned from leave at 23.59 hours on Saturday 2nd September and the following morning were once again on the Operations Order. Take-off was scheduled for around 15.30 hours and, as they discovered at briefing, the target for eighteen of the squadron's Halifaxes was to be another Luftwaffe airfield, this time at Venlo in southern Holland. Once again this was part of a large scale raid involving 675 heavy bombers attacking six Luftwaffe bases - for the loss of only one Halifax. All 578 Squadron crews experienced light but accurate Flak over the target, in fact the anti-aircraft gunners at Venlo proved to be very unfriendly (not really surprisingly), knocking out both starboard engines of the Lancaster flown by the Master Bomber, Squadron Leader A. J. Craig. He was forced to hand over control of the raid to his deputy, Flight Lieutenant F. Wilson, and head for the emergency landing ground at Woodbridge. Wilson fared little better, as Flak damage caused one of his engines to seize and jammed his bomb doors open. The Halifaxes of 578 Squadron also had their share of Flak damage, but the luckiest escape of the day fell to Flying Officer R. D. Davies and crew in MZ559, `F-Fox', which was hit by a bomb from another aircraft. The bomb went straight through the fuselage just aft of the mid-upper turret, smashing the interior of the aircraft as it passed through and no doubt causing the mid-upper gunner to require a change of underpants. Flying Officer Davies carefully nursed MZ559 back to the UK and landed at Old Buckenham where the Halifax was immediately written off. When the crew were collected and returned to Burn the following day, the Flight Engineer was wearing the Elsan seat around his neck!

Because of bad weather at Burn on the squadron's return from Venlo, only six of the Halifaxes managed to land at base, while the remainder were diverted to Shipham, Riccall or Carnaby. 'H-How' went to the latter and returned to Burn the following morning, where the skipper found himself in hot water with the ground crew. They taxied the Halifax into its dispersal, switched everything off and were collecting their bits and pieces together prior to leaving the aircraft. LAC Joe Raby[57] – their engine fitter - had already commenced his after-flight inspection while the aircrew were still inside collecting their gear. Having discovered bits of broken tree branches embedded in the underside of 'H-How's' rear fuselage, he was waiting by the open hatch for Geoff to disembark. As Flight Lieutenant Sanders climbed out of the aircraft Leading Aircraftman Raby sternly demanded to know what ' Sir' had been doing with his aircraft. Geoff was temporarily non-plussed, not least because he had no bloody idea what Joe was on about. Joe pointed to the branches stuck in the rear fuselage underside. 'What's this here then?' he again demanded. Geoff gulped, 'Don't really know Joe,' he replied, 'Unless we clipped some tree tops while climbing to clear the cliffs on our approach to Carnaby.' Geoff thought this sounded fairly plausible because he honestly had absolutely no idea how the branches had gotten there. Joe Raby did not appear overly impressed and wandered off muttering

---

[57] *Joe Raby was a most dedicated chap. Whether on or off duty, he was always there to see Geoff and the crew off on an operation and, more often than not, there to greet them on their return too.*

something that sounded remarkably like 'Bloody Pilots, think they own the bleeding kite.'

For the next four days bad weather at Burn prevented any flying and on Friday 8th September the squadron was officially stood down. On Saturday they despatched twenty-one Halifaxes as part of a 272-aircraft strong force to bomb German positions in front of Allied lines, while on Sunday, twenty-four of the Squadron's kites joined a total force of 992 aircraft in bombing eight different enemy strongpoints. All of these attacks were in the Le Havre area but Geoff and the boys were not asked to come out to 'play' on either occasion. They were however, called early in the morning of Monday 11th September to prepare for a daylight raid to the Ruhr, although Jack Munn missed this one, being replaced by Flight Sergeant Harrison.

The squadron contributed twenty-three aircraft to a 379-strong attack on three synthetic oil plants, Castrop-Rauxel, Kamen and Gelsenkirchen-Nordstern. The three forces were escorted by twenty squadrons of Spitfires and three squadrons each of Mustangs and Tempests and, because of this, no Luftwaffe fighters were encountered. Twenty-three Halifaxes of 578 Squadron participated in the Gelsenkirchen raid, in which 4 Group lost five Halifaxes and the Pathfinders lost two Lancasters. On arrival over the target the Nordstern plant was partially protected by a smoke screen so the Master Bomber was initially instructing all crews to bomb the greens and then later, ordering them to bomb the centre of the smoke and fires. Many of the squadron's crews managed to identify the target visually - the canals to the south of the plant being a good reference point - and at times the refinery buildings could be seen through the smoke.

Nordstern's Flak defences, although in barrage form, exacted a fairly heavy price from the attackers. Black smoke from the exploding Flak shells was so thick that, from a mile out, the target looked like a solid black thunder cloud. Two of the seven aircraft shot down belonged to 578 Squadron; LL584, E-Easy', (Warrant Officer D. L. Wood) and NA568, 'Q-Queenie' (Pilot Officer T. S. Coran), while another sixteen received Flak damage to some degree. `H-How' received several holes from Flak splinters as Geoff held her steady on the bombing run. Dick had just released their sixteen 500 lbs GP bombs on the target and advised 'Bombs gone', while his skipper kept the Halifax straight and level for the Aiming Point photograph. Just as Dick got up onto his knees on the bomb aimers couch and turned around to ensure that all the

F/O RD Davies brought his Halifax MZ559, LK-F, of 578 Squadron safely back from the target at Venlo after the aircraft was hit by a bomb from a higher flying aircraft.

bombing control switches were in the right position, 'H-How' went through another patch of Flak. Suddenly he felt an almighty thump in his stomach, temporarily knocking the breath out of him. Pulling his gloves off, he quickly felt all around his midriff area, fully expecting to feel the stickiness of blood on his fingers. Nothing! Straining his head forward, he searched every inch of his stomach and associated bits and pieces but all he could find was a deep dent on the release buckle of his parachute harness. Looking around his compartment, he finally found a Flak splinter about the size of the top joint of his first finger lying on the couch at his knees and a correspondingly sized hole in the nose perspex. Just an inch or so either way, or if he hadn't got onto his knees when he did, Dick would have become another statistic and Geoff, with only a few more operations to do, would have been looking for a new bomb aimer. It was now fairly clear just who the crew's lucky mascot was!

As the squadron returned to Burn, the crews were welcomed back by their AOC, Air Vice-Marshal Sir Roderick Carr CB, CBE, DFC, AFC. Of the two squadron aircraft that failed to return, LL584 crashed at Lille, Belgium and all the crew survived although taken prisoner, while NA568 crashed at Lirchellen with the death of one crew member. Later that day, one of the armourers handed Gordon Heard a small Flak splinter.

'Where did that come from?' asked Gordon. 'Stuck in the armour plate under your bum, Sarge.' came the reply.

Geoff and the boys did not fly the next day, Tuesday 12th September, but LK809 was taken on a daylight raid to Munster by the squadron's tame American, Lieutenant J. L. Christenson who brought 'H-How' back with a hole in the port side of the fuselage. The squadron was stood down on Wednesday 13th so it was on the 14th that Geoff and crew took 'H-How' on their 37th operation. Fifteen aircraft from 578 Squadron were to join a further 118 Halifaxes and 51 Lancasters of 4, 6 and 8 Groups. Take-off from Burn was around 13.30 hours but, because of failing weather conditions over the target, the whole force was recalled while still over the North Sea, still leaving the crew with only thirty-six operations completed.

The next day, Friday 15th September, was the day on which the Lancasters of 9 and 617 Squadrons, flying from bases in Russia, so damaged the Tirpitz in Kaa Fjord that she would never again sail under her own steam. This, of course, was not known at Burn when twenty-four Halifax crews were briefed

F/L Geoff Sanders (third from left) and his crew on LK809 celebrate the end of their tour.

for a night attack on Kiel. The primary aiming point was south of the main dockyard area and was marked by the Newhaven method, although Wanganui was also laid on as a back-up. The evidence of returning crews and their aiming point photographs led the Command to record this attack as 'a highly concentrated raid', with the old town and the modern shopping centre being devastated. This was supported by the local German report, obtained after the war, which records severe damage in the town centre and port areas. Flight Lieutenant Sanders and crew landed back at base at 04.07 hours after almost six hours in the air. The last squadron aircraft to land did so at 04.24 hours and the unit was stood down for the rest of Saturday.

Sunday saw Geoff and the boys, again in LK809, setting of on their 38th operation. They got airborne at 09.10 hours to form part of a 762-aircraft attack on German positions around Boulogne. This was a softening-up operation in preparation for an attack by Allied ground troops. One Halifax and one Lancaster were lost on this raid, but the German garrison surrendered soon afterwards. Landing back at Burn in nice time for lunch, the whole squadron was very upset to learn that their old CO, Wing Commander D.S.S.Wilkerson, DSO, DFC, had been killed that morning in a flying training accident. He was not quite twenty-seven years old.

The squadron was stood down on the Monday and Tuesday, but on Wednesday 20th September twenty-four aircraft and crews were detailed for operations that were later cancelled. This happened again on Thursday and yet again on Friday, while on Saturday 23rd, the unit was stood down once again. On Sunday, 578 Squadron despatched twenty-one Halifaxes to attack the German defences at Calais, but Geoff and his crew were excused games this day. In any case the Master Bomber stopped the attack after only 126 out of a total of 188 aircraft had bombed because the target became completely covered by cloud.

With only two operations left to do to complete their tour (they had now been informed that their tour would consist of forty ops), the past week had not been conducive to calming any operational 'butterflies' that the crew may have been suffering, so it was probably a relief to find that Operation No.39 was on for Monday 25th September. As on the previous day, the target was once again German positions around Calais, but this time the attacking force comprised 872 aircraft, of which twenty-three were from 578 Squadron. Again cloud obscured the target after only some of the aircraft (287) had bombed and once again 578 Squadron's Halifaxes had to ditch their bombs in the North Sea. This time however, the weather had also clamped in at Burn and only seven aircraft managed to land before thick, low cloud closed the airfield completely. Six of the unit's aircraft landed at Rufforth and the other ten, including 'H-How', landed at Marston Moor. They all returned to base later that same day.

On Tuesday 26th September the target was Calais again, but again Geoff and crew were left off the Battle Order, so their final operation at last arrived on Wednesday when they were one of eleven crews briefed for yet another attack on Calais. `Last op' jitters were not helped by the non-availability of their trusty steed 'H-How' and no-one was happy at the prospect of flying a strange aircraft. Unfortunately this could not be helped and at 09.05 hours Geoff lifted NA574, `D-Dog', off the Burn runway and headed south for Calais. The total force of 341 aircraft from 1, 3, 4 and 8 Groups included eleven Halifaxes from 578 Squadron, whose specific aiming point was the area around a bridge in the docks. Once again cloud contrived to fox the attackers but this time the Master Bomber was not going to be beaten, calling the force down to 4,000 feet, below the cloud base, to bomb. Unfortunately, as most aircraft emerged from the cloud, they found that they had overshot the AP, so all had to orbit and come in again. With the Master Bomber warning against undershooting the markers, Dick guided Geoff into the Aiming Point for the last time before releasing their three 1,000 lbs GP, six 1,000 lbs SAP and four 500 lbs GP bombs slap on the target. The bombing was well concentrated and accurate, with at least one stick of bombs right on the bridge. One Lancaster failed to return from this operation, but at 12.35

hours, Geoff gently lowered D-Dog' onto the Burn runway to complete the crew's tour of operations.

Final debriefing was followed by a leisurely lunch which, in turn, was followed by a restful afternoon before the crew collected their ground crew and took them to the 'George' in Burn village for a first class celebratory booze-up. The next day, whilst nursing sore heads, they learned that the German garrison at Calais had surrendered. That's the way to end a tour!

Canadian Flt.Lt. Maxi Baer and crew celebrate the end of their tour with a low pass over RAF Burn's Flying Control building.

The Pendulum and the Scythe

`Not Forgotten Lady'

We first met in 1944, when I was twenty years old.
She was much younger than I, but I took to her on first sight.
There was no reaction from her, but then
I didn't expect there would be.
The relationship, as far as she was concerned,
was of a working nature,
As long as I carried out my part of the bargain to the best of
my ability I would hear no complaint from her.
Her function was to carry out the purpose for which
she and I had been engaged
And in doing just that, we would get along fine together.
We didn't spend all our time in each other's company,
I often went out with my pals
Whilst she was occasionally taken out by someone else.
This arrangement in no way affected the close relationship
which was forged between us.
I was with her on the eve of my twenty-first birthday and we
didn't get back home 'til early next morning.
There were times when our partnership hit a rough patch and
if it had not been for her tenacity, all my efforts
might have been to no avail
The relationship lasted for just over four months,
when I was obliged to move on
She passed into partnership
with one of my colleagues after I left.
It is now over forty-seven years since we severed our
relationship, but I shall never forget her as long as I live.
Farewell- LK809, 'H-How' Halifax Mk.III
- 'One of the very best!'

Ken W Marshall DFC (1991)

Chapter Ten

1944-45: Just when you thought you were home – and safe!

Bill Strachan was born in Sydney, New South Wales, Australia on the 20th December 1922. He left school at the age of 15 to take up employment as an accounts clerk with a local manufacturing company. At eighteen-and-a-half he volunteered for aircrew duties with the Royal Australian Air Force, was accepted as trainee aircrew, placed on the Reserve and then told to return home to await his call-up. Eleven months later, in June 1942, he was called-up - by the Australian Army! Bill contacted the RAAF without delay and, in order to save him from wearing out his feet while dressed in khaki, they immediately inducted him as ground staff. He got his transfer to aircrew training on Armistice Day 1942.

After three months at No. 2 ITS (Initial Training School) at Bradfield Park, Bill was posted to 8 EFTS (Elementary Flying Training School). On the successful completion of his Ab Initio flying training, he found himself on his way to Canada, under the Empire Air Training Scheme, to join 41 SFTS. He was on the move again at the end of this course, arriving in England in September 1943 where, after a period of several months during which he spent time at 11 PRDC (Brighton), a Commando course at Whitley Bay and at 23 ACHU (Wednesford), he finally reported to 20 (P)AFU (Advanced Flying Unit). On 24th May 1944 Bill, now a Flight Sergeant, was posted to 21 OTU at Moreton-in-Marsh for crewing up - destination Bomber Command.

Crewing-up took the usual form of putting about twenty members of each aircrew category (with the exception of flight engineers), into an empty hangar and telling them to sort themselves into six-man crews. Bill Strachan and his friend, Keith Anderson - another Aussie pilot - decided they were in no particular hurry to 'plight their troth' to five other blokes and stood with their backs to the hangar wall and lit up cigarettes, watching the general proceedings with quiet amusement. After about ten minutes, the friends were approached by two Sergeant wireless operators[58], also friends. It was Ted

---

[58] *Although they had joined up as wireless operators, they finished their course as 'signallers' and were consequently wearing the new 'S' brevet, which they'd had to*

The Pendulum and the Scythe

Bill Strachan and his crew.

Richards who opened the conversation, 'Do you need a wireless op, Flight?' Bill glanced at Keith who appeared to be thinking deeply about this question. Deciding that someone had better reply to the wireless operator's polite enquiry, Bill said 'Yeah. I suppose we do.' So the two 'talkers' adopted each other and Ted's friend, Les Lamb, joined Keith Anderson.

Shortly after this, a Sergeant navigator approached the group and spoke to Bill. 'Have you got a nav' or a bomb aimer, Flight?' The pilot's reply in the negative was met with 'Well you have now Skipper. I'm Cyril Keeton and I'll be back in half-a-mo!' True to his word, Cyril returned shortly with a Sergeant bomb aimer in tow and introduced Johnny Wakefield to Bill and Ted. By this time Keith Anderson and Les Lamb had moved off in search of more crew members and Bill, Ted, Cyril and John stood and chatted, finding out where each other came from.

`Excuse us Flight but ah cuddun't help noticin' thet youer short of two gunners, like!' The Geordie accent was unmistakable, as Bill turned around to see two Sergeant air gunners, both shorter than himself, who had closed up on the little group unobserved. 'Looks like you could be right, chum,' said Bill. 'You wanna join us?' Why aye Skipper' chorused the two - they were both Geordies, Alan Parrish and Arthur (Archie) Tait – and they'd already decided that when they moved on to four-engined heavies (21 OTU was still

---

alter from engineer's brevets themselves because although the trade had changed its name, no-one in authority had had the foresight to order the 'S' brevets.

flying Wellingtons) Archie would occupy the rear turret and Alan the mid-upper.

Lying in his bed that night, Bill Strachan mentally looked back over the last few years and thought how differently things had turned out from what he had envisaged. He'd joined the RAAF Reserve in 1941, been called up in 1942 with the idea of flying fighters against the Japs who, it was strongly believed at the time, were about to invade Australia. He was sent to Canada in 1943 to train to be a fighter pilot, then posted to England where he had learned to fly twin-engined Oxfords and now, in mid-1944, he was the captain of a six-man bomber crew, about to learn how to fly a Wellington. God alone knew what the future might bring - if indeed there was any future in Bomber Command.

After a couple of weeks of ground classes they were transferred to Enstone, a satellite of Moreton-in-Marsh, where `D' Flight was situated and from where they were to do most of their flying. Their first flight, purely for familiarisation, took place on 12th June when Flight Lieutenant Fardell took them along on an air-test. Bill's first real touch of the controls of a Wellington happened a few days later, when his instructor, Flying Officer Brookbank, told Bill to take his crew out onto the tarmac where an aircraft would shortly be available. While they were waiting, a Wellington landed, taxied in and the crew vacated the aircraft. As this `sprog' crew passed Bill and his merry men, the pilot - another Aussie whom Bill knew slightly - wiped his brow and said 'These contraptions are bloody hard to fly. Best of luck mate, you'll need it.'

With great trepidation Bill strapped himself into the left hand seat, with his instructor in the right. Fearing the worst, Bill taxied out and then, under the watchful eye of Flying Officer Brookbank, he opened up the throttles and took off. Certainly the Wellington was different to the Oxfords he'd flown at AFU, in fact it was a bit like driving a lorry after having got used to a large saloon car. After a couple of sessions that day, Bill couldn't help but wonder what all the fuss was about and, on 19th June, Flying Officer Brookbank sent them off solo.

Cyril Keeton was an excellent navigator. He was level- headed, intelligent and 'old' - he was twenty-five. He was also the only married member of crew. Cyril's navigation expertise was so good that Squadron Leader Benbow, OC 'D' Flight, asked Bill if he and his crew would consider applying for

The Pendulum and the Scythe

Pathfinders -and this before they'd even flown a four-engined bomber! Bill was not over-keen on the idea - he'd been swanning around long enough already and just wanted to get on with his operational tour. A move to PFF meant even more training - Bill was definitely not smitten with his OC's request. The question was raised several times until Cyril put up 'a black' and got them all off the hook.

Cyril's wife had just moved into lodgings in Enstone village and she was heavily pregnant. Early one evening the crew were being kept hanging around the Flight Office, waiting to fly – but 95% sure of a stand down. Cyril prophesied that there'd be no flying that night but Bill was not so sure. I'm sorry Cyril, you'll just have to wait with the rest of us' he told him. Cyril became increasingly anxious. Just before nightfall Bill was called into Squadron Leader Benbow's office and told that a night cross-country had been arranged for him and his crew, 'So you'd better get them together and make your way to the aircraft.' Bill saluted, about-turned, left the OC's office and returned to the crew room. 'Come on blokes, we're on. A bloody cross-country........ Where the hell's Cyril?' But Cyril was nowhere to be seen. Cyril was pedalling his push-bike toward the village as fast as his whirling legs could propel him.

Bill was right in it up to his neck. He couldn't fly a cross-country without a navigator so, despite not wanting to drop Cyril into hot water, the only thing to do was go back to the OC and own up to having lost his navigator. Squadron Leader Benbow, a short, plumpish gentleman with an RAF moustache, had obviously 'been around'. The 'Goldfish' badge on his lapel signified that he had survived a ditching at some time and he was not one to be lost for words -as Bill was about to find out. `You can't find your bloody navigator! What-d-ya mean you can't find your bloody navigator. You're supposed to be his captain, you should know where he is every bloody minute of every bloody day! Jesus Christ, call yourself a bomber captain? You're not fit to be a bomber captain, you can't even control your own bloody crew.' The tirade went on. Bill focused his eyes on the Squadron Leader's 'goldfish' badge and bit his tongue while he received the biggest, longest bollocking he'd ever had in his relatively short air force career. All that crossed his mind was 'Well, there goes my commission.'

The Squadron Leader eventually ran out of epithets and swear words and informed Bill that 'they would carry out their night cross-country exercise' that he'd find them a replacement navigator and 'get out of my bloody sight!'

The exercise duly took place but, as the whole point of a cross-country was to test the navigator's abilities, the whole thing seemed bloody pointless without Cyril. Bill had a few choice words with his navigator the next day but the incident was soon forgotten when Cyril's wife presented him with a son. Henceforth Cyril was known as 'Dad.'

OTU training proceeded apace with the crew undertaking a Nickelling operation to Saumur on Sunday 30th July 1944, one of only six OTU sorties carried out that night from which all aircraft returned safely. John Wakefield still plainly remembers a chateau standing out in the middle of the Loire and the leaflets drifting down around it. At the end of August, with the OTU daylight practice bombing record to their credit, the crew was posted to Acaster Malbis for the best part of a month – but to this day, no one is quite sure why. They finally arrived at 1652 HCU, Marston Moor, on Friday 29th September, to convert to the Halifax bomber and pick up a flight engineer. Once again they found themselves shown into an empty hangar where there were about twenty crews standing around in their groups of six with a larger group of men - all flight engineers –standing somewhat apart from the OTU crews.

It was 'Dad' Keeton who spotted the commissioned engineer with the DFM ribbon under his brevet and correctly assuming that this had to be a second tour man, Dad nudged Bill to draw his attention to the Flying Officer across the hangar and then made his way over to the group of engineers and approached the young man with the DFM. 'Excuse me sir,' he said politely, 'would you like to join our crew?'

The young officer looked at him pensively. 'Where's your skipper from?' he asked. 'Australia,' said Dad. 'Why?'

'Oh, I just fancied flying with an Aussie pilot' replied the engineer. 'OK, you're on - my name's Bob Stow.' They shook hands and Dad took him to meet the rest of the crew. Now they were seven.

Bob Stow was just starting his second tour. He had undertaken his first on 51 Squadron where he'd taken part in all the Battle of Hamburg raids and finished the tour with the Peenemunde attack from which he'd returned on three engines. Bob met with some rather pointed comments in the Officers' Mess because he had elected to join a non-commissioned crew with a 'colonial' Flight Sergeant pilot as skipper, but Bob had decided that he was going to fly with Bill Strachan and, as far as he was concerned, that was that. Bob worked on the principle that as it was his neck he was putting on the block (for the second time), it was up to him who was flying the 'block' he was putting his neck on! Once his taunters realised that Bob was paying no attention to them, their comments ceased.

About this time, some of the crew inherited nicknames. Cyril had been 'Dad' for some time now but Bill became 'Desperate Dan,' presumably because of his determined looks and someone in the crew obviously read The Dandy' comic regularly. John Wakefield was called `Krad' for some inexplicable reason, while Arthur Tait became 'Archie' and Ted Richards was rechristened `Lou the WOP' or `Lou' for short.

The first night the crew was allowed to do solo 'circuits and bumps' Bill was having trouble with his landings. First he would get the tail wheel touching down first thus making the main wheels come down with a thump. Next time around the main wheels would touch down gently and then the tail wheel would arrive with a thump. For eighty minutes Bill tried different angles on the approach before asking John to close the throttles but he just couldn't get the landing to his satisfaction. This worried him and all the way back to billet and lying in bed that night, he puzzled over the problem. The next night they went up to repeat the exercise and Bill couldn't do a thing wrong -every landing was smooth as silk and he never had trouble with landing the Halifax thereafter.

On one of their day cross-countries they got lost on their homeward leg. They were flying in 8 to 9/10ths broken cloud and both the radio and H2S were playing up. Bill eased the Halifax down to 2,000 feet where they could catch occasional glimpses of the ground. John, Cyril and Ted were frantically trying to get something out of the H2S and radio but to no avail, when through a small gap in the cloud Bill spotted and immediately recognised Enstone. Bill called Cyril on the intercom. Cyril gave Bill the course for Marston Moor and they flew safely home.

On a night cross-country, they had been airborne for about two hours when Bill felt in need of a 'pee.' He hung on for quite a while until the urge got really desperate. He asked Cyril how much longer the flight would last - 'too long' came the reply – so Bill asked the crew to look around for some sort of receptacle he could use to relieve himself. While they were searching Bill thought about switching in 'George' and going back to the Elsan but a large bank of ominous black cloud slightly to port made him reluctant to leave the 'office'. Why, he wondered, didn't British aircraft designers fit 'pee tubes' like the Yanks had provided in the Harvard he'd trained on and where the hell were the lads with something he could use. They eventually came back to tell him that there was nothing suitable in the aircraft. Unable to wait any longer, Bill removed his flying gloves and used one of them to do what a man's gotta do. The next thing was Ted on the intercom from his wireless station immediately below Bill's seat, 'Hey, Skip, shut your window, the rain's coming in!'

Conversion onto the Halifax then continued its full course with but one heart-stopping experience. They were returning to Marston Moor after completing a night cross-country exercise, only to find the ground around the base covered in fog. They could only see the runway lights at 1,000 feet out and as they descended to 200 feet on their final approach, they entered the fog. Bill couldn't see a thing but he very gingerly continued his descent on instruments until he decided that this was getting bloody dangerous and there wasn't much future in continuing. He opened up the throttles and started an overshoot, being surprised as he did so, to see the control tower flash past his starboard wing tip!

The next attempt at landing was successful because the fog had cleared enough to see the runway, possibly due to the slipstream from their first run. Bill taxied back to dispersal, switched the engines off and slumped into his seat in relief. Nothing was said to him on his return to the crew room so either no-one in the control tower noticed how close they'd come to meeting their maker or they were so used to inexperienced Halifax pilots rattling their windows that it wasn't worthy of comment. Either way, the near-miss had scared Bill witless. The rest of the course went without incident and they were posted to 158 Squadron at Lissett, not far from 'sunny' Bridlington.

It was already getting dark on the evening of Sunday 19th November 1944 when the train pulled in to Burton Agnes station. The crew got off the train and dragged their kit onto the platform. Bill wiped his forehead with the back of his hand and looked around him. He was standing in what appeared to be the coldest, most dismal place he'd ever seen. It seemed to be miles from anywhere and he was convinced they'd been sent to the end of the world. They hadn't expected to be greeted by the RAF's Ceremonial Band but they had thought that there would be the usual RAF open truck to take them to camp. There was absolutely nothing. They stood around waiting until their collective patience ran out then Bill went in search of the Station Master and asked him to telephone Lissett and organise some transport. The gentleman lifted the receiver and tapped the cradle rest a few times, waited a few seconds and then asked for 'Burton Agnes 50 please.' Having got through to the guardroom, the Station Master handed the phone to Bill and it did not take him long to learn that he and his crew were not expected but that the Orderly Sergeant would send a vehicle to pick them up.

Not too long after this, a blue open truck with RAF roundels and `B/4' on the front mudguard pulled into the station yard and Bill and the lads heaved their kit over the tailgate and climbed aboard themselves. They arrived at Lisset and were greeted by the Orderly Sergeant who made a herculean effort to find them beds in a Nissen but and some bedding for the night. Bill got to know this sergeant quite well during his tour as he was the man who handed out the `wakey-wakey' pills before an operation.

On waking up that cold, dreary Monday morning, Bill dressed and stepped outside the Nissen but to have a look around. There was no airfield in sight. He thought they must be miles away from the aircraft dispersals and was just about to go back inside and wake the lads when he saw a vaguely familiar figure approaching him. It was another Aussie pilot whom Bill had known in training, one Flying Officer Jack Krefter, who gave the new arrival directions to the airfield and Station Headquarters, before wandering on his way. Bill rounded up the lads and set off to the station proper, an exceedingly long walk. After the usual nauseating procedure of officially 'arriving' on the station whereby they all had to visit almost every section and office on the site - and some that were well off it! - the crew finally ended up in 'B' Flight, commanded by Squadron Leader G. B. Read, DFC. Most unusually this officer was an Air Gunner. The squadron CO was Wing Commander P. Dobson., DSO, DFC, AFC.

So the seven new men settled into 158 Squadron, six of them to embark on their first tour of operations and the flight engineer on his second. The crew had learned to work and 'play' together and all got on well, each recognising the others' competence at their jobs, Pilot - Flight Sergeant Bill 'Desperate Dan' Strachan; navigator - Sergeant Cyril 'Dad' Keeton; bomb aimer - Sergeant John ' Krad' Wakefield; flight engineer – Flying Officer Bob Stow, DFM; wireless operator (Signaller) – Sergeant Ted `Lou' Richards; mid-upper gunner - Sergeant Alan Parrish and rear gunner - Sergeant Arthur

'Archie' Tait. All were now as ready as their training could make them. From here on it would be up to their own abilities - and Lady Luck.

On Saturday 25th November the new crew were taken for a familiarisation flight by Flight Lieutenant New. They flew Halifax B.Mk.III serial no. MZ759 and after 25 minutes they landed and Flight Lieutenant New sent them off on their own for 15 minutes local flying. On Monday 27th they went practice bombing on the Flamborough Head range in NR240 and on Wednesday 29th they ferried NX340 to 1652 HCU at Marston Moor. Sunday 3rd December saw them undertaking a 3 hour 55 minute night cross-country in NR133 and the following day they ferried another 'tired' Halifax (LW677) to Marston Moor.

Their names finally appeared on the Operations Order on Tuesday 5th December. At this point in the war the squadron was no longer sending new pilots on `second-dickie' trips so Bill Strachan's first operation was as captain of his own crew. They were allocated NR174, coded NP-L and, after giving it a thorough check over and an air-test, they went to crew briefing. Their baptism of fire was to take place over Soest, to the east of Dortmund in the Ruhr, as part of a 407-aircraft strong attack on the railway installations situated in the northern suburbs of the town. 158 Squadron contributed twenty-two aircraft to this attack, although Warrant Officer A. W. Elley and crew in NP-A (NP991) had to return early when their navigator collapsed. The force was drawn from 1, 4, 6 and 8 Groups and comprised 385 Halifaxes, 100 Lancasters and 12 Mosquitoes.

The crew's apprehension at having to go to the dreaded Ruhr was pushed to the back of their minds as the hours of preparation had been busy ones. A crew's first operation was always one of the most dangerous, purely due to lack of experience - experience being something you don't have until just after you needed it! Just after dark they boarded the crew truck and were taken out to NP-L's dispersal where they were met by the ground crew. Final cigarettes glowed in the dark (Bill received a regular allowance of American cigarettes and was pretty liberal with them - the whole crew smoked at this time), before they were crushed underfoot and the lads clambered aboard the aircraft to carry out their final checks. The ground crew 'Chiefy' climbed aboard and worked his way up to the cockpit where Bill signed the Form 700. `Chiefy' seemed reluctant to trust 'his' Halifax to the tender mercies of this `sprog' crew, but finally wished them 'Good Luck' before making his way back down the fuselage dropping down through the crew door on the port side and securing it behind him.

Soon they were queueing up around the perimeter track and then it was their turn to line up on the end of the runway. As usual, the station CO, Group Captain Tom Sawyer, had a good collection of ground staff, including Waafs, to wave each crew off and, on receiving the winking green light from the caravan, Bill Strachan opened the throttles, released the brakes and they were off down the runway. This was the first time they had taken off with a full load of bombs and fuel and it seemed an eternity before the Halifax finally left the runway and started the long climb up into the dark night sky.

Approaching the Ruhr, Bob Stow was almost convinced that they were lost - this couldn't be the Ruhr, where's all the Flak? He'd done his first tour in 1943 and just couldn't believe the difference in the strength of the German defences. In reply to the diplomatically phrased question 'Are we on track, Dad?' Cyril Keeton assured the somewhat doubtful flight engineer that they were not only 'dead-on track,' but that the target was only about 15 minutes away. Despite their being in the first wave, the target was already well alight and visible from miles out. Soon, John `Krad' Wakefield had picked out the red and green markers among the seething cauldron of bursting bombs, fires and smoke and started to guide Bill into the aiming point, disregarding the occasional grey puffs of Flak that drifted lazily past the Halifax on its approach. 'Krad' felt a large responsibility as he lined up the green markers in the bombsight lens for the first time. 'Get it right first time laddo, no going around again - no dummy runs - or you're going to be as popular as a pork pie in a synagogue' was the thought that came into his mind as he let the TIs track down the lens. They were flying at 20,000 feet at 162 mph on a heading of 148 degrees true.

Krad re-checked all the settings on the bomb sight computer - all OK. Suddenly the green TI s were in the cross-wire, Krad pressed the bomb release tit with his right thumb at 21.23.5 hours and said 'Bombs gone!' The Halifax lifted noticably as the three 1,000 pounders and eight 500 pound bombs left the bomb bay. Bill Strachan held the aircraft steady for their aiming point photograph as Krad switched the jettison bars across and closed the bomb doors. Then they were doing a gentle turn to port out of the target area and setting course for home. They landed back at Lissett at 25 minutes after midnight, feeling exhilarated - partly from the relief of tension but more because their first sortie was behind them - they'd survived. Bill Strachan couldn't believe his luck, apart from the odd bit of Flak, he'd begun to think he was on just another night cross-country exercise.

This attack on Soest was successful, with the majority of the bombs falling on their intended targets, the railway installations to the north of the town. Approximately 1,000 houses and 53 other buildings were completely destroyed. The force lost only two aircraft, both Halifaxes and 158 Squadron had two more return with slight Flak damage.

There was not a lot of time to reflect on their first operation, for they were on the operations list again the following night, again allocated NP-L (NR174). The squadron contributed eighteen Halifaxes to a total force of 453 aircraft despatched to attack railway yards at Osnabruck, this town's first major attack since August 1942. The raid was only a partial success because of 10/10ths cloud, although four factories - including the Teuto-Metallwerke munitions factory - were unintentional recipients of many bombs. Krad Wakefield was very disappointed when they reached the target - there wasn't a TI to be seen. The cloud obscured everything bar a considerable glow beneath it This glow coincided with an H2S image resembling Osnabruck so, in the absence of any instructions from the Master Bomber Bill told Krad to release their load on the glow and he turned for home.

The trip back was a nightmare. There had been a fair amount of Flak over the target, although nothing too close, but on the way home they ran into a severe electrical storm. They were in thick cloud and the night was totally black beyond the dim glare of the instrument panel lights. Suddenly the whole aircraft was lit up with dancing flashes of blue light and all four propellers were giving off sparks like demented Catherine wheels as 'St.Elmo's Fire' took the Halifax in its grip. This was a big enough: worry to a 'sprog' skipper but by far the biggest problem were the flying instruments. Every needle on Bill's blind flying panel was going haywire - only the altimeter seemed to act normally - all Bill could do was to hold on and gradually lose height in the hope of descending out of the storm before Dan got really desperate.' Fortunately, they dropped out of the cloud and its accompanying electrical disturbances after about 15 minutes and finally landed safely at Lissett at 22.37 hours.

The squadron despatched eighteen aircraft to Essen on Tuesday 12th December but Bill and the lads weren't asked to partake. Thus they missed the last major raid of the war on this unfortunate city. On Monday 18th

December, Bill and crew took NR240 (NP-N) on a very early morning trip to Duisburg but again 10/10ths cloud prevented accurate bombing for all 523 aircraft on this attack. Fortunately, this was planned as an area attack so identification of the town by H2S was good enough to cause serious damage. Eight aircraft failed to return, one of those being `J-Jig' from 158 Squadron. The pilot, Flying Officer W. L. Lynd, his flight engineer and both gunners survived but the three men in the nose (Sergeants E. A. Rhude - navigator; D. S. Brown - bomb aimer and J. V. Grant - wireless operator) were all killed when the Halifax crashed near Brussels.

Again, the pleasure of the company of Bill and crew was not requested on the squadron's next operation to Cologne on 21st December but at 11.35 hours on Christmas Eve they lifted Halifax MZ480 (NP-K) off Lissett's runway on their way to attack Mulheim Airfield at Essen. It is believed that this attack, along with that on another Luftwaffe airfield at Lohausen (now Dusseldorf civil airport), was intended to hinder the air movement of supplies from the Ruhr to the Ardennes battle area. Both attacks took place in good visibility and the bombing was accurate.

The weather was actually quite typical for Christmas Eve, with most of Yorkshire covered in frost but with clear blue skies. As MZ480 crossed the North Sea and entered allied re-occupied territory, `Krad,' in the nose, observed the launch of a V-2 to the north of their track. On their approach to Mulheim airfield (now Essen's civil airport), they were greeted by a sobering scene. The sky was covered with black bursts of Flak, looking much more evil and dangerous in daylight. The target was soon visible, erupting under a deluge of bombs as the Halifaxes and Lancasters of 4, 6 and 8 Groups pressed home their attack. Despite this, the Luftwaffe Flak gunners had certainly got their eye in - shells were bursting just ahead of Bill Strachan's Halifax and spot-on for height. Krad Wakefield, lying in the nose, was convinced that the Jerries were out to get him personally as he watched the angry red centres of the Flak bursts and their dirty black smoke. Spotting the red and green TI's, Krad at last had something to concentrate on and was able to put the Flak to the back of his mind as he called for Bill to fly `straight and level.' A last check around, airspeed 170 mph, heading 074 degrees true, height 20,000 feet and then back to the bomb sight.

The Master Bomber came on air, instructing all crews to bomb the reds furthest from the smoke. So, with a slight correction from Bill, Krad lined up on these reds and let them drift up the sight. Suddenly a shell burst quite near, Krad could hear the 'Crump' as it exploded and he assumed that they had probably been perforated somewhere - he remembered being told that if you could hear the explosion, it was close enough to cause damage to some degree - but the reds were getting closer. Krad let them ease down to the cross-wire and then pressed the 'tit' to release their five 1,000 and eight 250 lbs bombs. He looked at his Watch as he called 'bombs gone,' it was 14.35.5 hours. Krad called out 'Bomb doors closed' and Bill held the Halifax steady for another thirty seconds for the aiming point photograph before turning away from the target. As they straightened up on the course home they spotted another Halifax trailing smoke and cavorting all over the sky. It was obviously in serious trouble and as they watched, its crew started to bale out. Almost holding his breath, Krad counted the 'chutes as they opened, `four - five - six - come on skipper - seven. Thank God for that, all out safely,' and he reported this fact to Cyril so he could note it in his navigator's log. No sooner had the pilot left the stricken Halifax, than it reared up on its tail, stalled and did a wing over dive in a pretty fair imitation of a stunting Spitfire, then it looped up, stalled again and once more winged over into a dive. It then continued to repeat this aerobatic manoeuvre until it was lost to Krad's view. They landed back at Lisset at 16.25 hours - in nice time for tea! An inspection of their aircraft revealed only minor holes here and there. Altogether ten of the squadron aircraft bore Flak damage to some degree, some quite serious - 'A Merry Christmas from Jerry,' said Krad.

The squadron was stood down on Christmas Day, not because the 'powers that be' were full of goodwill to all men, but simply because the weather was too foul to fly in - even the birds were walking! They were, however, called to action on Boxing Day. The weather improved sufficiently to allow Bomber Command to intervene in the Battle of the Ardennes - the 2nd Tactical Air Force was still grounded by the bad weather on the European mainland - so just after an early lunch, the squadron despatched fourteen Halifaxes as part of a total force of 294 aircraft from all Groups in an attack on German troop positions near St. Vith, some 35 miles southeast of Liege. This attack, the first occasion since mid-October that aircraft from all the main Bomber Groups had joined together, was accurate and well concentrated.

Bill Strachan and crew were allocated NP-K again but during their pre-flight checks Bill and Bob Stow noticed that their brake pressure was very low. The air pressure to operate the brakes was supplied by a Heywood compressor mounted on the port inner engine but even running the engine at high revs seemed to make very little difference to the indication on the 'triple brake gauge.' It was obvious to a blind man on horseback that they couldn't taxi without brake pressure - nor could they break radio silence to call up their ground crew for assistance, so Bill told Alan Parrish to leave the aircraft and roust the ground crew out of their hut and get 'Chiefy' to phone Flying Control for instructions. Fairly quickly a small truck was sent out with a large bottle of compressed air and the ground crew re-charged the pneumatic reservoir so that Bill could taxi out and take off. He was assured that the air pressure would build up during the flight.

Approaching the target the Flak picked them up quite early but fortunately it lacked the accuracy they'd experienced over Essen on Christmas Eve. The sky appeared to be full of aircraft, all jostling for bombing position but Krad had no difficulty in assessing the drift and lining up on red and green TIs marking the target. He hardly had to give Bill any corrections and the TIs were drifting nicely down to the bomb release point when Bill suddenly wrenched the Halifax hard to port and then straightened up again. 'What the bloody hell's happening, Skipper?' asked Krad. 'Do you see that dirty great Lancaster to starboard?' replied Bill, 'Well it was just about to unload the contents of its belly on top of us!' This lucid but brief explanation completely satisfied the bomb aimer who still managed to adjust his run without them having to go around again.

On their way home, Bob Stow pointed out that the indications on the 'triple brake pressure gauge' had not improved. 'Sorry, Skipper, we've still got no brakes.' Bill decided to head for the emergency landing ground at Carnaby, which was only six miles up the road from Lissett and they landed safely, albeit with a very long run, at 17.35 hours.

The squadron did not operate on Wednesday but on Thursday 28th December, Bill and the boys found themselves in Halifax MZ350 (R-Roger), heading for the marshalling yards at Opladen - just one of 328 aircraft from 4, 6 and 8 Groups. R-Roger had left Lissett at 03.21 hours on a cold, frosty morning and it arrived in the target area after a three hour flight. Krad Wakefield released their single 1000 pounder and twelve 500 pounders onto the red and green TI s from 20,000 feet at 06.38 hours. At 06.38.5 hours Flak knocked out the oil supply to their starboard outer engine and within seconds the engine temperature had risen almost off the clock. Bob Stow told Bill what was happening and they shut the engine down and returned on the remaining three, landing back at Lissett at 09.08 hours, more than ready for breakfast.

There is no rest for the wicked, so they say, and the next day they were off again, this time to attack the Mosel marshalling yards at Koblenz, while a 3 Group force attacked the Lutzel yards in the same unfortunate town. Both were believed to be main centres serving the Ardennes front. Krad obeyed the Master Bomber's instructions to bomb the red TIs just visible through a scattered layer of 8/10ths cloud and they returned to Lissett in time for tea after six hours in the air.

The next night, Saturday 30th December, Bill and the lads were once again on the Operations Order. This would be their third trip in MZ350, R-Roger', an excellent aircraft that Bill really enjoyed flying. He was feeling pretty pleased because he had just been informed that this would be his regular aircraft from now on. They carried out their pre-flight checks, climbed aboard and started the engines. Bill was just about to taxi out when Alan Parrish came on the intercom, 'Skipper, I've just trapped me bloody fingers in the breech.' Jesus Christ,' came the exasperated reply, 'Well, get your bloody fingers untrapped and get your arse down to the crew hut and get them to send me another bloody gunner - sharpish!' Alan did as he was bidden and within minutes a van arrived at dispersal and unloaded a new bod who climbed aboard, got into the mid-upper turret, wiped some blood off the breech blocks and settled down for the trip. The 'new bod' was Sergeant R. V. Formstone and the poor man did not even know what the target was. Fortunately, the rest of the crew did. They were going to bomb the Kalk-Nord railway yards in Cologne as part of a 25-Halifax contribution from 158 Squadron to a total force of 470 aircraft. Bill lifted R-Roger' into the air at 17.25 hours, Krad released their bomb load onto the red and green skymarkers (10/10ths cloud again) from 19,000 feet at 21.08 hours and they returned to Lissett at 15 minutes after midnight. A totally uneventful trip - thank God.

Another New Year's Day dawned clear, cold and frosty, the sixth of the war. Surely this couldn't last much longer? Don't the Germans realise they're beaten? Operations again tonight, sixteen aircraft and crews - including Flight Sergeant Strachan and his merry men. Briefing revealed the target to be a benzol plant in Dortmund. They were taxiing along the perimeter track when R-Roger' lost nearly all brake pressure. Bill had to get off the peri-track so as not to delay the following aircraft and pulled into the first dispersal he came to. The brakes were only just holding the Halifax stationary with her engines at tick over. It was very dark, but within minutes Bill could make out a single masked headlight making its way towards them from the tower. A small van arrived and Group Captain Tom Sawyer, the Station CO arrived at Flight Sergeant Strachan's side in the cockpit like a veritable whirlwind. Ordering Bill out of the pilot's seat, the Group Captain took control of the aircraft and started to taxi out.

It did not take him long to realise that Bill was 100% right. The aircraft had next to no brakes. 'You're right Skipper,' said the Group Captain, 'You can't taxi this kite like this' and he turned onto a runway not in use and tried to stop. R-Roger's' brakes had now given up the ghost completely. Their air pressure had definitely gone AWOL (absent without leave). No matter how hard Tom Sawyer applied the brakes, the Halifax just kept rolling forward, only slowly, but rolling forward nevertheless. 'Get some of your crew to take their parachutes and push them under the front of the main wheels Flight Sar'nt said the Groupie. Bill did as he was ordered and Ted, Cyril, Krad and Bob grabbed their 'chutes, piled out of the crew exit and, keeping a watchful eye on the propellers, pushed two parachutes under each mainwheel. R-Roger' then condescended to stand still. They weren't going to Dortmund after all.

Later that evening when handing their parachutes back into the parachute section, Bill informed the NCO in charge that he'd better give them a good inspection and told him why. The NCO got very annoyed, 'Parachutes aren't made to be used as bloody chocks' whined the 'Penguin'[59]. 'You can't do that with my parachutes, I'll report you, you see if I don't.' Bill had had a trying night. His Aussie background came to the fore. 'I don't give a stuff about your bloody parachutes you whinging pommie. You can report me to the bloody AOC for all I care, but suggest you start with the Group Captain, it was him who told us to use your bloody parachutes as chocks. They're a bloody sight cheaper than a Halifax!' With that Bill turned on his heel and left the 'penguin' standing there with his mouth agape.

They were on the Operations Order the next day, Tuesday 2nd January, again with `R-Roger' (MZ350). The target was the I. G. Farben chemical factories

---

[59] *'Penguin' is a derogatory RAF aircrew expression for non- aircrew - a bird that can't fly!*

in Ludwigshaven and, although take-off was at 15.23 hours in the afternoon, it was dark by the time they reached the Rhine, for their course took them south of the target before they headed 15 degrees east of north to bomb. It was a clear moonlit night and Bill Strachan warned both gunners to stay alert for nightfighters and as he did so he gently rolled the Halifax to the right and then to the left to give Archie a chance to check the blind spot under the tail. As the port wing was at its lowest point, Bill looked down and noticed the moon shining on the river below them - it was just like a silver thread winding northwards -a wonderful sight and one that was momentarily hard to reconcile with their current duty. Bill called his navigator, 'Hey Dad, you can forget your charts and navigation - I can take you direct to the target from here' and he switched his mike off chuckling into his oxygen mask as he did so. Cyril did not rise to the bait.

On reaching the target, Krad had to give very few corrections on the run-up and released their ten 500 pounders and six 250 pound bombs onto the centre of the red TIs from 20,000 feet at 18.46.5 hours. There were a number of very large explosions in the target area. The first, at 18.46 hours, appeared to be right in the centre of the red Tis, was orange and red in colour and lasted for about five seconds.

There was a second at 18.47 hours, which was a large yellow explosion and others followed at 18.49, 18.51 and 18.54 hours until finally at 18.58 hours, there came the largest of all. It was reddish-orange, lasted several seconds and lit up the whole sky, making every aircraft in the bomber stream clearly visible. The bombing was very accurate, causing severe damage to the main factory and to that at nearby Oppau. Estimated totals of 500 high explosive bombs and 10,000 incendiaries fell inside the limits of the two factories and production at both plants ceased completely because of loss of power. Archie reported that he could still see the target burning as they were over Belgium on the way home.

R-Roger' was being serviced on Friday 5th January, so they took (NR133) to Hannover as part of a 664-aircraft force carrying out the first large raid on the city since October 1943. The briefing for this raid was changed at the last minute. Instead of flying across the North Sea at low level as initially instructed, the crews were told to climb to 10,000 feet as soon as they had taken off. Apparently a Meteorological Flight Mosquito had reported a cold front with icing conditions and high winds over the North Sea and the new plan was to climb above this. The crews were not best pleased at the thought of being picked up on German radar so early and giving the enemy plenty of time to organise its defences.

They might have missed the icing conditions but they certainly met the high winds. 'Dad' was plotting winds up to 100 mph and they were off track quite a bit. GEE was completely `grassed over' but Krad was able to provide a pinpoint from the H2S as they reached the coast. Their reception from the Flak on crossing the enemy coast was predictable, given their briefed height over the North Sea and Bill could see aircraft falling out of the night sky everywhere he looked.

It was another 10/10ths cloud job when they arrived over Hannover and they were going to have to bomb on sky markers. Flak was slight to moderate and appeared to be being fired at the sky markers, hitting at least one of them. There were many nightfighter flares and much nightfighter activity on the last leg into the target, over the target and on the leg out, where it appeared to be most intense. While over the target, Krad saw a Ju88 silhouetted against the clouds below them but fortunately it didn't see them. Bill, Krad and the gunners saw many exchanges of fire.

While just starting to line up for the bomb run, J-Jig was accompanied by a strange phenomenon - some sort of flying object flew parallel to the aircraft, about thirty yards out on the starboard side. It was streaming flames from its rear and kept station with `J-Jig' for several minutes before going into a steep dive, breaking into several parts and disappearing into the clouds below[60]. Krad Wakefield watched this all the time it was alongside them. It definitely wasn't an aircraft. Perhaps it was a mortar shell from a Wfr.Gr.21 firing tube mounted under the wing of a Wild Boar single engined fighter. We shall never know.

Bill landed `J-Jig' back at Lissett at 22.16 hours after almost five and a half hours in the air and the crew was saddened to learn that the squadron had lost three crews -those of Flight Lieutenant A. Elliott (NR251, NP-B), Flying

---

[60] *The object that they had observed could well have been a Mosquito being shot down by an Me262 nightfighter. Oberleutnant Kurt Welter of 10./NJG11 is believed to have made such a claim this night and the object 'with flames coming from its tail' could have been his Me262.*

Officer D. H. Robinson (MZ395, NP-C) and Flying Officer A. G. Robertson (MZ432, NP-Q). A total of 31 aircraft failed to return this night.

There was another morning briefing the next day, Saturday 6th January and as R-Roger' was still unserviceable, they were again allocated `J-Jig'. Their target for the night was to be an important railway junction at Hanau, east of Frankfurt and the squadron, was despatching twenty-one Halifaxes as part of a total force of 482 aircraft. They left Lissett at 15.33 hours and headed south to their first turning point at Reading. The late afternoon sky seemed to be full of RAF bomber aircraft and it was comforting to know that you weren't alone - a feeling that soon vanished as darkness fell and you began to wonder just how close some of those other bloody aircraft were and were their pilots keeping their eyes peeled!

The trip to the target was uneventful and the PFF marking appeared to be well concentrated. Krad saw a burning aircraft go down in the target area and observed several running fights between bombers and nightfighters. As was getting to be usual of late, the target was covered in 10/10ths cloud with tops at about 8,000 feet, although by the time 'J-Jig' arrived, a red glow could be seen below the clouds. On a course of 136 degrees true, at a speed of 160 mph, Krad released the bombload onto red sky markers at 19.05.5 from a height of 18,000 feet. One very large explosion was observed in the target area at 19.12 hours, as `J-Jig' was starting to leave.

Keith Anderson, whom we last met leaning against the hangar wall at 21 OTU, had followed Bill Strachan to 158 Squadron at Lissett and he and Bill had a regular bet on who would land first. In order to win this bet, Bill was not above calling Lissett Flying Control a little early on occasions – usually as they were approaching Hull - with the idea of getting an earlier slot in the stack. It didn't always work, but it worked often enough to keep Bill ahead in the betting stakes! On this Friday night, however, Bill played it straight and didn't try to jump the queue. Final approach was quite tricky, with a cross-wind swirling a reddish mist across the runway from left to right, occasionally totally obscuring the runway lights and pushing `J-Jig' off the approach line. Bill adopted a standard cross-wind approach and came in crabwise, with the nose of the Halifax pointing to port, then straightening the aircraft up a fraction of a second before touchdown at 22.07 hours. Bill had taken all this in his stride and, having just heard Keith Anderson, in `M-Mother' (NP-M) call Flying Control for permission to 'Pancake', he permitted himself a little chuckle of dual satisfaction - a nice, smooth cross-wind landing and he'd beaten Keith back again!

J-Jig' had just cleared the end of the runway when Bill heard Keith call an overshoot. `M-Mother' did not land back at Lissett. Keith's Halifax (MZ366) lost an engine on overshoot and crashed heavily at North Frodingham - about five miles southwest of Lissett - throwing the bomb aimer, Sergeant Ken Sutton, out of the aircraft. All seven crewmen were taken to hospital but Ken Sutton succumbed to his injuries later the next day. As mentioned earlier, Keith Anderson's wireless operator, Les Lamb, was a big friend of Ted Richards and Ken Sutton had been on the same course as Johnny Wrad' Wakefield and they'd been close friends. All four gunners from both crews were also mates, so there were two crews mourning the death of Sergeant Sutton.

Another 158 Squadron aircraft failed to return from Hanau. NP195 (NP-I) was shot down at Grossauheim in the south-eastern outskirts of the target area with the loss of all on board. The skipper was the same Flying Officer Jack Krefter who had given Bill Strachan directions to the airfield on the crew's very first morning at Lissett.

Thick snow cancelled operations for the next eight days, but Group Captain Tom Sawyer kept all Station personnel - including most aircrew - hard at it trying to keep the runways and taxi-ways clear of the white stuff. There were a few aircrew missing from this little chore. When ordered to fetch his crew for snow clearing duties, Bill set off to their billet to roust them out. He was unable to find any of them - they'd all suddenly vanished into thin air! The attempts at clearing the snow continued without their assistance, but it was a pretty fruitless task because just as they got the job half finished, another blizzard would arrive and they'd all be up to their knees in the stuff again. There were, however, many snowball fights and much larking about, mainly to keep warm (at least that was the excuse) as their Nissen huts were so cold and there was a constant hunt for extra coal and wood for the pot-bellied stove in the centre of each hut, to supplement the meagre 'official' ration.

Operations recommenced with an attack on the railway yards at Saarbrucken on Sunday 14th January, when they were back in 'R-Roger' (MZ350) at last. Apart from having to orbit in the target area (a most unpopular pastime) on instructions from the Master Bomber, this seven-hour trip was uneventful. Two nights later, Bill and crew were up for their thirteenth operational sortie.

Briefing revealed an area attack on Magdeburg, with 23 Halifaxes from 158 Squadron joining 348 other aircraft on this raid. R-Roger' was airborne at 19.04 hours and reached the target area at about 21.30 hours. As they turned to starboard to start their run-in, Bill saw a solid wall of Flak ahead of him. For the first time in his tour he felt really scared, perhaps the '13th op' was preying on his mind, but he couldn't see how they could possibly fly into that wall of Flak and come through it unscathed. Fortunately, Krad started giving his bombing run instructions and, with something to concentrate on, Bill stifled his concern and got on with the job in hand. Down in the nose, Krad hadn't even noticed the Flak. The first thing that struck him was that Magdeburg was already suffering greatly. It was the first time he'd seen a large city under attack and he was surprised to see how easily he could pick out the outlines of the streets. The second thing that got to him was the searchlights - the first time the crew had experienced them. It was these that made Krad concentrate on his bombing run, the fear of being coned raised its ugly head and he was determined that their thirteenth operation would not be their first 'dummy run'. Ignoring the decoy TIs about four miles east of the target - their shade of red was nowhere near bright enough - Krad checked the positioning of the real TIs with H2S and then lined the bomb sight up on the centre of the reds. He released their load with a two second overshoot (as instructed by the Master Bomber) from 20,000 ft at 21.46 hours.

Their return route passed close to Hannover and searchlights and Flak were quite intense there too. At least one aircraft was seen to be shot down and one of 158's aircraft was coned and damaged by Flak. Although fighter activity appeared to be mainly on the two legs out of the target, at least one Ju88 was seen in the target area and a Dornier Do217 was seen to shoot down a Halifax with a long burst from 'upward firing' guns (Schrage Musik). Altogether seventeen Halifaxes failed to return from this attack - 4.6% of the total force, but 5.3% of the Halifaxes despatched - exceedingly high losses for this period of the war. One of the missing aircraft belonged to 158 Squadron. NP-Y (MZ927), skippered by Flying Officer J.A.S.Stewart, came down between Oschersleben and Hodorf, eighteen miles west- southwest of the target. Only the Navigator (Flight Sergeant H.G.Hall) and the bomb aimer (Flying Officer H. Parker) survived to become prisoners-of-war.

Bill Strachan carried out an air test on Thursday 18th January but he then had to go to London. He discovered that he'd been commissioned with effect from 2nd January and he had to visit Australia House to obtain the distinctive dark blue material for his RAAF uniform and then have it tailored by Carr, Son & Woor Ltd. of 9 Saville Row. Because of this little jolly to the smoke', the crew missed the squadron's next call to arms, when they despatched 21 aircraft to Gelsenkirchen on the 22nd January. All returned safely and one of them, LV907, NP-F, otherwise known as Friday the 13th ', completed its 100th operation.

The last large-scale Bomber Command attack on Stuttgart took place on the night of Sunday 28th January, when 602 aircraft from 1, 4, 6 and 8 Groups attacked in two waves with a three-hour interval. 158 Squadron put up 22 Halifaxes for the first wave attack, one of which was MZ350, R-Roger', flown by Pilot Officer William Strachan and crew. The first wave of 226 aircraft was briefed to attack the important railway yards at Kornwestheim, a town just to the north of Stuttgart, while the second was directed at the northwestern suburb of the city, known as Zuffenhausen, where the main target was the Hirth aero-engine factory. The targets were mostly cloud covered for both attacks and the bombing, on sky-markers, was somewhat scattered over Zuffenhausen with bombs falling in many parts of the city's northern and western suburbs, although the Bosch works in the suburb of Feuerbach were hit. The earlier attack on Kornwestheim was the worst suffered by the town during the whole war and fires burned for up to twelve hours. Eleven aircraft failed to return.

This trip did not have an auspicious beginning when Bill, Dad, Bob and Krad were told at briefing that, because of the duration of the trip (eight hours) and the fact that R-Roger' was not fitted with a bomb bay overload fuel tank, fuel would be at a premium and that they may have to land in southern England on their return. Then they had to take off down a runway with cleared snow piled up on both sides. Sitting in the fold-down seat at Bill's side for the take-off, Krad looked forward as Bill released the brakes and thought 'Now is not a good time to swing on take-off.', but as usual, Bill kept R-Roger' as straight as a die and they were safely airborne at 16.55 hours.

On arrival at the target, the crew found 10/10ths cloud – yet again - with tops at 12,000 feet. PFF marking was slightly late but Krad lined his bomb sight up on a solitary red and yellow sky-marker, the position of which he confirmed with H2S and bombed it from 18,000 feet at 20.41 hours. Leaving the target and remembering the fuel warning, Bill asked Bob how much flying time they were likely to have remaining on reaching base. Bob

The Pendulum and the Scythe

Destination Stuttgart on 28ᵗʰ January 1945. 158 Sqn's Bill Strachan keeps MZ350 NP-R straight between the banks of snow. This aircraft failed to return from Chemnitz on 14ᵗʰ February 1945. F/O Gapes and his crew survived.

calculated that they should have about twenty minutes left on arrival over Lissett. Figuring that this was enough for him to land, Bill decided to head straight back to base, but he asked Bob what he would do in the circumstances. Bob had not survived one-and-a-half tours without learning to be circumspect, 'You're the skipper,' he replied 'It's your decision.' Working on the principle that if their fuel consumption was heavier than it should be, he could always lob in at any one of the hundreds of airfields in East Anglia or Lincolnshire, Bill asked Dad for a course for Lissett.

They landed safely back at base at 00.51 hours, taxied to their dispersal and switched everything off. Bill took his helmet off and relaxed in his seat for a moment. Bob spoke softly in his ear, 'I've been keeping my fingers crossed since you started your landing approach, hoping like hell you didn't call an overshoot.'

`Why?' asked Bill, 'How much fuel have we got left?'

'Not a lot.' replied Bob. Only five of the squadron's Halifaxes landed back at base, most of the others diverted to Upper Heyford because of fuel shortage.

Four days later, on Thursday 1ˢᵗ February, they were on the operations list again, along with another twenty-six squadron crews. Their target was Mainz and the Command despatched 340 aircraft to this target, 396 to Ludwigshaven and a further 282 to Sieger, giving a total of 1,273 sorties for this one night, a new record for the Command. As usual at this time of year the target was cloud covered - 7 to 8/10ths, with tops at 10,000 feet and rising. Crews bombed on TIs when visible through gaps in the cloud or on sky-markers. The crew of R-Roger' identified the target by the red and green sky-markers and Krad released their bombs into the centre of two of these at 19.33 hours from 20,000 feet. Krad put the jettison bars across and tested for hang-ups as usual but, for the first time in his operational career, he was amazed to find that one 500 pounder had hung up! He told Bob Stow what station it was on and Bob set about removing inspection panels above the bomb bay to have a `shufty'. He finally managed to release the stubborn little `so'n'so' in one of the standard jettison areas about fifteen miles east of Skegness, just off the Wash, and they landed back at Lissett at 22.59 hours.

The next night they went to the oil refinery at Wanne-Eickel and once again found the target covered in 10/10ths cloud. Again Harris split his attacking force, the Wanne-Eickel raid was carried out by 323 aircraft from 4, 6 and 8 Groups, while 507 aircraft went to Wiesbaden and a further 261 attacked Karlsruhe. On Sunday 4th February they took R-Roger, (MZ350) to bomb the Nordstern synthetic oil plant at Gelsenkirchen as one of a 120 aircraft attack, again through 10/10ths cloud. Three of the squadron's aircraft were damaged by moderate heavy Flak but `R-Roger' returned unscathed.

They were then given two nights off before finding their names on the operations list for the night of Wednesday 7th February. At briefing the twenty-six assembled crews heard that they were to attack Goch as part of a 464-aircraft force, while a further 305 aircraft attacked the neighbouring town of Kleve. Both attacks were to soften up the strong Nazi defences in this area of the German frontier near Reichswald in order to prepare the way for an advance by the British XXX Corps.

Again flying 'R-Roger' (MZ350), they left Lissett at 19.14 hours and set course on the first leg to the target. Arriving in the Goch area just before 22.00 hours, the Master Bomber could be plainly heard discussing - with his navigator - the courses he intended to steer and then gave a time check. Krad identified the target by the red and green TIs from 20,000 feet and these were tracking nicely down the bomb sight when the Master Bomber instructed 'Basement 5' (Come down to 5,000 feet) to all aircraft. Bill Strachan started a very precise 360 degree diving turn to port, going down through the cloud. He had to keep a close watch on the airspeed indicator, rate of turn and rate of descent indicators and the altimeter - all had to be monitored closely - as well as keeping a wary eye out of the cockpit for other aircraft whose pilots were attempting the same manoeuvre. Krad down in the nose and Bob with his head in the astrodome helped the gunners to keep a sharp look out while

Bill completed this very risky descent through cloud. The Master Bomber was not a popular chap!

At 5,000 feet they were still in thick cloud so Bill continued on down, finally breaking clear of the 'clag' at 3,000 feet. His turn and descent must have been spot-on because there, directly in front of them, was Goch. Bill rechecked his altimeter, yes, it did read 3,000 feet, but it seemed more like 300. Even the tracer from the light Flak seemed to be coming at them horizontally. Lying in the nose, Krad Wakefield picked out the target again straight away and began to track in once more. The major problem was that Halifaxes seemed to be milling about all over the sky. Even in just the light coming from the target's defences Krad could see four-engined bombers everywhere he looked. Mid-air collision was an ever present danger at night and with possible closing speeds in excess of 400 mph there was very little time in which to take avoiding action. Krad was also being distracted by the light Flak now being aimed, it seemed to him, at the bomb aimer of MZ350 personally. He watched almost spellbound as the tracer arced lazily into the night sky and meandered towards the aircraft before suddenly speeding up and passing his nose position like the clappers of hell.

Suddenly the Master Bomber's voice interrupted his preoccupation with the tracer. 'All aircraft abort - all aircraft abort. Do not bomb, I repeat, do not bomb!' A few choice epithets were heard to come from the nose of 'R-Roger' - and no doubt from many another bomb aimer in the attacking force. The raid was stopped after only 155 aircraft, including only four from 158 Squadron, had bombed. The Master Bomber was obviously concerned that with so many aircraft milling around all over the target area there was a serious danger that some bombs might be accidently released onto the British soldiery massing below, not to mention the high likelihood of losing bombers in collisions. It was the only sensible decision in the circumstances, but nevertheless frustrating for those crews who had hauled their bombs all that way, only to have to haul them all the way back again. R-Roger' landed at Lissett at 01.08 hours and before the crew got to bed Bill learned that another Aussie skipper, Flying Officer Jack Beeson, had failed to return. His body, along with those of another three members of his crew, were discovered lying in woods between Geldern and the village of Lullingen. All four are now buried in the Reichswald Forest War Cemetery. The squadron was losing Australian pilots – and their crews - at quite a rate. Bill couldn't quite make up his mind whether he should be worried, or just assume that he was leading a charmed life!

Having completed eighteen operations, their names came to the top of the leave roster and Bill and the lads vamoosed pretty quickly. Bill had no relations in England so Johnny `Krad' Wakefield took him home with him. Ten glorious, carefree days soon came to an end and they returned to Lissett to learn, that Flying Officer Jimmy Gapes had taken their aircraft (MZ350) to Chemnitz on the night of 14th February and had not returned it. Gapes and crew all baled out safely near Givet in France and returned to the squadron within a matter of days but Bill Strachan was really 'cheesed' at losing his favourite aircraft. It was not long before the squadron provided him with another one - MZ917. Another Halifax B.Mk.III, MZ917 had already 'got some in' with 51 Squadron (Bob Stow's first tour unit), serving as MH-K. Because of this, her port side nose carried a painting of a scantily-clad young lady sat astride a bomb, with the caption Krazy Kate and twenty small bomb symbols denoting ops with her previous unit. On 158 Squadron she became 'R-Roger' as a direct replacement for MZ350, but the crew elected to retain the nose art and adopted the Krazy Kate name. Little did they know, but Krazy Kate was not to stay with them for long.

Their first trip in MZ917 took place on Saturday 24th February when they joined another 339 aircraft in a daylight attack on the synthetic oil plant at Bergkamen, just north of Kamen. Again the target was cloud covered and

Bill Strachan and crew with Halifax B. MkIII MZ917 NP-R 'Krazy Kate'.

the attack was based on Oboe and H2S marking. On Tuesday 27th February they took part in another daylight raid, this time to Mainz and yet again the target was covered in cloud and all bombs were aimed at Oboe-dropped sky-markers. This was Mainz's last and heaviest raid of the war, with a total of 1,545 tons of bombs being dropped and 5,670 buildings destroyed. The town had received fourteen major raids by the RAF and USAAF during the course of the war. Krad Wakefield released Krazy Kate's bombload onto green smoke markers from 18,000 feet at 16.36 hours, but two incendiary clusters hung up and once again Bob Stow had to delve into the inspection panels above the bomb bay. They were finally jettisoned at 18.55 hours about ten miles due east of Skegness, before Bill landed Krazy Kate back at at Lissett at 19.33 hours. Flight engineer Bob Stow had finished his second tour and, with a DFC to add to the DFM from his first tour, he was posted back to instructor duties at an HCU.

A two-day respite followed Bob's departure but Pilot Officer Strachan and crew were woken up very early in the morning of Friday 2nd March. Cologne was now almost in the front line, with allied troops poised to take the city. At the request of SHAEF, Bomber Command laid on an attack, split into two parts, by a total of 858 aircraft that was aimed at softening up the Nazi defences for the advancing Allies. Take-off was scheduled to begin at 07.00 hours and 158 Squadron were included in the first part of the attack, to be carried out by 703 aircraft. The second attack was carried out by 155 Lancasters of 3 Group but this had to be abandoned after only fifteen Lancasters had bombed because the G-H station in the UK was experiencing technical problems - those bloody gremlins again!

The main raid, the last RAF raid on Cologne, was highly destructive, with PFF marking the target in - for a pleasant change - clear weather conditions. The city's warning sirens did not sound until just two minutes before the first bombs fell - such was now the pathetic state of the Nazi's early warning system with the rapid advance of the Allied ground forces – and hundreds of civilians and at least 160 soldiers (mainly SS) were killed. Many German military units were affected by the bombing and the city was captured by American troops four days later.

The squadron despatched twenty-two aircraft on this attack and Bill Strachan and crew, with a stand-in flight engineer, took off at 07.13 hours. Arriving in the Cologne area, all the crews found excellent visibility and the 2/10ths cloud, with tops at 7,000 feet, could be almost totally ignored. Krad

The Pendulum and the Scythe

Wakefield picked out the Rhine quite easily and Cologne was already enveloped in smoke, with very little more than the twin spires of the Cathedral sticking out through it. The Master Bomber came on the R/T, 'All Pickwick aircraft, Pickwick aircraft, undershoot the reds by 200 yards.' Krad lined the bombsight up as instructed and released their load from 20,000 feet at 10.10 hours. No sooner had he said 'Bombs gone' then the Master Bomber amended his instructions to overshoot the reds by 200 yards. Some crews heard only the first instruction, some heard only the second and some heard both. It was little wonder that returning crews reported that bombing seemed to be all over the area within the outer ring road and not just on the AP.

Despite the weight of bombing, the local Flak gunners put up a spirited defence and Flying Officer Kuperman lost the propeller from his starboard outer engine. Fortunately he managed to limp into Woodbridge Emergency Landing Ground. Flying Officer Houston, a fellow Canadian, landed at Carnaby on three engines after losing his starboard inner engine. Bill Strachan eased Krazy Kate onto Lissett's runway at 12.49 hours in time for a late lunch.

The next day, Saturday 3rd March, Pilot Officer W. P. Strachan and crew, plus Krazy Kate, appeared on the operations list again. This was the 2,000th night of the war and while 5 Group were to send 212 Lancasters and 10 Mosquitoes to the Dortmund-Ems Canal again, 4 Group prepared to despatch 201 Halifaxes along with 33 PFF aircraft in another night attack on the synthetic oil refinery at Bergkamen, just north of Kamen. This was the night on which Halifaxes LW587 (LK-A) and MZ527 (LK-D), both of 578 Squadron, logged their 100th sortie.

For Bill Strachan, this was to be his 22nd operational sortie and his second visit to Kamen, which he had previously attacked on 24th February. But for the first time he was to fly without 'Dad' Keeton, who had a bad head cold. His replacement was a Canadian, Pilot Officer D. H. MacKirdy. Take-off was at 18.29 hours and the flight to the target area was uneventful. Krad Wakefield latched onto the good concentration of red and green TIs and checked their position with H2S. Bill kept Krazy Kate on a heading of 150° true at an indicated airspeed of 160 mph while Krad allowed the TIs to ease down the sight and, at 22.06.5 hours, he released their bombload from 19,000 feet. They took their aiming point photograph and headed for home.

The Pendulum and the Scythe

As the crews returned to their bases, leaving Kamen severely damaged in a very accurate raid that stopped all production at the oil refinery for the rest of the war, they were not to know that the Luftwaffe had chosen this night to carry out *Operation Gisella*. Approximately one hundred Ju88 nightfighters had crossed the North Sea at low level and were awaiting the RAF bombers return, circling as close to the bomber bases of Yorkshire and Lincolnshire as they could without raising a premature alarm. Krazy Kate crossed the English coast at Orfordness and headed almost due north towards Lissett. Krad Wakefield was sitting on the folding seat alongside his skipper, thinking of his tot of rum and bacon and eggs. As they passed over the Wash, he saw what at first appeared to be two shooting stars falling to earth and drew Bill's attention to them. They speculated about them for a brief minute and then tracer fire to starboard brought them to the sobering conclusion that they must have been aircraft going down in flames. Just then, Lou Richards picked up a message from Lissett Flying Control warning all squadron aircraft that there were bandits in the area. There were sharks in their pool - and bacon, eggs and rum were instantly forgotten as Bill warned the crew to keep their eyes peeled for intruders. As Bill steadied Krazy Kate at 1,000 feet on the downwind leg of the landing circuit he reiterated his warning to keep all eyes peeled for intruders. The words had only just left his lips when their Halifax was engulfed in white tracer for about three to four seconds. The worst of the attack seemed to be down the starboard side of the aircraft but it was the port outer engine that burst into flames.

To the undying gratitude of his crew, Bill Strachan remained perfectly calm. As the tracer started to fly past the starboard cockpit window, Bill jinked the Halifax to port. As the port outer burst into flame he pressed the button to operate the built-in Graviner extinguisher system and feathered the propeller. The controls felt sloppy but Krazy Kate still responded fairly well. Lissett was now instructing all 158 Squadron aircraft to divert to Middleton St. George but, with one engine still on fire and only limited control of the Halifax, Bill decided this was not on.

He called Flying Control and briefly explained their predicament. Base replied that if they could come straight in they would put the runway lights on for a short time only. Bill told them he was coming straight in, did a quick turn to port and started his final approach. He called for undercarriage and thankfully it came down and locked - the three green lights on the instrument panel testified to that. He called for flaps and they also came down - perhaps his luck was holding – he couldn't contact the crew at all, obviously the intercom had been shot out. Fortunately Krad Wakefield had helped him with landing often enough to know exactly what to do and a nod from Bill was enough to tell him when to do it.

At about 500 feet they were attacked again. To his dying day Bill Strachan could not work out how the Luftwaffe pilot missed a sitting duck from almost point-blank range but most of this second attack went wide. The crew felt only a slight judder through the airframe and then a Ju88 flashed past them and vanished into the night.

Bill crossed his fingers and continued his final descent. He approached at the normal 120 mph IAS, dropped back to 100 at the beginning of the runway and pulled back on the control column to flatten out for touch-down. There was no response! The second attack had obviously damaged the controls in the tail. Krazy Kate hit the deck with an almighty thump and then bounced. There was nothing Bill cold do but hope and was greatly relieved when the Halifax settled down again safely. As soon as he could feel the rumble of the tyres on the runway, Krad throttled back the three remaining engines. The port outer engine was still glowing so Bill parked the badly damaged Halifax away from any buildings, thinking to himself that 'miracles do happen sometimes.' Then he learned that both of his gunners had been wounded, Archie Tait seriously. Bill used the R/T to call the tower and organised an ambulance before leaving his seat to go and see how 'Arch' was. Johnny 'Krad' Wakefield was already at the rear crew entrance trying to open the door but the fuselage was distorted and the door was jammed. Bill grabbed a fire axe and hacked at the door but no luck, it wasn't going to budge. As he'd passed the mid-upper turret it seemed to be in a right mess with Perspex everywhere but when he gave up on the door and went back towards the rear turret, he found Alan Parrish with one wounded arm, helping to get Archie out of the rear turret.

Krad Wakefield was to the fore in extricating the badly wounded rear gunner. As he tried to open the turret doors the rear of the Halifax suddenly seemed to be full of milling bodies. Archie was in a bad way, a shell had entered his chest, passed through one of his lungs and emerged from his back. He was bleeding quite badly. With the main door jammed, they had to carry Archie up the fuselage and gently lift him up through the escape hatch, lower him onto the starboard wing and then onto the ground before making him as comfortable as possible while they waited for an ambulance.

Meanwhile, the Ju88 was still flying around the aerodrome, firing shots at anything that moved. One of the crew noticed that Archie's bleeding was getting worse so Bill got two of the lads to give him a bunk-up back onto the wing and made his way to the radio. 'Where the hell is that bloody ambulance he demanded of the tower. 'Hang on,' they replied, 'it shouldn't be long.' Bill returned to the group around Archie and the ambulance finally arrived, the MO leaping from the cab even before it had stopped. 'Where the bloody hell have you been?' Bill wanted to know and immediately regretted his outburst when told that the Ju88 had strafed the ambulance off the road on its way to them.

They quickly loaded Archie into the ambulance and whisked him off to sick quarters and from there to Driffield Hospital. He ended up in Northallerton Military Hospital. The crew visited him while he was still at Driffield but Arthur 'Archie' Tait's flying days were over. By the time he was fit again the war was well and truly over. In any case, a lung wound of the sort 'Arch' had received was enough to remove the 'fit for aircrew' medical category for a long time, if not for good. Contrary to at least two published books on Bomber Command, Archie Tait was not 'mortally wounded' in this attack. Sadly, Archie died on 26th January 1994, just 36 days short of the 49th anniversary of his being 'mortally wounded.'

After the ambulance had departed, the Ju88 was still 'popping off' at anything that took its fancy so, deciding that they'd had more than enough excitement for one tour (never mind one night), they took shelter behind a brick-walled area[61]. Bill at last had a chance to look at his crew. Alan Parrish's arm wound was fortunately not serious. A cannon shell had smashed the mid-upper turret's perspex, sliced through the sleeves of Alan's flying jacket and his battledess jacket and merely grazed his arm. Their stand-in navigator was minus his flying helmet. Bill asked what had happened to it and looked at Ted Richards as he started to laugh. 'What's so bloody funny Lou?' he asked. Ted's laughter increased as 'Mac' Mackirdy tried to look nonchalant. Finally Ted managed to get out the explanation. `After the first attack, that mad bugger opened the escape hatch and stuck

---

[61] *They later discovered they'd been sheltering in the bomb dump!*

his head out to look around. The slipstream whipped his helmet off!' and he burst into laughter again, this time joined by the rest of the crew.

Krazy Kate (MZ917) was so badly damaged that she never flew again. The Halifax was broken down into her major component parts and shipped off to be repaired but was finally struck off charge on 14th March 1945.

Operation Gisella was quite a success for the Luftwaffe. In all, the German intruders shot down twenty bombers: two Lancasters from 5 Group, three Halifaxes, one Fortress and one Mosquito belonging to 100 Group and three Lancasters and two Halifaxes from the HCUs. But 4 Group suffered the greatest number of casualties with eight Halifaxes falling to their guns and a further six damaged. 347 and 466 Squadrons lost two each while 158 and 346 Squadrons lost one each. The Group lost 26 aircrew killed. The 158 Squadron aircraft shot down was Flying Officer Rogers' PN437 (NP-X), which crashed in flames near Sledmere Grange, not far from Driffield, with the loss of all on board.

Three German nightfighters crashed in England due to excessively low flying. Not one of them was shot down. Long after the war, Arthur 'Archie' Tait set out to discover which aircraft it was that had caused the damage to himself and Krazy Kate. He was convinced that the Ju88 responsible was Werke Nummer 621586, belonging to 13./NJG 3 and coded D5+AX. This aircraft was a Ju88G-6C and its pilot was Hauptinann Johann Dreher, the Kapitein of the 13th Staffel. He had been born in 1920 and had been a bomber pilot on the Eastern Front before volunteering for nightfighters. He was credited with two confirmed kills before the night of 3rd March 1945. His crew were Oberfeldwebel Hugo Boker, Feldwebel Martin Bechter and Feldwebel Gustav Schmitz. They were all killed this same night when their aircraft struck a farmhouse (killing two occupants) and crashed into a field at the junction of the Elvington/Dunnington road. This was the last German aircraft to crash on British soil during the war. In 1993, Arthur Tait laid a wreath, in remembrance of his ex-enemies, at the spot where their Junkers finally crashed.

There was no such thing as 'trauma counselling' in 1945 so less than 48 hours later Bill and the crew (with a replacement rear gunner) were taking off in absolutely appalling conditions to go to Chemnitz. At the briefing the met. officer had given the usual `bull.' Right chaps, bit of 5/10ths cloud over the North Sea, tops no higher than 10,000 feet. May be a bit of icing at low level but you should clear that just after take-off. Should be nice and clear at the target..........' They'd gone into thick cloud as soon as they were airborne and Bill was maintaining their briefed rate of climb on instruments only - there was no point in looking out of the 'office,' all that could be seen was thick 'clag' swirling past the cockpit.

Only ten minutes into the flight, the engineer reported problems with the port outer engine - oil pressure dropping and temperature rising - and just to make Bill's evening the controls were starting to stiffen up and he could just about make out the ice forming on the wings. Bill told the Engineer to keep an eye on the port outer while he tried to continue the climb, hoping to break out of the cloud at the promised 10,000 feet, but at 11,000 feet they were still in the 'clag' and the oil and cylinder head temperature gauges for the port outer were almost off the clock. Bill instructed the flight engineer to close the recalcitrant engine down and he reluctantly decided to abort the operation and started a descending turn back towards base.

Bill was not happy, he'd carried out twenty-two operations without once 'boomeranging' and he certainly did not want to start now. He was brassed off with the port outer, he was brassed off with the icing and he had a few choice words for the met. officer. Descending through the cloud on three engines, Bill was worried to feel that the controls were getting worse, obviously the icing was not decreasing with their loss of height. They finally broke out of the cloud base but with their ice accretion and only three engines, the first priority was to jettison the bombload to maintain height. Even after this, the Halifax was still losing height, albeit only slowly, but losing height nevertheless.

Bill decided that their best chance was Carnaby, which was slightly closer than Lissett. As they approached the Yorkshire coast, it looked as if it would be touch and go whether they made it over the cliff tops so Bill ordered the crew to their crash Positions. Ted Richards switched the IFF to distress and sent out an SOS before leaving his wireless set and heading down the fuselage.

The Halifax just scraped in over the cliffs and Bill put her down gently on the wide runway and breathed a sigh of relief. He taxied off the runway and onto one of the dispersals and closed down the three remaining engines. They'd been airborne for just 36 minutes but it had seemed like a lifetime.

Another Halifax landed just behind them and Bill met the pilot in the Flying Control. He was another Aussie, Ron Swain from 466 Squadron and Bill had known him on a course during training. Ron had also experienced severe icing, so severe in fact that he'd lost control of the aircraft and ordered his crew to bale out. He'd then regained control of the Halifax and landed it by himself. His crew were safely picked up from the drink by the Bridlington lifeboat.

On the 7th March the squadron sent twenty aircraft to Hemmingstedt but for once Pilot Officer Strachan and crew were left off the operations list. Perhaps their Flight Commander decided they'd had two rough experiences on the trot and deserved the night off. He was certainly a happy man because that very day he had been promoted to Wing Commander and given command of the squadron. A very rare appointment for an air gunner!

Bill and crew were back on the operations list on Thursday, 8th March, but without their trusty bomb aimer. Krad Wakefield was having a spot of ear trouble and the MO had grounded him for two days. His replacement for the night was Pilot Officer P. A. J. Carroll. With the sad demise of Krazy Kate (NP-R, MZ917), the RAF had supplied Bill Strachan with a brand new Halifax - PN379 had just arrived on the squadron and been coded NP-R, becoming Bill's third R-Roger.'

Briefing revealed that the squadron was despatching sixteen Halifaxes to join a further 298 aircraft from 4, 6 and 8 Groups in an attack on the Blohm and Voss shipyards in Hamburg. The purpose of the raid was to damage or destroy as many Type XXI U-boats (or their sub-assemblies) as possible. With its Schnorkel and a new battery-driven electric engine, the Type XXI could remain under water almost indefinitely and was capable of a high submerged speed. Its production in any numbers would present major problems for the defence of allied convoys so once again, the RAF came to the rescue of the Royal Navy.

The new 'R-Roger' had been air-tested and handled like a dream. Inside it had the almost 'strange' smell of new aircraft, a smell that was somehow difficult to define but nonetheless obvious. Bill and the lads jumped off the crew bus at the dispersal, unloaded their gear and with a cheery 'Good Luck' the WAAF driver graunched into first gear and drove off. By 18.40 hours they'd carried out all their pre-flight checks, run-up the engines, Bill had signed the Form 700 and they were taxiing around the perimeter track to the end of the runway. At 18.46 they were airborne.

Yet again the target was completely cloud covered and the stand-in bomb aimer had to content himself with releasing the bombload onto a cluster of sky markers from 19,000 feet at 21.34 hours. The Master Bomber was clearly heard instructing crews to bomb the skymarkers. R-Roger' returned to Lissett at 00.40 hours after an uneventful six hour trip.

Bill Strachan's promotion to substantive[62] Flying Officer came through shortly after this visit to Hamburg, but he and his crew were not asked to fly on the next two squadron operations - to Essen on 11th March and Dortmund on the 12th. There were no squadron losses on either raid. In fact, they had not officially 'lost' an aircraft since 23rd February. The fact that Krazy Kate had been written off by enemy action and that NP-X had been shot down with the loss of all on board that same night, didn't appear in official figures. After all, they knew where both aircraft were therefore they weren't 'lost.'

On Tuesday 13th March, Bill and crew (Krad had returned), went to Wuppertal in daylight. Again cloud hid most of the target from view and Krad released their load onto blue smoke markers from 20,000 feet at 16.03 hours. They returned safely to Lissett after five and a half hours in the air. All 354 aircraft involved in this raid returned without loss and the sorties brought the Command's total for a three-day period to 2,541 daylight sorties to the Ruhr, during which 10,650 tons of bombs had been dropped, all through cloud, with sufficient accuracy to cripple two cities and one town (Essen, Dortmund and Wuppertal). Total losses on all three attacks amounted to five aircraft - just 0.2%.

Ever since Bob Stow had finished his second tour after 20 operations, the crew had had the same replacement flight engineer. Unfortunately, this gentleman -fine engineer though he may have been - just didn't fit in with the rest of the crew. There had been some friction and after four raids together, Bill decided that in the interests of efficiency and harmony, he'd ask the Flight Commander for another engineer. So the following night, Wednesday 14th March, they took Pilot Officer G. Jenkins to Homberg. The

---

[62] *Bill had been promoted to Acting Flying Officer the day after he was informed that he had been commissioned!*

following day the squadron sent nine aircraft to Mathias-Stinnes oil refinery at Bottrop and a further twelve to Hagen that night. Flying Officer Strachan and crew were not called for either raid.

They undertook their 26th operation on Monday 19th March as one of 324 aircraft from 4, 6 and 8 Groups carrying out an area attack on Witten. 'R-Roger' left Lissett at 00.53 hours and returned after six hours and twenty minutes in the air. This was a successful raid carried out in good visibility (for a change) and the force dropped 1,081 tons of bombs, destroying 129 acres (62%) of the built-up area and severely damaging the Ruhstahl Steelworks and the Mannesman Tube factory. Eight aircraft failed to return. Their flight engineer for this trip was Pilot Officer Ernie Fleming.

The next day, again with Ernie Fleming, they took R-Roger' to Recklinghausen as part of a 153-aircraft attack on the railway yards. Yet again cloud, this time aided by a strong wind, contrived to reduce the accuracy of the raid. On their way home they spotted another Halifax streaming smoke from its port inner engine. It was a good way below them but Bill dropped down and they escorted the damaged bomber for a while. Eventually the engine stopped smoking and, as the aircraft was maintaining height and they were now over Allied-held territory, they waved goodbye and resumed course for base, landing at 15.34 hours after 5 hours and 12 minutes in the air.

Flying Officer Bill Strachan's 28th operation took place on Wednesday 21st March and the crew featured a new Pilot Officer navigator - Cyril Dad' Keeton had been commissioned. Ernie Fleming was the engineer again and they were to take `R-Roger' to Rheine in daylight. Once again the Command split its attacking aircraft into three forces, with 160 Lancasters of 3 Group attacking Munster and 139 aircraft from 1 and 8 Groups going to Bremen while 178 aircraft from 4, 6 and 8 Groups attacked the rail yards and surrounding area in Rheine.

158 Squadron detailed eighteen aircraft but NP-Z failed to take off and one other returned early. All the squadron crews map-read right up to the target without difficulty in the clear conditions and the marshalling yards were easily identified. TIs were well placed and easily seen and the Master Bomber's instructions were clearly and precisely given. Heavy Flak was moderate but very accurate and two of 158's Halifaxes sustained slight damage. One aircraft was seen shot down over the target but seven

parachutes were seen to emerge. At 17.36 hours Krad Wakefield released their bombs into the centre of a group of yellow TIs as instructed by the Master Bomber and they had an uneventful return to Lissett, landing at 19.56 hours. A 143-aircraft attack on Bochum the same night brought an end to the second Battle of the Ruhr, leaving virtually the whole area a smoking heap of ruins with all production at a standstill - awaiting the imminent arrival of allied troops.

The squadron operated again on Saturday 24th March, but again Bill Strachan and crew weren't 'asked to the party'. They were included the next day, however, with an early morning take-off for a daylight to Munster. Ernie Fleming was stood down for this raid, his place being taken by the squadron Engineering Leader, Flight Lieutenant J. R. Coates DFC. Bomber Command's operations on this day were directed at towns on the main reinforcement routes to the Rhine battle area. Heavy attacks were made on rail routes through these towns and on their surrounding areas. Hannover was attacked by 275 aircraft from 1, 6 and 8 Groups and 156 aircraft from 4 and 8 Groups went to Osnabruck while 158 Squadron contributed twenty-two Halifaxes to the 175 aircraft attack on Munster.

Few results were seen on the Munster raid because the target rapidly became covered in smoke. This was somewhat disappointing because the attack started in good visibility with no cloud. TIs were seen on approaching Munster but, by the time 158's crews started their bombing runs, these were obscured by the smoke. The Master Bomber was clearly heard and his handling of the attack was praised by several crews. In the early stages of the raid he instructed crews to bomb the TIs but later he told them to 'bomb the centre of the brown smoke – be careful not to overshoot.'

Heavy Flak was moderate to intense and six of the squadron's aircraft sustained minor damage and three aircraft were reported shot down in and around the target area (three Halifaxes failed to return). Krad Wakefield identified the target visually and, although the smoke completely blotted out the town, the railways and canals outside the city were clearly recognised. As ordered by the Master Bomber, Krad released their load from 17,000 feet at 10.19 hours into the centre of the brown smoke. They landed back at Lissett at 12.18 hours to complete operation number 29.

Sir Arthur Harris was now having a problem. At this stage of the war he was having difficulty in finding enough suitable targets to send his aircraft to and sufficient bombs to drop on them. In particular there was a severe shortage of 1,000 pounders and 158 Squadron, among others, had a ten-day rest. During this welcome break, Allied troops captured the towns of Paderborn and Lippstadt, bottling up the complete strength of Field-Marshal Model's Army Group. Almost a quarter of a million men were trapped in the Ruhr area and, although some industrial towns continued to function, their end products couldn't leave the area because of the vast damage to road and rail communications.

Bill's next operation finally arrived on the night of Wednesday 4th April. The night's efforts were mainly directed at the German oil industry with 341 aircraft going to Leuna, 272 to Lutzkendorf and 327 to the Rhenania oil plant at Harburg, south of the Elbe not far from the ruins of Hamburg. 158 Squadron participated in the Harburg attack, despatching twenty Halifaxes. Their total contribution should have been 22 aircraft but Pilot Officer J. W. Furness in NP-D swung on take-off and crashed into another Halifax that was minding its own business, sitting on its dispersal, with its engines running. Both aircraft were completely written off but miraculously, no-one was killed. 'R-Roger' was airborne at 20.14 hours.

Arriving over the target to find 3/10ths cloud with tops at 6,000 feet, the PFF TIs were clearly visible. While on the bomb run, Krad reported a large explosion, lasting several seconds, on the ground at 22.30 hours and, at 22.33 hours from a height of 19,000 feet, he added R-Roger's' contribution onto the well placed TIs. Two minutes later there was another large explosion on the ground. Heavy Flak was moderate and scattered as was the searchlight activity. One Me410 was seen in the target area and considerable light Flak was witnessed on the homeward leg. Bill eased 'R-Roger' back onto the runway at Lissett at 01.10 hours to complete his - and Ted Richards - 30th operation. But were they screened? Were they hell!

Four nights later, Flying Officer Strachan's name appeared on the operations list again - against Halifax MZ480, 'R-Roger' was being serviced and would not be ready for the night's raid so Bill had to settle for another aircraft. Aircrew were superstitious about their 'own' aircraft and no-one liked flying in someone else's. Too many crews had got the chop flying a strange aircraft and Bill and the lads clearly remembered losing their first 'R-Roger' when she was taken to Bohlen by Jimmy Gapes while they were on leave. Still, what couldn't be helped, couldn't be helped and at 19.45 hours, Bill lifted

'K-King' off the runway and started to climb prior to setting course for Hamburg.

When the target was first revealed at briefing, Bill wondered what the hell there was left to bomb in Hamburg but he soon learned that the attack was to be directed at what remained of the shipyards and 158 Squadron was despatching twenty-one Halifaxes as part of a total force of 440 aircraft drawn from 4, 6 and 8 Groups. The squadron's aircraft were distributed among the force's three waves and 'K-King' was to attack in the third and final wave.

Although the target was covered in 10/10ths cloud with tops at 2,000 feet, TIs were just visible through the cloud and seemed to be well concentrated. As 'K-King' approached, the target was already an inferno but this didn't seem to stop the Luftwaffe gunners putting up a tremendous heavy Flak barrage. Krad Wakefield was tracking down onto the target with H2S because of the cloud but he could see more TIs than he'd ever seen over one target before. The Master Bomber's transmissions were very faint but Krad just heard him order all crews to 'slightly overshoot the greens'. With 'K-King' flying at 18,000 feet on a heading of 188 degrees true, Krad followed this instruction at 22.38 hours. Many explosions were reported in the target area, including one at 22.39 hours. There was some nightfighter activity in the target area and the crew of Halifax NP-U reported firing on a Ju88. Yellow fighter flares were another major feature of this night sky over Hamburg. This was the last major Bomber Command raid of the war on Hamburg - and it turned out to be 158 Squadron's last night operation of the war.

Nuremberg was the squadron's target on Wednesday 11th April, a relatively quiet day - operationally speaking - with only 4 and 8 Groups operating. One hundred Halifaxes, together with 14 Lancasters and 8 Mosquitoes went to Bayreuth and carried out a very good attack on the railway yards without loss, while 158 Squadron contributed 25 aircraft to a force of 129 Halifaxes from 4 Group plus 14 PFF Lancasters in a very accurate attack on the railway yards at Nuremberg, again without loss.

The squadron aircraft were all scheduled to attack in the first phase, between 15.05 and 15.07 hours. Weather over the target was clear (a pleasant change) and red TIs were clearly visible, as were the railway yards themselves. The Master Bomber controlled the attack well, with directions changing from

'Bomb the reds' through 'between the two reds' to 'all Pickwick aircraft bomb the centre of the smoke.' This smoke eventually rose to about 10,000 feet over the marshalling yards, giving the attacking crews great satisfaction, although Flak was intense and six squadron aircraft returned with varying degrees of Flak damage.

Bill Strachan and crew, back in their trusty steed 'R-Roger' approached the target at 15,000 feet, heading 083 degrees true at 143 mph. Krad Wakefield followed the Master Bomber's last instruction, releasing their load into the centre of the smoke at 15.06 hours. As he pressed the 'tit' there were several considerable explosions in the target area. They landed back at Lissett at 18.24 hours after just over seven hours in the air.

Exactly one week and five minutes after their take-off for Nuremberg, the crew were once again leaving Lissett's runway to do battle with the enemy. The target was Heligoland. This small island, situated about 45 miles due north of Wangerooge, the most northern of the Frisian Islands, guards the sea approaches to the northwestern coast of Germany, with ports like Wilhelmshaven, Cuxhaven and Bremerhaven. It was a serious thorn in the flesh of the Royal Navy and the enemy forces stationed there posed a threat to all allied sea traffic. It was about to be neutralised.

On this Wednesday, 18th April, the Command assembled a force of 969 aircraft from all Groups for this attack on the naval base, airfield and town on this small island. The civilian population had been removed from Heligoland long before this attack took place, so the complete island was a wholly military target. 158 Squadron's contribution to the attacking force comprised twenty-eight Halifaxes, a number only equalled on three previous occasions in its whole operational existence (Berlin on 23th August 1943; Caen on 18th July 1944 and Essen on 29th November 1944). These 28 aircraft were made up of five Halifax B.Mk. VIs (D, H, K, S & W) and twenty-three B.Mk IIIs (A, B, C, E, F, G, I, J, J2, L, M, N, O, P, Q, R, S2, T, U, V, X, Y and Z) and all bombed in either the fifth (13.23 to 13.28 hours) or sixth wave (13.38 to 13.49 hours). The squadron were led into battle by Squadron Leader H. F. Watson DFC (OC 'B' Flight) and Squadron Leader L. B. Reynolds RNZAF (OC 'C' Flight).

'R-Roger' had left base at 11.24 hours and just under two hours later Bill and the crew were approaching the target at 18,000 feet on a heading of 175 degrees true. Visibility was about twenty miles but there was patchy cloud over the area with a base of 15,000 feet but with some further patches of cloud below this. As they approached Heligoland, the outline of the island was clearly visible, with a heavy pall of dark brown smoke drifting across the southern end. Token Flak bursts littered the skyline. Just as they commenced their run-in the Master Bomber ordered 'Basement 14, bomb the centre of the smoke.' Bill dropped 'R-Roger' down to 14,000 feet and Krad Wakefield continued to track down onto the target, ignoring the danger of being bombed by aircraft above them who either had not heard, or chose to ignore, the Master Bomber's instructions. Krad released their bombs at 13.28 hours and Bill turned the Halifax for home. One bomber was seen to crash into the sea near the target after being hit by bombs from another aircraft.

Bombing was very accurate and all target areas were turned into crater-pitted moonscapes. Three Halifaxes failed to return but all 158 Squadron's aircraft made it back safely to Lissett. 'R-Roger' landed at 15.15 hours. The next day the crew was sent on leave and all rushed off at a great rate of knots, leaving only Bill Strachan on camp. It was not until they'd gone that Bill was told he'd finished his tour and was being repatriated to Australia. To say he was brassed off at not being able to organise an end-of-tour booze-up was putting it mildly. He went to stores to hand in his flying gear before departing and tried to explain the situation to the WAAF in stores. She was married to Corporal Jimmy Moore, the NCO in charge of 'R-Roger's' ground crew. Bill asked ACW Moore to give his apologies to Jimmy and tell him what had happened. Bill managed to see Johnny 'Krad' Wakefield before he left for Australia but it was only at the squadron reunion, in Bridlington, in 1989 that he got to see Ted 'Lou' Richards, Bob Stow and Arthur 'Archie' Tait (plus Krad) again. Cyril 'Dad' Keeton had died in an accident in 1987 and Alan Parrish had emigrated to Canada in the meantime.

Additional Notes to Chapter 10

1.   158 Squadron carried out only one more op after Bill Strachan finished his tour. They despatched 27 aircraft to Wangerooge on 25 April as part of a 482 aircraft attack on the coastal batteries. This was also the last attack undertaken by 4 Group. The war ended on 7 May.

2.   Bill Strachan, Cyril Keeton and Bob Stow were awarded the DFC and John Wakefield a DFM. Bill could never understand why Ted Richards, who was the only one of his crew to complete all 33 ops with him, did not also receive a DFM.

Epilogue

The following order was issued on 8th May 1945 by Air Chief Marshal Sir Arthur Harris:

SPECIAL ORDER OF THE DAY

Men and Women of Bomber Command,

More than five-and-a-half years ago, within hours of the declaration of War, Bomber Command first assailed the German enemy.

You were then but a handful. Inadequate in everything but the skill and determination of the views for that sombre occasion and for the unknown years of unceasing battle which lay behind horizons black indeed.

You, the aircrews of Bomber Command, sent your first ton of bombs away on the morrow of the outbreak of war. A million tons of bombs and mines have followed from Bomber Command alone. From Declaration of War to Cease Fire a continuity of battle without precedent and without relent.

In the Battle of France your every endeavour bore down upon an overwhelming and triumphant enemy.

After Dunkirk your country stood alone - in arms but largely unarmed - between the Nazi tyranny and domination of the world.

The Battle of Britain, in which you took great part, raised the last barrier, strained but holding, in the path of the all-conquering Wehrmacht, and the bomb smoke of the Channel ports choked back down German throats the very word 'invasion': not again to find expression within these narrow seas until the bomb-disrupted defences of the Normandy beachheads fell to our combined assault.

In the long years between much was to pass.

Then it was that you, and you for long alone, carried the war ever deeper and ever more furiously into the heart of the Third Reich. There the whole might of the German enemy in undivided strength, and the scarcely less a foe - the very elements, arrayed against you. You overcame them both.

Undismayed

Through those desperate years, undismayed by any odds, undeterred by any casualties, night after succeeding night, you fought. The Phalanx of the United Nations.

You fought alone, as the one force then assailing German soil, you fought alone as individuals - isolated in your crew stations by the darkness and the murk, and from all other aircraft in company.

Not for you the hot emulation of high endeavour in the glare and panoply of martial array. Each crew, each one in each crew, fought alone through black nights, rent only, mile after continuing mile, by the fiercest barrages ever raised and the instant sally of the searchlights. In each dark minute of those long miles lurked menace. Fog, ice, snow and tempest found you undeterred.

In that loneliness in action lay the final test, the ultimate stretch of human staunchness and determination.

Your losses mounted through those years - years in which your chance of survival through one spell of operational duty was negligible. Through two periods, mathematically nil. Nevertheless survivors pressed forward as volunteers to pit their desperately acquired skill in even a third period of operations, on special tasks.

Grievous

In those five years and eight months of continuous battle over enemy soil your casualties over long periods were grievous. As the count is cleared those of Bomber Command who gave their lives to bring near to impotence an enemy who had surged swift in triumph through a continent, and to enable the united nations to deploy in full array, will be found not less than the total dead of our national invasion armies now in Germany. In the whole history of our national forces never have so small a band of men been called to support for so long such odds. You indeed bore the brunt.

To you who survive I would say this. Content yourselves, and take credit with those who perished, that now the 'Cease Fire' has sounded countless homes within our Empire will welcome back a father, a husband or a son whose life but for your endeavours and your sacrifices, would assuredly have been expended during long further years of agony to achieve a victory already ours. No allied nation is clear of this debt to you.

Your attacks on the industrial centres of Northern Italy did much toward the collapse of the Italian and German armies in North Africa, and to further invasion of the Italian mainland.

Easier prey

Of the German enemy, two or three million fit men, potentially vast armies, continuously held throughout the war in direct and indirect defence against your assaults. A great part of her industrial war effort went towards fending your attacks.

You struck a critical proportion of the weapons of war from enemy hands, on every front.

You immobilised armies, leaving them short of supplies, reinforcements, resources and reserves, the easier prey to our advancing forces.

The Pendulum and the Scythe

You eased and abetted the passage of our troops over major obstacles. You blasted the enemy from long prepared defences where he essayed to hold. On the Normandy beaches. At the hinge of the Battle of Caen. In the jaws of the Falaise Gap. To the strongpoints of the enemy held Channel ports, St Vith, Houffalize and the passage of the Rhine. In battle after battle you sped our armies to success at minimum cost to our troops. The commanders of our land forces, and indeed those of the enemy, have called your attacks decisive.

You enormously disrupted every enemy means of communication, the very life blood of his military and economic machines. Railways, canals and every form of transport fell first to decay and then to chaos under your assaults.

You so shattered the enemy's oil plants as to deprive him of all but the final trickle of fuel. His aircraft became earthbound, his road transport ceased to roll, armoured fighting vehicles lay helpless outside the battle, or fell immobilised into our hands. His strategic and tactical plans failed through inability to move.

From his war industries supplies of ore, coal, steel, fine metals, aircraft, guns, ammunition, tanks, vehicles and every ancillary equipment dwindled under your attacks.

At the very crisis of the invasion of Normandy, you virtually annihilated the German naval surface forces then in the Channel, a hundred craft and more fell victim to those three attacks.

You sank or damaged a large but yet untotalled number of enemy submarines in his ports and by mine-laying in his waters, you interfered widely and repeatedly with his submarine training programmes.

With extraordinary accuracy, regardless of opposition, you hit and burst through every carapace which he could devise to protect his submarines in harbour.

By your attacks on inland industries and coastal shipyards you caused hundreds of his submarines to be still born.

Your mine laying throughout the enemy's sea lanes, your bombing of his inland waters, and his ports, confounded his sea traffic and burst his canals.

From Norway throughout the Baltic, from Jutland to the Gironde, on the coasts of Italy and North Africa you laid and relaid the minefields. The wreckage of the enemy's naval and merchant fleets litters and encumbers his sea lanes and dockyards. A thousand known ships, and many more as yet unknown, fell casualty to your mines.

You hunted and harried his major warships from hide to hide. You put out of action, gutted or sank most of them.

By your attacks on experimental stations, factories, communications and firing sites, you long postponed and much further reduced the V weapon attacks. You averted an enormous further toll of death and destruction from your country.

With it all you never ceased to rot the very heart out of the enemy's war resources and resistance.

Continuous

His capital and near 100 of his cities and towns, including nearly all of leading war industrial importance lie in utter ruin, together with the greater part of the war industry which they supported.

Thus you brought to nought the enemy's original advantage of an industrial might intrinsically greater than ours and supported by the labour of captive millions, now set free.

For the first time in more than a century you have brought home to the habitual aggressor of Europe the full and acrid flavours of war, so long the perquisite of his victims.

All this, and much more, have you achieved during these five-and-a-half years of continuous battle, despite all opposition from an enemy disposing of many a geographical and strategical advantage with which to exploit an initial superiority in numbers.

Men from every part of the Empire and of most of the Allied Nations fought in our ranks. Indeed a band of brothers.

Epilogue

In the third year of the war the Eighth Bomber Command, and the Fifteenth Bomber Command U.S.A.A.F. from their Mediterranean bases, ranged themselves at our side zealous in extending every mutual aid, vying in every assault upon our common foe. Especially they played the leading part in sweeping the enemy fighter defences from our path and, finally, out of the skies.

Nevertheless nothing that the crews accomplished - and it was much, and decisive - could have been achieved without the devoted services of every man and woman in the Command.

Those who tended the aircraft, mostly in the open, through six bitter winters. Endless intricacies in a prolonged misery of wet and cold. They rightly earned the implicit trust of the crews. They set extraordinary records of aircraft serviceability.

Those who manned the Stations, Operational Headquarters, Supply Lines and Communications.

The pilots of the Photographic Reconnaissance Units without whose lonely ventures far and wide over enemy territory, we should have been largely powerless to plan or to strike.

The Operational Crew training organisation of the Command which, through those years of ceaseless work by day and night, never failed, in the face of every difficulty and unpredicted call, to replace all casualties and to keep our constantly expanding first line up to strength in crews trained to the highest pitch of efficiency; simultaneously producing near 20,000 additional trained aircrew for the raising and reinforcement of some 50 extra squadrons, formed in the Command and despatched for service in other Commands at home and overseas.

The men and women of the Meteorological Branch who attained prodigious exactitudes in a fickle art and stood brave on assertion where science is inexact. Time and again they saved us from worse than the enemy could ever have achieved. Their record is outstanding.

The meteorological reconnaissance pilots, who flew through anything and everything in search of the feasible.

Meticulous

The Operations Research Sections whose meticulous investigation of every detail of every attack provided data for the continuous confounding of the enemy and the consistent reduction of our own casualties.

The scientists, especially those of the Telecommunications Research Establishment, who placed, in unending succession, in our hands the technical means to resolve our problems and to confuse the every part of the enemy. Without their skill and their labours beyond doubt we could not have prevailed.

The Works Services who engineered for Bomber Command alone 2,000 miles of runway track and road, with all that goes with them.

The Works staffs, designers and workers who equipped and re-equipped us for battle. Their efforts, their honest workmanship, kept in our hands indeed a Shining Sword.

To all of you I would say how proud I am to have served in Bomber Command for four-and-a-half years and to have been your Commander-in-Chief through more than three years of your saga.

Your task in the German war is now complete.

A.T.HARRIS

Air Officer Commanding-in-Chief,

Bomber Command

In Memoriam

We've erected a statue to Harris,
We've unveiled a statue of 'Butch'.
Our governments couldn't be bothered,
For a man who gave Britain so much.
We've erected a statue of Harris,
The men of Bomber Command
Butch's 'old Lags' have never forgotten
The man for whom they'd still stand
But it's not just a statue of Harris,
It's in memory of all those who died,
The fifty-five thousand five hundred
Who gave of their all for 'our side'.
It's a constant reminder of honour,
Standing up there in the Strand
Of the selfless devotion to duty
By the men of Bomber Command.
We've erected our statue of Butch,
A leader of stature so tall.
We've put up a memorial to Harris,
Who did what he did for us all
A symbol of all our endeavours,
A memorial to all those who fell.
To a man who did what he had to,
And he did it so bloody well.
The Germans and others objected,
From somewhere they found the sheer gall,
To complain that we shouldn't remember
The man who made Germany fall
They all got up and protested;
With moans about Dresden, Cologne
And Berlin and quite a few others,
Forgetting the guilt that they own.
And what if that shiny black jackboot
Had been on the other foot?
They'd have erected their statues to Goering,
And Goebbels and Hitler to boot.

The Pendulum and the Scythe

But they wouldn't have confined them to Deutschland
That we all could tell,
They'd have stuck them in occupied countries,
We'd have had them in London as well!
We could understand all the furore,
If we'd put Harris up over there.
If we'd stuck him in Essen or Hamburg,
Somewhere we'd bombed from the air.
But we've erected this statue of Harris,
We've put him outside Clement Danes.
We've put him up here in London,
Which was bombed by Luftwaffe planes.
We've erected our Memorial to Harris
And to each and every 'Old Lag',
For the things we remember and others
We can't, that at our memories nag.
Yes, we've unveiled our statue of Harris,
It's up there so noble and new,
For the chaps whom we knew that didn't come back,
It's for them and Bert Harris too.

Written by Ken J. W. Marshall shortly after the unveiling of the Bomber
Command Association's statue of Sir Arthur Harris, by H.M. Queen Elizabeth the
Queen Mother on Sunday, 31st May, 1992.

Appendix 1: Senior RAF Commanders 1939 to 1945

1. Secretary of State for Air:

The Rt.Hon. Sir Kingsley Wood, MP.   16 May 1938 - 5 Apr 1940

The Rt.Hon. Sir Samuel J G Hoare, Bart., GCSI, GBE, CMG, MR

5 Apr 1940 -11 May 1940

The Rt.Hon. Sir Archibald Sinclair, Bart., KT, CMG, MP.

11 May 1940 - May 1945

2. Chief of the Air Staff:

MRAF Sir Cyril L N Newall, GCB, CMG, CBE, AM.

1 Sep 1937 - 25 Oct 1940

ACM* Sir Charles F A Portal, KCB (later GCB) DSO,MC.

25 Oct 1940 - May 1945

* Later MRAF.

3. Air Officer Commanding-in-Chief, Bomber Command:

ACM Sir Edgar R Ludlow-Hewitt, KCB, CMG, DSO, MC.

12 Sep 1937 - 3 Apr 1940

AM Sir Charles F A Portal, KCB, DSO, MC.   3 Apr 1940 - 5 Oct 1940

AM Sir Richard E C Peirse, KCB, DSO, AFC.   5 Oct 1940 - 22 Feb 1942

AM Sir Arthur T Harris, KCB, OBE, AFC.   22 Feb 1942 - May 1945

4. Air Officers Commanding Groups in Bomber Command:

No.1 Group:

AVM A C Wright	3 Sep 1939 - 27 Jun 1940
A.Com. J J Breen	27 June 1940 - 27 Nov 1940
AVM R D Oxland	27 Nov 1940 - 24 Feb 1943
AVM E A B Rice	24 Feb 1943 - 12 Feb 1945
AVM R S Blucke	12 Feb 1945 - May 1945

No.2 Group:

AVM C T Maclean	16 May 1938 - 17 Feb 1940
AVM J M Robb	17 Feb 1940 - 12 Feb 1941
AVM D F Stevenson	12 Feb 1941- 17 Dec 1941
AVM A Lees	17 Dec 1941 - 29 Dec 1942
AVM J H D'Albiac,	29 Dec 1942 31 May 1943*

* When No.2 Group became part of 2TAF.

No.3 Group:

AVM J E A Baldwin	29 Aug 1939 - 14 Sep 1942
AVM the Hon. R A Cochrane	14 Sep 1942 - 27 Feb 1943
AVM R Harrison	27 Feb 1943 - May 1945

No.4 Group:

AVM A Coningham	3 Jul 1939 - 26 Jul 1941
AVM C R Carr	6 Jul 1941 - 12 Feb 1945
AVM J R Whitley	12 Feb 1945 - May 1945

No.5 Group:

A.Com. W B Calloway	17 Aug 1937 - 11 Sep 1939
AVM A T Harris	11 Sep 1939 - 22 Nov 1940
AVM N R Bottomley	22 Nov 1940 -12 May 1941
AVM J C Slessor	12 May 1941 - 25 Apr 1942
AVM W A Coryton	25 Apr 1942 - 18 Feb 1943
AVM the Hon. R A Cochrane	18 Feb 1943 - 16 Jan 1945
AVM H A Constantine	16 Jan 1945 - May 1945

No.6 Group:

| AVM G E Brookes | 25 Oct 1942 - 29 Feb 1944 |
| AVM C M McEwen | 29 Feb 1944 - May 1945 |

No.8 Group:

| AVM D C T Bennett | 13 Jan 1943 - May 1945 |

No.100 Group:

| AVM E B Addison | 8 Nov 1943 - 1945 |

Printed in Great Britain
by Amazon